Prime Time Soap Operas on Indian Television

Prime Time Soap Operas on Indian Television

Shoma Munshi

Routledge
Taylor & Francis Group

LONDON AND NEW YORK

First published 2010
by Routledge

2 Park Square, Milton Park, Abingdon, Oxfordshire OX14 4RN
52 Vanderbilt Avenue, New York, NY 10017

Routledge is an imprint of the Taylor & Francis Group, an informa business

First issued in paperback 2019

Transferred to Digital Printing 2010

Copyright © 2010 Shoma Munshi

Typeset by
Star Compugraphics Private Limited
D-156, Second Floor,
Sector 7, Noida

British Library Cataloguing-in-Publication Data
A catalogue record of this book is available from the British Library

ISBN 978-0-415-55377-3 (hbk)
ISBN 978-0-367-17645-7 (pbk)

For my parents,
Anil and Sreela Munshi,
and my sister, Poroma Rebello,
My home in the world

Contents

Acknowledgements

A book that has come about as a long term interest in studying the media in India owes much to many people. My greatest intellectual debt, for this project in particular, is to Dale F. Eickelman, who has kept track of my research and writing over the years, and read through and commented on various papers, including drafts of chapters in this book. He has been a constant source of intellectual debate and inspiration; and above all, friendship and support. For that, I am truly grateful.

My heartfelt thanks to Patricia Uberoi, whom I admire as a scholar and value as a friend and colleague. Her work on popular culture in India has always held the greatest appeal for me, not just for its convincing arguments, but also for her lucid style of writing. I am doubly grateful to her for agreeing to go through the manuscript on a tight schedule and provide invaluable comments. I am also grateful to the other anonymous reviewer of the manuscript.

I cannot forget Peter van der Veer, under whose supervision, as a postdoctoral research fellow, I first started researching in this field. Peter has remained a steadfast friend and support in all my academic endeavors, always reading my work with a rigorous and analytically critical eye.

Research of this kind requires establishing contacts in the field of media production. As always, writer and journalist, and a friend of long standing, Kishore Singh, supplied me with many contact details for people in television production in Mumbai. Kishore remained interested all along in how my research was progressing, repeatedly asking me to find out "how old is Ba in *Kyunki Saas Bhi Kabhi Bahu Thi*." I hope this book answers some of his questions. Special thanks to Ritu Vajpeyi-Mohan for putting me in touch with Routledge, and to Abhilasha Ojha as well.

I have accrued countless debts in Mumbai where I carried out most of my fieldwork. People whom I met for the first time welcomed me and found long hours to meet with me, despite the punishing schedules they keep in the frenzied world of media production. My debt to them is immense, because without their inputs, this book would not have been possible. They include, among others, Shalija Kejriwal, Sandiip Sikcand, Kamlesh Pandey,

Rama Bijapurkar, Anil Wanvari, Shobhaa De, Ravi Chopra, and Rakesh Roshan. Special thanks to Shailja Kejriwal, who, even after the interview, made time for a long telephone conversation late in the evening, providing me invaluable data and insights on the K soaps. Shailja was a magician and fixed an appointment with Shobha Kapoor at very short notice. My grateful thanks also to Rama Bijapurkar, whose writing I always enjoy, and who was very supportive of my writing on soaps.

In content production houses, Rajan Shahi of Director's Kut, Sunjoy Waddhwa of Sphere Origins, and Balaji Telefilms' Shobha Kapoor, Chloe Ferns and Nivedita Basu received me warmly and gave willingly of their time to discuss production processes and the conceptualizations of soaps. They also allowed me to see first-hand how production houses function and made sure that I could attend shootings of various soaps. Rajan Shahi and Sunjoy Waddhwa continued to answer all my additional queries long distance, and always responded in a timely fashion. My grateful thanks to Rajan Shahi and Sunjoy and Comall Waddhwa for visuals of their shows and for procuring the TV channel's permission to use them in the book.

An exceptional note of thanks to Rajan Shahi for inviting me to the party to celebrate the success of *Bidaai*, for calling me many times in Kuwait, and for discussing his future productions with me.

Yash Khanna of STAR India Pvt. Ltd has remained unfailingly helpful and gracious. He answered many questions, big and small, and sent me tapes of shows, visuals and other data whenever I requested it. I would like to express my deep gratitude to Yash for everything, as also to the team at Star TV, who sent visuals of their shows included in the book. I deeply appreciate the invaluable help and support Yash provided throughout the researching and writing of this book.

L. V. Krishnan of TAM Media Research Pvt. Ltd was a fount of information. Charming and kind, LV very generously shared his experience of many years and valuable insights on television viewership and ratings, discussed soaps in detail, and also supplied data and graphs. Thank you, LV.

Stars of soaps like Sakshi Tanwar, Ronit Bose Roy, Smriti Z. Irani and Achint Kaur received me on the sets where shooting was going on and at various outdoor locations. I spent entire days on the sets. They took enormous amounts of time to sit with me between takes and be interviewed, and made sure that I was kept supplied with food, tea and coffee. They also took me around and introduced me to other stars of the soaps. All of them are big stars in their own right, and they were wonderfully gracious and charming. Being with them during filming allowed me to observe, up close and personal, how master shots and close up shots are taken, how costumes and make-up function, how inventive the production process is, and how the entire production process moves from take-to-take in what seems to be a completely chaotic situation, but appears to be seamless and effortless on screen. It was an exciting learning experience.

I must acknowledge, with deep gratitude, Dhananjay Date, longtime friend, who left me the keys to his apartment in Mumbai, even when he was away, traveling on work. Thank you, Date, for being such a good friend.

I was fortunate to present earlier versions of a couple of these chapters at a talk sponsored by the Annenberg School of Communication Studies and the Center for the Advanced Study of India, University of Pennsylvania, during Fall 2005. Comments received there opened up new lines of inquiry. I would like to specially mention Francine Frankel, with whom working at Penn was an enriching and exciting experience, and whose continuing friendship means a lot to me.

At the American University of Kuwait (AUK), where I am now privileged to work, my grateful thanks to President Marina Tolmacheva, who has always been supportive of my work. Meetings on other issues inevitably concluded with her telling me about the soaps she manages to watch once in a while, and discussing aspects of my work, thereby providing insights that enriched my thinking. I cannot thank Margaret Combs enough for taking the trouble to buy, and carry back, many books from the USA for me. Margaret has always been an invaluable source of friendship and support whose "inner voice," as I always tell her, is similar to that of Parvati's and Tulsi's (whom I hope she gets to know after reading this book!). The library staff at AUK provided critical and timely support in accessing many articles for me. My thanks to Amna Al-Omare, Asma J. Yacoub and Hana Kaouri. I would like to acknowledge, with the greatest thanks, Micheline Zouein, without whose superb administrative support I could not have stayed home to work on the book on my non-teaching and non-meeting days. I would also like to acknowledge, with gratitude, Mada Hammoud, who, with her expertise in graphic design, created a version of the book cover. Special thanks also to Kimberly Al-Suffi, Juliet Dinkha, Astrid Al-Hadeedi and Malini Mittal Bishnoi — friends and colleagues — who made sure that I actually got out of the house for dinner at least one evening every week in order to stay sane! For the many evenings that I was at home for dinner, my thanks to Mary, who made sure that I ate properly and who told me to get up from my work because it was time to switch on the TV for my daily dose of soaps.

Over the years, I have received inspiration from friends and colleagues who have discussed my work and provided inputs that have sharpened my thoughts and arguments. Mostly, they have remained a constant source of friendship. I would like to pay tribute to Shohini Ghosh, Aditya Behl, Wim Stokhof, Gananath and Ranjini Obeyesekere, Kevin Robins, Dipesh Chakrabarty, Satadru Sen, Lorraine Gamman, Neera Burra, Jyoti Grewal, Monroe Price, David Birch, John Knight, Cynthia Chou, Deborah Tooker, Laurie Sears, Paule Gentot, Maurice Aymard and Christophe Jaffrelot.

The team at Routledge has been wonderful to work with. A special note of thanks to Omita Goyal, who immediately saw the importance of this project, and provided constant support and feedback throughout. My thanks also, in particular, to Pallavi Narayan for her meticulous copy editing, efficient follow-up and excellent professionalism throughout (including sitting with me at the typesetters' office for an entire day, through a Delhi power cut).

My family, to whom this book is dedicated, is my greatest inspiration and support. I wish that my grandmother, (late) Renuka Bhattacharya, could have read this work. Her courage and generosity continue to inspire me. My uncle, Anjan Bhattacharya, while not quite understanding my passion for soaps, still recorded episodes that I missed and was happy to discuss them with me.

My debt to my parents, Anil and Sreela Munshi, and my sister, Poroma Rebello, is immeasurable. Their love and support is the strongest dynamic and the one constant in my life.

List of Graphs and Illustrations

TAM data and graphs
Courtesy: TAM Media Research Pvt. Ltd. Used with permission.

Charts of Sphere Origins
Courtesy: Sphere Origins. Used with permission.

List of Visuals

(Between pp. 112 and 113)

Visuals from *Kyunki Saas Bhi Kabhi Bahu Thi*
Courtesy: STAR India Pvt. Ltd. Used with permission.

1. Tulsi Virani
2. Mihir and Tulsi Virani
3. Mihir and Tulsi
4. Tulsi and Mihir
5. Karan and Nandini
6. Krishnatulsi (KT) and Ba
7. Mihir Virani
8. The two Tulsis
9. Tulsi
10. Tulsi
11. Virani family
12. Mihir and Tulsi offering prayers with the Virani family
13. Older Tulsi
14. Virani family in *chawl*
15. One of the title shots of *Kyunki*

Visuals from *Kahaani Ghar Ghar Kii*
Courtesy: STAR India Pvt. Ltd. Used with permission.

16. Parvati Om Aggarwal
17. Om and Parvati
18. Parvati and Om
19. Aggarwal family
20. Parvati with Aggarwal family children
21. Parvati
22. Parvati as Janki Devi

Visuals from *Kasautii Zindagi Kay*
Courtesy: STAR India Pvt. Ltd. Used with permission.

23. Prerna
24. Mr Rishabh Bajaj
25. Prerna
26. Anurag Basu and Prerna
27. Prerna

1

Introduction

On 3 July 2000, a soap opera, with little known actors, debuted on prime time on a struggling television channel. That soap opera was *Kyunki Saas Bhi Kabhi Bahu Thi* (Because the Mother-in-Law Was Also Once a Daughter-in-Law, henceforth *Kyunki*), the production house was Balaji Telefilms, and the television channel was Star Plus. A few months later, on 16 October 2000, Balaji Telefilms launched their second prime time soap on Star Plus, *Kahaani Ghar Ghar Kii* (The Story of Every Home, henceforth *Kahaani*). At that time, no one expected what came to be termed the "*saas–bahu* sagas" (mother-in-law–daughter-in-law sagas) to become the *chhotey parde ki bari baat* (the big thing on the small screen), transforming the fortunes of the production house and the television channel, making their leading stars household names, and millions of Indians, both in India and overseas, part of the extended Virani (*Kyunki*) and Aggarwal (*Kahaani*) families.

The first serials to be aired in India were *Hum Log* (We People, 1984) and *Buniyaad* (Foundation, 1986). Both were telecast on the state-sponsored channel, Doordarshan, and became very popular with audiences (see Brown and Cody 1991; Das 1995; and Mankekar 1999 for details). But times change, and a generation that was enjoying the fruits of India's economic liberalization since the beginning of the 1990s started looking for something new. This was the period that marked the entry of prime time soaps on Indian satellite television channels. These soaps raised the bar for production values; introduced catchy title songs and the opening montage; brought in aspirational lifestyles, but one that espoused *parivaar aur parampara* (family and tradition); expensive and stylized sets; and an upmarket look, reminiscent of popular Bollywood films of the 1990s. Nothing like this had been seen before on TV.[1]

Tulsi of *Kyunki* and Parvati of *Kahaani* became the ideal wives and *bahu*s. They, along with the negative women characters, set fashion trends in saris, blouses and jewelry. Even the men got their share of fan following and adulation. When Mihir, Tulsi's husband in *Kyunki,* was killed, women took to the streets in protest. So many e-mails came in, both to the offices of Balaji Telefilms and Star Plus, that their computers crashed.[2] The producers had no choice but to resurrect Mihir's character, this time played by another actor.

After multiple twists and turns of the plot — generation leaps, plastic surgery, amnesiac bouts, rapes, murders, extra-marital affairs, and illegitimate children — *Kahaani* bid the audiences goodbye on 9 October 2008; and *Kyunki* aired its last episode on Star Plus on 6 November 2008; but left the question of its continuing on a rival channel wide open, given the to-be-continued way that the Thursday, 6 November 2008 episode concluded with.[3]

This, however, is no indication that the soap bubble has burst. Newer soaps such as *Saat Phere: Saloni Ka Safar* (henceforth *Saat Phere*)[4] on Zee TV, *Sapna Babul Ka ... Bidaai* (henceforth *Bidaai*),[5] and more recently, *Balika Vadhu* (Child Bride) on Colors are alive and doing well.

Soap, Serial and Series

It is in the storytelling format that we can differentiate between the soap, serial and series, though the difference between these is not always distinct.[6] A serial is spread over many episodes but tells a complete story. It may use the device of a hook, sometimes also called the cliffhanger, to lure audiences back to the next episode. *Ramayan, Mahabharat, Hum Log,* and *Buniyaad* are examples of serials. They differ from soaps in that there is a closure to their narratives.

The series format resembles a soap in offering a set of characters and often, a specific place with which audiences become familiar. Generally one hour long, the narrative structure, however, is such that the main story is resolved in a single episode. The audience is thus offered a satisfactory resolution each time a series is aired. Each telecast is thus complete in itself. Shows such as *CID* (Crime Investigation Department) and *Man Mein Hai Vishwas* (There is Faith in My Heart) are examples of series on Indian television.

In soaps, as Christine Geraghty observes, "stories are never finally resolved and even soaps which cease to be made project themselves into a non-existent future" (1991: 11). Soap stories do not encourage a final resolution, and a lack of narrative closure is key to soaps.

Locating Indian Prime Time Soaps

The genre of the soap opera, as it is understood, has its origins in 1930s America in the form of daytime serials broadcast on radio and sponsored by giant soap manufacturers such as Proctor and Gamble, from whence the name. Cantor and Pingree's work has shown how radio soap operas were the front runner of television soap operas: "the story of the soap opera ... after radio became a 'mass medium' in 1930 is the story of American manufacturers' need to find nation-wide consumers for their products, and of a few individuals' applied creativity and imagination in response to that need" (1983: 34).

Since its beginnings, the study of soap opera came to occupy an important space in discussions of genres of popular culture and in debates about television as a whole. There already exist comprehensive accounts of overviews of work previously carried out in this area (see, for example Creeber 2001; and Geraghty 2005: 308–23). Here, I will note what is of importance for this study. To begin with, Geraghty's observations of the following have resonance: "firstly, defining soap opera [is] one way of separating the characteristics of television drama from drama in theatre or cinema and of assessing distinctions within television drama itself by setting soap opera against other forms such as the series or the serial ... secondly, how soap opera has been studied and defined has been affected the development of television studies itself and continues to shape the way we look at certain kinds of issues. Work on soap opera allowed an entrée for feminist work on television ... finally in debates about the mass media, soap opera continues to brand television as a whole as a mass medium which produces particular kinds of products. That the term 'soap opera' is often used as a metaphor for rather tacky activities in other spheres — politics, sport, business — tells us something about how the pleasures and possibilities of popular television are defined" (2005: 308).

What is important for this study is the moment when in soaps was seen a feminine-oriented narrative in which women were central. Charlotte Brunsdon (1997) theorized that soap operas, far from being without merit, actually required feminine competencies. This analysis was highly influential as was the idea that soap narratives paid attention to the complexities of the private sphere that tended to be overlooked in other genres. Further, "the centrality of women, and in particular the predominance of stories about families, was an important element in work which ought to situate soap operas into the larger category of melodrama" (Geraghty 2005: 316).[7]

Some academics trace the development of soap operas as a woman's genre and in reception studies examined it in connection with women as audiences (see, for example, Ang 1985; Brown 1987; Gledhill 1987; Seiter 1989 and 1999; Geraghty 1991; Nochimson 1992; van Zoonen 1994; Mumford 1995; Dow 1996; Brunsdon 1997; Mankekar 1999; McMillin 2002a; Hobson 2003; Abu-Lughod 2004; Spence 2005; Klein 2006; McCabe and Akass 2006; and Lotz 2006). The soap opera, however, is one of the main texts of television that has broken down the boundaries between high and low culture (Brunsdon 1990: 41). The genre has also evolved as an area of vital importance to the television industry.

This book focuses on prime time soaps on Indian television, what I term "urban family soaps," and analyzes them as an important resource for insights into contemporary social issues and practices. It is also important because it studies the "popular" and "everyday" (and profitable!) while also concentrating on the middle class.

The "urban family soaps" I focus on are *Kyunki*, *Kahaani* and *Kasautii Zindagi Kay* (The Trials of Life, henceforth *Kasautii*). All three are produced by Ekta Kapoor's Balaji Telefilms and aired during prime time on Star Plus. *Kyunki* and *Kahaani* began in the year 2000, and *Kasautii* began in 2001. All three came to a close in 2008. This book also focuses on two other soaps, *Saat Phere* (Zee TV, produced by Sphere Origins) and *Bidaai* (Star Plus, produced by Director's Kut) that were the first to dislodge Balaji Telefilms' supremacy with TRPs (Television Rating Points). All of them are aired four days a week, Monday–Thursday, on prime time slots in the evenings.[8]

A few important points need to be noted at this juncture: *First*, by terming these soaps "urban family soaps," I do not imply that these soaps are watched only in urban areas by the middle class. The penetration of satellite television into smaller towns and rural areas as well as, very importantly, the overseas market, such as the Middle East, Europe, the US and Canada, is increasing. *Second*, it has been noted elsewhere, "while the soap opera audience contains men as well as women, the genre 'soap opera' carries heavily feminine connotations in contemporary culture, as it has been marketed and addressed to women since its early twentieth-century broadcast origins. Scholarship on soap opera viewing generally takes this for granted ..." (Warhol 1998: 2. See also de Lauretis 1987 for her argument on "technologies of gender").[9] In referring to the "feminine", I do not mean that only women watch soaps. Viewership surveys detail that the soaps I am examining are in fact viewed by the family, slotted into what is termed, by the television companies like Star, Sony and Zee, as "family viewing time", from 8 pm–11 pm. During this time, however, the woman has charge of the remote control.[10] This puts prime time soaps under pressure to appeal to an evening family audience and this book investigates how this necessity impacts their themes and structures.

Third, India's middle class, often referred to as important only for their consumer base, numbers more than 400 million now, a substantial body of people to base research on.[11] In this regard, Ekta Kapoor, the young and successful producer of Balaji Telefilms, often referred to as the "Queen of Soaps" in India, said in a recent interview that she makes soaps for the middle and lower middle classes, not for women who live in the posh seafront localities of Mumbai (Ekta Kapoor interview on the *Koffee with Karan* show, Star One, 27 June 2007). This seems to endorse Patricia Uberoi's view, and one that I am in agreement with, that "a finger on the pulse of India's middle and lower middle classes is a finger on the pulse of modern India" (2006: 7). It is important to remember here that these soaps are also watched avidly by families in rural areas.

Fourth, more than one-third of India's billion inhabitants regularly watch Indian television soaps. In India, and in the Indian diaspora worldwide, they are a feature of life — a source of pleasure, discussion and shared identity.[12] This is, in one respect, how the media, in this case television soaps, help in the creation of alternative modernities (see, for instance Martin-Barbero 1988;

Morley and Robins 1995; Sreberny-Mohammadi 1996; Larkin 1997; van der Veer 1998; Munshi 1998 and 2001; Gaonkar 1999; and Uberoi 2006). Satellite television is making huge inroads into the Indian entertainment market and giving Bollywood competition in viewership and profits. In such a scenario, the soaps I focus on are worthy of serious academic inquiry, keeping pace with the growing legitimacy of the study of poplar culture in academia. It is doubly important because there is a scarcity of methodologically sound empirical studies, with an anthropological/sociological perspective, in this area.[13]

This enterprise is, as Patricia Uberoi states, "about engaging seriously — and ... also *joyfully* — with the stuff of everyday life and popular culture in India" (2006: 3, emphasis in original). My focus is on one genre of popular culture — prime time soap operas from 2000–2008 and their production — to try and understand their importance in the business of television. This is a large enough time span to analyze soap form and narratives as they increasingly explore the representation of women, family and family values, and other social issues in contemporary India.

Each genre of popular culture — films, advertising, romance fiction, soaps, etc., — has its own specificity. But genres of popular culture also borrow from, and within, each other "according to the mode and mechanics of production, as well as considerations of distribution and consumption" (Uberoi 2006: 6). Also, different genres attract different methods of analysis, sometimes borrowing from several fields. Indian prime time soap operas have their origins in a variety of sources, yet have their own unique specificities. I will now outline some of the forms that soap production in India draw from as I attempt to develop a theory of genre for Indian prime time soaps.

Melodrama and Realism

It is useful to employ Ien Ang's straightforward definition of melodrama here when she says "there is a name for cultural genres whose main effect is the stirring up of emotions: melodrama" (1985: 61) that draw on "a tragic structure of feeling."[14] Not always highly regarded, melodrama is often regarded as "a sentimental, artificially plotted drama that sacrifices characterization to extravagant incident, makes sensational appeals to the emotions of its audience, and ends on a happy or at least morally assuring note" (Thorburn 1976: 78).

Soap operas, providing continuous narratives, require a stable framework of reference. That is provided by the family being central to soaps. Soaps are also largely considered to be addressed to women and their competencies in the personal sphere. Thus, "in both cases a family history, it is tempting to say family melodrama, seems to provide the ideal format, a long-running saga of emotional entanglements with the home as the stable centre" (Geraghty 1991: 60).

In referring to family melodramas, I am drawing on a wide body of theoretical work on film melodrama which took place in the discipline of film studies in the 1970s.[15] The 1950s Hollywood films do not provide a model for Indian prime time soaps in the twenty-first century, but the theoretical work that led to the genre's re-evaluation offers useful pointers as to how the family is structured in Indian prime time soaps. Of particular importance is Laura Mulvey's reappraisal of Douglas Sirk's films and melodrama. Mulvey argued that melodrama operated as a safety valve for the contradictions created by the family in bourgeois society: "no ideology can pretend to totality ... [the excitement in] fifties melodrama comes from conflict not between enemies, but between people tied by blood and love" (1987: 75).

So it is in Indian soaps, where melodrama is played out by the emphasis on the functioning of characters in situations that push their emotion to extremes. "In real life we are rarely called upon to feel so intensely, and never in such neatly escalating sequences. But the emotions dramatized by these improbable plots are not in themselves unreal ..." says David Thorburn about television melodrama (1976: 83).

We have already noted that the family is central to the soap opera, and thus, "melodrama needs to be read metaphorically to understand its typical focus on the family ..." (Dwyer and Patel 2002: 29).[16] Creative heads in production houses, such as Sandiip Sikcand and Shailja Kejriwal, said that research has shown them that "our audiences in India love the melodrama in daily soaps ... we Indians are people who love being melodramatic ... look at the overly dramatic way in which we react to even regular everyday situations." This bears out how critics point to the melodramatic nature of social existence in Asian countries.[17] Sikcand and Kejriwal added that "our audiences even enjoy a kind of release by crying at situations their favorite characters get into. Part of it is also the relief that their own lives are not beset with all the problems they see in the fictional soap families."[18] This observation underlines Steve Neale's (1986) argument that the pleasure of melodrama, or the pleasure of being made to cry, involves family members and the community. In these pleasures, audiences can find meaning for their own lives.

Melodrama "foregrounds language, as it makes all feelings exterior, with the characters verbalizing their feelings and creating discourses on their emotions" (Dwyer and Patel 2002: 29). In the "world of soap opera," observes Ang, "characters go through all kinds of calamities as though it were the most normal thing in life" (1985: 63).[19] Grandiloquent dialogs are mouthed by soap opera characters. Parvati and Tulsi are, in fact, known for their monologues when holding forth about *sachhai* (truth) and *bhalaai ki jeet buraai par* (the triumph of good over evil). The overt display of emotions is accentuated through the use of the swish pan shot when the camera zooms in and out, mostly three times, accompanied by loud music (see Chapter 3 for details). Very often, storms and rain outwardly manifest a character's internal emotional state. Strong, howling winds, windows flying open, and curtains billowing is a common scene in soaps. There have been innumerable occasions in *Kahaani* when, in such situations, the light from the *diya* (lamp) at the altar has started flickering dangerously, and Parvati has always rushed to safely cradle the flame between her cupped hands. In the episode of 4 November 2008 of *Kyunki*, when Ba died, a copiously weeping Tulsi could not keep the flame of the *diya* lit; and just as she heard Ganga howling out Ba's name in despair, the *diya* went out, symbolizing that the light of their lives, Ba, was no more.

The use of melodrama in soaps often draws censure. Jostein Gripsrud, for instance is critical of *Dynasty* and other soaps because in such dramas, "melodramatic devices are used as pure instruments for 'stirring up emotions'" (1995: 248). I am, however, in agreement with Christine Geraghty when she argues that "it is surely preferable to accept that melodrama has a place in popular culture ... and to ascribe value to certain kinds of acting, visual style, writing style or narrative formulations which can broadly be defined as melodramatic. An academic reassessment of soaps has recognized their importance as a narrative space in which emotion finds expression. But the discussion of how that is done does not as yet allow us to make finer distinctions between different uses of melodramatic conventions" (2003: 32–33). The end of the narrative is always problematic for melodrama. As Laura Mulvey observes, "the strength of the melodramatic form lies in the amount of dust the story raises along the road, a cloud of over-determined irreconcilables which put up a resistance to being neatly settled in the last five minutes." (1978: 54). In principle, soaps go on endlessly.[20] As Ien Ang states, "this lack of an end, this constant deferment of the ultimate 'solution' adds a new dimension to the tragic structure of feeling" (1985: 74). Since delay is the norm, the audience is pushed into a position of wondering "what next?," or what Roland Barthes refers to as "disorder ... what is forever added on without solving anything, without finishing anything" (1976: 76).

The realism in Indian soaps is largely drawn from middle-class sensibilities. Producers of soaps all point out that they tackle "real issues" such as the problems of being a dark-skinned girl in India; and even deal with issues such as marital rape, euthanasia, and a romantic love among the older generation.[21] Chapter 7 will deal with these issues in greater detail.

Influence of *Ramayan* and *Mahabharat* Epics

Prime time soaps in India "represent a continuation of their culture's pre-cinema dramatic forms and stories, transformed by the capitalist economy of scale and the power of the mass media. Where they differ from their Western counterparts is in the dramatic traditions from which they emerged" (Booth 1995: 172).[22] For most Indians, drama traditionally draws from the two epics of the *Ramayan* and *Mahabharat*, the *Puranas* and other Indian legends, as well as a constellation of genres that share an amalgamation of dramatic narrative, song and dance that take different regional manifestations and names. These include the north Indian *Ramlila, nautanki, khyal,* and *svang*; the eastern Indian genre of *jatra*; the *bhavai* of Gujarat; the *burrakatha* of Andhra Pradesh; the *tamasha* and *natyasangeet* of Maharashtra, etc.[23] All were performed by peripatetic professional or semi-professional troupes, usually in outdoor settings; and all emphasized music and dance.

What I am suggesting, in particular for the K soaps of *Kyunki* and *Kahaani*,[24] that first defined the parameters of prime time soaps in India, is that there are many links and connections with the large body of epic stories, in both oral and written form, particularly the *Ramayan* and *Mahabharat*. Asked how she had conceptualized *Kahaani*, Ekta Kapoor is known to have answered that she "wanted to make a modern *Ramayan*. Doesn't every home have a Ram? That's how *Kahaani* ... took shape" (Lalwani 2003b). Indeed, when *Kahaani* aired its last episode on 9 October 2008, the central protagonist, Parvati, explicitly reminded audiences that "*hamari is kahaani ka adhar Ramayan raha hai*" (the basis of our story has been the *Ramayan*). Content borrowed from the *Ramayan* and *Mahabharat* and other pan-Indian tales frequently broadens characterization and interpretation of plots in daily prime time soaps. This is in line with aesthetic theories found in Indian epic narratives. Interpersonal relationships, which are the backbone of soaps, suggests the Indian epic structure.

Sara Mitter writes of the *Mahabharat* that it is "the epic of epics, the longest poetic composition in world literature, eight times the length of the *Iliad* and *Odyssey* combined. It recounts the lifelong rivalry between two clans of warrior princes. Interspersed in the narrative of intrigues and battles is much independent material: legends, instruction manuals for kings, and philosophic discourses, the best known of which is the *Bhagavad Gita*" (1995: 91). Psychologist Sudhir Kakar notes of the *Ramayan* that "the popular epic contains ideal models of familial bonds and social relations to which even a modernized Hindu pays lip service, however much he may privately question or reject them as irrelevant to the tasks of modern life" (1982: 63–64).

Such observations were borne out in my interview with Ravi Chopra of B. R. Films, whose family production house, B. R. Films, first serialized the *Mahabharat* on Doordarshan in 1998–99, and in 2008 started producing and directing the new *Ramayan* on NDTV Imagine. Chopra told me that "no other country in the world has a value system so deeply and permanently entrenched in its mythology as India ... the way these two epics their plots and sub plots, conceptualize and represent their strong characters is unique ... nowhere else, in no other body of literature, do values play such a pivotal role as they do in the *Ramayan* or the *Mahabharat*." Chopra added that "in these epics, characters give their word and lose everything while keeping their promise; they choose exile, hardship and deprivation as an act of obedience to honor an elder's promise. You have valor, family unity, respect and honor for elders, romance, elegance, art ... every facet of life has an exquisite expression in these epics. *Most important to every generation of Indians are the value systems reflected by the relationships of the various characters."* [25]

The epic content in the K soaps usually forms a secondary subtext, except in situations when the central protagonist, for example Tulsi in *Kyunki*, or Parvati in *Kahaani*, are fighting the battle of good over evil and then the epics function as the principal text, for a few episodes at least. *Kahaani* used the technique of a "leap," and Parvati returned in the avatar of Janki Devi in November 2007 to right the wrongs done to the Aggarwal family, with Narayani Devi as her mentor. In this new avatar, direct and constant reference was made to the battle of Kurukshetra in the *Mahabharat*, with Parvati as Arjun asking for advice from Narayani Devi as Lord Krishna, and Narayani Devi advising her that this is a fight between truthfulness and wrongdoing and that, like Arjun, she must carry out her *karma*. Not only were episodes replete with verbiage from the Bhagvad Gita, the visual scenes of Parvati and Narayani Devi were fast cut, and sometimes superimposed by pictures of Arjun and Lord Krishna on the battlefield. Generally speaking, however, the epics act as a secondary subtext.

Epic content also interacts with soaps through a variety of visual frames imposed by the conventions of filming soaps. The standard opening credits of *Kyunki* and *Kahaani* are framed in a distinctly Indian dramatic convention. *Kyunki* has Tulsi pouring water into the *tulsi* (holy basil plant) and *Kahaani* focuses on the deities of Lord Ram, Sita and Lakshman, and Parvati and Om's hands guarding the sacred flame of the *diya* at the altar. These shots immediately lend meaning to the plots, characters and narratives and establish the intertextual connections between the epics and the soaps. Both couples — Mihir–Tulsi in *Kyunki* and Om–Parvati in *Kahani* — are referred to as the *Ram–Sita ki jodi* (the Ram–Sita couple) by the elders in the family. [26] With such references, Ekta Kapoor is obviously relying on the audience's understanding of the intertextual relationship between Ram–Sita of the *Ramayan* and television's Ram–Sita to augment their positive reception of the stories and their characters (cf. Booth 1995: 174).

Filming conventions of soaps, with their reliance on many lengthy frontal close up shots of central iconic characters such as Parvati and Tulsi, call to mind the cultural practice of *darshan* that is most often used in the context of religious worship, where it is a two-way look between the deity and devotee (see Babb 1981; Eck 1985; Lutgendorf 1991; Prasad 1998; Vasudevan 2000; Rajagopal 2001; Brosius 2005; Uberoi 2006; and Rester n.d.). Simply put, *darshan* is an act of seeing and of being seen by a divine image. Just as many visual representations of deities in India are depicted straight on from the front so that both eyes directly face the devotee, so also most close up shots of Parvati and Tulsi film them with faces directly at the screen where the camera lingers for long moments, "arranged by the directors according to iconographic prescription" (Lutgendorf 1991: 327). The end of each day's episode, nine times out of ten, also freezes the picture directly on the faces of Parvati and Tulsi. By means of direct address to the viewer, the television images of Parvati and Tulsi allow themselves to "constitute itself and its viewers as held in a relationship of co-present intimacy" (Ellis 1999: 388). This form of direct address blends well with the dramatic conventions of soaps. Similar to audiences watching the telecast of the epic *Ramayan* on Doordarshan in 1987, audiences of soaps also enter into "visual communion" with soap characters and where emotions are conveyed through close up shots, and intense emotions by repeated zoom shots (Lutgendorf 1995: 230).

The *Ramayan* and *Mahabharat* also involve conflicts within the family. In the *Mahabharat*, initial weaknesses of good characters, the Pandavas, leads to war. In *Kyunki*, it is the inherent weaknesses of Sahil, for instance, that leads to turmoil and dissension in the Virani household when he forsakes his faithful wife, Ganga, for the scheming Trupti; and later in the episodes from June–October 2008, forsakes Ganga due to the machinations of Shiv Singhania. In the *Ramayan*, filial unity between Ram and Lakshman in particular is of the utmost importance. In *Kahaani*, the elder brother Om is referred to as the "*Aggarwal parivaar ka Ram*" (Ram of the Aggarwal family) and his younger brother, Kamal, is constantly referred to as Lakshman. The triangular relationship of Ram–Sita–Lakshman is reflected throughout the history of *Kahaani*'s narratives in the characterizations of Om–Parvati–Kamal.

Plots in epics are often interrupted by subplots, which branch off from the main narrative and then return to it. Narratives are frequently extended in the epics over a wide range of characters and a number of generations. All the soaps under study in this book show generations of each family and numerous characters that take the narrative forward. The special episode on *Kyunki*, aired on the television news program, *Saas, Bahu aur Saazish* (Mother-in-Law, Daughter-in-Law and Intrigue) on 5 November 2008, on Star Plus noted that *Kyunki*, in its eight-year run, had aired close to 1,900 episodes, with 76 actors playing different roles.

Blackburn and Fleuckiger (1989: 4) have observed that Indian epic stories can broadly be classified as martial, sacrificial and romantic. While all three epic types can be found in Bollywood cinema (see Booth 1995), the one that applies to all the soaps examined in this book is the sacrificial category. It has been noted that sacrificial epics emphasize the preservation of social norms or mores. Conflicts are usually emotional and internal, and are resolved either through sacrifice or superhuman endurance and perseverance. Of soap operas, Horace Newcomb says that "most of the problems forming the centre of soap opera plots can be defined best as being in the areas of ... emotional pain" (1974: 137).

Beck (1989: 168) discusses how in sacrificial epics, " ... a heroine is more likely to play the role of protector and guardian of the status quo." Sacrifice and perseverance in sacrificial epics is undertaken by the women: Tulsi, Parvati and even the more romantic Prerna of the K soaps undergo innumerable trials and hardships *parivaar ke bhalaai ke liye* (for the good of the family). Saloni of *Saat Phere* deals with trials and tribulations in order to keep her family intact. The *Bidaai* heroines are also no exception. Sadhana, the beautiful, fair-skinned sister, gets married to the mentally challenged Alekh Rajvansh to prevent her maternal home from being sold. Ragini, the dark-skinned sister, who has suffered all her life due to her complexion and looks, is willing to sacrifice her love for Ranvir Rajvansh and their future together (October and November 2008 episodes) in order that his mother, the sharp-tongued Vasundhara Rajvansh, will stop insulting her family and have her brother, Vineet, released from jail from the trumped up charges of fraud against him.

The importance of the central figure of the woman has also been noted in the sacrificial epics (see, for instance Kinsley 1988). He suggests that the virtuous and long suffering Sita in the *Ramayan*; and the firm, determined, revenge seeking Draupadi in the *Mahabharat* provide the central models of behavior in most Indian narratives.[27] Sita is of course to be found, in one way or another, in all representations of soap heroines. Draupadi is especially found in the characterizations of Parvati and Tulsi.[28] Ekta Kapoor taps into the audience's knowledge of these narrative trends which led almost everyone I interviewed to allude to her soaps as "they are the *Ramayan* and *Mahabharat* retold."[29]

One important point needs to be noted here. Patricia Uberoi, in her superbly lucid and accessible work on popular culture in India, defends it in allowing for "a creative dialogue between the modern mass media and genres of folk culture — something [she believes] to be very important in the context of a society like India — the emphasis being on their common *vernacularism*. ..." Uberoi notes that the three genres of "calendar art, Bollywood cinema, and magazine romance" in her analysis are *not* folk-art forms ... "[but] on the contrary ... are 'popular' by virtue of their wide distribution as products of the modern *mass media*." This holds true for the genre of prime time soaps as well, all of which "are produced and marketed by formidable 'culture industries' for nationwide popular consumption, and intimately connected with and inflected by global flows of technologies, images and meanings" (2006: 4–5, emphasis in original).

Influence of US Prime Time Soaps

When satellite television first came to India, audiences were able to watch prime time US soaps such as *Dallas*, *Dynasty* and *The Bold and the Beautiful*. These had very high production values and were lavish treats visually, similar to Bollywood films of post-liberalization India. They also had ingredients that are common to soaps such as emotions and everyday life, even if the focus was on enormously rich families. They also contained "one of the vital ingredients for success in relation to audiences for soap operas — personal problems and emotional entanglements. They [were] set in exotic locations but they are still about problems, the difference being that they are about problems of extremely rich and privileged people" (Hobson 2003: 13).

US prime time soaps became part of the experience of Indian viewers[30] and influenced Indian soap opera production, particularly in their lavish spectacle and presentation, narrative structure and content. Columnist Shailja Bajpai noted that *"The Bold and the Beautiful* is certainly the inspiration for our daily and weekly soaps. It is basically about a family and there is the *saas–bahu* angle to it. Beyond that, Indian soaps have moved in many directions and Ekta Kapoor's serials are very *Indian and original in treatment and themes"* (2003, emphasis mine).

Influence of Bollywood

Prime time soaps are greatly influenced by popular mainstream Bollywood cinema in several aspects. Kamlesh Pandey, writer of several Bollywood films, and who also writes for television, said of the K soaps that "Ekta grew up watching the films of her father, Jeetendra. She is not analytical, but she is very smart and intuitive. She recycled the opulent family dramas in films and packaged them for TV. Now, most soaps that have followed — and which are successful — spare no expenses in maintaining high production values."[31]

It must be noted here that producer–directors like Karan Johar of Dharma Productions and Aditya Chopra of Yash Raj Films are both born into well known film families. Both are reputed for making films on a lavish scale, with beautiful costumes and jewelry and spectacular sets, often filmed overseas, which has led to the comment that they pander to the NRI (non-resident Indian) audiences. Most of their films — such as *Dilwale Dulhaniya Le Jayenge, Kuch Kuch Hota Hai,* and *Kabhi Khushi Kabhie Gham*[32] — have been spectacular hits; but over the past few years, some films have not worked, due mainly to loose narratives. This led Pandey to comment "Karan Johar and Aditya Chopra's films have not worked in recent times — see *Kabhi Alvida Naa Kehna, Ta Ra Rum Pum* and *Jhoom Barabar Jhoom.* Ekta does a much better job of these kinds of stories than they do."[33]

The big budget films of Chopra and Johar present "endless rounds of parties, beach dances, wedding celebrations, festive occasions, and an all-round feeling of well being" (Kripalani 2001: 45). The films mentioned above "allow their audiences to share in the extravagant lifestyles of the elite classes and cross the threshold of their luxurious homes, whether Western style mansions or traditional *havelis*" (Sharpe 2005: 61). With the exception of *Kabhi Alvida Naa Kehna* (which was not exactly a feel-good film, focusing, as it did, on extramarital affairs), Chopra and Johar's films are usually feel-good films with a glossy and stylish finish.[34]

Similarly, in prime time soaps, the family mansions are huge and lavish and richly appointed, in particular the mansions of the Virani (*Kyunki*), Aggarwal (*Kahaani*), Basu and Bajaj (*Kasautii*) and Rajvansh (*Bidaai*) families. Furniture, décor and upholstery are sourced both from India and overseas.[35] Each soap has a separate set dedicated to it that is immediately recognizable as to which soap it belongs to. Each set costs several millions of rupees. The costumes, accessories and jewelry of the stars are expensive and have spawned a secondary market to copy their costumes, jewelry and even make-up. This lavish display of opulence in soaps is "accepted without guilt, and with no indication ... that affluence might be corrupting or ill-gained ..." (Uberoi 2006: 149). If anything, it was first Ekta Kapoor's soaps that made watching television akin to the experience of watching a lavishly produced Hindi film. Prime time soaps in India look chic and stylish and are made with filmic expertise, which is visually pleasurable for audiences. This is what led Kamlesh Pandey to remark, "*what Ekta does on TV, Karan Johar and Aditya Chopra do in films*. The only difference is the names of the stars ... and TV stars like Sakshi Tanwar, Smriti Irani, Ronit Bose Roy and Hiten Tejwani are very big in their own right today."[36]

It has been noted above how soaps draw from sacrificial epics. Popular Bollywood films have also used the trope of sacrifice for the attainment of a larger good through personal sacrifice, where social duties and bonds of kinship outweigh personal desires (cf. Thomas 1995: 164–66; and Uberoi 2006: 150–52). Thus Parvati and Tulsi, in their avatars of *ma, bhabi, bahu, aur patni* (mother, sister-in-law, daughter-in-law, and wife) are constantly sacrificing their own personal interests — even going to jail, or being thrown out of the family home — *parivaar ke bhalaai ke liye* (for the good of the family). Even the two sisters of *Bidaai* — Sadhana and Ragini — make many personal sacrifices for their family.[37]

In films such as *Hum Aapke Hai ... Koun!* (Who Am I To You!, 1994, dir. Suraj R. Barjatya), the "truth-telling voice in the film" came from a " ... rather unpleasant character, who at every turn in the plot, questions the sanitized ideal of the joint family and of affinal relationships that the film Is seeking to construct and project" (Uberoi 2006: 159–60). As creative heads of soaps told me repeatedly, "we have to show the bad with the good. Without evil, there can be no good."[38] The truth of multiple liaisons and marriages, illegitimate children that are endemic to soap narratives is brought to the fore by the negative women characters. It was Trupti, Sahil's second wife in *Kyunki* who, warning the family against pointing a finger towards her being married while also being married to Sahil, detailed, at length, how many triangular romantic relationships existed in the Virani family (almost an entire episode in November 2007). Similarly, it was Pallavi who pointed out to Parvati that there were many reasons behind their enmity, including Parvati getting her married to Kamal without her knowledge, and later taking her adopted son Krishna away from her. Just like *Mamiji* (maternal uncle's wife) in *Hum Aapke Hai … Koun!*, characters like Trupti and Pallavi give "voice to a range of opinions that strike at the very basis of the joint family as a moral institution. [They] demonstrate … that family members can be selfish, rather than selfless …" (Uberoi 2006: 162).

Bollywood family melodramas of the 1990s also foreground what both producers and audiences see as "Indian culture, values and tradition," or what I term the *parivaar aur parampara* (family and tradition) phenomenon. The emphatic assertion of an "Indian" identity in these films may be considered as a response to a globalizing, "modern" India by rejecting so-called "Western values" and embracing "traditional Indian" values. Television executives emphasized that their research shows that "audiences of soaps longed to see family relationships, not so much as they *are* now, but more as they *should be*." Writer of several soaps herself, Shobhaa De said, "what soaps tap into is something very basic. There is a lot of nostalgia, life as we no longer recognize it. Some of us may be wanting to turn the clock back because large families were our security blanket. It is undoubtedly a highly idealized, romanticized version of family life. But in the hurly-burly of today's world, it satiates our own hunger because we no longer have it."[39] The audience response cell at television channels like Star and Balaji Telefilms archive how viewers write in with praise for self-sacrificing *bahus* like Parvati and Tulsi in upholding the family order. Audiences have also written in with praise for Sadhana and Ragini in *Bidaai* who, despite being young girls, "don't act modern" and know the value of "respecting one's family and elders and respecting tradition."[40]

An important point to note here is Bollywood films post-1990 display a remarkably consistent pattern in producing an Indian identity that is Hindu, wealthy and patriarchal in nature. "The terrain of who gets included in the signifier 'Indian' has shifted significantly to include the wealthy among the diasporic Indian community [who] now find a prominent place within that signifier provided they conform to a particular articulation of Indian identity and traditions. Consequently, certain minorities like Muslims and Christians find themselves excluded ... from this terrain ... this cultural conflation (of Indian *with* Hindu and wealthy), the product of particular socio-political and economic trends (*Hindutva*, global capital flows and regressive gender politics) ... marginalises and often erases the experiences of religious minorities and the poor who do not fit this constructed norm ..." (Malhotra and Alagh 2004: 19; see also Uberoi 2006, especially Chapter 6). A similar trend can be discerned in prime time Indian soaps where all stories are set within a Hindu context, most times, a wealthy one.

Tradition and Modernity

Scholars of colonial and postcolonial cultures have analyzed how modernity is not so much the negation of tradition, but rather the basis for its formation (see, for instance Makdisi 1995; Mani 1998; and Grewal and Kaplan 2001). As Appadurai *et al.* argue, "tradition is a reflective and reflexive discourse. In it, and through it, societies explore the limits of their histories, and replay the points of tension in these histories. It is a metadiscourse, which allows the past to cease to be a "scarce resource" (Appadurai 1981) and allows it to become, to borrow an adjective from ecologists, a renewable resource. Tradition is another zone of contestation ... about temporal boundaries themselves" (1991: 22).

Here, I would like to add that I subscribe to the idea that "tradition, like modernity, is a *process*, including the taken-for-granted background understandings of family and gender, attitudes toward which are difficult to change in any society. These ideas and practices are contested, shifting and uneven, and change in them comes from two directions. From the top ... [and] an even more powerful impetus for change is from below ... [such as] the new media ..." (Eickelman 2008: 146, emphasis in original).

Stuart Hall suggests that cinema is not "a second-order mirror held up to reflect what already exists, but ... that form of representation which is able to constitute us as new kinds of subjects" (1996: 221). All the chapters in this book examine the real and symbolic functioning of the family and central woman protagonist. Often, in the realm of Indian soaps, modernity is negotiated tradition.[41]

Genre

The term "genre" is derived from French, meaning simply type or kind. While drawing on all the forms mentioned above, prime time soaps in India are mainly produced according to certain conventions that belong to the specific genre of producing soaps. Ien Ang observed that "a genre is ... a complex of themes, narrative structures and styles that groups of individual films or television programmes have in common with one another" (Ang 1985: 51; see also Neale 1980; and Geraghty 1991).

Focusing on daytime soaps aimed primarily towards a female audience, Mary Ellen Brown (1987: 4) provided a list of eight generic characteristics of the form.[42] Veena Das, in one of the earliest theorizations of soap operas in the particular context of India, wrote that "soap opera came to India through *Hum Log* (We People), which was modelled on the educational soap operas telecast in Mexico in the middle of the 1970s" (1995: 169). Das further noted six important generic characteristics through which *Hum Log* approximated the soap opera.[43] Thus, genre is, in many ways, a formula and each individual genre is a general application of the conventions of the genre (cf. Ang 1985: 51).

Prime time soap operas in India share some of the generic features of the soaps outlined in Brown and Das' works. But they have certain important differences that have to do with the particular social, economic and cultural context in which they are produced and telecast. Indian prime time soaps, broadcast from the year 2000 onwards, share the following generic features:

1) Open-ended narratives told in serial/episodic form which resists narrative closure
2) Multiple characters, plots, and sub-plots
3) Use of time at a dual level — one, which parallels actual time and implies that soap characters' lives go on whether we watch or not; and two, when the narrative takes a generational leap to introduce new characters and new story lines
4) Emphasis on dialog and attempt at resolution
5) Mixing of genres of melodrama, myth, realism and entertainment
6) Hook, Recap and Precap
7) Male characters whose actions move the narrative forward
8) Women as the central protagonists
9) The family home as the main setting for the show

Each chapter in this book deals with these genres in greater detail so as to be able to outline a theory of genre for Indian prime time soaps.

The importance of generic conventions cannot be over emphasized. They are of vital significance " ... because they are a way of understanding and constructing [the] triangular relationship between producer, text and audience" (Fiske 1987: 110). Thus, in her important work on genre, Jane Feuer (1992:145) summarizes three approaches to genre in television which she summarizes under three labels — aesthetic, ideological and ritual. The aesthetic approach confines itself to textual characteristics (cf. Geraghty 1991, chapter 2; and Hobson 2003, chapters 2 and 3). The ideological approach explains how genres provide audiences to advertisers and structure the dominant ideology into their codes and conventions. The ritual approach "sees genre as an exchange between industry and audience, an exchange through which a culture speaks to itself" (ibid.). Shared cultural concerns are thus negotiated, locating genres firmly within their socio-cultural context (cf. Newcomb and Hirsch 1983; see also Brown 1987; and Das 1995).

Brown and Das both importantly note that the generic characteristics of soaps differ within the different cultural and social contexts of different countries. Thus, Brown notes that "these characteristics vary ... from country to country, but it is largely the programmed time slot, and therefore its intended audience, which determines its production conventions and content" (1987: 4). Das makes a similar point when she writes: "not only are important variations in theme and character in soap operas produced in different countries in accordance with local cultures, but also the same soap opera may be very differently received in different parts of the world ... at the level of both production and consumption of meaning, the anthropological approach is to reinstate the importance of the integrity of local moral worlds" (1995: 170–71).

Thus, prime time soap opera in India must be viewed and analyzed within a context of other media texts, programs and discourses in the changing economic, political, social and cultural conditions in India during which they are being produced and aired. The soap will only make sense through its network of connections with other cultural forms and within the practices of everyday life (cf. Silverstone 1989; Lozano 1992; and Lozano and Singhal 1993). Chapters 2, 3, and 4 will examine these generic characteristics, codes and conventions in detail.

One of the pitfalls of working on a genre, as Christine Geraghty points out, is "the search for the perfect example. Genre theory then becomes a question of elimination and exclusion ... it is essential to have a wide definition of soap opera, to see soaps as programmes in which similar issues are variously played out and which offer, within the same broad area, a spectrum of different styles and occupations" (1991: 5). Two of the K soaps I examine are overtly based on the epic *Ramayan*, while the third is more a romance. Two others have at the center of the narrative the debate on fair and dark skin in India, particularly for women. Thus, it is crucial to remember that "what is at stake is not the pure examples of a particular genre but a range of programmes which, when together, represent a whole which can never be entirely consumed of played out" (ibid.)

Prime time soaps also mix different genres and work with elements of melodrama, myth, realism, and entertainment (cf. Fiske 1987; and Geraghty 1991). This study will look at the different ways in which Indian soaps mix their generic factors, and thus approach major themes differently. This mélange of attributes have at time provoked criticism, but they are what mark the *Indian* specificity of prime time soap operas.[44]

Importance of this Study

The study of soap operas on television gained currency in Western academia from the 1980s onwards, due in large measure to growing academic legitimacy of the study of the media texts of popular culture (such as television soaps), and feminist research on the media that helped sensitize gender issues while viewing media texts as a site of struggle over meanings. Historically, soaps have been patronized and criticized in the West, going so far as to be labeled "chewing gum for the eyes" (Kilborn 1992: 9). In India, they have faced criticism from scholars, journalists and activists who have rather continuously labeled them, in both print and televisual media, as "regressive" in their portrayal of women, particularly those from the Balaji bouquet. Landmark studies on various aspects of television in the Western, and other contexts, include, among others, Brunsdon (1981 and 2000); Morley (1988); Hobson (1982); Modleski (1982); Geraghty (1991); Ang (1991 and 1996); Gillespie (1995); Armbrust (1996); Abu-Lughod (2004); and Chua and Iwabuchi (2008).

In the Indian context however, studies of television came later. This is, of course, tied to the fact of India's opening her doors to economic liberalization only from 1991 onwards and the consequent transformation the Indian mediascape. Research on Indian television has focused on the earlier years of satellite broadcasting in India, and dealt mainly with religious and nationalist themes such as the televising of the epics *Ramayan* and *Mahabharat*, and serials such as *Hum Log* and *Buniyaad* (see, for instance Das 1995; Gupta 1998; Mankekar 1999; Brosius and Butcher 1999; Rajagopal 2001; Butcher 2003, etc.).[45]

This is the first book that addresses the issues I am analyzing. *First*, soaps are obviously popular, the proof being in high TRPs. Still, no detailed research has been undertaken so far on the soaps analyzed here. Only passing reference has been made to these long running prime time soaps (see, for instance Gokulsing 2004, chapter 4). *Second*, research on television in India has largely focused on state-sponsored programs (for example Mankekar 1999; and Rajagopal 2001). By contrast, the soaps I focus on are not state-sponsored, but are produced by private production houses that are often run like family businesses. Chapter 2 sets out a history of the production houses that produce these soaps and describes how they are different from the West. It also details the relationship between production houses and the television industry, and the importance of viewership ratings. The discussion is contextualized in a socio-economic context in India in which these soaps were conceptualized and telecast.

Third, the soaps I focus on are broadcast during prime time, i.e. from 8 pm–11 pm IST (Indian Standard Time), from Monday–Thursday. They are different from daytime soaps in that they need to appeal to a larger, more varied audience than the daytime soaps, which are said to cater traditionally to women audiences. Prime time programming requires that their structure, narrative, aesthetics, etc. are critical issues in their long running success. Questions such as will Om, who "died" 20 years ago, but who has been back since end-September 2007 in the avatar of Rishabh Rai Choudhuri (episodes of *Kahaani* from 20 September 2007 onwards); how old is Ba (*Kyunki*); should Prerna marry Anurag when her presumed dead husband, Mr Bajaj, returned with a loss of memory on *Kasautii* (episodes from 24 September 2007 onwards); will Ragini and Ranvir ever get married (episodes of *Bidaai*, October 2008 onwards) are, like it or not, questions which are part of the public domain, highlighting the capacity of these urban family soaps to implicate audiences in their plots and narrative structure. Chapter 3 deals with these issues in greater detail.

Fourth, the capacity of prime time soaps to engage their audiences in the narrative and their ability to open up a space for discussion is another feature that the book will address. All the soaps I focus on amply demonstrate this capacity to engage the audience to an extent that they start interpreting their real life experiences with reel life situations. The book, in particular Chapter 4, will also examine how, despite a high level of engagement, audiences also distance themselves from soap narratives.

Fifth, this book will analyze how soap women are conceptualized (Chapter 5) and how their roles are a source of pleasure to the intended audiences of the programs. In so doing, I do not just focus on representations of women, but also argue that their central role, whether positive or negative, needs to be studied within the framework of the theme of the whole narrative (Chapter 4) and the formal conventions that structure soap opera production. As Geraghty says, "in looking at the role of women in soap operas … we need to examine the programmes' narrative organization and aesthetic characteristics since it is the combination of certain thematic preoccupations with a particular kind of engagement with the viewer that forms the basis of the soap's appeal" (1991: 6).

Sixth, this book (Chapters 5 and 6) will examine the way in which prime time soaps extend the boundaries of the genre by making the women the central protagonists, but making the male characters, and their actions, the engines that drive the narrative forward. Chapter 7 takes up in detail the portrayal of soap heroines, not merely essaying the principal roles, as in soaps worldwide, but also as strong women. It locates soaps as sites of contestation and analyzes how prime time soaps relate, in complex and refined ways, with epics and Indian folk genres, particularly women's genres, including gossip and oral culture.

Seventh, this book examines how soaps address the theme of "Indian-ness" and a pride in "being Indian" (Chapters 2 and 7), [46] but also foreground issues such as marital rape, old age romance, the obsession with having a fair-skinned daughter, etc. that have their origins in the personal sphere of *ghar* and *parivaar* (home and family), but which spill over into the public domain.

A Personal Note

A few words are necessary at this juncture to clarify my research and writing on this topic. I truly enjoy watching soap operas and Bollywood films. As a self-respecting academic, I reckon I am supposed to shy away from admitting this, but for reasons I hope this book will make clear, I am stating this at the outset. I am one of those people who have devotedly followed most primetime soaps from 2000 onwards when Indian television programs became an entertaining pastime in India, but who have always remained particularly loyal to the Balaji bouquet of *Kyunki, Kahaani* and *Kasautii* and, in recent times, *Saat Phere* and *Bidaai*.

Since 1985, when I first left India, I have lived and worked in five different countries. This histoire mouvementé is fairly common among academics. The important thing however is that since the year 2000, one set of characters have always been there with me, particularly those playing the lead roles in the soaps I speak about in my book. Indeed, meeting them — in person on fieldwork in 2007 and 2008 — was akin to stepping into a soap opera myself! When at home in New Delhi, I have at times watched these soaps in my parents' mode of disbelief against their (sometimes) implausible narratives, my sister's and friends' amusement, yet incisive observations, whenever I have forced them to watch the soaps with me, or talked with them about it. But mostly, I have delighted in the soaps' lavish representations, their drama and narrative strategies. It comes as little surprise, then, that I should research and write in this area.

At the same time, I am aware that I am putting myself "out there" for (perhaps) a flurry of criticism from both scholars and activists on a few counts. Most studies on television, whatever the disciplinary approach, tend to privilege the act of consumption, i.e. how audiences make meaning of media texts (see, for example Ang 1985; Morley 1988; Mankekar 1999; McMillin 2002; Abu-Lughod 2004, etc.).[47] Indeed, I have just detailed above my own enjoyment of soaps. But to those studying the anthropology of media, and the claim that "media anthropology ... comprises of ethnographically informed, historically grounded, and context-sensitive analyses of the ways in which people use and make sense of media technologies" (Askew and Wilk 2002: 3), I have the following question: does anthropology only enter at the level of audiences producing meaning? Surely, if meaning is actively invented during reception, it is also actively invented during production? Jostein Gripsrud (1995: 14) astutely observes "... it is logically impossible to arrive at an understanding of historically produced interpretations without performing an interpretation of the texts in question"; and further, "[while] ... theoretically acknowledging the importance of reception studies, [one must argue] in favor of emphasizing the powerful role of production in the process of media communication" (1995: 18). Very importantly as well, it would behoove us to remember that producers of media texts, apart from keeping the obvious profit motive in mind, also have to take into account political, economic, social and cultural conditions. If they did not, no matter the ideology of profit, their product would not work and be off the air, much less leave space for ethnographic studies of audiences making meaning.

This emphasis on reception and active audiences has, in turn, made the other side of producers and production forgotten and neglected.[48] Indeed, media producers have now become the anthropological "Other" for many studies on the media. As

Christine Geraghty observes, "it seems important that in the urge to speak to 'real viewers' the pendulum should not swing so much the other way that textual work which is sensitive to the positions offered to the audience is no longer feasible. It seems important that the patina of authenticity that glows over the statements produced by audience research does not mean that this method becomes the only way in which the products of popular culture can be discussed" (1991: 7). By focusing on the production side, therefore, my hope is that this book will help correct some of this skewed balance.

My research and writing has always been interdisciplinary, drawing from anthropology, history, gender studies, media and communication studies, cultural studies, feminist research, and sociology. My arguments will continue to draw on interdisciplinary strands.

My analysis of prime time soaps will show how the chief women protagonists are represented not only as strong, but indeed, at times superhuman in their strength and fortitude. What might fell others in real life only seems to give greater strength and forti-tude in reel life as they overcome crisis after crisis. This comes in face of the sustained criticism, from many scholars and activists, that the urban family soaps face for their so-called "regressive" portrayal of women. My argument, as the book will demonstrate, is more to the contrary.

I am also aware that writing about these soaps is risky in that their plots and narratives are constantly evolving. In the course of researching, fieldwork and writing, generational leaps have occurred, "dead" heroes have returned though remain to be reunited with the heroines, some soaps have concluded, and we will no doubt see further twists and turns by the time this book goes to press. It is therefore not possible for readers to check back on episodes that I refer to unless they, like me, regularly watch these soaps. I have added in brief synopses, at the end, of the soaps under study in this book. My hope is that this book will fill a critical space in the study of soap operas in India and con-tribute to the ongoing research in the field.

Although I mention my own soap opera viewing, I hasten to add that the book will not be about my viewing habits. Nonetheless, I do not know how to write about prime time soaps without my own enjoyable experience that has alleviated loneliness on many evenings away from home. While admittedly a follower, and fan, of the particular soaps this book deals with, I will maintain an academic rigor throughout my analysis.

The soap opera is a form that rouses strong, contradictory feelings — loved by its fans and scoffed at by its critics. Its history can be considered as vignettes of the social lives of our times. For television channels, the soap opera is their flagship program and even works as a brand for the channel. As Dorothy Hobson says, "for broadcasters, the soap opera is the perfect television form: it achieves and retains audiences, gains press coverage, creates controversy, brings in advertising revenue, supports a public service ethos and generates discussion, dissection, analysis and astonishment at its survival and evolution ... it is its role within the broadcasting industry and its relationship to other broadcasting forms which accounts for its unique relationship between its producers and its audiences" (2003: xii).

The cultural product that is prime time soaps in India from the year 2000 onwards have borrowed from several sources and have brought its own conventions and traditions of performance to bear on the form, giving it a distinctly *Indian* identity. The story of prime time soaps in India, that are the flagship programs of TV channels, is a fascinating one. It is as compelling as the narratives in the soaps that continue to bring back audiences day after day and keep them engaged for years on end. This genre has retained its top position in viewership ratings. Prime time soaps have made the small screen a big medium in reaching out to people. How that has been achieved will be the subject of the rest of this book.

Notes

1. See also Raaj (2008).
2. Interviews with Shobha Kapoor, Shailja Kejriwal and Yash Khanna (2007 and 2008). This was also reported in the *Kyunki* special episode *on Saas, Bahu aur Saazish* (Mother-in-Law, Daughter-in-Law and Intrigue) program on Star News, 5 November 2008.
3. Mandvi Sharma, writing in the *Times of India*, 6 November 2008, states: "industry sources, say that Balaji has been in talks with 9X to air Kyunki ... because its other shows on the channel have been doing well. However, when contacted, 9X representatives refused to respond to the speculation. Balaji also remains mum on the topic of

shifting channels." The website www.tellychakkar.com first reported similar news via the grapevine on 25 October 2008 (http://www.tellychakkar.com/y2k8/oct/25oct/grapevine_kyunki.php).

4. *Saat Phere*, literally seven rounds, refers to the seven circles taken by a Hindu bride and groom around the scared matrimonial fire. With every round, they make a vow to each other.

5. *Bidaai* refers to the moment of farewell and departure when, after the wedding ceremony, the new bride leaves her paternal home (*babul ka ghar*) to go to her new home, her in-laws' house.

6. See Geraghty (1991), especially pp. 10–12, for a distinction between soaps, serials and series. Most people in India, when referring to soap operas, term them "serials."

7. See also Modleski (1984); Ang (1985); Gledhill (1987); Geraghty (1991); Seiter *et al.* (1991); Brown (1994); Mumford (1995); Brunsdon (1997 and 2000); Mankekar (1999); Abu-Lughod (2002); and McMillin (2002).

8. *Bidaai*, one of the prime time soaps under study in this book, added a fifth day. As of 23 January 2009, *Bidaai* started airing on Star Plus from Mondays–Fridays in the prime time band of 9 pm– 9:30 pm. Yash Khanna, corporate communications head, Star TV, told me that from February 2009 onwards, soaps run for five days a week, from Monday–Friday, and prime time has been extended to 7 pm–11 pm in the evening (personal communication, February 2009).

9. Teresa de Lauretis argues that gender is "the product of various social technologies, such as cinema, and of institutionalized discourses, epistemologies, and critical practices, as well as practices of daily life and not a property of bodies of something originally existent in human beings" (1987: 2–3). See also Raheja and Gold (1996) for women's performative traditions in Uttar Pradesh and Rajasthan; and Appadurai *et al.* (1991).

10. Interviews with executives of Star TV, Sony TV and Zee TV (2007 and 2008).

11. For research on India's middle class, always a challenging concept, see Munshi (1998 and 2008). See also Fernandes (2000); Deshpande (2003); and Ganguly-Scrase and Scrase (2009).

12. For a discussion of the articulation of Indian identity in a globalizing world see, for example Appadurai (1996, especially chapter 1); Mehta (2006); Manuel (1998); Dusenbery (1997); Grewal (1994); Rai (1995); Shukla (1997); Visweswaran (1997); Jayaram *et al.* (2004); Vertovec (2000); Ghosh (1989); Jain (1997); and Brown (2007).

13. A notable exception is Patricia Uberoi, who has always argued for the importance of studying popular culture in the Indian context, especially in the face of resistance to studying popular media texts as a serious academic endeavor in Indian academia. See also Dwyer and

Pinney (2000); and Das (1995). Works such as Purnima Mankekar's monumental *Screening Culture, Viewing Politics: An Ethnography of Television, Womanhood and Nation in Postcolonial India* (1996) deals with women's engagement with state-sponsored (Doordarshan) entertainment serials in India that are different from the ones examined in my work. My research deals with far more recent texts, i.e. television soaps produced by the privately owned Balaji Telefilms, Sphere Origins and Director's Kut (not Doordarshan) that started being screened eight years ago, as compared to the ones examined in Mankekar's research, which deal with those screened in the late 1980s and early 1990s. No work on the aspects I am studying with an anthropological perspective has been carried out in the Indian context so far (to the best of my knowledge).

14. Ien Ang (1985, particularly pp. 61–68) offers an excellent analysis of the functions of melodrama.

15. A classic work on melodrama is Peter Brooks' *The Melodramatic Imagination: Balzac, Henry James, Melodrama and the Mode of Excess* (1976). Thomas Elsaesser (1987) made one of the first influential attempts to track its course through its multiple traditions in literature and drama to Hollywood drama in the 1950s. Elsaesser's analysis of finding its origins in oral narrative and folk songs, medieval morality plays, romantic drama, sentimental novels, and historical epics can be said to echo a similar trajectory in the Indian context. What is important to note for the purposes of this study from Elsaesser's analysis is how, under certain historical conditions and the capacity to deploy mise-en-scène and narrative cleverly, melodrama can be mobilized for social criticism. See also Nowell-Smith (1987); Halliday (1971); Sirk and Halliday (1972); Willeman (1972/73 and 19778/79); Gledhill (1987); Mercer and Shingler (2004); Neale (1986); and Newcomb (1974).

16. Rachel Dwyer and Divia Patel's work deals with Hindi films, but many of the characteristics present in mainstream popular cinema are also present in prime time daily soaps. The influence of Bollywood on soaps is discussed later in this chapter.

17. Here we see an example of television executives extending melodrama as a metaphor to better analyze social processes. Wimal Dissanayake (1993) provides a number of useful essays elaborating this point.

18. Interviews with Sandiip Sikcand and Shalija Kejriwal (August 2007).

19. To the constant critique of soap heroines being "regressive," my sister Poroma told me that "they are not weak or regressive. They go from one life-changing crisis to another. Even one such crisis might fell an ordinary person, but not them. If anything, they are super human!"

20. When soap operas are terminated, like the three longest running K soaps of Balaji Telefilms, it is not because the narrative has ended, but mostly because of other outside factors such as organizational and commercial reasons, a change of scene at the television channel that airs the soaps with the departure of creative heads and program directors, falling TRPs, etc. This has led to the narratives of the three K soaps turned off, without much warning, sometimes in a rushed and arbitrary manner. This is unsatisfactory for their viewers (including myself).

21. Interviews with Sunjoy Waddhwa, Rajan Shahi and Shobha Kapoor (2007 and 2008).

22. Gregory D. Booth's lucid and clearly argued article deals with the influence of the epics and other folklore traditions on popular Bollywood cinema. The same argument can be extended to cover prime time soaps in India as well, particularly the K soaps.

23. For a fuller discussion of definitions and folklore traditions see, for example Claus *et al.* (2003). See also Hogan (2008) for an analysis of how Hindi films draw on a wide range of South Asian cultural traditions.

24. The reason for my emphasis on these two soaps in particular is that, liked or disliked, there is no denying that these redefined prime time viewing of entertainment in India and maintained the highest TRPs (Television Rating Points) for close to eight years running.

25. Interview with Ravi Chopra (August 2007, emphasis mine).

26. Further references to the elision of the sacred and secular, in particular for the K soaps, will be made throughout the book.

27. See Mankekar (1999, especially chapter 5) for a discussion on Draupadi's rage.

28. These points are further elaborated upon throughout the book.

29. Interviews with Shailja Kejriwal, Shobha Kapoor, Nivedita Basu, Sandiip Sikcand, Yash Khanna, Kamlesh Pandey, Smriti Z. Irani, Sakshi Tanwar, Achint Kaur, Ronit Bose Roy, Rama Bijapurkar, L. V. Krishnan, and Shobhaa De (2007 and 2008).

30. To the inevitable question that will be raised here as to only English-speaking viewers watching US soaps, I would like to add that the people working in my parents' home in Delhi, who spoke no English, avidly watched them. They were their daily doses of "*natak*" (drama), as they referred to the US soaps. They now make sure to watch the Hindi "*natak*s," and are happy to discuss them at length with me. It is important to note here that even in 2008, "despite positive media coverage and the large number of prints [of Hollywood films] being released, Hollywood still accounts for a slender five per cent of the cinema pie in India. Despite Hollywood's keenness to integrate with Indian culture and its valiant attempt to dub in every regional

language, the domestic taste still prefers the local flavor" (Iyer 2008). The same holds true for the television landscape in India. People prefer to watch Hindi or regional language programs (interview with L. V. Krishnan, CEO, TAM India Ltd, August 2008).

31. Interview with Kamlesh Pandey (August 2007).

32. *Dilwale Dulhaniya Le Jayenge*, also known as DDLJ (The Brave Hearted Will Take the Bride, 1995, dir. Aditya Chopra), *Kuch Kuch Hota Hai*, also known as KKHH (A Little Something Happens, 1998, dir. Karan Johar), and *Kabhi Khushi Kabhie Gham*, also known as K3G (Happiness At Times, Sorrow At Times, 2001, dir. Karan Johar). Patricia Uberoi has examined films like DDLJ and *Hum Aapke Hain Kaun*, also known as HAHK (Who Am I To You, 1994, dir. Suraj R. Barjatya) from various aspects, including that of conspicuous consumption and lavish display of wealth as well as the disapora's negotiation of an "Indian" identity. See Uberoi (2006, especially Chapters 5 and 6). See also Malhotra and Alagh (2004).

33. *Kabhi Alvida Naa Kehna*, also known as KANK (Never Say Goodbye, 2006, dir. Karan Johar), *Ta Ra Rum Pum* (2007, dir. Siddharth Anand), *Jhoom Barabar Jhoom* (Dance, Baby Dance, 2007, dir. Shaad Ali). Kamlesh Pandey called *KANK* "a bad episode of an Ekta soap on 70 mm" (interview with Kamlesh Pandey, August 2007).

34. Anupama Chopra (1997) stresses the point of the glossy finish in 1990s Bollywood films. See also Anupama Chopra and Nandita Chowdhury (1999), where they identify Aditya Chopra and Karan Johar as being part of the Bollywood Gen-Next brigade: "Raised on Hollywood, but firmly grounded in Bollywood, the new kids on the block — directors, writers, musicians, choreographers, art directors, editors, stylists, distributors, publicists — are serving up a clever cocktail of *desi* values wrapped in Yankee slickness." (The term *desi* is derived from *des/desh*, meaning one's own country.)

35. Interview with Shobha Kapoor (August 2007). See also chapter 3 on key elements of production.

36. Interview with Kamlesh Pandey (August 2007, emphasis mine). Sakshi Tanwar plays the role of Parvati in *Kahaani*; Smriti Z. Irani plays the role of Tulsi in *Kyunki*; Ronit Bose Roy plays the roles of Mr Bajaj in *Kasautii* and Mihir Virani in *Kyunki*; Hiten Tejwani plays the role of Karan Virani in *Kyunki*, and also played the role of Anurag Basu when he "came back from the dead" in *Kasautii*.

37. Greater details on the issue of sacrifice can be found throughout the book.

38. Interviews with Sandiip Sikcand and Shailja Kejriwal (August 2007).

39. Interview with Shobhaa De (August 2008). De was author of the soaps *Swabhiman* (Self-respect) that first aired in 1995 on Doordarshan, and later on Star Plus. She also wrote *Kittie Party* that was telecast

on Zee TV; and *Sarrkkar: Rishton Ki Ankahi Kahani* (Sarkar/Chief: The Untold Stories of Relationships) that was telecast in 2005 on Zee TV.
40. Archives of audience response letters at Star TV, Balaji Telefilms and Director's Kut. This material is also gleaned from interviews with Sandiip Sikcand, Shailja Kejriwal, Yash Khanna, Nivedita Basu, and Rajan Shahi (2007 and 2008). For an excellent discussion on how all the ceremonies shown in *HAHK* are presented in their non-Sanskritic idioms, see Uberoi (2006, especially pp. 153–54).
41. I am grateful to Rama Bijapurkar for making this observation (August 2008).
42. These are "serial form which resists narrative closure; multiple characters and plots; use of time which parallels actual time and implies that the action continues to take place whether we watch it or not; abrupt segmentation between parts; emphasis on dialog; problem solving and intimate conversation; male characters who are 'sensitive men;' female characters who are often professional and otherwise powerful outside the home; the home, or some other place which functions as a home, as the setting for the show."
43. They are as follows: "1) The serial form is considered to be the genre most suited to telecasting. The continuity of the story more than a year allowed a continuous interaction between viewers and the projected images. 2) The setting was clearly domestic with all the episodes revealing themselves in interior spaces. 3) The episodes moved through conversation rather than action. 4) The action was located in the present. 5) The soap opera, as a genre, is dependent not on individual actors but on the entire community of actors and actresses, both for aesthetic effect and popular appeal. *Hum Log* demonstrated the typical features of soap opera in that character, actor, and interaction had the stiff, unchanging quality of a cast-iron cartoon. 6) In the conclusion of each episode, the educational content was conveyed by the foregrounding of a celebrity as celebrity" (see Das 1995: 173–74).
44. Though not directly related, an article which provokes thought is A. K. Ramanujan's "Is There an Indian Way of Thinking?: An Informal Essay" in McKim Marriott (ed.), *India Through Hindu Categories*, 1990, New Delhi: Sage Publications, pp. 41–58. See also Philip Lutgendorf (2006).
45. Works on the Indian media, expanding the scope from just television, will include a longer list of authors. To mention just a few, Uberoi (2006); Dwyer (2006); Kaur and Sinha (2005); Mishra (2002); Dudrah (2006); Dudrah and Desai (2008); Jeffrey (2000); Munshi (1997, 1998, 2001, 2004, and 2008); Mazzarella (2003); Brosius and Butcher (1999); Brosius (2005); and Nigam (2007). Recent publications

include Derne (2008); Thapan (2009); Pauwels (2008); and Gokulsing and Dissanayake (2009).

46. Witness the celebrations when India won the Twenty20 World Cup, defeating Pakistan in the final game in Johannesburg on 24 September 2007. Shah Rukh Khan, the Bollywood superstar of the hit *Chak De! India* (Let's Go! India/Come on! India) was at hand, with son Aryan, to personally congratulate Team India which has since then been lauded for their wonderful achievement. *Chak De! India* (Yashraj Films, 2007, dir. Shimit Amin) achieved cult-like status in India. Based loosely on the life of Indian hockey player Mir Ranjan Negi, who had been disgraced for his alleged links with Pakistan, *Chak De! India* restored Negi's credibility, gone on to (re)popularize Indian hockey, and reiterated a pride in being Indian. *Chak De! India* seems to be the new national mantra for anything that has to be achieved, especially for sporting teams.

47. A noteworthy exception is Dale F. Eickelman and Jon Anderson's *New Media in the Muslim World: The Emerging Public Sphere* (1999) that deliberately stepped back from the consumption approach to looking at the subtle interplay between production, censorship and the changing art of the possible.

48. Patricia Uberoi also raises a similar point in her *Freedom and Destiny: Gender, Family and Popular Culture in India* (2006: 8), when she writes that "whether by contingency or disciplinary persuasion, most analysts are able to concentrate on only a single facet of the communicative triangle." See also Note 28, p. 40. Ferdinand de Saussure argued that a communicative act comprises three elements of the speaker, the utterance and the listener (de Saussure 1916). For analyses of semiotics, see Culler (1976) and Leech (1974). For studies that address all three dimensions of the communicative process, see Radway (1987) and Hobson (2003). Stuart Hall and others argued, as early as the 1970s, for the politics of cultural production in their agenda for Cultural Studies, as formulated at the Birmingham Centre for Contemporary Cultural Studies papers (see Hall *et al.* 1980). Some studies that have focused on the production side include Sullivan (1993); Armbrust (1996); and Ganti (1999 and 2004). Some correction to this trend of over emphasis on the reception side has been taking place in recent years. See, for instance Ginsburg *et al.* (2002), where the authors, while introducing some of the essays in the volume, write about " … the impossibility of separating ideas of the audience from the process of production" (2002: 17). See also Ang (1991 and 1996); and Dornfeld (1998).

2

Milieu of Production

Much has been written in tracking India's mediascape from the state-run channel Doordarshan to a dizzying array of channels once the airwaves were opened up to private broadcasting (see, for example Ninan 1995; Dyal 1992a and 1992b; Melkote *et al.* 1998; Brosius and Butcher 1999; Butcher 2003; and Mehta 2008). Rather than detailing once again the history of television in India, an appendix provides the major events in the Indian televisual landscape since the airwaves were opened up in the 1990s to satellite broadcasting. Suffice it to say at this juncture that "a unique confluence of technological, political and economic factors in the 1990s drove the transformative process and fast-forwarded Indian television through and beyond the process of development that had taken nearly five decades to mature in developed western economies … so much so that we are now seeing the beginning of a gradual re-ordering of global media flow, with India transformed from a mere receiver to a major supplier. A great deal of evidence is now emerging to show that the rise of India … as [an] economic power has been accompanied by its parallel rise as a new global 'media capital' — the centre of production where information flows originate and are circulated around the world" (Mehta 2008: 59–60).

Data gathered from the offices of TAM (Television Audience Measurement) Media Research Pvt Ltd shows that "prior to the year 2000, there were 116 television channels in India. This number has risen to 427 channels in the first quarter of 2008" (August 2008). How fast the television industry is growing in India is testified to by the fact that by the end of 2008, these numbers had grown! It was reported on 24 December 2008 that "a total of 357 private television channels have been uplinked up to the end of 2008, including as many as 197 news channels. [The] year-end review of the Information and Broadcasting Ministry [states that] the country at present has a total of 450 channels including 417 private channels and 33 Doordarshan and Parliamentary channels. Of the uplinked channels, a total of 160 are non-news and current affairs channels. A total of 60 channels including 13 news channels have been given permission to downlink into the country, the remaining being non-news and current affairs channel" (www.indiantelevision.com headlines).

The number of cable and satellite (C&S) homes in India has increased by 26 per cent to 66.54 million, according to the latest Indian Readership Survey (IRS) report. Urban India has 39.21 million C&S homes; the number is growing by 20.67 per cent. There are 27.33 million C&S homes in rural India, an increase of 25.26 per cent from the prior round of survey by IRS.

C&S penetration is highest in the state of Tamil Nadu (10.33 million), followed by Andhra Pradesh (9.84 million), Maharashtra (8.41 million) and West Bengal (4.6 million). Delhi and the surrounding urban environs reaches 3.22 million households. C&S penetration is lowest in Jammu Kashmir (131,000 homes).

The total number of TV homes (one TV set) in India has grown from 90.69 million to 100.38 million. In urban areas, the number of TV homes has increased to 48.98 million (from 45.04 million), while in the rural areas it has touched 51.39 million (from 45.65 million). The number of color TV sets has increased from 55.40 million to 73.98 million (details from www.indiantelevision. com, 8 November 2008).

A Reuters India article dated 13 November 2008 reports that "annual revenue for television in India, which is seeing an ex-plosion of new channel launches, is forecast to more than double to $11.6 billion by 2012, according to research firm Media Partners Asia."

The television industry in India today is an intensely com-petitive market, where those channels or shows that do not make the cut have a short shelf life. It is audiences who have benefited the most from this dazzling array of channels and variety of programs, and are now spoilt for choice. Within this, *it is prime time soap operas that are the flagship programs for general entertainment channels (GECs) and a measure of their success.*

This chapter will detail the importance of soap operas in prime time programming for television channels, television rating points (TRPs), a history of the production houses that produce the con-tent for the soaps discussed in this book, their similarities, and differences with production in the West. The chapter will conclude

The number of channels growing exponentially over years

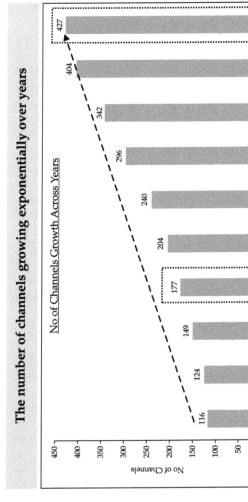

No of Channels Growth Across Years

Pre 2000	Yr 2000	Yr 2001	Yr 2002	Yr 2003	Yr 2004	Yr 2005	Yr 2006	Yr 2007	Yr 2008 [Q1]
116	124	149	177	204	240	296	342	404	427

No of Channels

Years

Source: TAM Peoplemeter System

fueling media insights that drive businesses

Courtesy: TAM Media Research Pvt. Ltd

Number of Hindi Based Channels and Regional has currently doubled from 2002

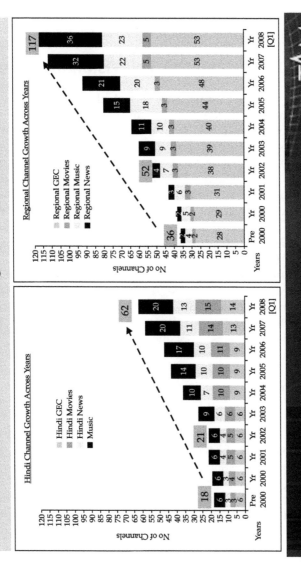

Courtesy: TAM Media Research Pvt. Ltd

with a section on the changing relationship between television channels and production houses in India today. The function of this chapter is, then, to establish the role of the genre within the television industry, which is critical to the understanding of the popularity and continuing importance of soaps.

Soap Operas and the Television Industry

Soap opera viewers take pleasure in watching them, and often, soaps become a part of the viewer's daily habits. At the same time, it is television channels which need them for the success of their channels. As Dorothy Hobson writes, the broadcasting industry needs soaps for bringing "audience share, and audience share and ratings are what soaps deliver to the broadcasters. But then they need to do it over and over again, and to keep being able to get a high score week after week, month after month ... [the role of soaps] in a multi-channel era has and will become even more important. *Soaps are essential to broadcasters. They are the lifeblood of the schedule*" (2003: 39, emphasis mine).

Yash Khanna, Corporate Communications Head of Star TV, says that "soaps are the flagship program for a channel, particularly those broadcast on prime time. The prime time band for television channels is 8 pm–11 pm. Soaps are aired four days of the week and they are the mainstay of the channel."[1] For seven of the eight years under study in this book, 2000–2008, Balaji Telefilms' mega soaps *Kyunki* and *Kahaani* pulled in the audiences for Star Plus. TAM ratings are testimony to this. On being asked about Star giving preference to Balaji soaps, Shailja Kejriwal, creative director of Star Plus in the honeymoon years of Balaji and Star (2000–2007), replied, "why shouldn't we? Ekta is a wonderfully creative person and she has given us most of our hit shows. But she's not the only person producing shows for us ... [there are] others doing shows on our channel" (www.gmagazine.com, 2005).

Such has been the impact of the K soaps produced by Ekta Kapoor that I reproduce below excerpts from two articles that detail how Tulsi, Parvati and Komolika are household names in far flung parts of the world such as Afghanistan and Brazil. Reporting about Afghanistan, Jayalakshmi Sengupta writes that "the soap queen of Indian television, also labelled Asia's most powerful communicator ... perhaps has no idea how she is creating waves in Kabul and other parts of Afghanistan ... her influence in moulding and shaping the minds and tastes of the next generation, binding the countries of India and Afghanistan in a common kinship ... the K-series has perhaps got the biggest TRP ratings and a fan following that will take considerable effort to repel ... The K-series has undoubtedly been one of its most successful ventures where five of Ekta's major serials are being constantly dubbed in Dari (a local dialect) and relayed to the Afghan public with a time handicap of a year ... people go to all lengths to enjoy the serials. The two-lakh population of Faizabad, the capital of the northernmost province of Afghanistan, depends on the local micro hydel project to supply them with a meagre 3000 watts power every evening. Electricity is scarce in these parts. Naturally, just about two per cent are its beneficiaries. But the rest have garnered enough money to buy cheap Chinese generators to bring a little light in their life. These generators, despite consuming a fair amount of diesel, help them to connect to the happenings in the rest of the world. Happenings not as serious as nuclear pacts. What interests them most are the soaps from India! ... Kabul literally stops from 6.30 to 8.30 pm, and so does life in most of the other remote towns of Afghanistan where people have access to electricity. You will find little girls curling their locks and saying 'nekka' imitating Komolika, and young boys whistling signature tunes from the various serials at street corners. Girls may even set up a *pooja thali* (plate with prayer offerings) and play with *diyas* (lamp), (which are all un-Islamic so to say) and boys get together to water tulsi plants, just as they see being done in the serials ... Hindi serials affect people's fashion sense as well. During the most recent celebrations of Id, the hottest trend for men in these parts was the 'Anurag Kurta'... Invariably, the first question from the besotted viewers to an Indian visitor will be, 'What's happening (to so and so)?' ... The women in *chadri* (burqa) even have a word of advice for Tulsi who is the favourite. 'She shouldn't be such a forgiving diva, it is not good for her' ... So great has been the Indian influence on Afghan culture in recent times that it has made the Afghan Parliament debate on it. Despite being touted as a threat to local culture by the conservatives, *Afghanistan TV*, perhaps under Ekta's influence, has recently launched its first indigenous homemade commercial serial in Dari and Pushto. *Palwasha*, which is scheduled to be aired from this month, is a serial "that follows the parallel line of entertainment of tear-jerking actions, melodramatic theatricals, echoing dialogues of Indian soaps,' says *Khaleej Times*" (Sengupta 2007).[2]

Most recent is the report on how a Brazilian soap opera, *Caminho das Indias* (roughly translated as Passage to India), that has been on air just for six weeks as of 1 March 2009, capitalizes on the *saas–bahu* formula of the K soaps, demonstrating " ... that it's not just *Slumdog Millionaire* (2008, dir. Danny Boyle) that's successfully selling an Indian story abroad ... the Brazilians are lapping it up." Topping TV ratings in Brazil, in *Caminho das Indias*, "the actors are all Brazilian, but the characters manifestly indian" (Kurup 2009). Partly filmed on location in Jaipur and Varanasi in India, Brazilian actors play Indian characters of "Maya Meetha and Bahuan." It is noted how the writer of the soap, Gloria Perez, "researched Indian customs, costumes and culture, showing not just the 'joint family system,' but also 'modern India' with some of the main characters working in the IT industry and call centres." Kurup further notes that "an estimated 30 million Brazilians watch the hour-long spectacle of mystic figures, palaces, temples and Indian costumes and customs six days a week." Bright, colorful fabrics for costumes are sourced from India, and the soap uses a large number of Hindi words and terms "including *namaste, firangi, gora, chai* and *chalta hai*."[3] For added authenticity, the soap portrays "... traditional Hindu customs such as touching the feet of elders ...." Brazil's consul-general in Mumbai, Paulo Antonio, is reported as saying that "we [the Brazilians] don't feel that we are watching a very different culture because Brazil also has a multi-racial society ... and the soap shows what's common between Brazil and India, not what's different." Florencia Costa, India correspondent to *O Globo*, Brazil's biggest newspaper, is cited as saying that the huge success of *Caminho das Indias* is also due to the fact that in Brazil, "TV serials are the main source of entertainment and TV actors are huge stars [who] set trends for fashion, music and lifestyle." Kurup further notes that "the serial has also popularised the idea of 'how to be an Indian'. Brazilians are learning to wear saris ... and bangles, how to apply *mehndi* and do the *bhangra*[4] ... the serial's actors are teaching all this through their blogs — how to prepare Indian food and do make up, Indian-style, and dress like Indians" (ibid.; see also http://caminhodasindias.globo.com for further details on the soap).

Such reports bear out Yash Khanna's observations, when he told me, during interviews, that "we (Star TV), as a channel, are about being inclusive … bringing dispersed people together, not just in India, but also those who watch our soaps overseas … *Kyunki, Kahaani* and *Kasautii* are at the heart of that proposition."[5]

Two things are happening here: "the first importance of the soap opera to television executives is that it *connects* with their audience. It speaks to them and it brings to the channel a regular and committed audience" (Hobson 2003: 41, emphasis in original). Second, these committed and sometimes dispersed audiences are what Benedict Anderson proposed in his influential thesis in "an anthropological spirit" as being "an imagined community" (1991: 5–6).

Once a soap becomes successful, television executives make it the keystone of their scheduling. Thus *Kyunki* and *Kahaani* were the backbone of Star Plus's prime time scheduling for eight years, from 2000–2008. In October 2008, however, with falling TRPs of these two soaps, Rajan Shahi's hugely successful *Bidaai* became the backbone of Star Plus' prime time scheduling. From 13 October 2008, when a special episode with leading Hindi film star Hema Malini was aired, *Bidaai* started occupying a crucial one hour time slot (9 pm–10 pm) on Star Plus. Star Plus has been careful not to conflict with the timings of *Balika Vadhu* (Child Bride) on the new channel, Colors, that airs from 8 pm–8:30 pm, and follows *Bidaai* closely in TRP ratings. This kind of programming clearly shows "the *value* of soap opera as a commercial tool in the armoury of the scheduler" (Hobson 2003: 42, emphasis in original).

Speaking of the significance of soap operas for Indian television and how they become brands for channels, Yash Khanna said, "all major TV channels in India — be that us [Star] or Zee — have soap operas that we air for our audiences, and in prime time. Our soaps are born from stories about families that are so central to the Indian imagination. So, for Sony, it was *Jassi Jaisi Koi Nahin* (There is No One Like Jassi) earlier, for Zee it is *Saat Phere* and *Banoo Mai Teri Dulhan* (I Will Be Your Bride); for us, it was *Kyunki* and *Kahaani* earlier that were crucial for our success, now it is *Bidaai*. These soaps become *brands* for our channels."[6] This function of soaps operating as a way of branding the channel was also underlined by L. V. Krishnan, CEO, TAM Media Research Pvt. Ltd. Krishnan observed that "one of the major functions of soaps is to set one channel apart from the next one. News and soaps provide similar opportunities in that they are aired every night. Reality shows draw audiences, but they have a finite time limit, when the final event takes place, 15 or 16 weeks down the line. The significance of soaps in India is that they run for four days throughout the year."[7] Of course the audience loyalty factor also counts, so *Kyunki, Kahaani* and *Bidaai* are critical components of the Star Plus brand; and now *Balika Vadhu* is working as a brand signifier for Colors. What this means is that these are shows that audiences immediately connect in their minds with the particular channel and that sets one channel apart from another. These comments bear out Hobson's observation that "crucial is the role in the *branding* of the channel because it is to the brand of the channel that broadcasters think that viewers react. *Frequency* and *regularity* are also functions which are fulfilled by the soap opera and, like news, they are always part of the output of the channel" (2003: 45, emphasis in original).

Soap operas also play an important role in attracting viewers to other programs on the channel. Yash Khanna made this point when he stressed that "audiences who watched soaps on Star Plus would more or less automatically find out what shows would be broadcast Friday–Sunday on the same channel. In this way, Star Plus has been able to attract audiences for reality shows such as *Amul Voice of India* (a singing contest) and two reality dance shows, *Nach Baliye* and *Aaja Mahi Vay* that are aired in the weekend prime time slot."[8] Similarly, soaps like *Saat Phere* and *Banoo Main Teri Dulhan* on Zee TV on weekdays attract audiences to their weekend reality singing contest *Sa Re Ga Ma Pa*. So, popular soaps often act as a *tool* for leading audiences to other programs that they may not necessarily have watched (see also Hobson 2003: 48–50 for similar programs aired on BBC1).

Almost everyone I interviewed — television executives, actors and actresses, audience and market research experts — spoke about soaps in their relation to current trends in society. All of them felt that soaps deal with social issues and keep abreast of current news and events. Also, significantly, they present ideas and themes that may have been forgotten by the young generation, such as the importance of family, various festivals, etc. — in short, what I term *parivaar aur parampara* (family and tradition).[9] Thus, soaps also act as agents for discussion of relevant social issues. This, in turn, underlines the accessibility of the genre.

The continuous process in the production of soaps also means that there is a continuous opportunity for employment of people. Production houses such as Balaji, Director's Kut and Sphere Origins audition all over the country for fresh faces to act in their shows. For example in 2002, Balaji Telefilms placed advertisements "calling out to 'pretty faces and handsome men in the age-group of 18 and 28' in the Sunday morning papers. [This] saw about 900 aspirants make a beeline for the studios ... the mass audition was held in Sankraman Studios, in Goregaon, a suburb in Mumbai" (www.indiantelevision.com, 30 September 2002). When Rajan Shahi began producing his second soap for Star Plus, *Yeh Rishta Kya Kehlata Hai* (What Is This Relationship Called), "the production house held a nationwide search" before zeroing in on the girl to play the lead role" (www.tellychakkar. com, 13 October 2008). Production houses of successful soaps also provide a large number of jobs to writers, directors, creative teams, costumes and make-up artists, cameramen, technicians, light boys, spot boys, security staff, and many others. In the unstable word of showbiz, production houses play an important *functional* role in providing employment for many thousands of people.

Academic definitions of soap opera, including my own in Chapter 1, attempt to assimilate all features of the genre. But how do the actual practitioners define soaps? Their answers, outlined below, were always more direct and succinct.[10] Nivedita Basu said, "continuing, never-ending story;" Shailja Kejriwal defined it as "narratives without closure and permanently in the channel's scheduling"; Sandiip Sikcand, previously creative head with Balaji Telefilms and now freelance consultant, sees soaps as "multi-episodic, with viewer loyalty"; and Shobha Kapoor of Balaji Telefilms sees them as "long-running stories without any visible ending in sight."[11] What becomes obvious from these comments is how soaps bring together the channel and the audiences. As Dorothy Hobson observes, "it is the soap opera and its frequency and permanence which gives the audience an anchor point within the schedule and provides the broadcaster with ... their most valuable scheduling tool" (2003: 53).

Scholarship on television in India has not always been charitable about soap operas. In a volume celebrating India's 60 years of independence, the following observations were made. One author states that "television programming is now aimed at the lower middle and working classes with a few exceptions, such as news bulletins. The majority of the programming has little appeal to educated middle classes as it consists mostly of soap operas, reality TV and various competitions, with little serious drama, documentary and educational broadcasting" (2007: 229). A second author, writing in the same volume, states that "the public agenda on state television ... has moved from being primarily development-oriented to being market-oriented at prime time, with imitations of the TV genres pioneered by the satellite TV channels: maudlin, almost regressive fiction ..." (2007: 249). Such observations do not fully take into account the importance and significance of the role that soaps play, both in the lives of their producers *and* their consumers, the audiences, not just in India, but also overseas. One look at ratings for channels, even in relative channel share, proves that audiences of soaps are drawn from all socio-economic classes in India. The point about their being "regressive" is one that I have always taken issue with; I hope to be able to argue otherwise in the course of this book.

One last point needs to be made. For all the years of study in this book, from 2000–2008, Star Plus has retained its numero uno position both in relative channel share and in the general entertainment market, despite many new channels entering the fray. Zee follows closely. Media data underlined the fact when they report: "there is still no argument. Star Plus, as has been the case for the last seven-plus years, holds firmly onto pole position, despite Zee TV's best efforts at tipping the ratings scales in its favour" (Dubey 2008; see Tables 2.1 and 2.2 as well).

Even towards the end of the year, in September 2008, "Star Plus continues to lead the GEC space with 287 GRPs while sister channel Star One is at fifth spot with 85 GRPs. NDTV Imagine follows with 80 GRPs while Sahara One is seventh with 66 GRPs. 9X takes the eighth spot with 57 GRPs while Sab has 33 GRPs" (www.indiantelevision.com headlines, 25 September 2008).

Launched in the summer of 2008, Viacom 18's new channel in India, Colors, is now providing competition to Star Plus and Zee in the GEC market. With its smart programming, Colors has forayed "into the mythological space with *Jai Shri Krishna*" in the 8:30 pm–9 pm time band. "Another bold move on the part of Colors was to take up a topic like child marriage through *Balika Vadhu*.

While the programme might not appeal to an urban audience, it is expected to find instant audiences in states such as Rajasthan, Madhya Pradesh and Uttar Pradesh. This programme is seen by experts as a potential lead soap in days to come" (Phadnis and Aga 2008). Indeed, Colors' *Balika Vadhu* bagged a number of awards at television award ceremonies by the end of the year 2008. *Bidaai*, however, still retained top position in many of the popular award categories.

Table 2.1: Relative Channel Share in 2007

Channel	Jul	Aug	Sep	Oct	Nov	Dec
Star	36	36	36	39	39	38
Zee	29	29	32	32	30	29
Sony	14	15	14	11	11	11
Star One	7	7	7	6	6	7
Sahara	9	9	9	8	8	8
Sab	5	4	3	3	4	3
9X	0	0	0	0	2	4

Source: TAM Media Research Pvt. Ltd.

Table 2.2: GRP January 2008, Weekdays — Prime Time

Channel	Week 1	Week 2
Star	226.65	192.42
Zee	169.04	170.84
Sony	52.51	46.77
Star One	37.05	41.93
Sahara	27.13	27.74
Sab	12.08	12.59
9X	15.47	17.02

Source: TAM Media Research Pvt. Ltd.

Television Audience Measurement (TAM)

Television audience measurement (TAM) media research is the TV viewership analysis firm of India. It is a 50–50 joint venture company between AC Nielsen and IMRB International. Details of TAM are available on http://www.tamindia.com. In addition to measuring measuring TV viewership, TAM also monitors advertising expenditure through its division AdEx India. It exists in the PR monitoring space through another division — Eikona PR Monitor.

The viewership cell runs what is one of the largest Peoplemeter TV panels in the world, with approximately 30,000 sample individuals representing all the Class-I towns (towns with population more than 100,000) polled every week for their viewership habits. This division measures television viewership of audiences for the 300 plus TV stations operating in India.[12]

Viewership details are tracked through TRPs and GRPs, as L. V. Krishnan explained. GRPs, or Gross Rating Points, are "an aggregate of the total 'ratings' of the schedule against the target group. Thus, percentage reach multiplied by average frequency equals GRPs." TRPs are average set of audiences watching a program. They commonly refer to people rating points. TRP is the criterion that indicates the popularity of a channel or program and this data is very useful for television channels and advertisers. In a highly clustered market, targeting audiences is problematic because of the presence of numerous channels with a variety of programs catering round the clock to a vast and scattered population. Television ratings provide information about the viewers' TV watching habits and the socio-economic background of the audience. TRPs not only help decide the advertising rates on different programs and which programs should continue airing on TV, they have also been instrumental in changing the course of the direction of the narratives of some soap operas.

Krishnan explained that TAM measures "only the urban Indian market which now numbers close to 400 million in a country of a billion plus people."[13] He provided the following details: 95 per cent homes in India are still single TV set homes. Women spend 160–170 minutes daily watching television, while the rest of the family spends 120 minutes on television consumption. Afternoon programs are mainly targeted towards women; children's viewing time is from 5:30 pm–7 pm. 8 pm–11 pm is what the television industry considers prime time, and there is, in this time band, an increase in the number of daily soaps and other entertainment content. Most families in India beyond the metro cities are still joint families, and women take control of TV viewing from 8:30 pm–11 pm. In the advertising breaks, the woman is multi-tasking — going to the kitchen, laying the dinner. Men use ad breaks to surf channels. Post 11 pm, the shows is skewed to male viewing. Weekends, i.e. Friday evenings — Sunday evenings, are counted as family viewing time, when films, game shows, and reality shows pick up in a more dramatic fashion.

Krishnan made it clear that "very importantly, prime time viewing is divided in a balanced fashion, with 54 per cent of female viewership and 46 per cent male viewership." It is "the engagement level of viewing that differs. If you index it for women, their engagement level is 200 per cent, and for men, it is about 50 per cent. Therefore, *there is a huge difference in the way that both genders watch soaps.* We come to know of this when the viewer is asked to recall names, clothes, jewelry, décor, etc."[14]

History of Production Houses

Balaji Telefilms

Balaji Telefilms Limited was started in 1994 by Jeetendra Kapoor, a big star of Hindi cinema from the 1960s–1980s, his wife Shobha Kapoor, and daughter Ekta Kapoor. It is one of India's leading entertainment content providers. Jeetendra, who has acted in over 200 films in his career, is the Chairman of Balaji Telefilms and the company's main person for interaction with television channels for the company's programs. Shobha Kapoor is the Managing Director and is instrumental in shaping the company's diversification strategy and looks after its overall administration and management. She also handles the production functions. Ekta Kapoor is the Creative Head. On 24 October 2008, Puneet Kinra was appointed group CEO of Balaji Telefilms (headlines on www. indiantelevision.com, 24 October 2008).

Ekta is the face of Balaji Telefilms but in reality, the success story is in equal measure her mother, Shobha Kapoor's, as well. Born on 7 June 1975, Ekta was not interested in academics. She wanted to do something on television from the age of 17, and around the same time, Shobha wanted to produce soaps for television because she was smart enough to see that this was where the future of television was headed. Balaji Telefilms was set up in 1994. Kapoor told me that another important reason "for going into television was that Jeetendra was going through a dull phase in his career as a film star at that time. He was getting offers to work in TV … but why work in TV when you can produce it? We got the finance from Jeetendra, and started in our basement of 4,000 square feet, where we worked for six years."[15] Ekta and Shobha Kapoor produced six pilots with three episodes each, but none of them worked. Then came a sitcom in 1995, *Hum Paanch* (We Five), that was aired on Zee TV, and it was a success. The plot where Balaji Telefilms has their office, said Kapoor, "had been purchased by Jeetendra. But instead of leasing to outsiders, we leased it to the family as Balaji House. Initially, the first two floors were offices, there were two floors for editing and three more for shooting." The Balaji Telefilms office is heavily guarded. Entry is allowed after multiple checks. A *mandir* (temple) of *Mata Rani* (mother goddess) stands in the lobby of the entrance. A Lexus parked there informed me that Shobha Kapoor was in, and later a bur-gundy colored BMW testified to Ekta Kapoor's presence on the premises. Pictures of the god Balaji are at the entrance, and a flick of a switch allows *shlokas*[16] to be sung as one touches the feet of the god. Paintings and statues of gods and goddesses are everywhere with garlands of fresh flowers and burning incense sticks. After the evening *aarti*[17] was performed, when I was in Shobha Kapoor's office, someone entered with the scared flame and I was also given *prasad*.[18] This happened the second time as well while I interviewed Nivedita Basu, second in command to Ekta Kapoor as creative head.

What struck me was that most of the people working at Balaji — creative heads, associates, assistants, secretaries — were all young women. The men were mainly security staff, cleaning personnel, and serving tea and coffee to visitors. If prime time soap operas in India are women-centric, then there was no better proof than at one of their main production houses, Balaji. Not only are women the central protagonists in their soaps, Balaji Telefilms itself is headed by women, and seems to employ women in large numbers! In fact, when I asked Shobha Kapoor about this, she con-firmed my observation, saying that there are more women than men in Balaji.

Shobha Kapoor said that in the initial years, budgets were low, so they undertook shootings at the office itself. She reminisced that her office room was often used for shots of offices, and the mandir that they have at the entrance was used for many *mandir* scenes, especially for their first soap, *Kyunki*. She stated that "many Tulsi and Ba scenes at the *mandir* were filmed in our office *mandir* … though initially built for shootings, it eventually became a real *mandir* … I called in a *pundit* (priest) to perform the prayers."[19]

Balaji ran its sets from Balaji House for the first two and a half years. Shobha Kapoor said, "Ekta's office used to be next to mine. As we grew, I moved her offices up to the fifth floor.[20] Also, after the initial period, Ekta wanted bigger sets. So now we have 32 state-of-the-art studio sets." Details of sets and locations sets can be found in Chapter 3. Balaji has regional shows on the Sun network in South India, with shows in the Tamil, Telugu, Malayalam, and Kannada languages. Its Hindi soaps are not dubbed when telecast in south India. Special shows are produced for the south India market. Shobha Kapoor stressed that "Balaji has time and again been made to perform, made to regain TRPs that channels have lost with their wrong decisions of promoting other productions."

Adding that "all our prime time shows are with Star due to our contract with them," she also said that "channels are quite an insecure lot. A slight drop in TRPs and they start suggesting *'yeh karo, woh karo'* (do this, do that). First they get in touch with the executive producers (EPs) of the show concerned. If required, Ekta steps in. After all, it's her concept. If Ekta is not convinced about their call, they get in touch with me. I am dealing with them on an almost daily basis — arranging press conferences, delivery of tapes, production values, uplinks, finance...."[21] (see also Lalwani 2003c).

The process of production at Balaji is detailed and thorough. Shobha Kapoor explained the process to me in detail, stressing on the importance of the Kapoor family in handling the reins and taking all major decisions. Ekta Kapoor oversees the creative department entirely while Shobha Kapoor has full charge of the production details. She was clear that they "preferred not to go out of Mumbai for logistical reasons." 95 per cent of the work is done on their sets. All people in production are in-house. Balaji has its own editing department, graphic department, music department, and music rights. Nim Sood, Shobha Kapoor's sister, is the fashion stylist on all Balaji shows. Jeetendra liaises with television channels on how to take their business forward. Balaji also has departments for audit, accounts, operations, executive producers, and creative heads. The "executive producer is on the sets, the creative head works with Ekta on the next 20 episodes, then sits with writers who prepare the script. The writer has detailers who look after minor details such as who will enter the scene now, etc. After the script is detailed, it is given to the production head who then calls the production manager, executive producer and the entire team, and sits down and plans the shoot. Creative heads also have associate creative heads who go for shootings. The associates tell the directors what kind of performance Ekta and the creative heads want. The associate also talks with the dress department, and narrations to actors. The associate creative heads and executive producers inform the art department if cars are required for outside sequences such as airport sequences."[22]

Everyone I interviewed spoke of Ekta Kapoor's instinct and intuition in conceptualizing her soap stories and for being able to judge the pulse of the audience. It is a little known fact that when Ekta Kapoor and Jeetendra approached Sameer Nair, then Executive Vice President, Content and Communications, and later CEO of Star TV, with their soap *Kyunki*, it was originally titled *Amma*. Then Ekta Kapoor's aunt suggested the title *Saas Bhi Kabhi Bahu Thi*, but this title was already registered with actor Sachin Pilgaonkar. On being approached, however, Pilgaonkar gave the name to Balaji Telefilms. Ekta's fixation with the letter K added the first word *Kyunki*, and Sameer Nair, also known to be instinctive and intuitive about what will work, suggested that the soap go ahead with the title of *Kyunki Saas Bhi Kabhi Bahu Thi*, feeling that "this title had the widest range of appeal, and that all mothers-in-law and daughters-in-law would check it out."[23] Nair proved to be correct. Mihir Virani's character was named after Ekta's school friend, Mihir Shah. The name of Tulsi was adopted from Gujarati novelist Harkishan Mehta's work *Jad Chetan*.[24]

What was brought out repeatedly in interviews was that fact that "not a single episode goes on air without Ekta Kapoor's permission, unless Ekta herself might have handed over charge of a production to a senior deputy creative head like Nivedita Basu who was trained with Ekta for the past nine years."[25] Famous for working seven days of the week, Ekta Kapoor is known to be a hands-on boss for every show of hers. Basu, her long time deputy creative head, called her "a one-man team who is totally into her work, she never takes a break from it. Work is her passion, her whole life." When a show is being tweaked and reworked, Ekta's involvement is even greater. "For instance when *Kahaani* went in for its second generational leap in November 2007, Ekta Kapoor worked on every detail of the representation of Parvati herself, including her dress, jewelry, hairstyle with designer Manish

Malhotra."[26] The creative department also works every day of the week. Shootings take place everyday. There are times when shooting for the next day's episode takes place the day before. That is what is called a "cut-to-cut situation" in the television industry.[27] Ekta Kapoor holds "episode meetings" and "creative meetings" everyday with her team that decide on how to take the narrative forward.

Part of Shobha Kapoor's work is when Ekta gives her a remit for what kind of set is required. Shobha Kapoor told me, "Ekta says 'I want a huge set.' If I tell her that the *Kasautii* set is free, she will reply that she wants a brand new set. We consult catalogs from all over the world, choose what we think will suit our story, then I discuss details with the art director depending on size and location. This is entirely my decision after Ekta tells me what she wants. Everything outside the creative side is my responsibility."[28]

Aspiring actors leave their portfolios at Balaji offices. The casting department goes through them and contacts Ekta Kapoor with a short list. Balaji also advertises and auditions for shows across the country; huge numbers of people turn up for these. Ekta Kapoor takes the final decision regarding the lead actors; others are decided by the casting department. She is reputed to have an unerring eye and persisted in casting Sakshi Tanwar in the role of Parvati in *Kahaani* when she spotted her auditioning for another pilot.[29] Gauri, the heroine of *Karam Apna Apna* (Everyone's Own Karma) was spotted by Ekta in the background of another show.[30] Generally, actors with Balaji sign an exclusivity contract, unless stated otherwise at the time of joining, and give 20–25 block dates to Balaji for shooting.

On a personal note, Shobha Kapoor said that "though there are no Sundays in [her] own working week," she "worries as a mother at the punishing schedule Ekta keeps. She is in the Balaji offices from early afternoon till midnight with the creative team. At midnight she comes home, and goes jogging for an hour … security personnel are detailed with her for that hour of night. After coming home, she works at home, watching episodes and having other meetings till 6 am. She says she works better at night, it is less disturbed. Ekta sleeps from 6:30 am till about noon, after which her working day starts again."[31]

Balaji productions, whether in television or film, begin with the letter "K." It is alleged that celebrity numerologist and personal friend Sunita Menon has advised Ekta to do so since this alphabet supposedly brings her good luck. Ekta Kapoor regularly visits temples and shrines. It was a Tuesday when I first went to the offices of Balaji Telefilms and I was informed by Shobha Kapoor that Ekta was at the Siddhivinayak temple where she goes every Tuesday.

It will not be an exaggeration to say that Ekta Kapoor "... single-handedly changed the way the nation spends its evenings" (Balaji Telefilms company profile). Ekta Kapoor's impact on the television landscape in India has been like no one before her. She pioneered prime time soap opera viewing. Producers from rival production houses like Sunjoy Waddhwa and Rajan Shahi, in interviews with me, praised Kapoor's contributions for being first in the field of producing content of long running soaps. The company profile further lists its "core strengths" as "creativity as a discipline, targeted content, constant improvisation, exploring new vistas, strong management, skilled talent pool and conducive environment". *Kyunki* and *Kahaani* are Ekta Kapoor's first two soaps. Both went on to create television history. Tulsi and Parvati became household names and their families became our families. They enjoyed unprecedented success and top TRPs for several years consecutively.

Ekta Kapoor has since widened her scope of production to include the production of reality shows such as *Kahaani Hamarey Mahabharat Ki* (The Story of Our Mahabharat) and *Kaun Jeetega Bollywood Ka Ticket* (Who Will Win the Ticket to Bollywood) on the channel 9X; and films such as *Krishna Cottage* (2004, dir. Santaram Varma), *Kya Kool Hain Hum* (How Cool We Are, 2005, dir. Sangeeth Sivan), and *C Kkompany* (2008, dir. Sachin Yardi). All the films star her brother, Tusshar Kapoor, and Ekta herself did a cameo in *C Kkompany*.

At a young age, Ekta Kapoor has been the recipient of several honors and awards. She was chosen to lead the entertainment committee of the Confederation of Indian Industry (CII). At the sixth Indian Telly Awards 2006, she bagged the Hall of Fame award for her contribution to the Indian television industry. Other awards she has received include the Ernst & Young Entrepreneur of the Year in 2001, the Corporate Excellence award from Bharat

Petroleum, and the Rajiv Gandhi Award in 2002. She was named as one of the 50 most powerful communicators in Asia by *Asiaweek* magazine in 2001. The *Asiaweek* survey on the region's most influential communicators, technologists, artists, entrepreneurs, and politicians praised Ekta Kapoor, saying: "Since producing her first blockbuster television programme at 19, Ekta Kapoor has rewritten the script on TV entertainment for the masses. She has created more than 20 soaps on 10 major Indian networks; a comedy series she created ran for five years. The Indian showbiz community watches her every move, and older, more experienced producers are quick to copy any new Kapoor concept" (www.indiantelevision.com, 11 June 2001).

Sphere Origins

Sunjoy Waddhwa started his working life as part of the family business in the export of handicrafts. He started his media career in 1996 when he set up a company called Karnik Communications, where he produced a few shows like *Niyat* (Intention), *The Thief of Baghdad* and *Arth* (Meaning) for Zee TV; *Ek Mulaqat* (A Meeting) and *Aatish* (Fire/Splendor) for Star Plus; and *Nirnay* (Decision) for Doordarshan.

In 2002, Waddhwa restructured and set up Sphere Origins. He recalls the brief Zee sent him: " 'We want a serial on the dark skin theme. Give us a dark girl's story.' The call from Zee TV meant my independent venture Sphere Origins' debut on the channel."[32] *Saat Phere* catapulted Sphere origins into the big league. Currently, Waddhwa has further strengthened his position with his show *Balika Vadhu* on the new channel, Colors, that is in competition with Rajan Shahi's *Bidaai* on Star Plus for top ratings. Other productions include a telefilm *Phir Se* (Once Again) for Sahara. Waddhwa had also taken over *Des Mein Nikla Hoga Chaand* (The Moon Must Have Risen in My Country) from Aruna Irani for Star Plus.

He is helped in his work by his wife, Comall Sunjoy Waddhwa. Similar to the Balaji set-up, the husband–wife duo split work responsibilities between them. Sunjoy "handles the creative and marketing sides entirely, including story ideation, development of narratives, channel liaison, marketing, as well as overseeing technical and commercial aspects, creative feedback and providing overall support to the team." Comall has "overall charge of administrative and production functions of the company." Like Shobha

Kapoor, it is Comall's role to "interact with the architectural and design teams and she is actively involved in the look and design of all the shows. Her experience as a designer and exporter of Indian furniture and accessories stands her in good stead to carry out her responsibilities."[33]

The production office of Sphere Origins is located in Andheri, where many television offices are to be found. Covering an area of approximately 6,500 sq. feet, the office premises are fully equipped, and houses its "core creative team, core production team, writers, research and ideation team, production office staff and other support staff."[34] The company's "in-house production facilities include four permanent sets at Charcop in Mumbai, three indoor sets at Dahisar, and a large warehouse that stores props and costumes. As and when required, we put up new sets, new studios." Post-production facilities are located in Andheri. The company has tie-ups with some of the best studios in Mumbai for special effects and computer generated imagery.[35]

Waddhwa said that "compared to Balaji, we are younger in the field." He added that Sphere Origins are "good content providers," but distanced himself from Balaji in that they "did not do *saas–bahu* soaps." Sunjoy made special mention that not just *Saat Phere*, but his other stories also "manage to hold audience attention sometimes with dramatic disguises and sometimes with sheer pace ... the suspense does not linger more that it is necessary ... there is not a moment when audiences feel that the track is getting repetitive or a thought is being stretched too far. *We expand our story, but we always stick to the plot.*"[36] He explained to me that "Sphere Origins' reporting is structured in a pyramid fashion, with Comall and himself at the top of the pyramid."

Actors are contracted "on more or less uniform contracts. With main leads like Rajshri Thakur, who plays the lead role of Saloni in *Saat Phere*, we have exclusivity contracts. The range of payment for actors can range from Rs 5,000 per day up to Rs 50,000 per day or more."[37] Sunjoy admitted that stars moved between production houses, but that he was sure of the loyalty of his lead actors. A year after I met him, www.indiantelevision.com reported on 23 October 2008 that Rajshri Thakur, the lead actress playing the role of Saloni in *Saat Phere*, was leaving the show. There were conflicting claims about her departure. The news item reported that the "reclusive Rajshri [informed] 'I'm not being sacked but I

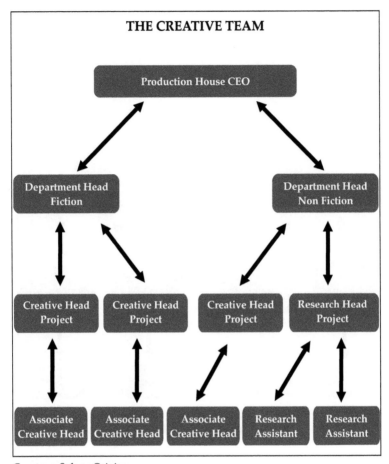

Courtesy: Sphere Origins

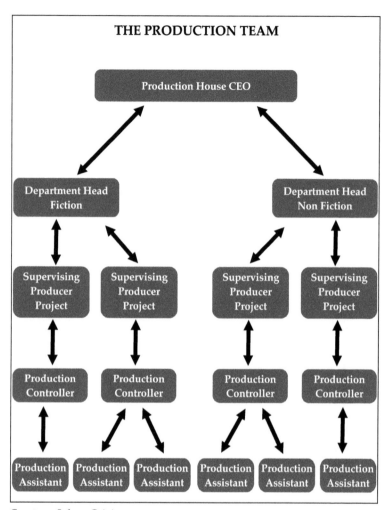

Courtesy: Sphere Origins

have quit the show two days back. I just felt that I needed more time for me and I also have certain family commitments,' said the actress. Seconding Rajshri's claim a source from the production says, 'Rajshri [has] been struggling to balance her professional and personal life. All this has taken its toll on her and that's the reason we find her indulging into tantrums.' [Rajshri's response is to say that] 'in the past too, I had expressed my desire to leave but the production house and channel kept telling me that they would work out a solution. However, being the protagonist you are required to be there in virtually every scene thus it's difficult to have a solution'" (Lookhar 2008). *Saas, Bahu aur Saazish,* the program that reports on the television industry on Star News, reported on 24 October 2008 that "*Saloni set par nakhrewali ban gayi hai aur Saat Phere par unka safar tham jayega*" (Saloni has become fussy and troublesome on the sets and her travels on *Saat Phere* are coming to an end). This was obviously not true, since Rajshri Thakur is still very much around, continuing to play the lead role of Saloni in *Saat Phere*. The loyalties of his actors and actresses, as Waddhwa pointed out, are clearly not in question.

Working hours at Sphere Origins are equally long, but not through the night like at Balaji. Sunjoy said that their "working hours are from 9 am till midnight and sometimes past that." He underlined that they are producing "60 episodes per month and several others are in the pipeline. The office works 24x7 … we have to deliver every day's shows."[38]

When I asked him about the unusual spelling of his and his wife's names, Sunjoy said, "you must have figured it out by now. I believe in astrology and numerology. We were told to spell our names this way, and we did, and we have reaped the benefits."[39] Shows produced by Sphere Origins have received many television awards.

Director's Kut

The newest kid on the block is Rajan Shahi's company Director's Kut. Influenced by his maternal grandfather, veteran Hindi film actor P. Jairaj, a recipient of the Dadashaeb Phalke Award, the idea of being a part of the entertainment industry fascinated Shahi from a very young age. After completing his schooling from St Columbus, New Delhi, and graduating in English Literature from Hindu College, University of Delhi, Shahi shifted base to

Mumbai. He has assisted Gulzar, Lekh Tandon, Sanjay Khan, and Mahesh Bhatt in their film productions.

Shahi has been the director for a number of hit shows on television, including being the series director of *Saat Phere* on Zee TV, and later *Ghar Ki Lakshmi… Betiyaan* (Goddesses of the Home … Daughters), also on Zee TV. He "launched these shows, saw to their scripts, dialogs, costumes … the whole pattern of the shows."[40] In 1999, Shahi directed his first independent venture of 58 episodes titled *Dil Hai Ke Maanta Nahin* (This Heart Does Not Listen) for Sony television.

Shahi set up his own production house, Director's Kut, of which the hit soap *Sapna Babul Ka … Bidaai* is the first production launched on 8 October 2007. Shahi credits the idea of *Bidaai* as having come "from Vivek Bahl's vision," with whom he "shares a very good equation."[41] Bahl earlier worked at Zee TV where he started a new phase for them with shows such as *Banoo Main Teri Dulhan* (I Will Be Your Bride) and *Kareena Kareena*. He has been working with Star TV since 2007 and is famously known for sticking to regular working hours and not carrying a cell phone. Shahi shares a long-term comfortable working equation with Bahl, and they trust each other's instincts and views.

Despite being on air for a relatively short time, *Bidaai*'s place in the television industry is secure. At the last Star Parivaar awards aired on 8 June 2008, the show was accorded a lot of importance in the theme of *naye parivaar ki nayi lahar* (the new family wave). The two lead actresses, Sara Khan and Parul Chauhan, playing the roles of Sadhana and Ragini respectively, were in the limelight, and picked up awards for their portrayals. Senior stars like Smriti Z. Irani, who was welcomed back into the Star *parivaar* fold with her return to *Kyunki*, gestured towards the two heroines of *Bidaai*, saying that it would be for them to carry the work forward.

Director's Kut has offices in Bandra and Andheri in Mumbai. When I visited the office in Andheri, there was a long queue of young hopefuls with their portfolios for a chance to audition in Shahi's next production.

Due to date problems that Shahi faced with actors he had originally cast in *Bidaai*, he has now "made it mandatory for all actors to produce an NOC (no objection certificate) establishing that they are free to do his show and commit the required dates.

Shahi says, 'I have made a company policy that all actors will have to give an NOC with details of the contracts with any other production house, to avoid clashing of dates. Actors cannot manipulate and create differences between production houses. I have told my entire unit that nothing is more important than the show'" (Shah 2008a).

Regarding his role as director, Shahi is on record saying that "a director should have the ability to skillfully balance all tools — script, screenplay, dialogues, actors etc. — required to tell a story as effectively as possible. He should be able to bring about cohesion between creativity and the right packaging required to market creativity. A director is like the captain of the ship and more than anything else, he needs to be extremely patient with all his crew members" (Amar, n.d., interview with Rajan Shahi, www.indiantelevision.com). Shahi said more or less the same things to me when I interviewed him in August 2008.

The one important point that sets Shahi apart from his peers in the business is that he "concentrates on one show at a time and is involved in the whole production aspect, from sets to choosing actors to story ideas to spot boys ... right down to the color of the heroine's nail polish." He is a "one-man monitoring show." He feels that "this is not a popular concept with other producers who focus on multiple shows, but he gives all his time and energy to one show."[42] It is perhaps because of his attention to every little detail on one soap at a time rather than multiple soaps that it has been written of Shahi that "he is a master craftsman, an artist, a technician, a visualiser, all rolled into one. He is the man who lends his artistry to create path breaking scenes and dramatic sequences. He is the director, who directs the cumulative energy of his work force towards one creative whole — he is the captain of the shows that make us laugh and cry" (Sengupta 2005). Shahi's production *Yeh Rishta Kya Kehlata Hai* (What Is This Relationship Called) started being telecast from Mondays–Fridays in the prime time slot of 9:30 pm–10 pm on Star Plus from 12 January 2009.

Similarities with Each Other

One main point of similarity between all production houses is the passion and commitment to work. Rajan Shahi, Sunjoy Waddhwa and the Balaji team drive themselves with unrelenting passion and dedication. A common theme that ran through all conversations was the "desire for perfection." Shahi said that "the stakes for daily soaps are very high because if one is not careful with the way the narrative is developing, they can get repetitive." What drives him is his "biggest fear that the magic might not work this time ... that fear motivates you."[43] Ekta Kapoor is described as "a bundle of nerves each time a new show of hers goes on air. Competition, even in the slightest form, is said to set her teeth on edge" (Lalwani 2003a). Shobha Kapoor told me that she "leaves home every afternoon and does not return before nine or ten at night." She added "I have a lot of money. Do I really need to slog so much? Real passion is a continuous process. I have real passion for work. So does Ekta."[44]

A second point of similarity is the loyalty that production houses command, especially from their lead actors. Nowhere is this truer than for actors whose identities have been carved from the roles they essay in successful soaps. Sakshi Tanwar, Ronit Bose Roy, Achint Kaur, Hiten Tejwani, Ram Kapoor, and even Smriti Z. Irani, who ventured away on her own for a while in between, credit Ekta Kapoor with giving them characters to play that have brought them instant recognition and fame. Rajshri Thakur, who plays Saloni in *Saat Phere*, is under an exclusivity contract with Sphere Origins.

There was a recent controversy that erupted with news of Ekta Kapoor trying to lure away lead actresses Sara Khan and Parul Chauhan (Sadhana and Ragini, respectively, in *Bidaai*) to act in Balaji productions. This news hit the headlines even as I was sitting with Rajan Shahi in his office on 12 August 2008, and one of his associates walked in with the newspaper *Mumbai Mirror* reporting that "two newcomers, just a show old, got calls from Ekta Kapoor inviting them to be part of the Balaji stable, by acting in her new show, and also attend her party on Saturday. That's Sara Khan (Sadhana) and Parul Chauhan (Ragini), the two female leads of *Sapna Baabul Ka ... Bidaai*. However and here's the crux of the story — both of them preferred to stick with *Bidaai* rather than attend Ekta's party and do her show! When contacted, Sara Khan said, 'around 11.30 pm, I got a call from Ekta. It took me a while to realise that it was actually Ekta Kapoor herself who was calling me! I was really surprised. She said that she wanted to do a show with me, which would replace *Kyunki Saas Bhi Kabhi Bahu Thi*, and a separate show with Parul as well. She also invited us to a party at her house on Saturday night. We said that we would love to work with her, but right now we are busy with *Bidaai*.' Parul Chauhan sounded as happy about receiving a call from Ekta, but as firm about not leaving her parent show. She said, 'Ekta wanted us to do her show, which means that we would have to leave *Bidaai* which we would rather not do. We have no intention of leaving our show and joining Ekta right now. We've achieved name and fame due to *Bidaai*, so we can't leave it midway. Besides, we got a call from Ekta, on the strength of *Bidaai*, right?'" (Shah 2008b). Reaction from Ekta Kapoor was swift, with the next day's edition of *Mumbai Mirror* reporting that "the two girls will be sued by Ekta Kapoor, who says that the girls' claim is a blatant lie. She is now in the process of sending them a legal notice for using her name to promote themselves and their show" (Shah 2008c). Shahi told me later that the matter was resolved between him and Kapoor.

At television award ceremonies, stars receiving awards on stage always thank the relevant producer by name and credit them with their success. Television stars are no longer small stars. It does not matter that they do not act in Hindi films. What is significant in India's changed mediascape is that they are very big names on their own now.

A third point of similarity is that no expense is spared in the making of TV soaps. A look at some statistics will reveal this.[45] The cost of each indoor set ranges from Rs 2–4 crore.[46] Costumes are also expensive affairs. Shobha Kapoor told me that "there are times when we spend anything upto Rs 1 crore on saris and *lehanga*s (long skirts) in one month just for one show alone." The jewelry and clothes worn by characters in all the soaps under study are the most expensive designer ones in the market today. Rarely are costumes repeated in successive episodes. The production houses stock costumes and accessories in their warehouses. A rain sequence uses about 3–4 tankers of water, each with 20,000 liters of water. Vanity vans are hired for stars on outdoor shoots at the cost of Rs 6,000–7,000 per day. Technical equipment that these production houses use can equally well be used for making big budget Hindi films. Each camera costs upto Rs 20 lakh and usually three or four cameras are used for shooting. The Jimmy Jib camera crane costs Rs 15 lakh. Recording equipment can cost anything between Rs 7–9 lakh. Shobha Kapoor also told me that they "spent upwards of Rs 50 lakh to shoot the famous sequence of Tulsi shooting her son Ansh" because they had to use "rotating cameras" and what is termed the "bullet time effect, made famous in the film *The Matrix*."[47] Stars are paid handsomely, especially the lead actors. It is said that they can command upto Rs 50,000 per day of shooting. It is reported that "people who board local trains to reach Balaji sets drive out in BMWs" (Ojha 2007).

On the visual presentation being lavish and glamorous on TV soaps, Shailja Kejriwal, head of programming at Star Plus from 1998–2007, says, "unlike films, television is close to you, it sells aspirations and dreams which are achievable. Entertainment is nothing but an escape into a world of dreams. It provides hope. Visually, a serial has to be appealing. Presentation is important. I will give you a simple example. When a person wants to celebrate, he will take his family to a five star restaurant. The food in a three star hotel is maybe better but he will prefer a five star. The reason is simple, it provides a good ambience and setting. It's the same logic that works here. The story may be seeped in ordinary middle class family values but the projection is visually rich" (interview with Shailja Kejriwal, 2 March 2005).

On the kinds of stories they make and the audiences they cater to, all the producers want to reach the maximum number of viewers with "stories that appeal to the sensibilities of all Indians."[48] Ekta Kapoor said that she "does not make shows for the upper strata of people sitting in their comfortable homes in Malabar Hill in Mumbai because they don't know about the problems that ordinary people face. Therefore, [she] makes her soaps for the masses who identify with the problems of joint families that [her] soaps are based on" (*Koffee With Karan*, Star One, 27 May 2007). Similarly, Sunjoy Waddhwa's and Rajan Shahi's soaps touch upon the problems of dark-skinned girls is a problem that is faced by many families in India.

Differences with the West

A few important points need mentioning here that have differences with the milieu of production in the West. *First*, production houses in India are mostly family run businesses. Ekta Kapoor and her mother Shobha Kapoor are the producers of Balaji soaps; discussions with television companies are conducted with the help of Ekta Kapoor's father, Bollywood actor Jeetendra; the fashion stylist on all Balaji soaps is Nim Sood, Shobha Kapoor's sister. Sunjoy Waddhwa and his wife Comall Waddhwa are the producers of Sphere Origins. Rajan Shahi owns Director's Kut.

Second is the belief that Indians have in astrology, numerology and *vaastu*,[49] when it comes to success in their professional and personal lives. For instance the soaps produced by Balaji Telefilms are often referred to as the "K soaps" (because all their titles inevitably start with the letter K). Both Ekta Kapoor, who is often referred to as the "Karan Johar of the small screen," and Karan Johar himself share the same numerologist, Sunita Menon, whose advice to them is that the titles of their productions should start with the letter "K." Sandiip Sikcand, creative head at Balaji and a freelance consultant for other television channels, also spells his name in the way he does thanks to numerology, as do Sunjoy and Comall Waddhwa (instead of the more usual "Sanjay" and "Komal").[50]

Most recently, Ekta Kapoor, whose serial on the epic *Mahabharat* started being broadcast on the channel 9X in July 2008, made sure that the title began with the letter "K." The serial is called *Kahaani Hamarey Mahabharat Ki* (The Story of Our *Mahabharat*). Ekta Kapoor said that she "chose a few titles ... and sent them to her astrologer Sunita Menon for approval. 'I value Sunita's opinion a lot. Surprisingly and luckily, the title with the best sounding aura was *Kahaani Hamarey Mahabharat Ki*.' The title was later sent to numerologist Sanjay B. Jumaani for spelling correction" (*The Times of India*, 4 June 2008).

The extent to which Ekta Kapoor believes in astrology can be understood from the lengths to which she has reportedly gone to choose the actor to play the role of the god Krishna as a child in *Kahaani Hamarey Mahabharat Ki*. *The Times of India* reported that "To play the role of Lord Krishna, Ekta ordered that only those kids born on *Janmashthami*[51] last year could apply. Not only that, Ekta even ordered seven pundits from different parts of India to match the *kundlis* (horoscopes) of those kids with Lord Krishna's. The *kundli* of the child that matched the most with Lord Krishna's bagged the role. The pundits have been put up in Mumbai and Ekta's company, Balaji Telefilms is bearing the cost of their lodging and boarding" (Lalwani, 19 June 2008). When contacted, Ekta apparently confirmed the story, saying "Yes, it is true. I have assigned my staff to call for pundits who would have to look into the *kundlis* of all those who applied for baby Krishna's role. We received 150 entries and it was not an easy job ... it was necessary that the kid's *kundli* matched Lord Krishna's. We are talking about God and we can't be anything but authentic. In fact, I am taking special care to see that the kid's attire and accessories like the *mor pankh* (peacock feather) and *sudarshan chakra*[52] are also sent by *pujaris* (priests) from various temples of India" (*ibid.*).

The fixation with the letter "K" seemed to have undergone a temporary change in October 2008, with both Karan Johar and Ekta Kapoor titling their next ventures without the omnipresent "K." Johar's latest production is *Dostana* (Friendship, 2008, dir. Tarun Mansukhani) and Ekta's next soap, slated to take *Kahaani*'s slot from Mondays–Thursdays at 10 pm on Star Plus, is titled *Tujh Sang Preet Lagayi Sajna* (I Give My Love to You). A news report in early November 2008 reports that seeing the dire straits that the K soaps have fallen into with Star Plus, "Ekta had a closed door meeting with her astrologers and numerologists. Ekta follows her good friend Sunita Menon's advice closely. And according to her, Ekta is now being told to name her shows starting from the alphabet T, B and M" (Kapoor 2008a).

Astrology and numerology seem to have worked well in everyone's favor so far, if the success of their soaps and films are anything to go by! Numerologist Jumaani adds a realistic and practical note here by saying that "let us not discount the fact that good luck smiles only on those who work hard. Ekta is a workaholic and that's why our numerology on the spellings of her serials hits the bull's eye more often than not" (Lalwani 2003b).

Third, is a belief in the strength of prayers and the visibility of statues and deities in all the offices of production houses. All the offices have statues of Hindu deities with offerings of fresh flowers and burning incense sticks. The Balaji office is like a shrine. The temple of *Mata Rani* (mother goddess) greets one at the entry, and there are statues and paintings everywhere of gods and goddesses with fresh flowers and garlands. The smell of incense permeates the atmosphere. Most workers have a *tilak*[53] on their foreheads and all pictures of Ekta Kapoor show her with the *tilak* on her forehead.

Fourth is the incredibly long working hours that production houses keep. I cannot speak with a 100 per cent certainty for production houses in the West, but from my own experience of the sanctity of weekends in Europe and America, would hazard a guess that at least Sunday would be a holiday. This is not generally the case in India. Both Sphere Origins and Director's Kut keep long working hours, though they do not work through the night like Ekta Kapoor and some Balaji creative heads like Nivedita Basu. Working seven days of the week is quite normal. Even national holidays like 15 August (Independence Day) are not a day off for production houses. I interviewed Ronit Bose Roy and Sakshi Tanwar on the sets of their respective shows on 15 August 2007. The sets were a hive of activity with stars, creative heads, cameramen, tea boys and spot boys, tailors and those ironing clothes milling around. It is reported that the Balaji "crew works round the clock, often moving from shift to shift without a break. [Shobha and Ekta Kapoor's] attitude with employees — many of whom they appear to have plucked out of thin air — is said to be feudal" (Lalwani 2003b).

Fifth is the manner that television soaps are watched in India. Shalija Kejriwal finds it a "unique situation." Overseas, particularly in the US, there are season breaks before a show returns; in India, there are no season breaks. "People watch soaps 28 days in a month. It is a unique situation where the characters become a part of your family. The experience of viewing is completely different in India, you watch without a break, they are one's daily *dal–chawal*" (lentils and rice, often a staple diet in India). Ekta Kapoor observed that "*Kyunki* continues to be amongst the first three slots in the TRP ratings almost every week. *Its characters have become like family members to everybody*" (Lalwani 2003c, emphasis mine). In 2008, the same could be said of the characters in *Saat Phere* and *Bidaai*. In October 2008, the program *Saas, Bahu aur Saazish* (Mother-in-Law, Daughter-in-Law and Intrigue) airing five days a week on Star News, had many callers telephoning in to talk to the characters Ragini and Ranvir in *Bidaai* to know when they would actually meet up and how their love story would progress.

Sixth is a constant allusion to family. The Star Parivaar Awards, instituted by Star TV in 2002 to give television awards for all the shows aired on their channel, also make constant reference to family. The title itself alludes to family. This award show has proved to be a TRP gainer, and Shailja Kejriwal went on to say, "The Star *parivaa*r has grown bigger and has seen a flurry of new faces joining the family. So, all in all it is a nice mix of old and new. The ratings are astounding, and this gives us the encouragement to make it even bigger next year" (Krishna 2005). The awards theme in 2005 was *"har parivaar, Star parivaar"* (every family is a Star family), and in 2008, given the new shows that have since been launched on their channels, became *"naye parivaar ki nayi lahar"* (the new wave in the new family). Their catchy, popular title track also makes multiple references to the soap characters becoming members of our families: *"aaye they hum ek roz mehmaan ban kar, kya thi khabar aap ke ghar ke hi ho jayenge; pardey pey joh rishtey nibhaye hain hum ne, yun aap se bhi sabhi naatey woh jud jayenge ...* (we had come one day as guests, little did we know that we would become members of your family, and the relationships that we portrayed on screen would also become your relationships ...). This track plays at the opening and in between breaks, with characters from all Star programs lip-synching the lyrics and dancing along in Bollywood style. When *Kahaani* broadcast its last episode on 9 October 2008, after eight years on air, the last 15 minutes had the central character, Parvati, talking with the audience, saying, *"hamare ghar ke rishtey aap ke ghar ke rishtey ban gaye hain ... hamara parivaar aap ka parivaar ban gaya hai ..."* (our family's relations have become your family's relations ... our family has become your family).

This reference to being part of one family is one that is also made by all the employees of different production houses, be they actors, creative heads, cameramen, costume designers, spot boys, and others. Interviews with TV stars on the news show *Saas, Bahu aur Saazish* broadcast on Star News always detail how unit members ask each other if they have had lunch, enquire about each other's families, exchange recipes and shopping tips. In November 2008, when *Kyunki* was nearing its end on Star Plus and Ba's death scene was being filmed, the *Saas, Bahu aur Saazish* show of 4 November reported that many unit hands waited outside till the scene was over. Many of them could not bear to watch a family member's demise (even on screen). "We are all part of one family" was the refrain that ran through all interviews that I conducted. Family ideology, then, is a prime mode of address of the soap opera genre, for both the production members and the viewers (see also Katja Valaskivi's work [2000] on Japanese TV drama).[54]

Conceptualizing Soaps

Soap opera stories are conceptualized keeping current socio-economic scenarios in mind. The Balaji Telefilms' bouquet on Star Plus beginning with *Kyunki* and *Kahaani* that came on air in 2000, followed by *Kasautii* in 2001, were the first long running soap operas on Indian prime time television. The reason behind their programming was detailed research carried out by producers at Star on "how they perceived society at that point of time, and the homes that had cable TV."[55]

The importance of planning and research before launching soaps is stressed by Shailja Kejriwal, creative head of programming at Star from 1998–2007 and the main contact person with Balaji Telefilms, when she says, "it is the most important factor. Without that I would be completely at sea. Your gut has to be substantiated by science. That minimizes mistakes. It does not ensure success, but it does minimize errors. You have to plan and be on the ball all the time" (interview with Shailja Kejriwal, 7 September 2004, www.indiantelevision.com).

When cable television first came to India, few people owned TV sets. Programming was geared more towards the elite. Star World's English programming was very popular with those middle-class families who owned TV sets. From 1995–97, color TV started entering middle-class homes in larger numbers. These families are referred to as the *"hamara Bajaj* families" by Kejriwal. Indeed, "in those days, [if] one had to picture a quintessential middle class Indian family, it would be a snap of a Bajaj scooter with the father driving, trying hard to concentrate on the task at hand — that of herding his family safely to their destination; the younger kid, standing in the front, wind rushing through the hair, elation written on the face at this chance of discovering the world outside; the mother, sitting sideways, clutching the stepney tire, with a rather vacant expression; and the elder kid sandwiched between both parents, twisting his head this side and the other, desperately trying not to miss the view on account of his position. Driving further this picture into the Indian psyche was the famous *Hamara Bajaj* (our Bajaj) advertisement; the idea behind which was clearly that a family isn't complete (or middle class enough) without a Bajaj" (Anonymous 2006).

I agree with Kejriwal's observation that "this *Hamara Bajaj* picture remains an important milestone in the history of Indian society." It signaled mass acceptance of an urban lifestyle and of the nuclear family which were important precursors to the widespread changes that liberalization of the economy entailed. In a country of such vast cultural differences, it remains one of the few symbols that was once understood all across the country. The *Hamara Bajaj* families were mainly government employees with job security. Their children had started getting jobs in the IT sector, the family could afford Nike shoes. For them, owning a good color TV set was still a luxury because color TV sets were still expensively priced at Rs 30,000. Buying a color TV set usually entailed a month long discussion — it was a luxury to be proud of, to be shown off. Kejriwal termed this state "buying a color TV, waiting for the Maruti[56] class" that seemed within reach. Glad to be out of Doordarshan's clutches with its state-sponsored agenda, they were happy to see the infotainment on TV. The Indian televisual space was opening up to glitz and glamor.

As the years went by, television became available to lower earning classes and started spreading to rural areas as well. During this period, 1995–2001, India's information technology sector grew by leaps and bounds and India became the preferred destination for off-shoring practices and outsourcing IT work. This period from 1995–2001 was called the period of the "dot-com bubble," sometimes also called the "IT bubble." The young Indian middle class, so far desirous of secure government jobs, faced job insecurity in a liberalizing economy, but also at this point had greater money to spend and took greater risks. By the time the IT meltdown started in 2001, television had become a necessity.

The IT bubble started threatening to burst by 2001, succumbing to the country's own economic slowdown and a global economy pushed further into recession after the September 11 terrorist attacks in the USA (United Press International 2001). The economic slowdown in the USA at this time forced once high-flying Indian companies to begin laying off software engineers. The mood in the job market was one of unease. "There was a discernible slowdown in hiring across all levels, with some companies implementing a postponement of hiring. Indeed, recruitment at most companies had been frozen" (Krishnadas 2001). Many small start-up companies that had been set up during the euphoria phase closed down and numbers of people were rendered jobless.

There was no coping mechanism and middle class Indians were seeing for the first time what it felt like to be part of a capitalist economy. It became a matter of shame for their families as well, since they were not equipped to deal with lay-offs. Shailja Kejriwal told me that "at this point, the family became the only support system, an area of solace." She added that she had "seen her own relatives leaving home in the mornings, spending the entire day at Marine Drive in Mumbai, and then returning home so that the kids did not know that Daddy did not have a job any more."[57] People were not going out in large numbers to movie halls either. There was a decline in socializing due to fear of embarrassing questions being asked. Television consequently became "the escape route to be entertained, yet one could be on his/her own. People needed the solace of the family and also needed to have their minds taken off their problems even for a while and be entertained. Women also needed to dream."[58]

The family thus became the central focus of people at this time and was both "idealized and idolized."[59] Audiences were looking for a comfort zone where the wife was ideal and supportive in the mold of Parvati and Tulsi, and mothers were unquestioning and loving like Ba and Ma-*ji*. Keeping this economic and social reality in mind, Star TV decided to "give their viewers the ideal family that they were looking for." *Kyunki* and *Kahaani* were born.

Kejriwal observed that "entertainment fills the gap between aspirations and fulfillment. At that point in time, the dream and aspiration was for an ideal situation ... *ek din mera bhi hoga* (one day even I will have this). Watching *Kyunki* and *Kahaani* at that time filled that gap."[60] TRPs for that period bear witness to Kejriwal's claim. It was reported that "Star Plus continues to reign supreme on the TRP charts. The top eight slots across all satellite channels belong to it, a company release states, quoting the latest AC Nielsen TAM ratings for the week ending 27 May. Looking at the TAM ratings as a whole, Star Plus has reached an all time high with 37 programmes in the top 50. Star Plus' 24-hour share is 9.9 per cent — the highest ever, the release states. And it is Star Plus' two superhit soaps, *Kyunki Saas Bhi Kabhi Bahu Thi* and *Kahaani Ghar Ghar Ki* which have carved out the top eight positions. Positions 1 to 4 have been taken by *Kyunki* ... with the

Thursday 24 May episode being the highest with a 14.7 per cent viewership. For *Kahaani* ... the Tuesday 22 May episode had the highest viewership coming in at 5 with a 10.9 TRP rating. Both series air four days a week Monday through to Thursday" (www. indiantelevision.com, 6 June 2001).

This dream run continued for a long time. Television industry news reports said, "if it was Star Plus' soaps that ruled the TRP charts in the year gone by, the tale was no different as Hindi entertainment television bid adieu to 2003. While a whole lot of people were letting their hair down on New Year's Eve, there was that loyal lot who was glued to the television too. And unsurprisingly most of them were watching Star Plus ... it wasn't the special events or programmes that were popular with the viewers on New Year's Eve but rather Star Plus' staple of daily soaps ... viewer fatigue or no viewer fatigue, Star Plus with its family sagas held sway in the numbers' game even on 31 December 2003" (www.indiantelevision.com, 12 January 2004). TRPs then also bear out Kejriwal's astute observations of *Kyunki* and *Kahaani* connecting with audiences at a basic comfort level and thereby keeping their attention.

A few years into the twenty-first century and with the Indian economy recovering from the dot com crash years, confidence started building anew. In 2008, leading marketing consultant Rama Bijapurkar was writing: "The *janata* (public) has given a clear thumbs-up for consumption. The best indication of sustained consumer confidence is the doubling of the pre-budget poll score on 'the budget will bring relief to the common man' to 43% ... Inclusive consumption is achieved: The 23-million lower middle class urban households ... have seen visible wealth and have a strong aspiration to consume. Between 2004 and 2007, they have had a 35% increase in consumption intensity, which is poised to continue ... the best indication that India's consumption story isn't about to dry up" (Bijapurkar 2008). L. V. Krishnan told me that "in India, television provides the biggest consumerist movement, aimed first at women, next at kids."[61] A young Team India, under the captainship of Mahendra Singh Dhoni, brought home the Twenty20 World Cup in cricket in 2007, having beaten arch rivals Australia in the semi-finals and Pakistan in the finals. Bollywood films are a success overseas and world tours of leading stars such as Amitabh Bachchan's "Unforgettable" tour in 2008 and Shah Rukh Khan's "Temptations" tour are sold out. India signed a nuclear deal with the USA in 2008, ending years of nuclear isolation. We also launched our first unmanned mission to the moon, Chandrayan I, in October 2008. Television channels have proliferated "from 116 channels prior to the year 2000 to 427 channels in the first quarter of 2008."[62] All kinds of programs — ranging from news, reality shows, direct telecast of sports events, especially cricket, serials, sitcoms, and soaps — now jostle for space. There is a new confidence everywhere that is palpable and a pride in "being Indian." Advertisers regularly use slogans such as "*Yeh hamara India*" (this is our India).[63] Santosh Desai, former COO of McCann Erickson, and now CEO of Future Brands, has rightly pointed out that "the idea of self-consciously calling oneself Indian and with pride is a recent phenomenon. Earlier, every time we talked about India, we talked about its glorious past. Today, we see our present as equally glorious."[64]

Bijapurkar pointed out that "earlier, it was cool to say 'I don't see Hindi films or television.' Now the coolest thing to see is Hindi films. It is cool to see *Jodha Akbar*, *Mughal-e-Azam* reworked in color and *Jab We Met*. Corporates in Mumbai booked the Inox cinema hall for a special screening of *Jodha Akbar* for their employees."[65] She added: "look at clothing stores nowadays, they are filled with ethnic clothes for men and women. Men are now wearing the *sherwani kurta*, like the actors in *Kabhi Khushi Kabhie Gham* (Happiness at Times, Sorrow at Times, 2001, dir. Karan Johar) and the actors in our soaps. Soaps, in fact, are like Hindi movies used to be earlier. Even politics and the stock market, which were never attention grabbers earlier, are now cool and sexy. Patriotism, nationalism, and philanthropy are all cool. Everyone is proud to be Indian."

It is a changed scenario. Kejriwal pointed out that "audiences of 2007 and 2008 are very different from audiences of 1999 and 2000. The current audiences are more upbeat and outgoing, different from the licking-one's-wounds audiences of 2000."[66] In this changed scenario, soaps such as *Kyunki* and *Kahaani* are yielding way to different stories that are being told. Maybe Raman Kumar, writer–producer and director of TV serials, was prescient when he said in 2001 that "the *saas–bahu* (mother-in-law–daughter-in-law) sagas are the in thing today but very soon they will have to go. But yes, programming on TV will remain women-centric, because the primary audience for TV constitutes women. Five years ago, we were talking about the woman of today, now we are talking about the woman of yesterday but very soon, we are going to start talking about the woman of tomorrow. That will be the change in programming in the coming years" (interview with Raman Kumar, www.indiantelevision.com, 16 August 2001).

L. V. Krishnan of TAM India says that "simple, social issues work best now. That is the common denominator that cuts across viewership patterns. The communication has to be simple and direct and the themes need to be those that people relate to more easily now."[67] It is perhaps no surprise, therefore, that *Bidaai* has been maintaining the number one position on a regular basis from the end of 2007, and *Saat Phere* was the first to give the K soaps a run in viewership ratings.

In a time of financial crisis, however, in 2008, with world markets crashing from September 2008, the Indian stock market touching its lowest levels in October 2008 during the festive season, and companies downsizing, there is a general sense of panic all over the world, including India. It remains to be seen what kind of programming will lure audiences at this time. Raman Kumar observed that "the audience watches TV, the content changes just like changes in fashion — for instance bell bottoms may get replaced by jeans and jeans by baggies over time. Similar is the change in the nature of TV programmes. But TV programming follows a cycle and the same kind of programmes resurface after a point in time" (interview with Raman Kumar, www.indiantelevision.com, 16 August 2001). It will be interesting to see which way the Indian viewer's preferences tilt now.

Relationship of Television Channels with Production Houses: A Shifting Space

The relationship between television channels and production houses is one of trust and confidence, and also, of course, that production houses deliver content that keep TRPs high for the channel. In 2003, television channel officials were on record saying, "advertisers love TRPs and the *saas–bahu* sagas deliver them ... family based dramas continue to occupy more than two-thirds of TV viewer's time on air. The present focus is then on creating dramas. That's what the viewer wants for the moment" (Kotian *et al.* 2003). Star Plus' bouquet of Balaji soaps during prime time — *Kyunki, Kahaani* and *Kasautii* — bear out the truth of this remark. The trio of these K soaps was hugely successful for Star, and helped in establishing the channel as a family brand. It has been rightly said that "the 3 Ks were born at the right time. Hindi programming at that stage had reached a juncture where audiences were on the lookout for something new. Besides, the shows raised the standards of Indian television in terms of production values, show packaging, the introduction of catchy title songs and opening montages. It brought in aspirational lifestyles, stylised sets and a very upmarket and glossy image which was never witnessed before" (Krishna 2004).

Akhila Shivdas, head of the Centre for Advocacy and Research, observed, "all these three serials came at a time when people were looking for something different. These offerings were unique. The experimentation with a new telling format also was an instant hit." Similarly, media analyst Sevanti Ninan stated that "the three serials were based on market research as Star was looking at widening their audiences and going beyond the metros. Focus group discussions that were conducted by the network gave them a fair idea of what viewers wanted — a glimpse of their everyday lives. Star also incentivised the production house on the delivery of ratings. So, if the ratings were good on a show, a percentage was given to the production house" (Krishna 2004).

It is no surprise, therefore, that Star and Balaji enjoyed a very comfortable and profitable relationship between 2000–2008. In 2005, Star group CEO, Michelle Guthrie, commenting on the relationship between Star TV and Balaji Telefilms, said, "Balaji as a production company is pretty unique in the sense of the leadership position it has in the market ... we have only recently invested in Balaji, though we have worked successfully with it before. After the equity participation, that relationship has become stronger. Balaji continues to work closely with us, while making programmes for others ... creating quality programming is the key to any successful television business, not just Star's TV business" (Mitra 2005). When I interviewed Yash Khanna, Head of Corporate Communications at Star, in 2007, he confirmed that "Star had taken 25.9 per cent equity in Balaji Telefilms. Separate from this was the understanding that Balaji's soaps on Star could not conflict with their soaps on other channels in the same time slot. If they did, Balaji would be competing with themselves."[68]

He also said that "there was a lot of interaction between producers and programming heads from Star and Ekta's team of creative heads" and was emphatic in adding that Star programming "monitor and research TRPs on a minute-to-minute basis, and this is discussed with Balaji. Star needs to do this from their marketing point of view and channel share in the market."[69]

When asked if a good equation with a channel helps Balaji, Ekta Kapoor herself is on record admitting that "of course, it helps. For instance, I have a good equation with Star Plus. But mind you, I have to deliver the TRPs. If my show does not deliver, my relationship would not help me to swim in smooth waters. I might even go for a toss." She also added that "serial making is not autocracy. It's meeting on common grounds. Why should a channel sail on a boat which does not know how to wade its way through troubled waters?" (Lalwani 2003a).

By 2008, the Balaji–Star relationship was beginning to feel the strain of dipping TRPs for the Balaji's flagship soaps, *Kyunki* and *Kahaani*. When questioned in April 2008 if "the low TRPs of the Balaji shows [were] sending out alarm signals," Star Plus General Manager, Keertan Adyanthaya, replied, "absolutely not," and added that "fiction shows have high and low points; Star is not unduly worried about it at all" (Sultana 2008).

By summer 2008, when I was in Mumbai for a second round of fieldwork, hints of brewing trouble between Balaji and Star were gradually becoming visible. At this time, Yash Khanna said that despite the many new channels that had opened up, "Star still retained its lead in the GEC (general entertainment category), followed by Zee and then all other channels." He did admit, however, that "business [had become] very competitive, [and that] time slots are given based on its probable delivery and not any more by guts. Programming has to generate mass viewership, better TRPs for our shows. Be it following a formula or breaking the mold, the result has to be better TRPs. One has to cater to the needs of the viewer." By then, Star had already been paying attention to why TRPs were declining for *Kyunki* and *Kahaani* and wondering whether "a story could be stretched for so long." In September 2008, *Kahaani* was not ranked in the top 40 shows in TRP ratings. In the week of 7–13 September 2008, TAM data shows that it had slipped to position 41 with a rating of 2.03. Publicly, Star senior creative director Anupama Mandloi said, "*Kahaani* ... is concluding after a successful span of 8 years. It is a time of nostalgia, sadness and yet a feeling of triumph for all those associated with the show" (Jain 2008). In the interview with me, Khanna explained that "managing TV programming is a commercial art. So commercial needs have to be taken into consideration. I feel these requirements are justified."[70]

By the middle of August 2008, however, the following news hit headlines: "Balaji Telefilms has snapped ties with Rupert Murdoch's Star Group. The Star Group held 25.99 per cent stake in Balaji Telefilms via Asian Broadcasting FZ LLC. 'The agreements entered into between Balaji and Star in April 2007 relating to the regional languages joint venture will also be terminated,' says a Balaji statement ... Star India CEO Uday Shankar said, 'Star and BTL (Balaji Telefilms Ltd) have agreed to determine all prior agreements such that each side is freed from all respective rights and obligations arising from such agreements. The relationship between Star and BTL as broadcaster and content provider will not be affected. The new arrangement allows both parties to take the best advantage of emerging opportunities in broadcasting and content creation.' An official statement says that the content supply agreements between Star and Balaji for various shows produced by it will be modified to remove the restrictions imposed upon Balaji relating to exclusivity on certain prime time slots" (headlines, www.indiantelevision.com, 19 August 2008).

Kahaani aired its last episode on 9 October 2008. Soon after, it was widely reported in the media that Star had decided to terminate *Kyunki* from 10 November 2008, and that Balaji Telefilms has moved the Mumbai High Court, challenging Star group's decision to terminate the longest running daily soap *Kyunki*, since Star was apparently in breach of contract for this early termination. All concerned parties from Balaji and Star refrained from comment (see www.indiantelevision.com headlines; www.tellychakkar.com; *Times of India; and Indian Express*, 20 October 2008).

Media reports have been raising the question whether "fresh concepts and storylines adopted by new channels had led to a decline in the popularity [of *Kyunki* and *Kahaani*]"[71] (*Times of India,* 24 October 2008). From 13 October 2008, Rajan Shahi's successful soap *Bidaai* had moved to a one hour time slot on Star Plus prime time, 9 pm–10 pm.

There is no doubt that Ekta Kapoor is going through a troubled professional spell in late 2008. Balaji Telefilms' "income from operations dropped 32.56 per cent in the second quarter of the financial year 2008–09, and its profits were down by 31.02 per cent from the corresponding quarter of the previous fiscal year" (headlines, www.indiantelevision.com, 25 October 2008). Media reports in October 2008 speculate that "stars, numbers and astrology, Ekta Kapoor's life and career have been ruled by them. The lady who was known to have a 'midas touch' is now going through a rough patch. First it was curtains for her flagship show *Kahaani Ghar Ghar Ki* and then came her fallout with Star Plus. Two big shows KGGK (*Kahaani Ghar Ghar Kii*] going off air and *Kyunki Saas Bhi Kabhi Bahu Thi* receiving stepmotherly treatment from the channel shows Ekta has been at the receiving end." The report goes on to ask, "complications and controversies, they just don't seem to leave her side. Wonder what do the stars have in store for Ekta Kapoor this year. Will she bounce back or topple down like the Indian Sensex?" (*Times of India,* 29 October 2008).

Rajan Shahi has maintained the top spot with *Bidaai* for Star Plus. News headlines on www.tellychakkar.com on 25 October 2008 observed that "*Bidaai* just didn't make Parul Chauhan a household name it also altered power equation in Star Plus. Star has been a bastion of Ekta but the channel seems to have found an equal ally in Rajan Shahi. So, out goes *Kyunki, Kahaani* and other ageing soaps of Balaji as Star welcomes another show from Rajan which surely will have TV pundits say '*Yeh rishta kya kehlata hai*'" (What is This Relationship Called).[72] In January 2009 as well, *Bidaai* scaled new heights in the TRP charts. "It reached a milestone with an 8.9 weekly TRP average, the highest in nearly 100 weeks in any channel in India. Two episodes were at 9.6 and 9.2, the highest rating on GECs, in more than 570 days across all channels in India" (personal communication with Rajan Shahi, 16 January 2009; see also headlines, www.tellychakkar.com, 10 January 2009).

By late October 2008, speculation had already turned rife about changed equations at Star Plus. *Times of India* reported on 30 October 2008, "with a very heavy heart Balaji bids adieu to its flagship show *Kyunki Saas Bhi Kabhi Bahu Thi* on the 10th November 2008. The production house and the star cast of the show, with a heavy heart will watch the last episode of the show on air together ... the show has fallen like a pack of cards and this has disturbed Balaji no end. [Star] has shows like *Bidaai* that is the current hot favorite. After the original creative team of Star Plus, like Sameer Nair and Shailja Kejriwal quit, the new team started giving Balaji stepmotherly treatment ... the buzz is that Ekta is not too happy with both her flagship shows *Kahaani ... and Kyunki ...* going off air in a span of one month" (Thapar Kapoor 2008).

Indeed, the beginning of January 2009 saw Ekta Kapoor return to her comfort zone of the television producer team of Sameer Nair and Shailja Kejriwal, the team which had made *Kyunki* and *Kahaani* household names. Nair and Kejriwal had left Star and moved to NDTV Imagine. Announcing the association with Balaji Telefilms, Shailja Kejriwal, executive vice president, content, NDTV Imagine, said, "we are delighted to be working with Ekta once again. She has a great understanding of the pulse of our viewers and together we will create stories that will refresh and delight our audience. It is also quite a coincidence that the first time we interacted with Ekta was for the 10.30 pm slot, just like this one." Ekta added, "this is like homecoming; to be back working with Sameer and Shailja. They are the ones who gave me my first break and I treat them like my bosses. I am pleased to be working with them again as they give me all the support and freedom and I will work with the same passion as I used to earlier" (http://entertainment.oneindia.in/television/top-stories/news/2008/imagine-balaji-tie-up-151008.html). Ekta's two new soaps — *Bandini* and *Kitani Mohabbat Hai* (How Much Love Is There) started being telecast on NDTV Imagine from 19 January 2009 onwards in the prime time bands of 10 pm–10:30 pm and 10:30 pm–11pm respectively.

This chapter bears out the fact of the importance of soap opera as a genre both for television channels and production houses. How this genre has developed in prime time programming on two of the top general entertainment channels — Star Plus and Zee TV — will be tracked in the course of the book.

Notes

1. Interview with Yash Khanna (August 2007).
2. By April 2008, however, K soaps and other Indian soaps such as *Kumkum: Ek Pyara Sa Bandhan* (Kumkum: A Loving Relationship) produced by B.A.G. Films were ordered by conservative elements in the Afghan parliament to be taken off air, as they were considered un-Islamic (www.Afghanistannewscenter.com, 21 April 2008).
3. *"Namaste"* is the Indian greeting for welcome with hands folded; *"firangi"* refers to "foreigner;" *"gora"* literally means "of fair skin," but is used here in reference to a white-skinned foreigner; "chai" means "tea;" and *"chalta hai"* is a term that means "it's carrying on."
4. *"Mehndi"* is henna, generally applied on the hands for festive occasions, especially on the bride's hand during weddings. *"Bhangra"* is a form of Indian folk dance and song that originated in the north Indian state of Punjab in India.
5. Interview with Yash Khanna (August 2007).
6. Interview with Yash Khanna (August 2008).
7. Interview with L. V. Krishnan (August 2008).
8. Interview with Yash Khanna (August 2008).
9. This point is discussed in more detail in a later chapter.
10. See Hobson (2003: 52–53) for a discussion on how TV executives in the UK answered the same question.
11. Interviews held in 2007 and 2008.
12. Details of TAM are taken from its website http://www.tamindia.com.
13. Interview with L. V. Krishnan (August 2008).
14. Interview with L. V. Krishnan (August 2008, emphasis mine).
15. Interview with Shobha Kapoor (August 2007).
16. A Sanskrit term specifically denotes a metered and often rhymed poetic verse or phrase. *Shloka* is the chief meter used in the epics *Ramayan* and *Mahabharat*.
17. *Aarti* is a Hindu ritual in which light from wicks soaked in *ghee* (purified butter) or camphor is offered to one or more deities. *Aarti* is generally performed two to five times daily, usually at the end of a prayer session.
18. *"Prasad"* literally means "gracious gift." During prayers, something edible like fruit or sweets are first offered to the deity and then distributed after the prayers are over.
19. Interview with Shobha Kapoor (August 2007).
20. Many Balaji employees refer to Ekta Kapoor simply as "fifth floor."
21. Interview with Shobha Kapoor (August 2007).
22. Interview with Shobha Kapoor (August 2007).
23. Interview with Shailja Kejriwal (August 2007).

24. Details from *Kyunki*, special program, *Saas, Bahu aur Saazish*, Star News, 5 November 2008.
25. Interviews with Chloe Ferns and Nivedita Basu (August 2007).
26. Interview with Chloe Ferns (August 2007).
27. Interview with Chloe Ferns (August 2007).
28. Interview with Shobha Kapoor (August 2007).
29. Interviews with Shobha Kapoor and Sakshi Tanwar (August 2007).
30. Interview with Chloe Ferns (August 2007).
31. Interview with Shobha Kapoor (August 2007).
32. Interview with Sunjoy Waddhwa (August 2007).
33. Interview with Sunjoy Waddhwa (August 2007).
34. Interview with Sunjoy Waddhwa (August 2007).
35. Interview with Sunjoy Waddhwa (August 2007). Further details on the company are available on its website www.sphereorigins.com.
36. Interview with Sunjoy Waddhwa (August 2007, emphasis mine).
37. Interview with Sunjoy Waddhwa (August 2007).
38. Interview with Sunjoy Waddhwa (August 2007).
39. Interview with Sunjoy Waddhwa (August 2007).
40. Interview with Rajan Shahi (August 2008).
41. Interview with Rajan Shahi (August 2008).
42. Telephonic interview with Rajan Shahi (October 2008).
43. Interview with Rajan Shahi (August 2008).
44. Interview with Shobha Kapoor (August 2007).
45. Details put together from interviews with Shobha Kapoor, Chloe Ferns, Sunjoy Waddhwa, and Rajan Shahi (2007 and 2008).
46. A lakh (sometimes also written as lac) is a unit in the Indian numbering system equal to one hundred thousand. A crore is a unit in the Indian numbering system equal to 100 lakh. Conversion rates as of 4 February 2009, list one US\$ being the equivalent of approximately INR (Indian Rupees) 50. Rs 1 crore, then, is approximately US\$204,265; and Rs 1 lakh is approximately US\$2043. (Conversion website — www.oanda.com.)
47. Interview with Shobha Kapoor (August 2007). Bullet Time Effect refers to a digitally enhanced simulation of variable speed photography. It is characterized both by its extreme permutation of time (slow enough to show normally imperceptible and un-filmable events, such as flying bullets) and space (by way of the ability of the camera angle — the audience's point of view — to move around the scene at a normal speed while events are slowed). These special effects have been used successfully in *The Matrix* (1999, dirs Andy Wachowski and Larry Wachowski).
48. Interviews with Shobha Kapoor, Nivedita Basu, Sunjoy Waddhwa, and Rajan Shahi (2007 and 2008).

49. *Vaastu shastra* deals with various aspects of designing and building living environments in harmony with the physical and metaphysical forces. *Vaastu* is conceptually similar to *feng shui* in that it also tries to harmonize the flow of energy, also called life-force, and prana in Sanskrit.
50. Interview with Sunjoy Waddhwa (August 2007).
51. Janamashtami is a Hindu festival celebrating the birth of Krishna, an avatar of the god Vishnu.
52. *Sudarshan chakra* is a spinning, disc-like weapon which serves as an attribute of the Hindu god Vishnu, also called Narayan. Lord Vishnu is depicted holding the *chakra* from a central hole with his index finger. The disc spins around his finger. According to the *Puranas*, he would release it and it would do the necessary and return back to his finger. It is revered as a divine weapon. Of all divine weapons, this is the only one which is constantly in motion.
53. The *tilak* is a mark, generally on the forehead, and may be made with sandalwood paste, vermilion and ashes (*vibhuti*) and applied after prayers.
54. An important question which arises is whether this emphasis on family, from both the production and reception sides, is more pronounced in Asian cultures.
55. Most of the details in this section on the soaps of Balaji Telefilms are taken from interviews with Shailja Kejriwal.
56. Maruti 800, modeled after the Suzuki Alto, is a city car manufactured by Maruti Udyog in India. Launched in 1984 and priced within reach of a large number of people, it quickly became the fastest selling car in the Indian market.
57. Interview with Shailja Kejriwal (August 2007).
58. Interview with Shailja Kejriwal (August 2007).
59. Interview with Shailja Kejriwal (August 2007).
60. Interview with Shailja Kejriwal (August 2007).
61. Interview with Rama Bijapurkar (August 2008).
62. Figures provided by L. V. Krishnan (August 2008).
63. This does not, in any way, imply that the picture in India is only rosy. The reality is far from it. We still have poverty, hunger and illiteracy to deal with, in addition to myriad other problems such as extremism, lack of transparent governance, corruption, lawlessness, etc. But this does not take away from the fact that we have come a long way, and that now there is a discernible pride in being Indian and things Indian that was not there till even as recently as about 10 years ago. In this context, see Ganguly-Scrase and Scrase (2009), which examines the complexity of the globalization process in India and the contradictory attitudes of the lower middle classes. The authors challenge the notion of a homogeneous Indian middle class

as being the undoubted beneficiaries of recent neoliberal economic reforms, showing that while the lower middle classes are generally supportive of the recent economic reforms, they remain doubtful about the long term benefits of the country's new economic policy and liberalization.

64. Rama Bijapurkar provided this quote. In a recent insightful article, Bijapurkar notes that in India, incomes of both the top and bottom rungs of the ladder have increased. What has not kept pace is the quality of life, defined as "access to basic amenities and services." She warns against confusing "consumption of consumer goods with quality of life improvement" and notes that this might be a fallout from referring to people at the bottom of the economic pyramid as "consumers and not as citizens." She ends the article by calling for government to act and build on successful models that have already shown results in India. She also calls for those in business to "revisit the metrics of progress and inclusive growth..." (Bijapurkar 2008b).

65. Interview with Rama Bijapurkar (August 2008).

66. Interview with Shailja Kejriwal (August 2007).

67. Interview with L. V. Krishnan (August 2008).

68. Interview with Yash Khanna (August 2007).

69. Interview with Yash Khanna (August 2007).

70. Interview with Yash Khanna (August 2008).

71. New concepts include shows like *Balika Vadhu* (Child Bride) and *Mohe Rang De* (Colour Me [Saffron]), on Colors; *Radhaa Ki Betiyaan Kuch Kar Dikhayengi* (Radha's Daughters Will Achieve Something), *Jasuben Jayantilal Joshi Ki Joint Family* (Jasuben Jayantilal Joshi's Joint Family), and *Main Teri Parchhain Hoon* (I Am Your Reflection) on NDTV Imagine. *The Times of India* (24 October 2008) reports that "most of these serials are a departure from the typical saas–bahu sagas that STAR Plus, Sony and Zee TV have sworn by. While *Radhaa Ki...* is about the struggle of a single small town woman and her three daughters, *Balika Vadhu* focuses on child marriage. *Mohe Rang De* is set in the pre-Independence era and *Main Teri Parchhain...* is about a 21-year-old girl, who chooses to be the mother of three children."

72. This is a double entendre, since it is also the title of Rajan Shahi's new soap.

3

Key Elements of Production: Characteristics of Soaps

Several different elements come together in the production and presentation of a soap opera. Soaps on prime time television share common features. This chapter indicates their significance in brief narratives of their function. They are fundamental issues to be considered in a discussion of the genre.

Role of the Producer

Dorothy Hobson rightly states that "television is a producer's medium and the soap opera is the form which clearly demonstrates their power. The strength and impetus for the soap opera comes from the producer" (Hobson 2003: 63).[1] In the case of soaps, the reference is to both sets of producers — the content production house and the producer at the television channel who, along with a team of co-producers, is the contact person with the production house.

Senior television executives made clear to me in interviews that executive producers and programming heads from the TV channel interact closely with production company heads like Ekta Kapoor, Rajan Shahi and others who produce shows for the channel.[2] For instance, Shailja Kejriwal was the main contact person between Star and Balaji Telefilms from 1998–2007. Kejriwal was trusted implicitly by the two producers of Balaji Telefilms, the mother and daughter team of Shobha Kapoor and Ekta Kapoor.[3] After Kejriwal's departure to join NDTV Imagine, it is now Anupama Mandloi who is Star's main contact person with Balaji. Similarly, producer Vivek Bahl, headhunted from Zee TV in 2007, is Star's main contact person with producer Rajan Shahi of Director's Kut. Despite having a team of associate producers and creative heads, it is the producers themselves such as Rajan Shahi and Ekta Kapoor who meet with the television channel's producers in order to discuss storylines, changes, etc. While TV executives say that theirs is the "ultimate decision," they also admit that they do not ride roughshod over the producer without first having detailed discussions with them as to how the soap narrative must progress. Rajan Shahi, the producer of *Bidaai*, for instance has a long history of producing shows for which his main contact person at the television channel is Vivek Bahl. Shahi directed some episodes of *Jassi Jaisi Koi Nahin* (Sony) and also set up hit shows like *Saat Phere* and interacted with Bahl and *Ghar Ki Lakshmi ... Betiyaan*[4] for Zee as series director when Vivek Bahl used to be Creative Head of Zee TV. With Bahl's move to Star, he roped in Shahi to produce *Bidaai*, the show that is currently topping TRPs in the country.[5] Star commissioned Shahi to produce the new soap *Yeh Rishta Kya Kehlata Hai* for Star Plus. As with anything else, the personal connection goes a long way in ensuring the comfort level on both sides, and so the television company is careful in choosing who interacts with the creative production head.

Television executives say that from the point of view of production and profits for the channel, they track the shows very closely, as in monitoring TRPs and audience feedback via letters, e-mails, etc. TV channels have separate departments to deal with audience feedback.[6] In case TRPs show consistent decline, this is immediately discussed with the production house, and steps are taken jointly, after discussion, to see how the storyline needs to proceed to grab audience eyeballs again. A few examples will illustrate this point. For instance, television executives go through national and regional figures which come in every week from TAM. So, for instance when Star Plus noticed that regional viewership in Kolkata had fallen for *Kayamath*,[7] the soap fast forwarded five years in the love story of the lead characters Prachi and Milind to Kolkata where Bengali characters and festivals such as Durga Puja have been introduced (*Kayamath*, Star Plus, September 2008 onwards).[8] Another very good example of this was the return of Smriti Z. Irani in 2008 to reprise the role of the nation's favorite *bahu*, Tulsi, in *Kyunki*. While TRPs had initially dipped after Irani had left *Kyunki* in 2007, Gautami Gadgil's essaying of Tulsi's role did not fare too badly for *Kyunki*. However, with the launch of *Bidaai* on Star Plus in October 2007, the Balaji bouquet started showing signs of wilting. *Bidaai*'s popularity has been stupendous. It has maintained the number one position since its launch till September 2008.[9] New channels also began proliferating and in

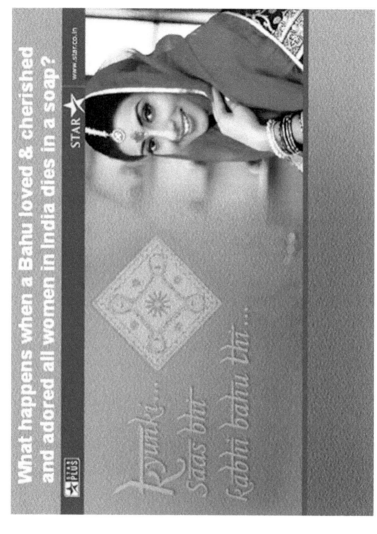

What happens when a Bahu loved & cherished and adored all women in India dies in a soap?

Kyunki...
Saas bhi
Kabhi bahu thi...

STAR PLUS

STAR ★
www.star.co.in

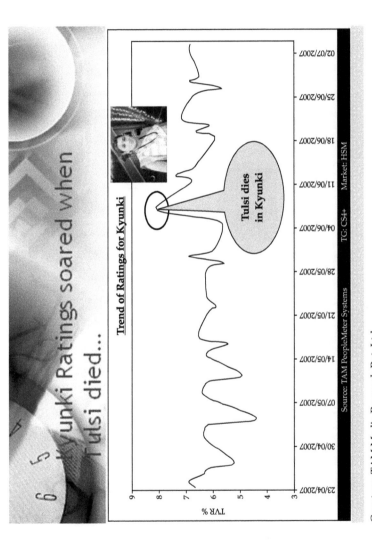

Kyunki Ratings soared when Tulsi died...

Courtesy: TAM Media Research Pvt. Ltd

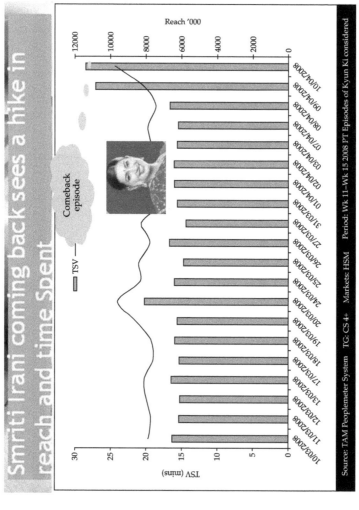

Smriti Irani coming back sees a hike in reach and time Spent

Reach '000

TSV (mins)

Comeback episode

TSV

Source: TAM Peoplemeter System   TG: C5 4+   Markets: HSM   Period: Wk 11–Wk 15 2008 PT Episodes of Kyun Ki considered

Courtesy: TAM Media Research Pvt. Ltd

such a scenario, Balaji needed something dramatic to regain its lost footing. After a series of discussions with Star executives, it was decided to invite Irani to reprise the role of Tulsi in *Kyunki*. A lot of media space was given up in discussing her return to the show. If one were to believe just the printed media reports, then there were many other reasons for her return, such as audiences wanting her back, Ekta Kapoor's much-publicized making up with her at the Balaji Telefilms Awards in Dubai in early 2008, etc.[10] *Kyunki*'s falling TRPs were never cited as the reason in the popular press, but behind-the-scenes research tells a different story.

The producer therefore, from both ends of the spectrum, "is the key to soap opera. The producer … is the overall controlling influence in the genre and in the day-to-day, week-to-week development of the series" (Hobson 2003: 66).

Writers

Writers of soap operas have been termed "the lifeblood of the series" (Hobson 2003: 77). They are the people " … who create the characters, think of the storylines and write the everyday dialogue which tells both the stories and gives the characters their personality and individuality" (ibid.). A lot of the work in writing is a collective effort, though there are individual writers who work on individual soaps from time to time. For instance Kamlesh Pandey, who is well known for writing film stories, notably the recent *Rang de Basanti* (2006, dir. Rakyesh Omprakash Mehra) that won critical acclaim and several awards, was called in to write for *Kahaani* in autumn 2007, to prepare for the generational leap that reintroduced Parvati back into the story as the glamorous Janki Devi. Kamlesh Pandey was responsible for conceptualizing the new Parvati, who had so far always been Sita of the *Ramayan*. In her new avatar, Parvati was molded like Arjun in the *Mahabharat* in a war against evil. Her mentor is Narayani Devi, who, like Lord Krishna in the *Mahabharat* shows her the right way to fight her battle, often making references to the Bhagvad Gita.[11]

Every soap produced by Balaji Telefilms has its own creative department with writers. Nivedita Basu, its long time creative head, and Chloe Ferns from Human Resources told me that "the writers have a large staff reporting to them that includes script heads, screenplay writers, associate screenplay writers, and 'detailers' who work on the script once the story is approved."[12] Writers and creative heads have meetings on how the story can proceed. These ideas are then taken to Ekta Kapoor. It was made clear to me repeatedly that "no episode goes on air without Ekta's permission. Every show is taken to Ekta who makes changes and then tells the creative team how she wants her ideas executed."[13]

Rajan Shahi, producer–director of *Bidaai*, is associated in a hands-on fashion with the writers and creative heads of Director's Kut regarding the development of the narrative of *Bidaai*. If Shahi feels strongly about changing the concept that the writers and creative heads have, he does so based on instinct and gut feel. Two examples of his insistence are casting Alok Nath in the pivotal role of Prakashchand Sharma; and changing the original concept of Sadhana as a bubbly extrovert to a more demure, shy persona after a few episodes when he noticed that Sara Khan, who plays the role of Sadhana, is a quiet person, but that on screen, a shy Sadhana worked equally well. This comes from a long experience of being associated with soaps that have proven to be hits on prime time Indian television. Sunjoy and Comall Waddhwa of Sphere Origins also monitor the development of the storyline of *Saat Phere* closely.

When asked about what factors a director takes into account most of all when producing a show, director Ashok Pandit[14] is on record saying that the "foremost concern is the writer because the writer is the star on TV ... if you observe carefully, TV is a medium where you can do without too much of technical finesse and sometimes even average performances. But the storytelling is one aspect which can never be compromised on. In fact ... for any successful project 60 per cent of the credit should go to the writer" (interview with Ashok Pandit, 3 August 2001, www. indiantelevision.com).

Even if writers take final direction from the producer of the soaps, their initial input is considered very valuable because it is they who provide the ideas which are worked around. Successful writers are paid much higher than average actors in soap operas (not the lead actors). Rumored to make between Rs 15,000–20,000 per episode, Dheeraj Sarna, a leading dialog writer of Balaji, says, "the soul of a show is its content. If your script is weak then the entire plot flops" (Kapoor 2008). Sarna adds, "If you have your screenplay and dialogue in place then your character is a sure shot hit. Mouthing dialogues is a cake walk for the actors, but it's a tough job for the writers. Everyday you live and grow with the character you're writing about" (ibid.).

There is no doubt that writers have created the iconic figures of Tulsi and Parvati, and have provided them with some of their finest dialogs. "Writers also pick up on actors' personal skills and mannerisms and write them into the characterization" (Hobson 2003: 77–78). These are two strong women of the small screen, yet the writers have used the strengths of the actresses who portray these roles (Smriti Z. Irani as Tulsi and Sakshi Tanwar as Parvati) to give them a definite and particular flavor in their characterizations.

Writer Mahesh Pandey, said to be the highest paid writer on television, says that he started his career "with a small amount of Rs. 500 per episode," but adds that "today the scenario is different" (Kapoor 2008).

It is true that writers of soaps in the Indian television industry work under impossible deadlines and tight schedules. Many times, they are writing for the episode to be shown the very next evening. Dialog writer Sharad Tripathi, who has been associated with many big shows, says that they "work under crazy deadlines. Actors can make mistakes and get away but if writers goof up then you're damned. It's the toughest job. Not many people aspire to be writers. Most of them want to be actors. But very few are aware that it's a writer who creates these larger-than-life heroes. In the course of it if they get more money then I think they deserve it" (Kapoor 2008).

Actors and Actresses

Actors and actresses in soap operas, and the characters they essay on screen, are the main pull that entice viewers to the genre and keep them coming back day after day to watch the soaps. They are held in the highest regard by loyal audiences, often to the extent that they are better known by their screen names than their real life names. Chances are that many viewers will recognize who Parvati (Sakshi Tanwar in *Kahaani*), Tulsi (Smriti Z. Irani in *Kyunki*), Mihir Virani and Mr Bajaj (Ronit Bose Roy in *Kyunki*

and *Kasauti* respectively), Karan and Nandini (Hiten Tejwani and
Gauri Pradhan Tejwani in *Kyunki*), and Prerna (Shweta Tiwari
in *Kasautii*) are, but will not know their real life names. This is
the nature of the relationship that is engendered between audiences and soap actors, in which the audience feels that they
actually "know" these people (cf. Hobson 2003: 67). Ronit Bose
Roy recounted an incident to me in which he said that when
he was in the hospital for a regular check-up and was lying in
bed, unable to move, having his electrocardiogram done, he was
accosted by a lady of grandmotherly age, who pounced on him
asking why he was being unfaithful to his devoted wife, Tulsi by
having an affair with the scheming Mandira (*Kyunki*). Roy said
that despite his protestations that it was just a character he played
on screen, the lady kept questioning and berating him till she had
to be dragged away by the hospital authorities.[15]

It comes as little surprise then that Smriti Z. Irani, who plays
the role of the iconic *bahu* Tulsi in *Kyunki*, was drafted into the
Bharatiya Janata Party (BJP) in early 2004 to contest the general
elections.[16] Journalist Bhawana Somaaya writes, "For the common
man, there is no dividing line between the image and the actor.
When they watch Amitabh Bachchan destroy anti-social elements
and emerge victorious on the big screen, they expect him to perform the same in real life ... now they will expect the same out of
Tulsi Virani" (2008: 13). Such is the power of audience identification
with the roles that actors portray on the screen!

While creative heads and writers craft the persona of the character, after the actor has portrayed the role for a while, the writers
build in the natural characteristics of the actor to assimilate
them into the character. For instance, as mentioned earlier, Rajan
Shahi told me that when conceptualizing the lead role of Sadhana
in *Bidaai*, he had originally conceptualized the character as bubbly
and extroverted. After a few epsidoes of *Bidaai* had been canned,
Shahi noticed that the actress portraying Sadhana (Sara Khan)
was quiet and more of an introvert. This somehow worked well
within *Bidaai*'s narrative, and after consultation with Vivek Bahl
at Star, Shahi continued with the portrayal of Sadhana as essayed
by Sara Khan.

Writing about British soaps, Dorothy Hobson observes that "for
the most part, actors in soap operas have to produce performances
that are understated and low-key, always less than 'actorly,' for

it is their job to create the illusion of the ordinary" (2003: 67). This observation holds true of British soaps which perhaps fall more within the realism genre (see Geraghty 1991; Hobson 2003; and Brunsdon 1997a and 2000 for details). Indian soap operas are dramatically different in this regard. There is nothing low key about most soap performaces in India. If anything, acting is in many close up shots and is dramatic for more effect. Ekta Kapoor's soaps are more like lavish mini productions of family saga Hindi films of the 1980s of her father, actor Jeetendra; and more recently, the Karan Johar variety of ostentation and glamor. The only possible exception among today's top rated shows may be *Bidaai*, which relies more on low key acting.

If actors find it relatively easy on British soaps to essay new characters, the same does not yet hold true of Indian soap actors and actresses. The latter, particularly those associated with a certain role, find it difficult to move out and portray other characters. Smriti Z. Irani left *Kyunki* in 2007, produced and acted in other programs such as *Viruddh, Thodi Si Zameen Thoda Sa Asmaan*, but could never rid herself of the Tulsi tag. Similarly, actor Kiran Karmarkar (Om in *Kahaani*) moved out of the soap by "dying" in a flood in Ahmedabad, Gujarat, declaring in the press that he was going to join Hindi cinema. Nothing transpired of that, and Karmarkar was brought back from the dead in *Kahaani* after a few months, with, needless to say, the same face, but amnesia, which has since been cured. After *Kasautii* ended in February 2008, Shweta Tiwari, who played the lead role of Prerna, found it difficult for a while to get other roles because of audience identification with Prerna. She seems to have found her footing, however, since she is currently a judge on the dance reality show *Aaja Mahi Vay* on Star Plus and portraying a role in *Ajeeb* (Strange/Unusual), a bi-weekly serial on the new channel 9X, and a lead role in *Jaane Kya Baat Hui* (Who Knows What Happened) on Colors TV. Ronit Bose Roy (Mihir in *Kyunki* and Mr Bajaj in *Kasautii*) is now playing the lead role in a Balaji Telefilms production, *Bandini* (literally, imprisoned), that started airing on NDTV Imagine from 19 January 2009, in the prime time slot of 10 pm–10:30 pm.

The two talented powerhouse actresses, Sakshi Tanwar (Parvati in *Kahaani*) and Smriti Z. Irani (Tulsi in *Kyunki*), have been less visible on the small screen after the closure of both soaps towards the end of 2008. The media in November 2008 was speculating about the future of *Kyunki,* that aired its last episode on 6 November 2008 on Star Plus, being aired in a new avatar on a rival channel. Irani is continuing her production work with her company, Ugraya Entertainment. Both actresses, however, have been roped in as brand ambassadors for Dabur India, a company that manufactures, among other things, home care products. Girish Kumar, senior general manager, Homecare, Dabur India is on record saying, "Both Smriti Irani and Sakshi Tanwar are well respected stars and symbolise true family women. We are confident that these associations will prove very fruitful for our home care brands" (www.indiantelevision.com headlines, 17 December 2008). It is noteworthy how Dabur is using the image of these two actresses in public memory as ideal homemakers in branding its products.

Costumes and Makeup

As Dorothy Hobson observes, "the creation of a character through dress and appearance is an important aspect of the fictional representation in television soap operas ... costume helps to create personality and register the changes in a personality. Costume can create the 'ordinary' or the most glamorous. The clothes have to be completely 'in character' for the soap opera and its style" (Hobson 2003: 68). In Balaji Telefilms' soaps, given that almost all of them have stories of rich industrialist joint families, all the actors wear expensive, designer clothes. The women are mostly decked out in the latest fashionable saris with matching jewelry and accessories. The younger generation women are sometimes shown wearing salwar kurtas or trousers with tops. The men's sartorial styles range from Indian clothing of knee-length formal coats like *sherwani*s and *kurta*s for most scenes of religious festivals and other ceremonies such as marriages, etc. and western clothes — suits, shirts and ties — as well. Balaji's costume designer Nim Sood's, (the sister of producer Shobha Kapoor) name appears in all Balaji credits. Shobha also informed me that Balaji has its own cupboards and trunks filled with expensive saris that they try never to repeat. Each sari costs anything upwards of Rs 15,000. When a sari is repeated, it is, more often than not, given to a minor character to wear in one of the new soaps.[17] Balaji actors and actresses are dressed and made up like film stars in an expensive Bollywood production. Even grandmothers in *Kyunki* and *Kahaani* wear the most expensive silk saris. When Balaji wanted a makeover for Sakshi Tanwar, playing the role of Parvati as a widow, with a white, or light colored sari, a low bun or plait, they brought in the services of designer Manish Malhotra, who is well known in Hindi film circles for dressing many stars in Hindi films, and also for being the preferred designer for many Bollywood stars. Thanks to Malhotra, Parvati morphed into the rich, powerful and glamorous Janki Devi, with designer saris, expensive matching jewelry and straight, shoulder length hair. The credits of *Kahaani* acknowledge Manish Malhotra with special thanks.

Despite the fact that the soaps span generations, no actor or actress ages in them. Even when the female characters become grandmothers, they look just slightly older than their avatars eight years ago. Only Smriti Z. Irani, playing Tulsi, started sporting grey hair when Tulsi became a grandmother. Irani feels that her courage in daring to appear "old" "stems from her understanding of her audiences," who, she says, "don't expect me to be a dressed up *gudiya* (doll)." She went on to add, "I am not in the industry to be a glamor doll, I am an actor, a director's tool. I have no fear that my career will end if I wear white. If anything, it helped me play my role convincingly as 60-year-old Tulsi."[18] On her return to *Kyunki* in 2008, Irani said in a much publicized interview with journalists of the *Indian Express* that "I am not sultry. I have to make do with housewife type of roles. Unfortunately, I am not a Bipasha Basu or a Katrina Kaif (leading Bollywood stars). I am comfortable wearing saris and only *bahus* get to do that. But I never feel that I missed out on anything." She added that "there are many stars, few actors and fewer brands. I am happy to qualify for the last two" (*Indian Express*, 13 April 2008).

Hobson noted that "one of the differences between American and British soap operas is that American soap operas are much more aspirational. Reflecting the 'American Dream' that hard work brings financial success and status recognition, the series are cast with so-called 'beautiful people' whose clothes are a reflection of the glamour and success that they have achieved and to which the audience can aspire" (2003: 69). Following this path of argument, one can safely say that Indian soap operas are also aspirational. However, they do not necessarily reflect the achievement of status and expensive goods through hard work. Most of the soaps I am dealing with in this book show rich, joint families which have businesses worth millions. People from such families will dress accordingly. It is also a long standing argument that Bollywood provides escapist fare. The prime time soap operas in Hindi that I am discussing also provide the same in their lavish representations of sets, décor, costumes, and make-up.

Such is the popularity of soap opera fashions that the soap *bahu* has become a brand for fashion sense. The soap has a popular appeal and mass reach. A *Times of India* article recently noted that real life "brides are going gaga to incorporate the look into their trousseau. From *Kyunki ... Kahaani* and *Prerna* saris to *Kavyanjali* jewellery, there's a telly touch to their D-day. Our bahus are already becoming brands not just in India, but overseas as well" (Amar 2008). Vamps in prime time soaps have made the biggest fashion splash. In its anniversary issue of 29 December 2008, *India Today*, one of India's leading English language weekly magazines, noted, in an article on "Trend-Setting Style Statements," that "Urvashi Dholakia as Komolika in *Kasautii Zindagi Kay* with her garish make-up, satin saris and stylish *cholis* [blouses] became the most copied TV star. Balaji stylist Nim Sood says, 'I wanted her to show skin, so I put her in off-shoulders, halters and backless blouses' ... on the small screen, fashion favours the evil" (Motihar 2008: 150).

This fact was underlined to me in an interview with L. V. Krishnan, CEO, TAM Media Research Pvt. Ltd, that measures television audience responses. Krishnan told me that many small shops have mushroomed in the suburbs of big cities that produce overnight what TV women are wearing. These are highly popular and fly off the shelves as quickly as they are made. This makes the task for the production unit of the soap opera that much tougher.[19]

Nim Sood, fashion stylist for all Balaji soaps, says, "When I started designing for serial characters, I never expected they'll become so popular. For women audiences, these serials are like 'home-shopping haunts.' They watch their clothes and jewellery week after week and gradually start following them since they are wearable and comfortable. There starts the brand building process" (Amar 2008).

Sets and Outdoor Locations

Each soap opera has its own visual style and this is largely established by the sets that the audience immediately recognizes. Balaji Telefilms has its own separate sets for each soap opera, so that whenever the audience sees the establishing shot of the house from the outside or a shot of the interior, it is immediately able to identify which soap opera this relates to. Balaji currently has 32 sets of its own — for offices, college corridors, classrooms, nightclubs, and shopping centers. It owns 12 sets in Aarey Milk Colony, Mumbai; eight in Killick Nixon studio premises; and some in Balaji Studios which are rented property in Goregaon. Shobha Kapoor stressed that Balaji does not rent out its sets, nor does it rent sets. This is because production values and continuity may suffer and they want their shows to have the same look.

For outdoors, certain houses are given out on rent and temple locations are also used within the city of Mumbai. For garden scenes, mountains and snow, Balaji uses Film City sets. For hospital shots, equipment is hired and Balaji only has a hospital corridor as a set. Shobha Kapoor explained to me that they do not maintain a hospital set since this is considered *"apshagun"* (inauspicious).[20]

Sphere Origins has permanent studio sets in Mumbai and Dahisar, a large warehouse that stores costumes and props. Sunjoy Waddhwa of Sphere Origins also said that they put up new sets and studios as and when required.[21]

Director's Kut in *Bidaai* uses the set of "Kaushalya Niwas" (Kaushalya's Abode), the family home of Prakash Chand Sharma, named after his wife Kaushalya; and the mansion of the Rajvansh family where Sadhana is a daughter-in-law in *Bidaai*. The interior of Kaushalya Niwas is so designed as to have doors opening out on to the streets of (presumably) Agra, where the soap is set, and where outdoor shootings take place. Through these open doors, the viewers see passersby, thereby lending the scene authenticity. Rajan Shahi, producer–director of *Bidaai*, says that they wanted to "give a feel of Agra and wanted a set in which one feels one is in the center of Agra with a house whose doors open out on to the street." Concentrating on the presentation of the show, Shahi was very particular about "passersby on the street." He also shows a character like *Mamaji* (maternal uncle) walking down the street and entering the house, and added that he had actually purchased horse-drawn carriages and bicycles from Agra to lend more of a patina of authenticity to the show. He underlined the fact that he "concentrates on the presentation of the show" and that "*Bidaai* has set a trend for this kind of realism."[22]

Opening Credits

The opening credits are a very important visual part of soap operas. Dorothy Hobson remarks that "the titles encapsulate the essence of every series ..." (2003: 72). The opening credits change over time as the narrative progresses, but an important feature of Indian soaps is that they always feature the central female protagonist. *Kyunki* and *Kahaani* are family sagas and reflect this in the opening credits. *Kyunki*'s original opening credits show Tulsi inviting the viewer in to the Virani family home and introducing them to the various family members, with the closing shot of the entire family. This has now metamorphosed into Tulsi pouring water into the *tulsi* (holy basil) plant and then standing with folded hands while a rangoli (colored powder decoration) comes up on the side. *Kahaani*'s opening credits depict vignettes of the Aggarwal family's life closing with the hands of Om, Parvati and their daughter Shruti guarding the sacred flame of the *diya* (lamp). After Om's presumed "death" and subsequent return, this morphed into the hands of Om and Parvati guarding the flame of the lamp. Since August 2008, when Parvati was (temporarily) outmaneuvered by Trishna and the various children of the family whose lives she has touched are trying to save her, the opening visual shows Parvati on one side and the five children, with references to the five Pandava brothers from the epic *Mahabharat* standing alongside with their hands atop each other's. *Kasautii* was conceived more as a love story and hence the focus on the family is less. Rather, it showcases the eternal romance between Prerna and Anurag with a red *chunni* (scarf) flying and enveloping the two central protagonists. Red is meant to depict the color of passion.[23] The *Saat Phere* title shot initially showed the heroine Saloni in bridal attire, and asked whether dark skin is auspicious or inauspicious. *Bidaai* shows vignettes of the two cousins, Sadhana and Ragini, growing up and closes with both of them in wedding finery framed against the backdrop of the Taj Mahal, geographically situating the story in Agra. All these are the ways that soap operas introduce to the audience the nature of the story and drama that will subsequently unfold.

Music

Dorothy Hobson refers to the music as the *"siren call to view"* to the audience; it has to be recognizable from outside the room where the television set is located as it heralds the beginning of the program and calls the viewers into the room to watch. "The signature tunes of all the soap operas are recognizable even from the first tune" (Hobson 2003: 71, emphasis in original). This holds absolutely true of Indian soap operas as well. The distinctive tunes and songs that herald the start of the soap, and also the restart after the advertising breaks, are what alert the audience that the show is beginning/the ad break is over.

Just as in Hindi films, music forms an integral part of the soap opera experience. Music does not simply announce the beginning of the program. Many characters in the show are associated with popular Hindi film songs, so if the audience hears some lines, they can immediately identify the character(s) with which a particular song is associated. For instance *Mere dil ka tere dil se rishta purana hai* (The relations of our hearts have old ties) from the film *Koi Aap Sa* (Someone Like You, 2005, dir. Partho Mitra) immediately recalls to mind Om and Parvati, the lead characters of *Kahaani*. The *Kyunki* songs include *Tere liye hum hain jiyen* (I live for you), title song of the hugely popular Hindi film *Veer Zaara* (2004, dir. Yash Chopra) and *Tere Naam* (In Your Name) from the film of the same name (2003, dir. Satish Kaushik) and recall Mihir and Tulsi. The song *Tere Bin* (Without You) from the film *Bas Ek Pal* (Only One Moment, 2006, dir. Onir) and *Beetey lamhe hamein jab bhi yaad aate hain* (When I remember past moments) from *The Train* (2007, dir. Hasnain Hyderabadwala) bring to mind Karan–Nandini; *Jeeney ke isharey mil gaye* (I have got signs for living) from *Phir Milenge* (We Will Meet Again, 2004, dir. Revathi) recall Lakshya and Krishnatulsi. Ragini and Ranbir of *Bidaai* are associated with the hit track *Ishq Hua* (Love Happened) from the film *Aaja Nach Le* (Let's Dance, 2007, dir. Anil Mehta). Music, therefore, forms an integral element in the way that audiences perceive characters and their relationships in soap operas.

The Swish Pan Shot[24]

This is a feature perhaps unique to Indian soaps. It is when, at a critical point, the camera and sound track go somewhat wild and a couple of things happen. For example if someone has been slapped, the same action is shown three times, with the camera panning, or swishing in and out rapidly. This is what producer–director Rajan Shahi calls the "swish pan shot." The shot is accompanied by loud music, signaling that something critical has occurred. That action is also shown in different colors — either the faces of the characters in the scene turn red and yellow; the villain's face almost always turns green; and the faces of the characters witnessing the event are shown consecutively, frozen in black and white, as if to register shock and horror.

The viewer is almost always startled and might dive for the remote control to lower the volume. It also hurts the eyes. The question as to why it is used so frequently is one that I posed to actors, writers and directors of soaps during my fieldwork. The common thread that ran through their responses was that the swish pan shot, accompanied by a change in music, was to attract the attention of the viewers back to the TV set. Since these are prime time soaps and many families are having their dinner at the time they are being screened, attention may be diverted. Someone may have even gone away from the TV set to bring something to the table. The sounds and music of the swish pan shot ensures that the viewer is alerted and rushes back to the TV set, knowing something important has happened.

One point is noteworthy here: only *Bidaai*, topping TRPs since the beginning of 2008, does not use the swish pan shot. Shahi says he did not want to use this because he "wants the actors to do the acting, not a situation where the camera does the maximum acting."[25]

Return from the Dead, Amnesia ... and Plastic Surgery

Christine Geraghty notes that "death in the US soaps has long been recognised as being by no means irretrievable" and that there are many possibilities of "returning from the dead" (1991: 19). Indian soaps follow the return from the dead with alacrity. Thanks to media reports elsewhere, especially in the print media, audiences are already primed and know that a certain character will leave the soap. References have been made earlier to the departure and subsequent return of Tulsi in *Kyunki* and Om in *Kahaani*. At one point, Parvati also left *Kahaani*. Audiences were shown her dead body entering the crematorium. But she returned a few weeks later as the glamorous Janki Devi, ably represented by designer Manish Malhotra. It was only at that time that audiences were taken "inside" the electric crematorium, so to speak, and they saw Parvati being rescued by a well wisher, who subsequently had plastic surgery done on her to keep her looking the same age as before to enable her return as a young and glamorous grandmother in her avatar of Janki Devi.

But how were audiences supposed to deal with the return of Om, whose dead body and final funereal rites occupied several days of screen space? Audiences also knew, from press reports, that Kiran Karmarkar, the actor playing the role of Om, wanted out of his contract with Balaji for the greener pastures of Bollywood in the summer of 2005, after *Kahaani's* completion of 1,000 episodes. In an interview given at the time, Karmarkar said the following: "I have been playing Om since five years. I had shot for its pilot in 2000. When the leap happened, I settled into my character. I have enjoyed playing the character for long. But as an actor, I don't want to remain Om for life. I have enjoyed my popularity and recognition. I need to move on career wise ... I have already got six or seven serial offers, but I have said no to all. I want to do films" (www.tellychakkar.com, 29 July 2005).

Here is where a particular to Indian soaps — that of plastic surgery — comes in very handy. Depending on the real life situation, it leaves the character with the same face (only younger!) or gives the character a new face. If the actor returns with the same face, add a dollop of amnesia to the surgery. Om was reintroduced back as Rishabh Rai Choudhuri, a rich industrialist with a new wife, Rishika, and three daughters. Viewers later learnt that Om's face had been transplanted on to another unclaimed dead body in the Gujarat floods and the real Om had been rescued by Rishika, who later fell in love with him and married him. Rishika also made sure that the real Om did not remember his past life with Parvati by medicating him. When Smriti Z. Irani left *Kyunki* (as it turned out, only for a year) to be replaced by Gautami Gadgil to play the central role of Tulsi, plastic surgery was used to give Tulsi's character a different face. Needless to say, the prison van in which Tulsi (Irani) was traveling met with a terrible accident; hence Gadgil's introduction as Tulsi, with a different face, could be easily explained with plastic surgery, since she had suffered so many burns.

Geraghty's observation certainly holds true for Indian soaps that "in soap opera, conventions can be stretched to breaking point precisely because they are understood to be understood to be conventions and that it is part of the fun for the audience to see how the programme can get out of the narrative web it has woven for itself and the viewer" (1991: 20).

Recap and Precap

The beginning of every episode starts with a recap of the previous day's events, bringing the viewer up to date with what happened, and then a voiceover inviting the audience with the words *"aaiye, ab dekhtey hain aagey"* (come, let us watch further). Indian soaps, however, use a ploy which is peculiarly Indian in order to lure their viewers to watch the next episode. This is termed a "precap" — a uniquely Indian term, literally the opposite of "recap." The "precap" is a preview of the next day's episode.

Precap is similar to the incorrect, though extremely handy "prepone," the opposite of "postpone." Instead of using the term "bring forward," a lot of people simply say "prepone" to contrast with "postpone." It is common parlance in India and has come to connote what is referred to as "Indian-English." Terms like this are perfectly understood and accepted in India.[26]

The Hook[27] — Especially on Thursday Evenings

The hook, also referred to as the "cliffhanger" (Hobson 2003: 69), is the tool at the end of the soap opera when the main narrative of the day reaches a climactic point. It, however, is specially used at the end of the week's episodes, leaving the audience with unanswered questions, wondering what will happen next. This also guarantees viewership on Monday evening when the soap resumes. Hindi soaps almost always leave the last freeze frame shot on the face of the central woman protagonist — Parvati in *Kahaani;* Tulsi in *Kyunki;* Sadhana or Ragini in *Bidaai.* At times, the freeze frame shot is on the face of the scheming woman villainess as she plots her next move — Trishna in *Kahaani;* Mandira and now since June 2008 Vaidehi in *Kyunki;* Malti *bhabi* in *Bidaai.* Interviews with television executives underscore the point that soap operas are the flagship programs of television channels. Television channels therefore announce forthcoming episodes at the bottom of the screen, or continuously during advertising breaks on the channel. All this forms part of methods employed to seduce audiences back to watching every episode.

The Importance of *Saas–Bahu* (Mother-in-Law–Daughter-in-Law)

All soaps in India now are referred to with one umbrella term as *"saas–bahu"* sagas/soaps/serials. Interestingly, all the interviews I conducted with writers and creative heads of television houses underlined that all soaps are not *saas–bahu* affairs, as indeed they are not. There is a reason for this madness however: *Kyunki Saas Bhi Kabhi Bahu Thi* was the first of its kind, the longest running soap opera on Indian prime time television. Sandiip Sikcand, in fact, referred to it as "the mother of all soaps, the mother ship … like every ship that sinks is the Titanic."[28] So every soap that followed *Kyunki* was handily referred to as a *saas–bahu* soap. The term *"saas–bahu"* has grown in popularity along with *Kyunki* and is now used as a metonym for various kinds of programming and as a handy catchword, even for Hindi films!

Saas, Bahu aur Saazish (Mother-in-Law, Daughter-in-Law and Intrigue) is a hugely successful program launched by Star News on 11 October 2004. It very quickly climbed to the top in TRPs. It was initially telecast from Monday–Friday at 2:30 pm IST (http://www.indiantelevision.com/headlines/y2k4/dec/dec29. htm) but is now aired every day of the week at the same time. It "propelled the channel share of Star News in its time-slot, recording a whopping 90 per cent growth from 0.6 (week 36–41 average) to 1.1 (week 42–47 average) in the C&S 15+ HSM category. *Saas, Bahu aur Saazish* now leads in the 2:30 pm slot" (ibid.).

Saas, Bahu aur Saazish is a program about daily soaps and other programs such as reality shows, as well as the current state of the television industry. It carries out a recap of the popular soaps on TV; has interviews with TV stars; has shooting coverage of popular shows; provides news about upcoming shows; and provides general gossip about the television industry.

Nalin Mehta, in his recent work on satellite news channels in India, reports that "it was the quest for ratings that spurred Star News in 2004 to start a new afternoon news show … that seeks to build on the popularity of popular soap operas on Star's sister channel, Star Plus … the Star News programme seeks to inform viewers who may have missed the previous days' episodes about the latest twists and turns in the plot, apart from featuring behind-the-scenes interviews with the stars of the shows. The idea is to leverage the huge popularity of the television serials, even in the choice of the programme's name, and to draw in viewers who are committed soap watchers" (2008: 188). An important point to be noted is that while it is telecast on Star News, the show covers updates on soaps and reality shows, not just of those telecast on Star's channels, but also of other channels such as Zee and Sony.

Mehta adds in excerpts of an interview with Uday Shankar, CEO and Editor of Star News, about *Saas, Bahu aur Saazish*'s ratings: "In terms of viewer attention and time spent per viewer on TV, TV soaps have now overtaken Bollywood in a big way. A soap is being watched everyday while the biggest movie buff watches a movie once or twice a week … there are households where 10, 15, 20 serials are being watched every day but there was no reporting being done. So, from my point of view, it makes sense" (2008: 188–89). Shankar also added in the interview that "[he is] just providing information … [and not] sitting in judgment to tell people that this information is relevant … good for you and this is not … would you never expand the definition of news?" (ibid.: p. 189).

The popularity of the show can be gauged by the fact that it has won several awards, including the Sansui Television Award for the best entertainment-based show for the second time in 2008.

August 2008 saw Star One start the telecast of a reality program, a dance competition titled *Saas v/s Bahu: Kaun Kisse Nachayega* (Mother-in-Law versus Daughter-in-Law, Who Will Make Whom

Dance [presumably to the victor's tune]). Bringing the eternal rivalry on stage, various *saas–bahu jodi*s (pairs) have been taking the floor to best each other in dance. The winner of the day gets the coveted keys of the house from one of the judges which she uses to open a safe where a gift awaits. Getting control of the keys, presumably of the house, symbolizes control over the household, particularly in joint families.

The recognition of this term has not been lost on the Hindi film industry either. How much soap operas have become a part of the Indian psyche since 2008 is clear from the fact that a recently released Hindi film is called *Saas, Bahu aur Sensex* (Mother-in-Law, Daughter-in-Law and the Sensex [referring to India's stock market], 2008, dir. Shona Urvashi). The film, as its very title indicates, taps into the current Indian pastimes of tracking both soaps and the stock market on a daily basis. In fact, several of the film's reviews have commented on this fact.[29] Director Shona Urvashi said in an interview that "*Saas Bahu Aur Sensex* is a fun film on the changing face of India." She added that the film is about "how [the characters] find their place in the *masala* (spice mix) of the New Mumbai world, [and how this] forms the crux of the story. Stock market fluctuations, kitty parties, soap operas and the changing tides of New India add to the film's soul" (interview with Shona Urvashi, www.screenindia.com/news/Saas-bahu-aur-sensex/359690/).

Another film, *Golmaal Returns* (Chaos Returns, 2008, dir. Rohit Shetty) has one of the heroines, Kareena Kapoor, named Ekta in the film; she is an ardent fan of K soaps and watches all of them. Her brother's role is played by Tusshar Kapoor, Ekta Kapoor's brother in real life. With tongue-in-cheek humor and making references to the complicated narratives of the K soaps, Ekta (in the film) starts suspecting her husband of having an affair and cooks up stories constantly. She is aided in this by her brother. Fed up of the situation, the husband starts telling white lies to his wife, and gradually, there is complete chaos all around. Audiences of films like this already have a stock of intimate knowledge of Ekta Kapoor and her K soaps, as well as her brother, Tusshar Kapoor. The involvement of the audience, therefore, works at a double level of engagement and distance here. The other important point to be noted is how the popularity of the K soaps has such immediate recognition now as to be comprehensible in different, unrelated circumstances as well.

Press

Daily newspapers in India have separate sections on entertainment. The *Times of India*, for example has different editions for cities such as *Delhi Times* and *Bombay Times* that report on the latest developments in the television industry, interviews with stars, etc. *Mumbai Mirror, The Indian Express, Business Standard*, to name just a few of only the English language dailies, all have separate sections on the film and television industries. Magazines also carry news of television stars from time to time.

In 1999, media analyst Anil Wanvari set up http://www. indiantelevision.com which was "the first online and interactive information service focusing on the Indian television and media business." The website offers "a 360 degree media service" (http://www.indiantelevision.com/aboutus.htm). Updated throughout the day, the website provides, among other things, trends and analyses of the television industry, interviews with producers and stars, broadcasting acts and regulations of the Indian government, databases and directories of production houses, weekly updates of TRPs, etc. In addition to this, Wanvari also set up http://www.tellychakkar.com that is advertised as an "exclusive peppery online destination for the hottest news on TV shows, tête-à-têtes with TV stars, spicy telly gossip and much more...." (http://www.indiantelevision.com/aboutus.htm). Both these websites are mines of information and handy tools for anyone researching, or simply reading about the television industry in India.

The *chhotey parde ki bari duniya* (big world of the small screen) is further testified to by the launch of an annual planner calendar featuring well known TV stars in January 2009 in Mumbai. This is the *first time* a calendar of TV stars has been inaugurated.[30] The annual planner/calendar is Global Indian Television Academy Awards' annual planner, and using the abbreviated form with the first alphabet from each word is called *Gitaa*. In its episode of 30 January 2009 on Star News, *Saas, Bahu aur Saazish* covered the launch of *Gitaa*, and reported that the 12 faces for each month of the year are "stars who are icons and household names in the country. Their achievements are looked up to, and *Gitaa* acknowledges the high standards set by them, by featuring them through iconic images photographed by well known photographer, Joy Datta."[31] Among others, the calendar includes Sakshi Tanwar

(Parvati in *Kahaani*), Chetan Hansraj (Sasha in *Kahaani*), Hiten Tejwani and Gauri Pradhan Tejwani (Karan and Nandini in *Kyunki*), and Rakshanda Khan (Tanya in *Kyunki*).

Television Award Shows

Awards for television shows have mushroomed. They include the Sansui Television Awards and the Global India TV awards, where, in 2008, Balaji Telefilms honored its artistes.

The Indian Telly Awards were established in 2001, and the first awards were given out on 6 July that year. These awards are sometimes described as "the most coveted recognition an Indian TV executive, artiste, programme and channel can receive for talent and performance during a year ... starting as just awards for the trade and for select performance, they moved on to honouring on screen performances and cover almost every aspect of television. They have been labelled at times as the Oscars of the Indian television industry, the Emmys of India, by artistes and executives alike. Winners are decided through a process that includes several juries and polling to get a fix on the most deserving candidate" (http://www.indiantellyawards.com/y2k5/indexpop.htm).

The Star Parivaar Annual Awards, established in 2002, have become a much anticipated annual event. Different companies sponsor the awards each year. For instance in 2007, the Awards were sponsored by Dabur's Vatika hair oil. In 2008, they were sponsored by Reliance Mobile. Yash Khanna, Corporate Communications Head, Star TV, described this annual show as "an event that celebrates the excellence and contribution of each and every member of the Star family... Star viewers vote for their favorite characters, rather than the actor playing the role."[32]

The most important thing to note about these award shows, particularly the Star Parivaar Awards, is that their platform is used to satirize and parody many of the things that audiences undoubtedly wonder about at times. The Star Parivaar Awards for 2008, broadcast on 8 June 2008 on Star Plus, had many such moments. On stage, Daksha *chachi* (*Kyunki*) and Robbie Sabharwal (*Kasturi*) pondered about the centrality of women even in the titles of soaps such as *Kyunki Saas Bhi Kabhi Bahu Thi* and *Ba, Bahoo aur Baby*, only to say that this makes sense because titling a soap *Baap, Beta aur Business* (Father, Son and Business) did not sound interesting or promising. Referring to multiple wives in the K soaps, Malti *bhabi* (*Bidaai*) on stage asked Kamal (*Kahaani*): "A*apkey kitne biwiyan hai?*" (How many wives do you have), to which Kamal, looking directly at producer and creative head Ekta Kapoor, replied, "W*oh toh sirf Ekta jaanti hai*" (Only Ekta knows that). Characters from the show like Gattu from *Ba, Bahoo aur Baby* poked fun at the "lady villains" in soaps for being lazy. Gattu said "*Yeh lady villains bade aalsi hotey hain. Kitchen mein jaa kar khana nahin banati, sirf doodh mein zahar milati hain*" (These lady villains are very lazy. They don't make food when they go to the kitchen, they only add poison in the milk). Gattu also added that "*Yeh lady villains dialogs nahin boltey, sab man mein boltey hain … mast hai*" (The lady villains don't even speak their dialogs, they "speak" in their minds [referring to the voiceovers of evil thoughts] … this is fun).

The program *Saas, Bahu aur Saazish* on Star News also parodies many soap moments. It has, in addition, made reference to the negative women characters and called them "lady *Ravanas.*"[33] Celebrating its fourth birthday on 11 October 2008 with a special one hour episode, it covered moments during shootings when leading stars miffed their lines during shooting. Referring to the ageless Ba in *Kyunki*, the show's gossipy cartoon character, known as *Chugal Khor*[34] Aunty, said "*khud Ba ko nahin maloom ki unki umr kya hai … dekho na, ab toh unki umr 250 saal hogi*" (Ba herself does not know her age … she must be 250 years old by now). *Chugal Khor* Aunty also said that if *Kyunki Saas Bhi Kabhi Bahu Thi* (The Mother-in-Law Was Also Once a Daughter-in-Law) continues for even another year, it would soon have to be called *Kyunki Par Dadi Bhi Kabhi Par Poti Thi* (Because the Great Grandmother Was Also Once a Great Granddaughter).

I have already noted how the stories and conventions of soap opera are stretched, at times, beyond believable limits. Such moments of parody and satire, by the producers of soaps themselves, is acknowledgement of this fact, and participation, along with audiences, in the humor also of such conventions.

Notes

1. I am indebted to Dorothyh Hobson's characterization of the essential features of soap operas in the UK and have followed her format for this chapter (see Hobson 2003: Chapter 2). There are some additions that are particular to Indian soaps.

2. Interview with Yash Khanna, (August 2007 and 2008).
3. Interviews with Yash Khanna (August 2007) and Shailja Kejriwal (August 2007). I can also personally vouch for Kejriwal's closeness to the Kapoors. In a single day, she managed to fix an appointment for me to meet Shobha Kapoor. Despite many attempts, however, even by her mother Shobha Kapoor, I was unable to meet Ekta Kapoor, who is famous for not meeting people.
4. Lakshmi is the goddess of wealth and prosperity. In the Hindu tradition, daughters and daughters-in-law are referred to as the Lakshmis of the house, whence *Ghar ki Lakshmi … Betiyaan*.
5. Interview with Rajan Shahi, (August 2008).
6. Interview with Yash Khanna (August 2007).
7. Kayamath literally means something devastating, bringing with it calamity/destruction. The term could also, in certain circumstances, have a positive connotation.
8. Interview with Yash Khanna (August 2007).
9. I was invited to a press conference and party in August 2008, hosted by Director's Kut and STAR TV, to "celebrate the number one show" — *Bidaai*.
10. Further details on Smriti Z. Irani's exit and subsequent return to *Kyunki* can be found in Chapter 6.
11. The *Bhagvad Gita* is a Sanskrit text from the chapter "Bhishma Parva" of the *Mahabharata* epic, comprising 700 verses. The verses use the range and style of Sanskrit meter (*chhanda*s) with similes and metaphors. The content of the text is a conversation between Krishna and Arjun which takes place on the battlefield of Kurukshetra just prior to the start of battle. Responding to Arjun's confusion and moral dilemma, Krishna explains to him his duties as a warrior and prince and elaborates on different Yogic and Vedantic philosophies, with examples and analogies. This has led to the *Gita* often being described as a concise guide to Hindu philosophy and also as a practical, self-contained guide to life.
12. Interviews with Nivedita Basu and Chloe Ferns (August 2007).
13. Interviews with Shobha Kapoor, Nivedita Basu and Chloe Ferns (August 2007).
14. Ashok Pandit produced *Filmi Chakkar* and *Tere Mere Sapne*, as well as *Muqammal* for Star Plus.
15. Interview with Ronit Bose Roy (August 2007).
16. Actor Ronit Bose Roy also made this observation when I interviewed him (August 2007).
17. Interview with Shobha Kapoor (August 2007).
18. Interview with Smriti Z. Irani (July 2007).
19. Interview with L. V. Krishnan (August 2008).

20. All details about the Balaji sets are from the interview with Shobha Kapoor (August 2007).
21. Interview with Sunjoy Waddhwa (August 2007).
22. Interview with Rajan Shahi (August 2008).
23. This was pointed out to me by Shalija Kejriwal when she detailed how they had conceptualized the various Balaji soaps for Star Plus.
24. This is a term that I first heard from Rajan Shahi, producer and director of Director's Kut (interview, August 2008).
25. Interview with Rajan Shahi (August 2008).
26. Books such as Binoo K. John's *Entry From Backside Only: Hazaar Funds of Indian-English* (2007) provide a useful, and hilarious, overview of Indian English.
27. This is a term that I first heard from Ronit Bose Roy (interview, August 2007). It is a term that refers to the critical moment that the story leaves off every evening, but never more so than on Thursday evenings, when the weekly episodes come to an end and the audience has to wait till Monday evening to find out what happens next. Producers try to make sure that the hook is a nail-biting one, keeping alive curiosity for the next few days, and also thereby ensuring viewership on Monday evening.
28. Interview with Sandiip Sikcand (August 2007).
29. Links to reviews of the film *Saas, Bahu aur Sensex* (2008, dir. Shona Urvashi) provided in the Bibliography.
30. In recent times, a series of calendars that have been grabbing news headlines in India with its publicised launch are United Breweries' Chairman Vijay Mallya's Kingfisher calendars. Shot by renowned photographers like Atul Kasbekar, the Kingfisher calendars have swimsuit specials, and feature top models and even Bollywood actresses. For academic research on various kinds of imagery in Indian calendar art, including the sacred and the feminine, see, for instance Guha Thakurta (1991); Pinney (1995); K. Jain (1997 and 2002); and Uberoi (2006, especially Chapter 2).
31. *Saas, Bahu aur Saazish*, Star News, episode of 30 January 2009. The annual planner features Sakshi Tanwar, Apurva Agnihotri, Shilpa Agnihotri, Chetan Hansraj, Gauri Pradhan, Hiten Tejwani, Hussain Kuwajerwala, Mohammed Iqbal Khan, Mona Singh, Rakshanda Khan, Sandhya Mridul, and Shabbir Ahluwalia. The Managing Director of *Gitaa* is Kiran Bajla, an entertainment and business strategist. She also produced the Sansui Television Awards 2007.
32. Interview with Yash Khanna (August 2007).
33. Ravana is the demon god in the epic *Ramayan*.
34. *Chugal khor* refers to someone who carries tales or spreads gossip.

4

Soap Tales

A close relationship exists between soap operas and their audiences. Regular viewers are knowledgeable about soap stories and their characters. This is, in fact, part of the pleasure of watching soaps. This chapter examines the formal narrative strategies that soaps use to invite audiences into the fictional world, and allow, at the same time, that they stand back and view the formal conventions through which that world is constructed, what Christine Geraghty terms the "double action of engagement and distance ... " (1991: 10).

Prime time programming requires that the structure, narrative and aesthetics of soap operas are critical issues in their long-running success.

Time

From the point of view of producers, a critical and practical component of programming is the time band in which the shows are aired. Television channels consider 8 pm–11 pm as the prime time slot. Prime time programming has specific conventions that television producers need to follow in terms of visualization, filming and narrative. The following discussion examines these issues in detail.

Star TV launched *Kyunki* on 3 July 2000, the same day that it launched the first season of the hugely popular *Kaun Banega Crorepati* (*KBC*) hosted by Amitabh Bachchan.[1] In fact, during the first show of *KBC* which was slotted from 9 pm–10 pm, Monday–Thursday, Star Plus advertised the launch of *Kyunki* from 10:30 pm–11 pm, with advertisements at the bottom of the TV screen.

KBC drew an unprecedented audience. In the first week that it was introduced, Star Plus featured in the top 50 shows on all four days it was aired. From 5.96 TRPs on 2 July 2000, *KBC*'s viewership almost tripled to 15.28 TRPs by 27 July 2000.[2] Star Plus, with its clever ploy of using *KBC's* launch to market *Kyunki*, paid off handsomely. As Shailja Kejriwal said, "we wanted to take advantage of *KBC's* lead-in of family viewing and lead out with *Kyunki* also being watched by the whole family. *Kahaani* was launched on 16 October 2000 in the time slot of 10 pm–10:30 pm. We knew we had the family audience hooked with *KBC* and *Kyunki*. So, with *Kahaani*, we wanted to continue the same trend ... keep the family, don't let them go elsewhere (i.e. surf channels)."[3]

This strategy worked very successfully for Star Plus. Three years into the running by 2004, *Kyunki* was still acing the ratings map. *Kyunki* saw these ratings "due to the way the story line took shape [for almost a year] in terms of Tulsi being blinded by her love towards her immoral son Ansh, where the plot peaks with her realization about his true character. What is awaited is the stance and the action that she will take against her son" (Krishna 2004). Kejriwal pointed out to me that "every daily soap follows a format of a new story that begins within the daily episode and the culmination point of that particular plot, after which a new one begins. The build up of characters on an average takes place in the first 30–40 episodes. Every soap has a lot of stories woven around it. Every story, on an average, goes on for about 40–45 episodes. By the 30th episode, one has to start sowing the seeds for the next story. For example, while the first 45 episodes in the case of *Kahaani* ... built up the protagonist, Parvati, the following episodes then focused on the antagonist, Pallavi. Then on began their clash which was the battle between the good and evil. This formed the essence and the soap played on this eternal conflict."[4]

Kasautii was launched a year after *Kyunki* and *Kahaani*, on 29 October 2001, in the time band of 8:30 pm–9 pm. Kejriwal was clear that "*Kasautii* was scheduled for 8:30 pm. At this time, the family is generally scattered around the house — the mother may be in the kitchen, dad is just back from work, the younger children are busy with homework. Research told us that the younger person was most likely to watch at this time, hence *Kasautii* was a love story."[5] *Saat Phere* on Zee TV was launched in October 2005 in the time band of 9:30 pm–10 pm; and *Bidaai* was launched on Star Plus on 8 October 2007 in the time band of 9 pm–9:30 pm. Both shows are aimed at family viewership, and hence are slotted into the family viewing time bands.

Regarding prime time programming of daily soaps, Kejriwal also makes the important point of the "manner in which soaps are watched in India," something she finds "totally unique."[6] In the West, particularly in the US, there are season breaks; there are none in India. Audiences watch soaps for four days a week every month throughout the year. In such a situation, Kejriwal finds that "the characters genuinely become a part of your family." Ekta Kapoor is on record corroborating this point when she says that characters in *Kyunki* "have become like family members to everybody" (Lalwani 2003b). Rajan Shahi made the same point about Sadhana and Ragini's lives in his hit soap *Bidaai*, where audiences are always keen to know what is going to happen next in their lives.[7] When I asked Shahi how he managed to garner — and keep — eyeballs with all the prime time productions he has been associated with such as *Saat Phere* on Zee TV, *Jassi Jaisi Koi Nahin* (There is No One like Jassi) on Sony TV, and now *Bidaai* on Star Plus, Shahi said "you need two things — continuity and habit. You may be habituated to having food at a given time. Similarly, audiences must want to watch a given TV program at a given time. The trick lies in forcing this habit upon viewers by giving them good content."[8]

Kejriwal said that "in the West, there is a far more distanced approach between the producer and television channel, and therefore also with the viewer. Here, the viewer is watching every day, and the producer is making it every day, and the channel responsible for it is working every day. Thus, there is an important daily interaction at all levels with the final consumer — the audience. It is very important to know about the changes in your final consumer's life and understand it before you produce prime time programming on a daily basis." The point about Indian audiences watching soaps in a "different manner" was also brought up by L. V. Krishnan, CEO, TAM Media Research Pvt. Ltd. The television industry considers the time band of 8 pm–11 pm as prime time programming. During this time, the housewife is multi-tasking — running to and from the kitchen, preparing and bringing dinner to the table. Thus, Krishnan said, "in a half hour daily soap, along with advertising breaks, the entire 21 minutes of content has music. So when the pitch of the music goes high, the woman comes back to the TV set, and producers make sure to have action replay like in cricket.

This is positive for the audience and also keeps production costs lower."[9]

Prime time programming by producers also takes into account the fact that sometimes they need to repeat prime time shows in the afternoon time band as well. Viewers are loyal to the soaps they watch and will not normally deviate during the prime time band. So how did a soap like *Balika Vadhu* (Child Bride), launched in the 8–8:30 pm time band on the new channel Colors, owned by Viacom and TV 18, get its initial viewership numbers? "Instead of forcing viewers who might already be watching another soap on the prime time, they repeated the soap at 2 pm in the afternoon. Viewers were thus invited, rather than forced to change. As long as there is no clash, viewers welcome new soaps," said Krishnan.

Prime time programming also requires that much greater attention be paid to visualization and presentation of the soaps. Prime time soaps in India stand out for their lavish spectacle and glamor. A great deal of attention is paid to the lavish sets, costumes, jewelry, and accessories of the stars. High production values are the norm and shows are produced with filmic expertise.[10] Creative heads, producers and writers underlined that no expenses are spared in production. Kamlesh Pandey said that Ekta Kapoor has "repackaged Hindi films of the 1970s and 1980s, especially the family dramas that Jeetendra, her father starred in, and repackaged it glamorously. She uses expensive sets, saris and jewelry, spares no expense. *Ekta was the first to make TV look as good as the movies. What Ekta Kapoor does on TV, Karan Johar and Aditya Chopra do in films* (emphasis mine)."[11] This tradition has been faithfully followed in prime time soaps, and *Saat Phere* and *Bidaai* also boast of high production values.

It is important to note that this spectacle of lavish glamor is a source of pleasure for audiences. This has two important consequences. First, soaps, as experienced in prime time programming, have become objects of consumption and pleasure; and second, the expensive sets and décor, where festivals and other celebrations regularly take place, contribute to a sense of "Indianness."[12] These points are examined in detail in Chapter 7.

Within the soap stories themselves, the structuring and ordering of time is one of the central characteristics. Robert Allen notes that " ... one of the distinctive ... features of the soap opera is its absence of ultimate narrative closure; it is, in fact, one of the

Kyunki Saas Bhi Kabhi Bahu Thi

1. Tulsi Virani

2. Mihir and Tulsi Virani

3. Mihir and Tulsi

4. Tulsi and Mihir

5. Karan and Nandini

6. Krishnatulsi (KT) and Ba

7. Mihir Virani

8. The two Tulsis

9. Tulsi

10. Tulsi

11. Virani family

12. Mihir and Tulsi offering prayers with the Virani family

13. Older Tulsi

14. Virani family in *chawl*

15. One of the title shots of *Kyunki*

Kahaani Ghar Ghar Kii

16. Parvati Om Aggarwal

17. Om and Parvati

18. Parvati and Om

19. Aggarwal family

20. Parvati with Aggarwal family children

21. Parvati

22. Parvati as Janki Devi

Kasautii Zindagi Kay

23. Prerna

24. Mr Rishabh Bajaj

25. Prerna

26. Anurag Basu and Prerna

27. Prerna

few narrative forms predicated upon the impossibility of closure" (1985: 69; see also Geraghty 1991; Brunsdon 1997; and Hobson 2003). Soap stories are never fully resolved. In Indian prime time programming, for example, when *Kasautii* aired its last episode on 28 February 2008, the story made a seamless transition into the next K soap taking over that time slot of 8:30 pm–9 pm on Star Plus, titled *Kis Desh Mein Hai Mera Dil* (In Which Country Does my Heart Live). The lead couple of *Kasautii*, Prerna and Anurag, who had been killed, were "seen" in their spiritual forms at the memorial of their dead son whom they called Prem (meaning love). *Kasautii* was conceptualized as a love story, so each told the other that true love never ends, just carries on in other forms, and lives on in others. The camera then panned to the new couple of *Kis Desh Mein Hai Mera Dil*, where the hero is once again called Prem and the heroine's name is Heer. The transition was doubly reinforced at the 8 June 2008 Star Parivaar Awards night. Prerna and Anurag (*Kasautii*) came on stage with their swan song and dance. Handing down the mantle to the new members of the *parivaar*, Prerna and Anurag danced their way to unveil the new lovers, Heer and Prem, of *Kis Desh Mein Hai Mera Dil*. So, as we can see, *prem* (love) is eternal and love lives on. But this Prem too made an exit from the soap on 2 October 2008. Making a reference to the real world, when bomb blasts ripped across the capital, Delhi, in September 2008, the soap showed Prem caught in the midst of one of the blasts. Thursday, 2 October 2008's evening episode ended with Prem's picture going from color to black and white, and the words *"zindagi khatam hoti hai, prem nahin"* (life ends but love does not). So once again, *prem* (love) lives on.[13]

Kahaani's opening montage has had the scared flame of the *diya* (lamp) guarded in the cupped hands of Parvati, her husband Om and daughter Shruti. When *Kahaani* aired its last episode on 9 October 2008, the last shot had Parvati pushing the *diya* afloat on its journey along a river; it came to rest in the hands of a young unknown girl. Audiences found out on 3 November 2008 that the young girl is Vrinda, the heroine of the new Balaji soap *Tujh Sang Preet Lagayi Sajna* (I Give My Heart to You) in the same 10.30 pm–11 pm time slot that *Kahaani* earlier had. Audiences, aware of visual cues, were able to understand that from now on, the young Vrinda would carry on with the task of guarding the traditions of a new family.

Temporal matters are also dealt with in other ways.[14] The time that elapses from one episode to the next plays a role in which audiences experience the narrative. As Christine Geraghty states, "the characters in a serial, when abandoned at the end of an episode, pursue an 'unrecorded existence' until the next one begins" (1980: 10). Thus, as Ien Ang (1985: 52–53) puts it, "... the lives of the characters go on during our absence — i.e. between two episodes."

The resumption of soap narratives is signaled at the beginning of each episode with a recap of the previous day's events, bringing the viewer up-to-date with what has happened, and then a voiceover, inviting the audience with the words "*aaiye, ab dekhtey hain aagey*" (come, let us watch further). At times, to keep the audience hooked, Indian soaps, as we have noted, use the ploy of the "precap", which, when the evening's episode ends, provides a teaser glimpse of a crucial scene from the next evening's episode.

In addition, the real passage of time is also clearly marked. All Hindu festivals are faithfully shown and references are repeatedly made to them. Nowhere is this more visible than in the K soaps. Ekta Kapoor, known for being very religious herself, faithfully depicts each Hindu festival in detail. For example all her soaps have references, spread over several episodes, to Ganesh Chaturthi,[15] the Navratras,[16] Dussehra,[17] Diwali,[18] Karva Chauth,[19] Basant Panchami,[20] Holi,[21] Raksha Bandhan,[22] etc. Muslim festivals, such as Eid,[23] are not depicted, though reference may be made to them. For example, one may be visiting a family friend for Eid celebrations when Ramadan, the Islamic holy month of fasting, ends.

Important events affecting the country also find reference. Earlier episodes of *Kyunki* and *Kahaani* made clear mention of the IT dot com crash.[24] Younger male characters whose careers had been affected by this were shown. The episode of *Kis Desh Mein Hai Mera Dil* of 1 October 2008 showed the hero, Prem, shopping at a Delhi market; the episode closed with a bomb blast, the following text coming up on a black screen: "In September, there were five bomb blasts in Delhi. We mourn every death, because with each loss, a family dies." The words were in white on a black screen, with the single exception of the word "family," which was in red.[25] The participation of soap characters in such events enhances the notion that the world of the soap families runs conterminously with the "real" world outside.

Indian soaps are organized time wise more on the line of British prime time soaps, being telecast for four days every week throughout the year. US soaps, by contrast, rely on the season's episodes. However, whether it is a weekly affair, or run by seasons, all soap producers ensure the hook, or cliffhanger, literally keeping the viewer hooked till the next episode airs.

Space

Since soaps apparently have no ending, their lack of closure and resolution can make them boring and repetitious. One way that producers deploy is to make this very repetition enjoyable, " ... to give the audience a sense of familiarity with setting and characters so that the return to them is pleasurable" (Geraghty 1991: 13). Soap operas establish dramatic space in such a way that the viewer knows in a detailed fashion the layout of the setting in which the story unfolds. As Dorothy Hobson points out, "locations for soap operas are likely to be purpose built sets with outside lots and studio sets. The sets are a very important part of the drama because they create the physical space in which the drama takes place" (2003: 70).

Audiences are by now completely familiar with the mansions and houses depicted in soaps. The master shot, as it is called in the television industry in India, is referred to for western soaps as the establishing shot.[26] It sets the layout of the episode for that evening. Sometimes it may be the house seen from the outside. In *Bidaai*, for instance when we see "Kaushalya Niwas" (Kaushalya's Abode), named after the matriarch of the Sharma household, one of the two main families in the soap, audiences immediately know that we will now enter the Sharma household to find out what is going on with *Mamaji* and *Mamiji* (maternal uncle and aunt), Ragini, the dark-skinned sister, and Malti *bhabi*. Similarly, when the Rajvansh family mansion is shown, audiences know that the narrative's perspective will shift to Sadhana, the beautiful, fair-skinned cousin of Ragini, and her in-laws. Similarly, in the K soaps, a shot of the Virani and Aggarwal family homes from the outside invites the audience inside the fictional space. At other times, the master shot may also be the interiors of any of these homes. It could be the living room of Kaushalya Niwas or the Rajvansh mansion in *Bidaai*. It could be the living room of the Aggarwal *parivaar* in *Kahaani,* with stairs demarcating entry into the house and going up to the family quarters on the first floor, with the deities of the gods placed on one side of the main living room. Such is the viewer's intimate knowledge, however, that even if one was not in the room when the soap started, one can immediately tell which family's home one has wandered into. It could be the tiled living room of "Shanti Niketan" (Abode of Peace),[27] the Virani family mansion in *Kyunki,* with a huge chandelier in the living room and the *tulsi* plant always visible through the main entrance door. It could also be a shot taken from a distance, or even aerially of a particular ensemble of characters, depending on the soap. The reason that this shot is taken from a distance is that often all the actors are not present, so body doubles, or "dupes," as they are called in television shorthand,[28] are used for such shots. These are generally of the same height and build as the character(s) they are standing in for, and are dressed in similar clothes. Wherever the master shot occurs, it fixes the location of the scene to follow and also signals to the audience what is likely to happen.

The world of the soap opera also relies heavily on two kinds of filming shots: the close up and the two-shot, or shot/reverse shot. This focuses viewer attention entirely on the facial expression of the character, the dialog and narrative information contained therein. A gesture, glance or facial expression can convey laden meanings, and the close-up catches all this.[29] The close up shot, as the camera moves in "elegiac movement" towards the character's face, has "the effect of bringing the viewer closer and closer to the hidden emotional secrets soap opera explores: stylized expressions of pity, jealousy, rage, self-doubt" (Timberg 1984: 166 cited in Hayward 1997: 156). Tania Modleski (1982: 99–100) argues that close-ups provide training in the feminine skills of "reading people" and also the ability to understand what is left unsaid. Every episode of soaps has close up shots of various characters, especially the central protagonists.

The two-shot, or shot/reverse shot as it is sometimes called, allows viewers to see two characters in the same shot. It is rare that both actors are actually physically present when the two-shot is taken. Viewers can only be sure of this if they are able to actually see the faces of both actors on the screen. Generally, for this particular shot, what the viewer sees is one actor's face and the other's back and shoulder with a part of the hairstyle or clothes visible. Once again, the body double, or "dupe," is in place. Usually during filming the close up or two-shot, the actor is cued into the dialog by anyone present on the set. Other actors for that day's shooting can be sitting around on sofas in the studio set, or even absent. Light and spot boys hold white reflectors and bright lights inches from the character's face. If emotion is called for, glycerin is put into the actor's eyes, then water is sprayed, so that when the shot is being filmed, "realistic" tears fall. The actor emotes in a vacuum, so to speak. I was told that it is not always possible for actors to synchronize their busy schedules, especially if they are the bigger names of Indian television, or shooting for more than one soap at a time, or at times, have personal differences with one another. Many times, after a master shot is taken of all the characters present for the scene, close ups are then filmed on the actors separately. For putting the scene together finally, the audio is taken from the master shot and different two-shots and close ups since the actors have already delivered those dialogs.[30] Still, while observing shootings, I never ceased to be amazed at the versatility of the actors who performed under these rather unreal circumstances, particularly when I viewed the same scenes later and saw how seamless the shot appeared.

A sense of geography of the program is perhaps established best in *Bidaai* whose story is set in the city of Agra, famous for the Taj Mahal. The Sharma family home, Kaushalya Niwas, is fashioned such that with the main door of the house that is always kept open, the viewers can easily see passersby on the street, vendors and others. Often, the characters are shown walking along the roads to enter the house. The opening credits show Sadhana and Ragini as little girls running with their school satchels, with the Taj Mahal in the foreground. Other shots are taken from a rooftop from where audiences can relish views of the Taj Mahal in the background, or during outdoor shootings in the Taj Mahal gardens, once again with the Taj Mahal clearly in view. For the episodes aired in October 2008, of Ragini and Ranvir meeting at the Taj Mahotsav (Grand Festival of the Taj), Shahi filmed on location in Agra, and is on record saying that they were "underlining and enhancing the romantic track between Ragini and Ranbir with the backdrop of Taj Mahal which is arguably the replica of eternal love" (www.tellychakkar.com, 5 September 2008). Such space is part of the visual and spatial strategy used by Shahi as a necessary backdrop for the romance of Ragini and Ranvir, symbolizing the Taj Mahal not just as a symbol of beauty, but also as a symbol of love.

Stories and Characters

Indian prime time soaps began with Ekta Kapoor's productions. As stated above, writer Kamlesh Pandey, as well as creative heads like Sandiip Sikcand and Shailja Kejriwal, made it clear that Ekta Kapoor draws heavily from the family melodramas of the 1970s and 1980s that Jeetendra, her father, acted in. Pandey added that "Ekta has grown up watching her father's films, the family dramas. She recycled what her father had done into TV."[31] Indian prime time soap operas, especially the K soaps, have similarities with US soaps like *Dynasty, Dallas* and *The Bold and the Beautiful* in that they tell stories of rich, industrial families. But beyond that, it is important to note that our soaps move in different directions in establishing a unique "Indian-ness" in both their treatment and themes.[32] *Bidaai* and *Saat Phere*, in fact, deal with the problems of a dark complexion for girls.[33]

The family is the central basis of structure in Indian prime time soaps. Underlining the centrality of the family, Ekta says of her "K" soaps that "[she] realised that one subject which holds eternal interest for us Indians is the family — every Indian family is bound by traditions, festivals, etc., and every family tends to celebrate occasions with relatives, every family has certain characters who are good and bad, or rather, have particular habits. Then, I weaved all this realisation together" (Lalwani 2003a).

The pivotal position of family in the telling of soap stories is similar to British soaps like *EastEnders* and *Brookside* (see Geraghty 1995: 66–80) and US soaps like *Dynasty* and *The Bold and the Beautiful*. Dorothy Hobson correctly observed that in soap stories, "family is a universal theme, dominating the series in Britain, America, Australia and many other countries" (2003: 113).

An important point to note is that the K soaps have had strong concepts in their initial conceptualization. Kejriwal says "the biggest reason for the success of these shows is the fact that they started off as concepts ... all the three K's are concept driven. *Kyunki saas bhi kabhi bahu thi* is a concept. It's basically about *saas* and *bahus* and does not revolve around any particular character in the story. Again *Kahaani Ghar Ghar Ki* is a story of every family. So any story can be incorporated into *Kahaani*; the story is not about any particular character. *Kasautii Zindagi Kay*, talking about the crossroads of life, is again a strong concept. That's the essential difference between these three K's and any other show across channels" (Krishna 2004).

Ekta Kapoor's comments bear out Kejriwal's observations. When asked how the by now iconic *Kyunki* and *Kahaani* were conceived, Ekta, "There's an old lady called Amma in my house. Looking at her, I realized how we tend to ignore and neglect the elderly people around us. That's how *Kyunki*... took shape ... " (Lalwani 2003b). Kejriwal, Star TV's creative head, who worked very closely with Ekta in conceptualizing these soaps, added that "an important part of when *Kyunki* began was to show how the new *bahu* of the house, Tulsi, saw that her mother-in-law's generation not taking good care of their elders. Tulsi was the one who brought Ba, her grandmother-in-law, to the head of the table when everyone was against her."[34]

About conceptualizing *Kahaani*, Ekta said that " ...[she] wanted to make a modern *Ramayan*. Doesn't every home have a Ram? That's how *Kahaani*... took shape" (Lalwani 2003b). *Kahaani's* last episode, aired on 9 October 2008, clearly stated this fact. The last 15 minutes of the show had Parvati telling the viewers: "*hamari is kahaani ka adhar Ramayan raha hai*" (the basis of our story has been the *Ramayan*. Parvati then went on to add that *Kahaani* was bidding the audience adieu on *Vijaya Dashami* (9 October 2008 was *Vijaya Dashami*/Dussehra that year according to the lunar calendar), on the most important day of the *Ramayan*, when good triumphed over evil with Ram's killing of the demon king, Ravan.

Being asked how she conceptualized *Kasautii*, Ekta Kapoor's reply was as follows: "unrequited love between Prerna and Anurag. I was inspired by a real life incident. A friend of mine ditched his girlfriend to marry as per his parents' wishes. I was disturbed. Why couldn't the other woman be positive? Prerna was born. Why can't the wife be negative? Komolika was born" (Lalwani 2003b). Ekta's observations echoed Kejriwal who said that "Star TV directed Ekta Kapoor to make a passionate love story."[35]

Saat Phere and *Bidaai* also keep the family as their central focus even while playing out the theme of the dark-skinned girl's problems in society. A. K. Bijoy (2006) reports that while conceptualizing the show, programming head Ashwini Yardi had said that she personally knew "many women who are suffering from skin colour complexes. Then take a look at the consumer market. How come all these fairness creams are doing so well? That means we have a sizeable section of our audience suffering from this skin complex. So, we decided to blend this social issue with a Cinderella story." Similarly, Ananya Sengupta (2006) reports that during the launch of *Saat Phere*, "Zee TV's programming head Ashwini Yardi had stated, 'this is the story of a dark girl and she will remain so till the end of the show...she will not have any makeovers!' Yardi has kept her promise and perhaps this is the reason why *Saat Phere* has, in six months, become the channel driver for Zee." Producer Sunjoy Waddhwa added that "Saloni is a middle class ugly duckling, even after being on air for some time now, we are not making her go through torturous times, and that's a surprise for viewers of the medium! Her life is normal — neither does her family want to kill her after her marriage, nor is her husband having an extramarital affair!" Waddhwa made reference to the *Ramayan* in his conceptualization of *Saat Phere*. He said that the "conflicts in *Saat Phere* come from outside. The family is not fighting, but they are fighting together against forces from the outside such as Saloni's marriage being threatened, Saloni's husband Nahar's problems, the family falling into debt. The family is united, they solve problems from outside factors. Also, good always triumphs over evil. Whatever Kaveri, the villainess, tries to do, she loses in the end. *Saat Phere* is like the *Ramayan* — every year, Ravan is burnt, but people see it anyway."[36]

The only producer–director who did not make reference to the two epics was Rajan Shahi. Talking about *Bidaai*, the story of two sisters faced with different societal pressures because of their skin color, Shahi lists the following points for the success of the soap. First, and above all, he says, "it is God's Grace which has helped the show run smoothly. Second is the positive energy of all the people working on the show. Third, *Bidaai* focuses on the content and the characters of the show. The characters have become stronger than the actors' faces and viewers have got attached to all of them. Fourth, it is the hard work of the entire team. Fifth, and very importantly, simplicity and everyday emotions work well with audiences. They like to see a marriage of emotions and beautiful moments brought together. People like to watch simple concepts, a good story, well told. Finally, the amalgamation is just perfect and no one aspect of the show outperforms another."[37] It must be noted that *Saat Phere* and, more recently, *Bidaai* are two shows that made serious dents in Balaji ratings.

Dorothy Hobson writes, "soap operas tell stories. The stories are told through the medium of characters in the series. Characters are the most important element in any soap opera ...characters have to be introduced; the audience needs to know who they are before any major stories evolve" (2003: 81). All the soaps mentioned above followed this format of introducing their stories and characters gradually.

One of the crucial ingredients that all production houses — Balaji Telefilms, Sphere Origins and Director's Kut — have paid attention to is characterization. Their soaps have built greatly on their characters. All three production houses picked talented, unknown artists. When they began, the audience did not associate these faces with previous shows on television. But such were the characterizations that within a few weeks of going on air, most of the stars began to be known by their screen names.

Kejriwal stressed this point greatly for the K soaps, saying that "an important ingredient was building on characters and not the story. The idea is making that character such a part of your life that you don't tire of seeing them. You can get tired of a story. For instance, Tulsi is a *pundit*'s (priest) daughter who got married to a rich man's son and her life evolves around the house. There is actually no story to her, if you look at it. But what we did was built her character as a strong ideal woman ... in a concept driven serial, small plots are created to build up characters. Once the character is built, you follow the character. You want to see every action of the character. If you go back to the beginning of *Kahaani* ... it didn't start off with Parvati's story (the protagonist) at all. It started with one of the daughters of the household, Chhaya, who was married, but was coming back to her natal home, leaving her husband and one followed Chhaya's story for the first 16–20 episodes. So, what was interesting was that Parvati's character was built by the stand that she took on the situation. The idea is to build small plots in a concept serial to build on the characters" (Krishna 2004).

Kejriwal further pointed out the "interesting chronological progression from *Kyunki* to *Kahaani* to *Kasautii*." *Kyunki* began with a poor girl, Tulsi, marrying into a rich family, doing all the right things like taking care of elders like Ba. There were no illicit affairs, and everyone did the right thing in terms of relationships. The issue of sexuality never came up. *Kahaani* went one step further, not with the main protagonists, Parvati and Om, but with Om's younger brother, Kamal. We (Star and Balaji) did this because we knew that in the beginning, viewers will not accept a relationship outside marriage of the lead couple. It was okay for the *devar* (younger brother-in-law) to meet up with an ex-girlfriend, have a sexual relationship and a child with her. Viewers accepted that, because they knew that the good *bhabi* will take the decision of what is socially right, and so Parvati gave the child, Krishna, to the childless Pallavi, wife of Kamal."[38] In *Kasautii*, aimed also towards younger viewers, Kejriwal said that the producers experimented a little further and thought "what about a girl who has a child out of wedlock? There are so many women who are taken advantage of. This woman is a different kind of underdog from the dark-skinned Saloni of *Saat Phere* and Ragini of *Bidaai*. Here is a girl who loves a man with all her heart. The man is not bad, but he is torn between his mother and his girlfriend. This girlfriend was the opposite of Tulsi, however. If Anurag had accepted Prerna, like Mihir married Tulsi, it would have become a clone of *Kyunki*. But Anurag did not accept Prerna in the beginning. With that one simple twist, destiny became different. Later we added a Cain and Abel twist to it as well ... that is why it is *Kasautii Zindagi Kay* (the trials of life)."[39]

The endlessness of soap narratives has an effect on the construction and development of its characters and the narratives. Christine Geraghty (1991: 14–15) observes that " ... [this way] the audience becomes familiar with the history of certain characters and has access to knowledge which is well beyond that given in a particular episode ... such awareness is based not only on knowledge of key events ... but also an understanding of the way in which a particular character fits in to the network of relationships which make up a soap."

But if there is a pleasure in predictability, "the audience is also invited to relish change and disruption ... a soap's endless future means that an ultimate conclusion can never be reached and soaps are thus based on a premise of continuous disruption" (Geraghty 1991: 15). For television channels, the logic behind this chaos is the logic of ratings. TV producers call this "course corrections" with which, "when the original plots fail to fire the TRPs, the channel and the production house together turn the stories on their heads, resulting in gratifyingly good ratings" (Joshi and Ghag 2003). Sony television's Executive Vice President, Sunil Lulla, is on record saying "it does become necessary to keep periodic checks on the way a show is moving, keeping in mind the audience tastes and the pace of the show. Since the ratings are the current currency of measuring success, these too are employed" (ibid.).

For creative heads like Shailja Kejriwal, ratings are of course important, but the logic is a little different. She observed that "television has an infinite style. Your product is constantly under scrutiny, so you have to reinvent. Not to reach the end is an art that requires a huge amount of creative and strategic planning, market research, social understanding, evolution of characters who are icons such as Parvati and Tulsi. Characters have to evolve to remain relevant. Why is this character relevant today? Not just that. As producers, we have to keep the story moving forward. The best way to do it is to continuously threaten the stability of a conclusion with another disruptive event — marital discord, sibling rivalry, property disputes, etc. And since family is the central focus, we, as producers, introduce complications and disruptions in the family."[40] Sandiip Sikcand added, "all our relationships are complicated. TV is an entertainment medium and therefore, this is always exaggerated, dramatized. Every relationship is complex, TV just dramatizes it more."[41] Nowhere was this better visible than in the episodes of *Kyunki* aired from 1–5 November 2007. When Trupti, Sahil's second wife, was accused by the Virani *parivaar* (family) of having committed bigamy, she made detailed references to the numerous other multiple relationships of the Viranis, such as the romantic triangles of Mihir–Tulsi–Mandira; Karan–Nandini–Tanya; Krishnatulsi–Lakshya–Eklavya; Archita–Abir–Billy Thakral; and Bhumi–Joydeep–Abir. Shobhaa De likened family relationships in India to the network of family relationships in the *Mahabharat* and asked, "we accept the *Mahabharat*, don't we? If we can accept that, then accepting soap narratives is a piece of cake!"[42]

In order to revitalize the stories, Indian soaps jolt audiences with several ploys of high drama and twists and turns in the stories. The program *Saas, Bahu aur Saazish* on 18 October 2008, reiterated a news item posted on www.indiantelevision.com barely three days before a "major twist in the tale" of *Saat Phere*. Nahar, the husband of the heroine Saloni of *Saat Phere*, "will die but his doppelganger will surface after a while. This track will probably come into play during the second week of November 2008" (Lookhar 2008).

Tarun Katial of Star TV says, "the characters on these serials are already well established, and these serials do have a stable viewer base. It is better to fashion a new story around them and take the serial to a new level than to kill it and start all over again with a new show" (Joshi and Ghag 2003). The strategy behind sustained ratings, Kejriwal explains, is about having a core and a shifting audience. She is on record saying that "some of your audience grows up. But then there is also a new set of audience coming in. So we have to always take into account the psyche of the newer audiences as everything changes in a four year cycle. This thought process has to be incorporated. One has to keep understanding this. The effort is really on how to make the shows constantly innovative and contemporary. Like in *Kahaani* ...we brought in some bikers who are dressed in leather jackets and funky clothes. We could have launched a new show with these people. But the idea is that once you have a brand that has a huge loyal following, you try to introduce a subtle change within to widen your viewership base" (Krishna 2004).

Ekta Kapoor is a producer well known for serving up change and disruption in her soaps. She is on record saying "The basic thing is that these serials have had many peaks, and believe me, there are more to come. By peaks I mean, the high drama and the surprise element which leaves you amazed. Now surely, you can't keep peaking a serial every week. Then, the surprise element would fade away. The viewer needs to be jostled, then allowed to rest and put to sleep, and then jostled again with renewed vigour. That is the secret of serial making" (Lalwani 2003b).

K soaps, in particular, use such tactics. Their family space is markedly different from the space of the family in films. Unlike the utopic resolutions of many Hindi films nowadays, Balaji productions, in particular, represent the space of family and conjugality as deeply conflicted. By representing the family, at times, as fraught with discord, extramarital relationships, sibling rivalry and property disputes, the K soaps rupture the utopic imaginary of "Indian family values" even as they attempt to invoke it.[43]

An important point that needs to be noted is that while all soap stories are about the family, they also focus greatly on problems in the family. Yet no one leaves the family home. They may get thrown out, but they return after a brief sojourn outside.[44] On the other hand, it is true that if there are no problems and conflicts, there is no continuous story possible. It is necessary to keep the narrative going. As Kamlesh Pandey said regarding familial discord, "no good story can be without a conflict. You need opposing forces ... it could be a villain, it could be the mother-in-law or sister-in-law, it could be society rejecting you because of your dark skin color. One needs these elements to make interesting stories."[45]

Ien Ang has made a similar observation about the US soap *Dallas*, saying that "family life is not actually romanticized in soap operas; on the contrary, the imaginary ideal of the family as safe haven in a heartless world is constantly shattered" (1985: 69). These observations underline Jane Feuer's (1984: 15) claim that "serial form and multiple plot structure appear to give TV melodramas a greater potential for multiple and aberrant readings than do other forms of popular narrative." Ekta Kapoor's explanation is "it's this twisted storytelling format that gets the maximum eyeballs. And if you know this is your forte, which is also the popular, most commercial form of entertainment for the television viewer — why not go for it?" (Ekta Kapoor, Talk Asia interview, 2007).

Kamlesh Pandey and Sandiip Sikcand are in agreement that "TV is about clichés, but it also aspirational. The family is sacrosanct. It keeps hopes alive in spite of all the negativity that is shown to garner ratings form time to time. Yes, there is rupture with family values, but in the end, good wins over evil. It inspires hope, and audiences live on hope."[46] Sikcand adds that "good is only good because there is bad. You need evil to enhance the good. Soaps use the message that no matter how difficult good is, stick to it. That lends hope."[47]

Unlike the utopic resolutions of Bollywood films, especially those made after 1990s India's economic liberalization, where the family and "Indian values" are valorized, soaps often have fissures and conflicts dominating their narratives and structure. Conflicts are mainly played out around control over a man's affections *and* for control over the *parivaar ki jaidaad* (family wealth and property). Most of these women have either been married to the man serially (Komolika and Prerna with Anurag in *Kasautii*); or have had an affair with him, for instance Mandira with Mihir, Tulsi's husband, and then had a son, Karan, who hates his birth mother Mandira, but loves Tulsi as his "real" mother. Regarding the issue of multiple wives, Sandiip Sikcand says this is "purely for drama. If TRPs are falling, we bring in another woman. The "other woman" is the biggest threat to the *sada suhagan*[48] Indian woman. You are watching soaps every day. You have to keep audience interest going, there has to be engagement on a daily basis. That is what gets ratings."[49] *Kahaani*'s episode of 13 November 2007 amply bears out this insight. Om, who had lost his memory, and was Rishika's husband as Rishabh Rai Choudhuri, has now regained his memory. He makes Rishika apologize to Parvati. As the two women hug, the camera pans in on Parvati's face over Rishika's shoulder, and she says in Rishika's ear, *"kabhi kisi patni ko mat lalkariyega, bahut pachtayengi"* (don't ever challenge a wife, you will repent greatly).

Control over the *jaidaad* is also a concurrent key theme alongside the romantic shenanighans. The 2007 episodes of *Kasautii* had Komolika enter the scenario to gain control of Basu Publications owned by ex-husband Anurag Basu, and the TV channel owned by Prerna Bajaj. The 2008 episodes of *Kyunki* showed the Virani *parivaar* literally turned into paupers, living in a Mumbai chawl (albeit in glamorous poverty) because one of the evil daughters-in-law, Trupti Virani, had schemed and plotted with her first husband (whom the Viranis of course knew nothing about) to gain control over the Rs 500 crore Virani *parivaar ki jaidaad* and then threw Ba, Tulsi and the rest of the family out on to the streets. In the April–June 2008 episodes, we had Mandira and Juhi Thakral (masquerading as Tulsi, who, for a while had lost her memory) trying to gain control of the Rs 500 crore *jaidaad* of the Virani *parivaar*, while Mandira also had the added intention of trying to reclaim ex-lover Mihir and son Karan's affections. All these schemes failed by the end-June episodes.

When, in the late 2007, in *Kahaani*, Parvati returned in her glamorized Janki Devi avatar (short hair, designer saris and jewelry — makeover by designer Manish Malhotra), she was rich, hence powerful, hence able to buy out any business that, in the meantime, had fallen into the hands of her evil daughter-in-law, Trishna Aggarwal, who, like her *Kyunki* counterpart Trupti, was also treating the older Aggarwals with contempt and disdain, referring to them as "refugee camp" while they lived off her *daulat*. Janki Devi, by sheer dint of her wealth (she referred to herself as being from a *rajware khandaan ki*, from a family of royal lineage) and of course her brains, regained control of the Aggarwal family's wealth — once again, comprising Rs 500 crore. The episodes of May and June 2008 showed how Om Aggarwal, due to his naïveté, lost control of the Aggarwal family fortune by signing away all the Aggarwal companies to a fraudster, Vijay Aggarwal, without checking that the papers of the "business deal" (as referred to in soaps) should read Aggarwal & Aggarwal, not just Aggarwal.

What I am emphasizing is that control over money and property is used as a trope for control over upholding family values and tradition. Money matters are discussed openly in soap narratives in the public as well as private spheres. Central protagonists like Parvati use the power of wealth to bring the bad to book, and thereby regain control not just of the money per se, but also of the *parivaar ki bhalaai* (good of the family) issues.

Soaps also take generational leaps when required. *Kahaani* took two generational leaps, the first one on 7 September 2003, and the second on 15 November 2006. The first saw *Kahaani* taking an 18-year generational leap forward, and a whole new bunch of Gen Next characters were introduced, including Shruti, the grown up daughter of Om and Parvati. "In the fast forwarded *Kahaani* ... Om and Parvati's daughter Shruti, the blue-eyed girl of the Aggarwal household, occupies center stage. In college, she makes friends with Monalika, the daughter of Avantika and Ajay. Then there is Aryan, Sanjay and Ambika's son and Shruti's boyfriend; Krishna, Kamal's son and a protective cousin to Shruti. The story then evolved along the lines that Shruti is greatly influenced by Monalika. She admires Monalika's confidence but the plot thickens when Pallavi, Ambica and their siblings begin to scheme to ruin the Aggarwal household" (Lalwani 2003d).

When Ekta Kapoor was asked for the reason of this generational leap, she said that "[they] wanted to move the story ahead and also wanted to introduce a host of new characters in *Kahaani* ... , and this was a good way. We have succeeded in creating more interest. We have started with the focus on Shruti, and I believe it's one of the most interesting tracks ever" (Lalwani 2003d). TRPs bore out that Ekta Kapoor's gamble paid off. Thanks to this generational leap, *Kahaani* climbed from the eighth and tenth positions in TRPs at the beginning of September to the first and second positions by the end of the month (ibid.).

In *Kahaani's* second leap on 15 November 2007, Parvati was given a glamorous makeover by designer Manish Malhotra. This time around, she came back as Janki Devi to reclaim her own lost identity. Her new identity was groomed by her mentor, Narayani Devi, who, like Lord Krishna in the *Mahabharat*, showed her the right way to fight her battle.

Kyunki has also featured several leaps. The one on 7 June 2006 took a much publicized 20-year leap, and introduced the fourth generation of the Virani family. Commenting on the occasion, Shailja Kejriwal justified that "it was absolutely logical to take this leap, as even after five years, *Kyunki* remains a clear leader amongst television soaps across channels, and to remain at that level its always important to constantly innovate, so it was essential to bring in freshness to the story, with this leap into the future" (report on www.televisionpoint.com, 6 June 2006). Apart from the older characters greying, the biggest change was the introduction of seven new characters, the most important being Krishnatulsi, the child Tulsi adopted during her exile in Benares. "The other new characters of the younger generation include Lakshya, son of Sahil and Ganga; Nakul, adopted son of Damini and Gautam; Bhumi, daughter of Tanya and Karan; Ansh's son Eklavya; Manthan, son of Karan and Tanya; and Joydeep, Sahil's adopted son" (www.rediff.com, 7 June 2006). Speaking about the importance of introducing Krishnatulsi to carry on Tulsi's legacy, Ekta Kapoor said that it was "time Tulsi passes on the baton to the younger generation. I was very particular about what I wanted from the actor as it is a very important role that she, as Krishnatulsi, will be playing and I am happy that I narrowed down to the best. I am quite sure she will do complete justice to the role. For six years *Kyunki* has been the No. 1 serial and the mix of characters will make the plot all the more interesting. Not only the new characters, but also the new sets and the new look of the existing characters will make the prime slot worth waiting for" (ibid.). Interestingly, *Kyunki*'s last leap, that of five years, was taken one day before the soap went off air on Star Plus. It showed the Virani family in disarray, and the introduction of a new character, Sugandhi, who now lives with Mihir and Tulsi while the rest of the family have left due to a misunderstanding over Ba's last will and testament. The last leap also reintroduced Parvati of *Kahaani* into the story of *Kyunki*, bringing Tulsi and Paravti face to face.

There is obviously truth in the observation that "the ability to handle both repetition and disruption, familiarity and change is important in establishing the audience's relationship with a soap narrative and its characters" (Geraghty 1991: 16). The departure of a well-established character may create problems, but interestingly, given that soaps use multiple tracks and characters, it survives. For instance when Smriti Z. Irani left *Kyunki* in 2007, the show did go on. Ekta Kapoor said, "when she wasn't on the show, she was missed by one and all. But she made no difference to the ratings. People love the show and Tulsi. They didn't stop watching without Smriti. The TRPs are decided by the content, not the actors. TRPs change from week to week" (interview with Ekta Kapoor, http://in.movies.yahoo.com/news, 2008). Ekta's observations are backed by data from TAM.

Thus, "the organization of space, time, narratives and characters means that an audience is engaged with the programme as a whole, with its overall narrative and its established space; it is no accident that the titles of soaps refer to a geographical space or group of people ..." (Geraghty 1991: 16). This is certainly true for Indian soaps — *Kyunki* and *Kahaani* make immediate reference to a group of people in a family; *Kasautii* makes reference to the travails of life; *Saat Phere* and *Bidaai* immediately invoke the journey of marriage.

Engagement and Distance

Though I did not carry out research with audiences in great detail, I discussed how viewers participate in soap narratives with producers of soaps, who also view them with an audience's eye to keep track of the product. I also spoke with executives at TAM Media Research who monitor viewership patterns and details. Ekta Kapoor, despite producing several daily soaps, is said to watch each and every episode, or have her mother, Shobha Kapoor, watch them.[50] Rajan Shahi and Sunjoy Waddhwa, or his wife, Comall, watch every episode of their productions as well.[51]

According to the sources mentioned above, viewers participate in a number of ways with soap operas. As Christine Geraghty points out, "the conventions of establishing space, time and character ... become so familiar that they are recognizable to soap audiences as formal strategies ... the aim of most narratives ... subject to conventions which quite overtly postpone resolution ... the audience learns to be aware of the rhythms of the narrative" (1991: 19). Producers of soaps concentrate on developing a subplot for a while before moving on to another. This has much to do with keeping audiences engaged and of course, maintaining TRPs. For instance from June–August 2008, *Kyunki* reintroduced the scheming Trupti back into the Virani household, but this time working through Vaidehi, her goddaughter, to take on Tulsi. In these months, viewers were treated to many schemes on Vaidehi's part, all of which of course ultimately came to naught, *kyunki sachhai ki jeet hamesha hoti hai* (because truth always triumphs). From September 2008 onwards, the subplot of Shiv Singhania and his obsession with Sahil Virani's wife, Ganga, was been introduced in *Kyunki*. Through this device, the viewer knows that a character who has featured strongly for a while (Vaidehi from June–August 2008) will give way to a new character (Shiv Singhania from September 2008 onwards).

Writer Kamlesh Pandey, who has worked with Balaji Telefilms, especially during times that the narratives were being tweaked, feels that "Ekta shows typical Indian middle-class families in more glamorous settings — *saas, bahu, devar, devrani,* the vamp — typical kitchen politics." Pandey added that "TV has to have multiple tracks going. Unlike films, you have to deliver content every day. The family space is shown as conflicted because this is the license TV takes. One should not take this too seriously. If you want reality, see your own life. But TV is for entertainment. Everybody loves a good gossip, especially women. Ekta knows well that psychologically, people love to gossip, it makes people feel better about themselves. People need to heal their own guilt."[52] Sut Jhally and Justin Lewis have observed in this regard that "TV images are not only trusted; they are given more credence than real-life experiences." Viewers tend to feel capable of conceptualizing TV fiction better in terms of realism than news or current affairs. The soap opera genre in particular seems much closer to our own lives and the worlds we live in than news programs (Jhally and Lewis 1992: 31).

L. V. Krishnan of TAM Media Research Pvt. Ltd said that "most of the time, audiences know what is going to happen in the soap. The woman particularly discusses it with family and friends and watches it to check if she had guessed correctly. Producers like Ekta Kapoor, Rajan Shahi and Sunjoy Waddhwa understand this and have made the guessing game pleasurable for the viewers."[53] Soap audiences thus recognize how soap narratives are built, and can enter into a play of that process by trying to guess outcomes through reading internal conventions (cf. Geraghty 1991). Christine Geraghty's observation finds verification from television audience measurement.

Another important way in which viewers recognize conventions of soaps " … is the readiness with which they can be stretched, parodied and broken. Death … has long been recognized as being by no means irretrievable" (Geraghty 1991: 19). So, we have Anurag Basu returning from the "dead" in *Kasautii*, both Om and Parvati in *Kahaani*, and Tulsi and Mihir in *Kyunki*. This point is dealt with in greater detail in the following chapter. Suffice it to say here that in Indian prime time soap opera, particularly the K soaps, conventions can be stretched beyond breaking point. This can be done because the audiences clearly recognize that these are stretchable conventions, and part of their fun and pleasure is to try and figure out how the story will maneuver itself out of this corner that it has painted itself into.[54]

The regular viewer can also keep track of the external pressures on soaps. Daily newspapers in India have a section devoted to entertainment where all the latest news about films and television are available. In addition, magazines, websites and blogs provide details of the television industry. It is important to note here, however, that viewers of soaps can read about actors' contracts and their relationships with producers, their financial and emotional situations, etc. For instance Kiran Karmarkar's (Om in *Kahaani*) departure and subsequent return received widespread press coverage. Thus, "rows on the set, the desire of a leading character to leave ... are all fed into the fictional world of the soap and become part of how its narrative is understood" (Geraghty 1991: 21). Smriti Z. Irani's (Tulsi in *Kyunki*) departure from the soap and her subsequent return a year later were widely reported in the media. A great deal of speculation also went on as to the relationship between Ekta Kapoor and Smriti Irani. Audiences who were aware of the above, for example thus also understood that at that time, the narratives of *Kahaani* and *Kyunki* had to be developed in such a way as to enable the departure of two key characters from the soaps.

Geraghty observes that "the double process of engagement with a soap and acute awareness of its narrative processes can be seen clearly in press interviews with soap actors" (1991: 21). When Irani left *Kyunki* in 2007, there were many interviews with her in the press, where she stressed her other avatars as an actress who could "do without Tulsi" and as producer and politician (see, for instance Roy 2007). In interviews given in 2008 when she returned to reprise the role of Tulsi, she said that she identified with Tulsi, and that she "grew up in a conservative family. Even today, we start our day with puja. So the so-called Virani culture of *Kyunki* ... wasn't alien to me. In fact, one day my father came to pick me up at the airport and I embarrassed him by touching his feet in full view of journalists and fans gathered there. It came naturally to me. So I was very comfortable playing Tulsi" (*Indian Express* online, 13 April 2008). The division in the interviews between the actress speaking both for herself and for the character is typical of press interviews with soap stars (cf. Geraghty 1991: Chapter 1). Geraghty describes this process as a "delicate balancing act of discussing characters as if they were real people with histories, motivations and futures while at the same time recognizing the formal conventions of the serial in which they appear" (1981: 25). This balancing act and the pleasure that audiences derive from figuring this out has also been noted by Robert Allen where he argued that "to a greater extent than any other fiction, the soap opera text constantly walks the line between one that can be read as fiction and one that spills over into the experiential world of the viewer" (1985: 91).

The double process of engagement and distance allows us to follow soap narratives closely, and indeed, "the narrative work of soaps is to create that double vision, that oscillation between engagement and distance, which enables us to be both a concerned follower and outside observer and which makes discussion of a soap almost as pleasurable as watching the programme itself" (Geraghty 1991: 23–24).

Notes

1. *KBC* is modeled on the successful program *Who Wants to be a Millionaire?* Hosted by Bollywood superstar Amitabh Bachchan for the first season, the show swept the country off its feet. In following seasons, *KBC* was hosted by Shah Rukh Khan.
2. Figures provided by Dimple Bhagatji, Manager Business Development, TAM Media Research Pvt. Ltd.
3. Interview with Shailja Kejriwal (August 2007).
4. Interview with Shailja Kejriwal (August 2007).
5. Interview with Shailja Kejriwal (August 2007).
6. Interview with Shailja Kejriwal (August 2007).
7. Interview with Rajan Shahi (August 2008).
8. Interview with Rajan Shahi (August 2008).
9. Interview with L. V. Krishnan (August 2008).
10. Ien Ang makes a similar point for the American soap opera *Dallas* (see Ang 1985, especially chapter 2).
11. Interview with Kamlesh Pandey (August 2007). Karan Johar and Aditya Chopra are known for making expensive films with high production values, with expensive sets, décor, costumes, scenic outdoor locations, etc. It is often said that their main target audience are the NRIs (non-resident Indians) who love the lavishness of the spectacle and the reiteration of "Indian family values." One of Johar's biggest hits, *Kabhi Khushi Kabhie Gham* (Happiness at Times, Sorrow at Times) had the opening tag, "It's all about loving your parents."
12. Simon Frith, writing about rock n' roll in the US, makes a similar point when he states, "America, as experienced in films and music, has itself become the object of consumption, a symbol of pleasure" (see Frith 1982: 46).
13. Prem has since returned, since December 2008, in *Kis Desh Mein Hai Mera Dil*, with the same face, but in the new avatar of photographer Gaurav Sharma.
14. For a discussion on this point in British soaps, see Geraghty (1991), especially chapter 2.
15. Ganesh Chaturthi is the day on which Lord Ganesh, the elephant-headed son of Shiva and Parvati, is believed to bestow his presence on earth for all his devotees. He is invoked at the beginning of all

Hindu prayers and is widely worshipped as the supreme god of wisdom, prosperity and good fortune.

16. "Navratri" or "Navratra" is a combined word which translated means nine nights; *nav* meaning nine and *ratri* or *ratra* meaning night. Navratra is a nine-day holy festival which is celebrated to propitiate the Goddess of Shakti or Divine Mother. Many devotees fast on all the nine days of this holy festival of nights. Navratri celebrations are observed very enthusiastically in the state of Gujarat where all nine nights of the Navratra are spent in vibrant *garba* and *rasa* dance. In West Bengal, Durga Puja is the most important festival. The festivities end on the tenth day, signaling the triumph of good over evil, coinciding with Vijaya Dashami in Durga Puja, and Dussehra, celebrated in the rest of India. In north India, en effigy of the demon god, Ravan, is burnt.

17. Dussehra, also known as Vijaya Dashami, is celebrated on the tenth day of the bright half of the Hindu month of Ashwayuja or Ashwina, and is the grand culmination of the Navratra. The legend underlying the celebration, as also its mode of celebration, varies by region; however, all festivities celebrate the victory of the forces of good over evil.

18. Diwali is the festival of lights, when lamps and lights symbolize the triumph of good over evil. In north India, it is celebrated as the homecoming of Lord Ram to Ayodhya after 14 years in exile, when the citizens of Ayodhya lit lamps all along his path to welcome him home.

19. Karva Chauth is a traditional Hindu festival for married women, and is celebrated mostly in north India. Married women fast for a whole day without food or water for the prosperity and long life of their husbands. The ritual signifies wifely love and devotion to the husband and to remain *sada suhagan* (eternal bride), also signifying a blessing for the woman in that if she is *sada suhagan*, she will not become a widow.

20. Basant Panchami is a Hindu festival celebrating Saraswati, the goddess of knowledge, music and art. It is celebrated on the first day of spring.

21. Holi, also known as the festival of colors, is a spring festival. It is celebrated on the day after the full moon in the Hindu month of Phalgun. It celebrates spring and commemorates various events in Hindu mythology. People celebrate and play by throwing colored powder and water on each other.

22. Raksha Bandhan (literally, the bond of protection) is a Hindu festival, which celebrates the relationship between brothers and sisters. The festival is marked by the tying of a *rakhi*, or holy thread, by the sister on the wrist of her brother.

23. Eid ul-Fitr, often abbreviated to Eid, is a Muslim holiday that marks the end of Ramadan, the Islamic holy month of fasting. Eid al-Adha, or the festival of sacrifice, is a religious festival celebrated by Muslims as a commemoration of God's forgiveness of Ibrahim from his vow to sacrifice his son, as commanded by Allah.

24. The "dot com bubble," sometimes also called the "IT bubble," was a speculative bubble covering roughly 1995–2001 during which value in equity markets grew very rapidly, fueled by the growth in the new internet sector and related fields. Many new internet-based companies, commonly referred to as dot coms, were founded during this period. India, particularly cities like Bangalore and Hyderabad, functioned as the back offices of many Western companies. However, a combination of rapidly increasing stock prices, individual speculation in stocks and widely available venture capital created an environment in which the dot com bubble burst, leading to a recession in the early 2000s.

25. I am making a guess here, but the concept of family is the backbone of all K soaps. Family is also of paramount importance in India. Hence the emphasis on singling out that particular word.

26. For a discussion on establishing shots and close up shots, see Allen (1985); Geraghty (1991); and Hobson (2003).

27. It has been remarked that given the number of battles fought in this house, it is truly incorrectly named.

28. Ronit Bose Roy first used this term in our conversations. Later, Shailja Kejriwal and other television personalities also used the same term (fieldwork in Mumbai, 2007 and 2008).

29. Robert Allen, in his work on US soaps, makes detailed reference to this. See Allen (1985). See also Hobson (1982); and Geraghty (1991: chapter 2).

30. This process was explained to me in detail by Manish, Assistant Director on the sets of *Virruddh* (Against), produced by Ugraya Entertainment and being filmed at Rajkamal Studios (July 2007).

31. Interview with Kamlesh Pandey (August 2007).

32. Columnist Shailja Bajpai (2003) notes that "*The Bold and the Beautiful* is certainly the inspiration for our daily and weekly soaps. It is basically about a family and there is the *saas–bahu* angle to it. Beyond that, Indian soaps have moved in many directions … " (http://www. indiantelevision.com/perspectives/y2k3/shailaja.htm).

33. On the question of physical appearance and beauty being important for a girl, Zee TV's successful *Jassi Jaisi Koi Nahin* (There is No One like Jassi) was modeled along the American *Ugly Betty*, right down to the braces and spectacles of the heroine.

34. Interview with Shailja Kejriwal (August 2007).

35. Interview with Shailja Kejriwal (August 2007).

36. Interview with Sunjoy Waddhwa (August 2007).
37. Interview with Rajan Shahi (August 2008).
38. Interview with Shailja Kejriwal (August 2007).
39. Interview with Shailja Kejriwal (August 2007).
40. Interview with Shailja Kejriwal (August 2007).
41. Interview with Sandiip Sikcand (August 2007).
42. Interview with Shobhaa De (August 2008).
43. I am grateful to Shohini Ghosh for making this very important point and sharing her thoughts with me on this.
44. I am grateful to Poroma Rebello for making this point and sharing her thoughts with me about soaps.
45. Interview with Kamlesh Pandey (August 2007).
46. Interview with Kamlesh Pandey (August 2007).
47. Interview with Sandiip Sikcand (August 2007).
48. *Sada suhagan* literally translates to a wife whose husband is always alive, i.e. she is never widowed. Elders generally bless a bride/daughter/daughter-in-law with these words, implying "May you always enjoy a happy married life."
49. Interview with Sandiip Sikcand (August 2007).
50. Interview with Shobha Kapoor (August 2007).
51. Interviews with Sunjoy Waddhwa (August 2007) and Rajan Shahi (August and September 2008).
52. Interview with Kamlesh Pandey (August 2007).
53. Interview with L. V. Krishnan (August 2008).
54. In her analysis of soaps, Christine Geraghty (1991: chapter 1) points out that this stretching of conventions is to be found more in US prime time soaps that in British ones which lean more towards realism.

5

Women: Similar Genre, Different Representations

Conceptualizing Soap Opera Heroines

This is a complicated domain, particularly in India, where criticism is often vociferous against the representation of women in prime time soaps. But, as Charlotte Brunsdon argues, a difference must be made "between the subject positions that a text constructs, and the social subject who may or may not take these positions up" (1981: 32; see also Kuhn 1987). I have argued elsewhere, regarding the representation of femininity in Indian media, that "... resistance can be read in many ways — both by audiences of media messages and by producers of the same" (Munshi 1998: 587, emphasis in original).

Within the soap opera family worldwide, women are the central protagonists. Indian soaps too tend to favor very strong — positive or negative — women characters.[1] This point was underlined in all the interviews I conducted.

This chapter will focus on different representations of the woman, who is the central protagonist, in the similar genre of the urban family soaps: starting in chronological order, as they began to be aired — Tulsi in *Kyunki*, Parvati in *Kahaani* and and Prerna in *Kasautii*. To these, I will add heroines of two new soaps — Saloni in *Saat Phere*, and Sadhana and Ragini in *Bidaai*.

The chapter will also deal with the negative side of the woman's persona in bringing out the representation of the villainess — Mandira in *Kyunki*, Pallavi in *Kahaani*, Komolika in *Kasautii*, Malti *bhabi* in *Bidaai*. This aspect is equally important because it offers the comparative angle when contrasting "good" with "bad."

The K Soap Heroines

In the longest running K soaps — *Kyunki* and *Kahaani* — Tulsi and Parvati's characteristics are derived from the hierarchal textual authority of the *Ramayan*, and these two iconic heroines have all the characteristics of Sita — dutiful and virtuous, the perfect example of loyalty and morality, the ideal daughter, ideal wife and ideal mother.[2] This "elision of the sacred and the secular" is what Patricia Uberoi rightly terms "a peculiar and distinguishing feature of ... calendar art ... Indian TV and popular cinema ..." (2006: 56).[3]

The sacralization of Tulsi and Parvati is highlighted in many ways. The first and most obvious are their names. Tulsi has multiple meanings. It refers to the holy basil plant, commonly found in many Hindu homes because it is considered very auspicious and is worshipped. There are numerous mentions of the tulsi in folklore and Indian mythologies. It also finds mention in many stories related to the famous Krishna devotee, Mirabai. The significance of tulsi is sketched out in a tale in which Krishna was weighed in gold and even the entire jewelry of his consort, Satyabhama, could not outweigh Krishna, until tulsi leaves were placed on the other scale. Parvati (meaning daughter of the mountain, the Himalayas), is the divine consort of Lord Shiv, and the benevolent aspect of divine *Shakti*,[4] the embodiment of the total energy in the universe. Parvati symbolizes many virtues such as fertility, marital felicity, devotion to spouse and family, and power in its beneficent aspect.

A second aspect of sacralization of the two iconic *bahu*s of the small screen are the opening credits of *Kahaani* and *Kyunki*. *Kahaani*'s opening credits are with Parvati's hands guarding the sacred flame of the *diya* (lamp) at the Aggarwal family altar with the deities of Ram, Sita and Lakshman. This depiction has changed over the years. At one time, Parvati, Om and their daughter Shruti's hands guarded the flame, then it was Om and Parvati's, and many times, just Parvati's. The one constant has been Parvati's hands, adorned with bangles, guarding the flame. The opening credits of *Kyunki* in the initial years showed a picture perfect joint family of the Viranis, all smiling and waving at the camera in front of a rangoli.[5] In recent times, it is Tulsi pouring water into the tulsi plant outside the Virani family home, folding her hands and bowing her head in prayer and then looking up and smiling at the audience even as a colored *rangoli* comes up on the side of the TV screen.

A third and very important aspect are the *shlokas*[6] and *bhajans* (devotional songs) that are recited or sung in the background when Tulsi and Parvati are on screen, especially when taking the stance of good against evil. The ones heard most frequently in the background score in reference to Parvati are "*Raghukul reet sada chali aayi, pran jaaye par vachan na jaaye*" (This is the eternal law of the Raghu clan, one's life can be forfeited, but never one's word); and "*Jai Jai Ram Ramaiyya, Ayodhya lauti Sita maiyya*" (Hail the Lord Ram, Mother Sita has returned to Ayodhya). Tulsi is constantly invoked with "*Jai Ma Tulsi Ma*" (Hail Mother Tulsi). Both Tulsi and Parvati are picturized very often with the famous *Devi stotras* (prayer for the goddess) "*Sarva Mangala Mangalye, Shive Sarvartha Sadhikey, Sharanye Triambake Gauri, Narayani Namostute*" (Source of All Blessings, Auspicious One, She Who Is Refuge, She Who Has Three Eyes, Golden One, Bestower of All Wishes, Blessed of All Blessed Ones, I pray to You and Honor You); and "*Om Jayanti Mangal Kali Bhadrakali Kapalini, Durga Kshama Shivadhatri Swaha Swadha Namostute*" (All-conquering Mother, remover of darkness, reliever of difficulties, loving, forgiving, supporter of the universe; I offer my respect and devotion to You).[7] When audiences see Om–Parvati and Mihir–Tulsi together, very often the background score is "*Mangal bhavan amangal haree, Dhravahu Sudasarath Ajar viharee*" (One who does good, and gets rid of what is not, worship that son of Dasharath).

When the Virani (*Kyunki*) and Aggarwal (*Kahaani*) family members refer to Tulsi and Mihir, and Parvati and Om respectively, the phrase most often used in reference to them is that of alluding to them as Ram and Sita from the *Ramayan*. Elders in both families constantly pray "*Mere Ram–Sita ki jodi ko banaye rakhna Thakurji*" (please God, keep this Ram–Sita couple together and safe). The symbolization of Parvati as Sita has an added dimension in that of Kamal, her brother-in-law, who has all the qualities of Rama's younger brother Lakshman in protecting his *bhaiyya* and *bhabi* (brother and sister-in-law). Numerous episodes have Kamal saying "*Yeh Lakshman ko seva ka mauka toh dijiye bhabi*" (Give Lakshman a chance to serve you *bhabi*).

It must be noted, however, that the third K soap heroine that I examine (Prerna in *Kasautii*) was not conceptualized, or represented, in the Sita mold, but more through the lens of romance, while maintaining her persona as a working woman.

Also, the two other soaps I deal with that first dislodged Balaji's supremacy with TRPs (*Saat Phere* and *Bidaai*) deal with the fair skin/dark skin thesis. Shobhaa De refers to these two soaps as "a brilliant stroke of tapping into the mass neurosis we have in India of a dark skinned daughter. Any parent with a dark-skinned daughter immediately connects with this reality."[8]

Creative heads and writers of soaps, as well as the stars who enact these roles on screen, all voiced the same opinion that each character had a different characterization and were completely different from each other. They admitted that characteristics of Tulsi and Parvati were drawn from Sita, but they also stressed that each representation was separate from the other. Shailja Kejriwal, creative head of Star and the main contact with Balaji Telefilms' creative head Ekta Kapoor, was very clear in how they had conceptualized the three heroines of the "K" soaps. "*Kyunki*'s Tulsi was conceived of as being in the Cinderella mold, with Tulsi from a middle class background marrying Mihir of the rich Virani family; *Kahaani*'s Parvati was conceived of as the goddess Lakshmi;[9] *Kasautii* was a more modern love story and Prerna is a career woman, torn between her love for Anurag and her duty towards the older man, Mr Bajaj."[10]

Sandiip Sikcand, earlier a creative head with Balaji Telefilms, and in 2008, freelancing on the creative side with Balaji and other production houses, finds the three "K" women "completely different characters."[11] Sikcand's characterization is interesting in that he finds Tulsi "a very progressive woman, someone one can make a suggestion of going to a disco with!" He went on to add that "Tulsi is someone one can be comfortable with, she is a *friend* one can share problems with, more like an *elder sister.*"[12] On the other hand, he finds Parvati more in the mold of "*a mother, a protector.*" He feels that other soap family members would not discuss their problems so openly with Parvati, because "Parvati's character is governed a lot by *sanskar* (values) and *parampara* (tradition)."[13] Different from the above two, Sikcand's characterization of Prerna is "that of a *girlfriend.* Prerna is someone who believes in love. She will *make mistakes*, she is not always right, she can be fallible. She is more human than Parvati or Tulsi."[14]

Anil Wanvari, founder and editor-in-chief of Indiantelevision Dot Com Pvt. Ltd, has been a media watcher and analyst since the last 14 years. He feels that Tulsi was conceived as "a traditional young girl from a small town who is a fighter. She threw her husband out of the house when she found out about his extra-marital affair." Smriti Z. Irani, the actress playing Tulsi, obviously agrees with this assessment. She stressed that she "identified completely with Tulsi, except that Tulsi tolerated another woman (Mandira) in her husband's life. In real life, I would have walked out. None of us have Tulsi's patience. I wish I did!"[15] Wanvari finds Parvati to "also be a fighter, but Parvati is more traditional than Tulsi. She takes a strong step against her husband, Om, but tends to forgive him much more easily. Prerna is a modern woman. She has been married more than once, is a career woman, she is modern yet traditional."[16]

Writer Kamlesh Pandey, who writes both for Hindi films and for television soaps, has a somewhat different take on the three characterizations. Pandey feels that the three women — Tulsi, Parvati and Prerna — are "reflections of each other, there are a bit of each one in the other." Pandey added that they are "basically three different faces of the same woman. The stories are different, but their inherent personalities and beliefs are not different, in that they all believe that *sachhai ki jeet hamesha hogi* (the truth will always triumph)."[17]

It was not possible to meet Shweta Tiwari, the actress who played the role of Prerna in *Kasautii*. At the time of my fieldwork in Mumbai in the summer of 2007, Tiwari was undergoing problems in her personal life, including a publicized marital break-up. By the time I was in Mumbai for another round of fieldwork in the summer of 2008, *Kasautii* had already aired its last episode on 28 February 2008. I have therefore relied on interviews with others in the conceptualization of Prerna's character, not with the actress herself. As recounted by Shailja Kejriwal, "*Kasautii* was conceptualized as a love story, and Prerna was visualized as a romantic. But she was also a professional girl, who was always a career woman, working in the BTN news channel."[18] As noted above, Sikcand thinks of Prerna as "a romantic, a girlfriend."

Fortunately, I was able to meet and extensively interview two of the actresses who play the small screen's iconic *bahu*s (daughters-in-law), Tulsi (Smriti Z. Irani) and Parvati (Sakshi Tanwar) for their understanding of the characters they have been portraying four days a week, for eight years continuously, on screen. It would not be an exaggeration to say that they are better known by their screen names now.

Irani feels that "women make for far more interesting characters in soap operas. They play multiple roles — unlimited caregiver and nurturer. They can also be wicked. There are many shades to a woman's persona. Men are more limited in that sense."[19] She underlined that "while Tulsi is traditional, still, she has her own voice." She is always "sensitive and aware" of the characters she portrays on screen, especially that of Tulsi, "because of the target audiences who are families." She stressed that "being a mother herself," she knew "very well what to say and what not to say, what to do, and what not to do, since *Kyunki* is watched by such a large audience." Irani also said that she had a free hand with Ekta in the development of the character of Tulsi, and if she felt that "something went against the grain personally, [she] would call the producer directly and cancel it. The production house was very understanding of what [she] was trying to say. Ekta always understood."[20]

Smriti Irani left *Kyunki* in a much publicized departure with a prison van accident in 2007 that audiences were alerted to all day long on Star News. At that time, when asked, in an article headlined "I can do without Tulsi," in the *Indian Express*, if "Tulsi [was] no longer indispensable for actor Smriti Irani?," the actress had replied that "it never was. Roles come and go; it's the actor who stays in the end. On March 25, Tulsi completed a seven-year bond with the audience. I have grown while playing Tulsi and the industry has accepted me as an actor. But I won't be complaining if her track terminates tomorrow. Finally, people know and address me as Smriti today, instead of Tulsi" (Roy 2007).

An interesting reversal of tone became visible just a year later in 2008 when Irani returned to *Kyunki*. This time, when quizzed by the *Times of India* about her return to the show, she was reported to be "amused" and asked, "Why is everyone asking me that? How am I supposed to feel? I never had a gap. No matter where I went, my audience stayed with me. I have been one of those rare actors who's managed to retain the love and respect of people. Stars come and go, actors remain. And among them very few manage to become family members" (14 May 2008). About producer Ekta Kapoor, Irani maintained, "I never question Ekta. When I was asked to leave the show, I didn't question her. When she said she wanted me back, I just agreed" (ibid.). When I interviewed her in the summer of 2007, she was categorical that no matter what is reported in the press, "she was still under contract with Balaji, and would return whenever the narrative required."[21]

Sakshi Tanwar recounted to me the story of her coming to Mumbai and meeting with Ekta Kapoor, who saw her shooting for another pilot, and the moment she saw Tanwar, told her "you are Parvati."[22] Ekta Kapoor told Tanwar that within a few weeks of *Kahaani* being launched, everyone would be calling her by her screen name of Parvati. Tanwar laughed and added that it took barely two weeks for people to start calling her Parvati. Tanwar sees a clear delineation of the way Parvati's character has "journeyed over eight years" and "how soap stories are told from the view of the women characters." Her observation was borne out by Shalija Kejriwal who said, "Parvati has evolved over the years. She has to evolve to remain relevant."[23] Tanwar said that "in the beginning, Parvati would keep suffering silently. But after the generational leap, and after her transformation into Janki Devi, she puts the problem out there on the table and asks 'what should we do about it?'"[24] She also added that it "simply would not do to have Parvati, who had come back to take revenge, have grey hair. This would not have conveyed the message successfully. Hence, the glamorous makeover by Manish Malhotra in Parvati's new avatar as Janki Devi."

Tanwar's understanding of Parvati's character is that it is an "identifiable one. Parvati is a normal person who makes mistakes. She is human, she has also told a white lie when it is for the betterment of her family. She has not treated Pallavi fairly. Pallavi was supposed to marry Ajay, but Parvati got her married, without her knowledge, to Kamal. Ultimately, this was the better decision, but not if you see it from Pallavi's point of view."[25] Her thoughts of Parvati having a "fallible, human side" have obviously found voice, because the episodes of *Kahaani* in September 2008 show Pallavi having gone to extraordinary lengths to rescue Parvati from a mental asylum where arch villainess Trishna Aggarwal had placed her. Audiences have seen unbelievable shots of long-time enemy Pallavi comforting a weeping Parvati in her arms, and Parvati having said the very rarely heard "I'm sorry, Pallavi," also adding "*Ab tak duniya ne jethani aur devrani ko sirf ladtey dekha hai. Ab duniya dekheygi kya ho sakta hai jab jethani aur devrani ek ho jaatey hain*" (Until now, the world has only seen the elder sister-in-law and younger sister-in-law fighting. Now the world will see what can happen when the two unite).[26]

Tanwar, too, says that she "keeps providing feedback to Ekta about her role. [She] meets people on the roads, in markets, she attends functions and shows, and people tell [her] what works and what does not. Balaji is open to suggestions."[27] She added that "Balaji has a very able creative team headed by Ekta Kapoor whose unerring instinct in the visualisation of her characters always works magic on the screen."[28] Tanwar negotiated directly with Ekta for her role and shoots very long hours, but only for 15 days in the month. She has also played the role of *Devi* (Goddess) in a serial of the same name on Doordarshan, but as Kejriwal astutely pointed out, "the character of Devi feeds off the character of Parvati."[29]

Dark-skinned and Fair-skinned Heroines of *Saat Phere* and *Bidaai*

Two newer soaps — *Saat Phere* (Zee TV) and *Bidaai* (Star Plus) — moved away from the conceptualizations of the K soaps' heroines. A basic premise that both soaps have dealt with is the fair skin versus dark skin issue for girls in India, albeit from two somewhat different viewpoints. One look at the Classifieds column in matrimonial advertisements in newspapers and the skincare market in India establishes the premium we place on fair skin in India, especially for girls.[30] This was, therefore, a natural line to be explored in soaps. Both soaps also enjoy high TRPs and were the first to dislodge the K soaps from their top positions.

Zee TV, where *Saat Phere ... Saloni ka Safar* airs Mondays through Thursdays at 9:30 pm, describes the soap thus: "*Saat Phere* is a story of a girl's struggles against the stigmas forced upon her by society and her quest for her unique identity ... [this is the story of] Saloni, a dark complexioned 24-year-old girl. Saloni's talent is overshadowed by her complexion. Faced with such a situation, Saloni is determined to not let society's will be imposed upon her and ruin her life and has the will, spirit and the courage to embark upon the journey to search for her own unique identity. *Yehi hai Saloni ka Safar* (this is Saloni's journey)" (http://www.zee-tv.com/ZeeSerial.aspx?zsid=56).

The Rajshri Films' website describes *Saat Phere* as follows: "One of Zee TV's most popular shows, *Saat Phere — Saloni Ka*

Safar explores this unreasonable preoccupation with the transparency of the skin over that of the mind and character of a person, through the eyes of Saloni. The protagonist Saloni (Rajshree Thakur), a dark-complexioned twenty-four year old girl, is faced with stigma forced upon her by society. She also finds that her talents are overshadowed by her complexion. Being a resolute young woman, Saloni decides not to get bogged down by the age-old myths and gathers the courage to search for her own identity. *Saat Phere — Saloni Ka Safar* is a heartwarming tale which is still popular for rendering intense emotions through its story and characters" (http://www.rajshri.com/zee/saatphere/index.asp).

Sunjoy Waddhwa's company is Sphere Origins, producer of *Saat Phere*, that turned around the fortunes of Zee TV. Waddhwa has had a career in the media, and has directed other soaps earlier. For *Saat Phere*, he was told by Zee TV that they wanted "to do something with mass appeal, something to do with the underprivileged."[31] Zee gave him a one-line brief that they wanted "to tap into an existing social concern, [so Zee asked for] *ek kali ladki ki kahaani*" (a dark-skinned girl's story)."[32] Waddhwa told me that he has traveled extensively over India and has seen children, especially girls, walk 5 kilometers to school. He also realized that "whether one subscribes to it or not, the color factor exists in India." In making *Saat Phere*, he decided that "*pehle aap samasya dikhaiye, aur phir uska samadhan*" (first show the problem, and then its resolution). So they cast Rajshree Thakur in the lead role of Saloni who faces problems due to her skin color, but whose strength and inner beauty shine through, and who fights for other's causes. Waddhwa said that "Saloni started off as an underdog, but see how she has come up in life ... now she has a perfect marriage, a good husband, a loving family."

Rajan Shahi, producer and series director of *Bidaai*, has had a successful innings in the television industry. In fact, it was Shahi who first set up *Saat Phere* on Zee TV and was the series director for *Ghar Ki Lakshmi ... Betiyaan*, another of Zee's successful soaps. Shahi credits the story idea of *Bidaai* as having originated with Star TV's Vivek Bahl, who moved from Zee to Star. Having worked with Bahl earlier, Shahi has a comfortable equation with him, reminiscent of Shailja Kejriwal and Ekta Kapoor. Initially, the film company, Rajshri Productions, which are known for making films providing good, wholesome family entertainment, was asked to do the show. This, however, fell through, and Shahi was offered the show with a month to its launch date.

Launched on 8 October 2007, *Bidaai* garnered top TRPs by January 2008. Television Point news online reported that "Star Plus' *Sapna Babul Ka ... Bidaai* is the most popular show on the channel with a TRP rating of 5.58, beating *Kyunki Saas Bhi Kabhi Bahu Thi* at 5.25, which was the most popular show on the channel for six consecutive years. A source at Balaji Telefilms says that Ekta Kapoor immediately called for an emergency meeting to evaluate the success of Rajan Shahi's *Bidaai* that was inspired by Sooraj Barjatiya's film *Vivah*" (www.televisionpoint.com, 15 January 2008). It was also rumored that Zee accused it of being a copy of *Saat Phere*. Shahi, however, refuted this and said that "the inspiration for *Bidaai* came from Rajshri Productions' successful film *Vivaah* (Marriage, 2006, dir. Suraj R. Barjatya). This is why the opening credits of *Bidaai* acknowledge Rajshri Productions."[33]

Shrugging off rumors, Shahi said that in *Bidaai*, he "moved away from multiple affairs and chose instead to focus on the fair girl versus dark girl complex." He added, "Let's face it, skin color is still an issue in India." But we have handled this theme in a sensitive way."[34] Indeed, what is noteworthy about *Bidaai* is that Ragini, the dark-skinned sister, is not represented as suffering from an inferiority complex next to Sadhana, her fair and beautiful cousin. Ragini is shown to be smart, confident and relaxed. The two sisters love each other unconditionally. It is through two other older womens' characters that *Bidaai* highlights anxieties and prejudices against dark-skinned girls. One is Ragini's mother, Kaushalya Sharma, who constantly worries about her daughter coming off second best when compared to Sadhana, to the extent that she ends up misunderstanding and ill-treating Sadhana. The other is Vasundhara Rajvansh, who has a fixation about being fair and good-looking. As *Bidaai*'s narrative unfolds, we find out that Vasundhara's younger sister-in-law, Ambika, in the Rajvansh household, is in actuality her own elder sister, but who has never been acknowledged as such. Ragini's being dark-skinned is one of her main reasons for opposing the marriage of her son, Ranvir, with Ragini.

Bidaai thus highlights how undeniably in India we suffer from such anxieties and prejudices. Rajan Shahi placed an advertisement in 13 major newspapers in India when *Bidaai* started airing. The results are there to see, underlining the unfortunate truth that " … we are driven by physical appearance and external beauty." The two dark-skinned actresses in *Bidaai* are on record saying that at times their real lives have mimicked their reel lives. Parul Chauhan, who plays Ragini, says that her maternal uncle "has two daughters. One is fair and the other is dark. The dark cousin always faces discrimination which I really condemn. They always worry about her marriage. I ask them to see my serial and hope that they will change with time" (Maheshwari 2008). Vibha Chibber, who plays the role of Ragini's mother, Kaushalya Sharma, says that, in real life, she has always had a supportive family, both before and after marriage, but "finds it very strange when society differentiates between fair and dark skin. No matter how the male skin is but the female has to be fair. A mother is always worried about her dark daughter's marital prospects. I just find the whole thing very gross. I like the serial *Bidaai* because it deals with this problem in the best way possible" (ibid.).

The weekly English magazine *Outlook India*, in its issue of 3 November 2008, reports that "the Indian obsession with 'white skin' begins early these days. Now, childless Indian couples aspiring for offspring have a large roster of demands: fairer skin, light hair and blue/green eyes. And they're thronging sperm banks and fertility centres across the country looking for '*firangi*' (foreign) donors to ensure they get it … with 40 million infertile couples in India, the market is, by any reckoning, huge. And the number of those who want their progeny to have characteristics different from their own physical profile is also growing." The article further reports that the highest demand is for "fair skin, lighter hair, blue/green or light eyes, and higher IQ levels"; and that despite no existing system of check and balances, the number of sperm banks and in-vitro fertilization clinics is growing in the country (Bakshi 2008).

NDTV 24x7, one of India's leading English news channels, aired a show on Sunday, 28 September 2008 titled "Not Just Skin Deep Prejudice: Why are Indians Obsessed with Fairness?" in its weekly program slot "We the People"(on Sundays at 8 pm) anchored by Barkha Dutt. In the program, actress Parul Chauhan of *Bidaai* openly recounted that when she was born, her maternal grandmother lamented to her mother, *"beti hui, woh bhi kali"* (not only has a daughter been born, but she is also dark), and this continued till she was in the seventh grade. Chauhan also admitted that while shooting for *Bidaai*, her "skin color is darkened to make her look three times darker than she is in real life."[35] The same program also featured men who said that they used fairness creams because "they wanted to look better."

Advertising for fairness creams is blatant in India. Sravanthi Challapalli's article (2002) on fairness creams in India states that "of the Rs 3000 crores cosmetics and toiletries market, the skincare segment accounts for Rs 1200 crores. Fairness products account for a whopping Rs 700 crores of this segment. The annual growth rate is between 10 and 15 per cent. Hindustan Levers, with Fair & Lovely, has a massive 53 per cent market share, followed by Cavin Kare (Fairever) with over 12 per cent share and Godrej Fair Glow with a 3.5 per cent share. Himalaya Drug Company recently made an entry into this segment and aims to capture two per cent share of the market. Other players such as Emami (Gold Turmeric and Naturally Fair) and Revlon (Fair & Glow) also have a presence."

But advertising for fairness creams is no longer limited to women. In 2007, Fair and Handsome, a fairness cream for men, was launched in India by Emami; this is advertised as "the world's No. 1 fairness cream for men." To fight off any possible ridicule, Bollywood superstar Shah Rukh Khan endorses the product. The website http://www.fairandhandsome.net also takes pains to explain "why men need fair skin." The four reasons given are because of "exposure to sun, pollution, stress factors and harsh blades." Thus, "Emami in collaboration with Activor Corp, USA, herbalists and dermatologists from India has created a unique fairness cream for Men with a breakthrough Five Power Fairness System to make skin fair and handsome in 4 weeks. It also helps in relieving stress and fatigue signs — gives men's tough skin a firmer look. Emami Fair and Handsome World's No. 1 fairness cream protects men's face from sun's UV Rays." The running ticker tape tab lists comments from media personalities. "Men are also under pressure to look better," says advertising guru Prahlad Kakkar. Writer Jerry Pinto observes that "most dark skinned men are as insecure as women, and go to equal lengths, albeit secretly, to achieve lighter skin."[36]

This new focus on men coming out openly on the use of fairness creams has caused some public debate in India. It used to be accepted wisdom that "looks" were important only for girls, and that this was part of the asymmetry of gender relations. This open attention to male grooming is a recent phenomenon in India. It is a fact that there are beauty salons and spas in India now that cater specifically to men. I have written elsewhere about the proliferation of gyms and beauty parlors and how discourses of body care shifted from the private to the public sphere in India from the 1980s onwards (Munshi 2004). I cannot enter this debate at length here, but will hazard a guess that this is in keeping with the global trends that India is exposed to in a liberalizing economy (see, for example books on male grooming, such as Flocker 2003; West 2006; and Bartky 2008).

To return to how the *Bidaai* heroines were conceptualized. Shahi made it clear that *Bidaai* is different from *Saat Phere*, of which he was originally a part. *Bidaai*, according to him, explores the fair/ dark issue from both viewpoints — from the viewpoint of Ragini, the dark sister and her mother, Kaushalya's concerns. At the same time, however, *Bidaai* also looks at it from the other angle, "how the beauty of Sadhana, the fair and good-looking sister, becomes her biggest curse." Shahi also attributes the success of *Bidaai* to other factors such as its "simplicity and innocence, and its res-onance to everyday problems that people face in their lives."[37]

Roles of Villainesses

Moving on from the representation of the heroines, creative heads and writers all underlined that "one needs the villainess" because "everything is comparative. Good is only good because there is bad. You need evil to enhance the good. There cannot be good without the bad."[38] As Patricia Uberoi has argued in writing about calendar art and Hindi films in India, "Against this image of the dutiful wife is counter-posed the figure of the temptress or 'vamp' … her existence is cognitively necessary to underline by way of contrast the opposite qualities of the good and obedient wife … the theme of female power, protective or destructive …" (2006: 62–63). Shailja Kejriwal stressed on this dichotomy by saying "*agar nirman hai, toh vinash bhi hai*" (if there is creation/ design, there is also destruction).[39]

In the world of soaps, unhappiness and crisis is the rule rather than the exception. It is these crises that act towards deferment and soap narratives resisting closure. Contradictions are never entirely resolved. Highlighting these contradictions are the villainesses in soap stories. They do not accept unhappiness as their norm and are presented as intelligent, scheming and (destructively) powerful. In her scheming and manipulations, the villainess constantly disturbs the patriarchal status quo (cf. Budge 1988).

Prime time soaps in India depict strong negative characters played by women. Actress Achint Kaur plays the pivotal roles of Mandira in *Kyunki* and Pallavi in *Kahaani*. She felt that while Tulsi and Parvati "get a graph of a couple of emotions such as duty and sacrifice, the villainess (as portrayed by her) is more natural." She rightly claimed that she had "never been over the top loud. [She] is natural. The people Pallavi and Mandira love, they love; those they hate, they hate. Pallavi and Mandira have a range of emotions allowed to them — love, anger, jealousy, betrayal." All these, feels Kaur, make them "real characters."[40] *Kasautii* had the much married, scheming and glamorous Komolika, whose sartorial attire set a fashion trend.

Like Alexis in *Dynasty*, Pallavi in *Kahaani*, Mandira in *Kyunki* and Komolika in *Kasautii*, the act of donning different hats at different times — that of business tycoon, lover, wife mother, daughter-in-law — constantly initiate intrigue. As Belinda Budge argues persuasively in this context (1988: 106), "her displacement from one fixed familial role represents a threat to the stable worlds of marriage, work and the family, and hence to their underlying dependence on female submissiveness ... [displaced] from the traditional family structure, whose bounds cannot contain her character." Thus Pallavi, Mandira and Komolika have all been (literally) displaced from their family homes as well.[41]

Tania Modleski (1982: 11–34) points out that in soap opera, "misery becomes not ... the consequence and sign of the family's breakdown, but the very means of its functioning and perpetuation." This is most obvious in the functioning of the characters of Pallavi, Mandira and Komolika in the three K soaps, and at different times, Vasundhara Rajvansh, Malti and Avani in *Bidaai*. These women, far from trying to hold the family together like Parvati, Tulsi, Sadhana, and Ragini, constantly exacerbate unhappy situations. *Bidaai* has the scheming Malti *bhabi* in the Sharma household and Avani in the Rajvansh household. It is through Malti *bhabi*'s role, with her trademark statement of *"jhoot toh main bolti nahin"* (I don't tell lies), and her many machinations, that wrongdoings are highlighted. Rajan Shahi told me that "it is through the situations that Malti *bhabi* gets into — like trying to draw her husband away from his parents; trying to wrest control from her mother-in-law in running the household; and in August and September 2008's episodes, maxing out the credit cards — that we highlight the fallout of negative actions." He said that by showing "how Malti played fast and loose with the credit cards, he was (also) trying to highlight a problem that many young people face nowadays with the plastic culture of money."[42] The characterization of soap villainesses challenges ideological assumptions about a woman's place in the family.

Two additional and important factors to be noted at this point about villainesses in K soaps: one, women like Komolika, Pallavi, Mandira, and Trupti are all successful businesswomen. They have, on occasion, divested the heroes of the K soaps from their fortunes. Prerna was portrayed as a successful businesswoman, and Parvati has on occasion tried her hand at business, especially to save the fortune of the Aggarwal family. The second point is that is through them that uncomfortable truths about the so-called perfect families come to light. For instance the episodes from 1–5 November 2007 of *Kyunki* had Trupti mouthing many unpalatable truths about the Virani *parivaar*. When accused of already having a husband while being married to Sahil, she pointed towards Sahil and said *"do auraton ke beech grilled sandwich bane tumhe 25 saal ho gaye"* (it has been 25 years that you are a grilled sandwich between two women [Ganga, his first wife, and herself]). When accused of having committed bigamy, Trupti detailed the other numerous bigamous relationships in the family.

Very importantly, and in a distinct departure from Bollywood films, women's bodies, even the slim, svelte ones of Komolika and Mandira, are not explored as sites of sexuality. As Mary Ellen Brown (1987: 19) argues in this context " … the image of the body as sexual currency is absent, but the spoken discourse of the power of the female body to create is given crucial importance." Being the mother of Mihir Virani's son, Karan, is the source of power that Mandira wields over Mihir, Tulsi and the Virani family. The fact of bringing up Krishna as his foster mother is what gives Pallavi strength in the Aggarwal household. Rishika Rai Choudhuri's hold over Om Aggarwal (then in his avatar of Rishabh, her husband who has amnesia) is the fact that they have three daughters together. Thus, "a woman's sexuality does not, in soap opera, result in her objectification for the male. Rather it is a ... means of her empowerment in a patriarchal world" (Fiske 1995: 345). The villainess' power to control the hero is never finally achieved. Still, it is a struggle constantly in process.

Films have closure, soaps do not. Lead actresses playing negative roles are finally contained within the film's narratives. They may excite, threaten, destroy, but are ultimately punished for their transgressions.[43] Soap villainesses, on the contrary, by virtue of the never-ending character of soap narratives, can scheme and fight on endlessly.

Soap villainesses turn feminine characteristics "... which are often seen as weaknesses ensuring her subordination into a source of strength ... she uses her insight into people to manipulate them, and she uses her sexuality for her own ends, not for masculine pleasure ... above all, she embodies the female desire for power which is both produced and frustrated by the social relations of patriarchy" (Fiske 1995: 346). The ultimate control that soap villainesses work towards is, as Tania Modleski argues, *control* not over men, but *over feminine passivity* (1982: 97, emphasis mine). Indeed, audience reception research (such as Seiter *et al.* 1989) shows how female audiences find the long suffering soap heroines to be "whiners" and "wimpy," whereas they evinced no dislike towards the villainesses.

Noted researcher on market strategy and consumer behavior in India, Rama Bijapurkar, observes that "the primordial force — television — has been the source of enormous change. Whatever may be the critical pronouncements of intellectuals on the retrograde stereotypes of women shown in serials, television has widened the frame of reference and given them the information resources to imagine and aspire. While many people decry the soaps that are the staple of Indian television as regressive and brainless, the fact is that they all have a subversive feminist discourse. The protagonists are all women, good or bad, they all take charge of situations, and they all deal with them in different ways. The virtuous heroine can, when required, be the vamp and the vixen and the message is that all is fair in the game of life and women have the power, if they choose to wield it" (2007: 218).

Fluid Space of Television

A few important points need to be made at this juncture. There are some points of similarity and some points of disjuncture with earlier research on media in India. Research on constructions of femininity on Indian television predates my work on prime time soap operas (in particular, see Mankekar 1999; McMillin 2002a and 2002b; Ahmed-Ghosh 2003). There are differences between representations of femininity of an earlier period on Indian television and now in prime time soaps. Purnima Mankekar's landmark work, focusing on Doordarshan's screening of serials such as *Hum Log* and *Buniyaad* in the 1990s, "... focused on middle class families and their struggles to acquire or maintain upward mobility and middle-class respectability" (1999: 114). This is at variance with the soaps that I examine. All the narratives are set within rich joint families and their trials and tribulations.

Second, Mankekar writes that "the sexuality of daughters was an important concern in many Doordarshan narratives that focused on the position of women" (1999: 117). As we have seen above, the sexuality of (even) soap villainesses is not a matter of objectification for the male, but rather the villainess' source of empowerment within the larger family. The sexuality of daughters is also not a matter of concern in prime time Indian soaps, with the passing exception of Tanu's desire to become a model in *Kahaani* (episodes of January–June 2008). Here, too, the context was to tap into a real life situation. Balaji Telefilms followed a current sensational news item, that of the (still unsolved) Arushi Talwar murder case in Delhi. The *Times of India* reported on 6 June 2008 about *Kahaani* that "the body of Tanu's boyfriend is found inside the house just as the body of the servant was found on the terrace, in Aarushi's case. The similarities do not end here. In the show, as in reality, Tanu's ashes will be immersed in Haridwar, just like Aarushi's. Also, the drama will focus on a family member's involvement in the murder. Like Aarushi's mother, Parvati will be shown giving interviews to the media. The show has also incorporated the element of the MMS from Aarushi's case and the CBI probe into the case."[44]

Third, Mankekar's work found that "dowry was a very common theme ... most frequently, in women-oriented narratives" (1999: 125). With the exception of an instance when Ragini, the dark-skinned heroine of *Bidaai*, herself turned away her husband-to-be and in-laws because they demanded dowry due to her skin color, was the only time that dowry was shown to be an issue. It is noteworthy that in 2008, the heroine herself is shown to be taking such a strong stance against the institution of dowry (and the plotting of her sister-in-law, Malti).

Mankekar further writes that " ... serials such as *Buniyaad* normalized the exploitation of daughters-in-law" (1999: 126). All the prime time soaps examined in this book, however, specifically mention how *"bahuwon ko beti jaisa pyaar aur izzat diya jata hai"* (how daughters-in-law are treated with love and respect like daughters of the family). Episodes of October 2008, for example in *Kyunki*, show Tulsi's strong stand on this matter. When Ganga, one of the daughters-in-law, is told to leave "Shanti Niketan," the family home, by the men in the family, it is Tulsi who tells her sons that Ganga is a daughter of the house and has equal rights just as the sons of the house do. Tulsi is supported in her stance by the other two daughters-in-law, Damini and Nandini.

Patricia Uberoi argues about the "iconization of women" in calendar art (2006: chapter 2, in particular, on calendar art). This is true for soap opera heroines. The above discussion has examined in detail, how, in the representations of Tulsi and Parvati, there is an elision of the sacred and the secular. Extending the point further, my own work on Indian advertising (1997) and research such as Uberoi's (ibid.) on calendar art talk of the fetishization and commodification of women. Writing about calendar art, Uberoi postulates that "reading the general social science literature on the 'status of women' in India (preoccupied, as it no doubt rightly is, with issue of 'victim', 'violence' and 'voice') leaves one rather unprepared for some of the themes that are very insistently foregrounded in the calendar art medium" (2000: 66).

What is different in prime time soaps is that issues of "victim, violence and voice" are not central to the narrative structure, thematics and conventions of the prime time genre of soaps. This, in addition to the argument above regarding villainesses, is perhaps another reason why women, and women's bodies, are not the subject of commodification or fetishization in soaps. It is more the lavish spectacle of the sets, filming of the soaps, fashion trends set by the actors, and overall glossy presentation that are commodified. This point is explored in greater detail in Chapter 7.

Finally, and very importantly, there is a vast body of literature on the "centrality of femininity in the symbolic constitution of an Indian national identity" (Uberoi 2006: 52) both in the colonial and postcolonial periods (see, for example Nandy 1980; Chakravarti 1988; Chatterjee 1989; Sangari and Vaid 1989; Tharu 1989; Mankekar 1999; Sarkar 2001; Munshi 2004; and Uberoi 2006).

Scholars such as Enloe (1989 and 2000); Jayawardena (1986); Jayawerdena and De Alwis (1996); Sarkar and Butalia (1995); and Kandiyoti (1996); and Ray (2000) have argued that women's bodies are used as sites of contestation in a discussion of nationalism, and that nationalism appropriates modernization, capitalism, postcolonialism, and feminist ideology to further a traditional agenda by using women as national symbols. The 1980s serials on Doordarshan in India represented women in roles of "upliftment" and social reformist efforts (Mankekar 1999). Arvind Rajagopal examines how the right wing Bharatiya Janata Party (BJP) used the telecasts of the *Ramayan* and *Mahabharat* as expressions of Hindu nationalism. Rajeswari Sunder Rajan warns that "femaleness is constructed, and that the terms of such construction are to be sought in the dominant modes of ideology (patriarchy, colonialism, capitalism). What is required here is an alertness to the political process by which such representation becomes naturalized and ultimately coercive in structuring women's self-representation" (1993: 129). Huma Ahmed-Ghosh, writing about beauty pageants and television serials in India observes, especially of the K soaps, that "transnational satellite television channels have also resorted to producing serials reflecting the 'traditional' Indian women in Hindu joint families to capture the viewing market. Most television serials propagate traditional Indian values of sacrifice, submission, and chastity of women ... propagating conservative views in the name of 'traditional' culture, most of these family serials also reinforce the 'corrupting' ideology associated with 'Westernization'" (2003: 215–16).

This "'stereotype-centred' approach" is, as Shohini Ghosh argues eloquently, "useful but limited. Useful because it unpacks oppressive patterns of prejudice to show that such reductions are not just errors of perception but forms of social control" (1999: 237). But such a "consciousness raising approach," as Ghosh terms it, entails other theoretical and political pitfalls (cf. Stam and Shohat 1994). "It reduces a complex variety of representations into pre-established categories and prescribes as 'corrective,' 'positive' images against 'negative' ones ... [but] women's responses to images are as diverse as women ... one woman's negative image may be another's empowerment. Making sense of representations and cultural praxis hinges on a recognizing of identities as multiple, unstable, historically situ-ated and products of on-going differentiation" (Ghosh 1999: 237).

The space of television in India that prime time soap operas are aired in is a fluid and fast evolving one. New channels regularly come up and new shows compete with each other. Femininity, as represented in prime time television, is constantly being redefined, re-presented, and re-negotiated. Patricia Uberoi's analysis of the "peculiar character" of femininity in calendar art can well apply for current prime time soap representations. Just as in calendar art, "the corpus is open-ended, the nation an entity still under negotiation," and representations of femininity those in which "sacred and secular images constantly interpenetrate — the 'iconic mode,'" as Uberoi terms it (2006: 70) — so also for prime time soaps. Characters like Tulsi and Parvati jostle on our screens for attention alongside different characters like Saloni, Ragini and Sadhana. They undoubtedly represent strong women (this is further discussed in Chapter 7).

We need to remember, however, that the emerging narrative movements in prime time soaps are just that — emerging. If they cannot be classified as "progressive"; they certainly cannot be called "regressive" either. At best, what we record as academics, in the changeable and unpredictable space of television, is a register of the times we research and write in. Also, no matter what our understanding, as academics and viewers of soaps may be, of representations of femininity, it is equally important to note what understanding and thought processes went behind the conceptualizations of these heroines of the small screen.[45]

Notes

1. See also article by journalist Shailja Bajpai on www.indiantelevision. com, 4 November 2003: "*The Bold and the Beautiful* is certainly the inspiration for our daily and weekly soaps. It is basically about a family and there is the *saas–bahu* angle to it" (http://www.indiantelevision. com/perspectives/y2k3/shailaja.htm, accessed 16 October 2007).

2. Two important points need to be noted here. One, that this construction of Indian femininity is almost always Hindu and, most often, with an emphasis on north India. For instance most Hindi films nowadays are made using Punjabi vocabulary and a liberal sprinkling Punjabi terms. A recent hit film titled *Singh is Kingg* (2008, dir. Anees Bazmee) starring Akshay Kumar could easily have been a Punjabi film, as most of the dialogs were in Punjabi. The point about conflating cultural tradition and the sacred with Hinduism has been made, for instance by Chakravarti (1988); Kapur (1989); Uberoi (2006); and Pauwels (2008). The second point is that apart from Tulsi and Parvati, the other soap heroines under study do not have names laden with such (Hindu) religious significance. In fact, the third K heroine in *Kasautii* is named Prerna (meaning inspiration). This is because they were conceptualized differently.

3. Patricia Uberoi (2006: 56) also cites the works of Das (1981); Mankekar (1999); Mitra (1993); and Rajagopal (1999).

4. A discussion on *Shakti* will follow in Chapter 7.

5. *Rangoli* is a form of art that uses finely ground colored powder to make wall or floor decorations, generally at the entrance of Hindu homes in India.

6. *Shloka* refers to a metered, poetic verse/phrase. It is the chief meter used in the epics *Ramayan* and *Mahabharat*.

7. I thank my father, Anil Munshi, for the ready and simple translations. Similar *shloka*s in Sanskrit are also recited for important second female leads, such as Ganga in *Kyunki*, who is named after the most sacred river of the Hindus. This chapter, however, focuses more on the primary leads in the soaps.

8. Interview with Shobhaa De (August 2008).

9. Lakshmi is the Hindu goddess of wealth and prosperity. In Sanskrit, Lakshmi is derived from its elemental form "laks," meaning to perceive or observe. This is synonymous with "lakshya," meaning aim or objective. Lakshmi is thus goddess of the means to achieving objectives, including prosperity in the lives of mankind. See Chakrabarty (1992); Lutgendorf (1990); Kong (2001); and Stevens and Sapra (2007).

10. Interview with Shailja Kejriwal (August 2007).

11. Interview with Sandiip Sikcand (August 2007).

12. Interview with Sandiip Sikcand (August 2007, emphasis in original).

13. Interview with Sandiip Sikcand (August 2007, emphasis in original).

14. Interview with Sandiip Sikcand (August 2007, emphasis in original).

15. Interview with Smriti Z. Irani (July 2007). This point will be elaborated upon in a later chapter.

16. Interview with Anil Wanvari (August 2008). For a fuller discussion on the modern yet traditional thesis, see Munshi (2004).

17. Interview with Kamlesh Pandey (August 2007).

18. Interview with Shailja Kejriwal (August 2007).
19. Interview with Smriti Z. Irani (July 2007).
20. Interview with Smriti Z. Irani (July 2007). It is to be noted that at the time I interviewed Irani, she had left *Kyunki* in a much publicized departure from Balaji, and was in fact shooting for her own production house's soap *Virrudh*. She returned to *Kyunki* in an equally publicized return after a year, in 2008.
21. Interview with Smriti Z. Irani (July 2007).
22. Interview with Sakshi Tanwar (August 2007).
23. Interview with Shailja Kejriwal (August 2007).
24. Interview with Sakshi Tanwar (August 2007).
25. Interview with Sakshi Tanwar (August 2007).
26. This might also have to do with rumors in the media, some of which I heard on fieldwork in Mumbai in the summer of 2008, that *Kahaani* was coming to an end in October 2008. The main reason cited for this decision was that the story could not be stretched much further and that TRPs were falling. See, for instance Lalwani (2008) and Jha (2008): If *Kahaani* has to end, then Parvati *bhabi*'s *ghar ki kahaani* (story of Parvati *bhabi*'s house) has to have a happy ending.
27. Interview with Sakshi Tanwar (August 2007).
28. Interview with Sakshi Tanwar (August 2007).
29. Interview with Shailja Kejriwal (August 2007).
30. A lot of work has been done on the politics of skin color and race. The point I am raising here is simply to do with the premium that is put on fair-skinned girls in India, particularly in the matrimonial market. See Tummala-Narra (2007). Prayusha Tummala-Narra's work shows that the idealization of light skin color even in mainstream white and ethnic minority communities in the US has impacted a wide range of societal and individual perceptions ranging from physical attractiveness to intellectual and social competence. See also Kishwar (n.d.); Lakshmi (2008); and Sullivan (2003).
31. Interview with Sunjoy Waddhwa (August 2007).
32. Interview with Sunjoy Waddhwa (August 2007).
33. Interview with Rajan Shahi (August 2008).
34. Interview with Rajan Shahi (August 2008).
35. The NDTV 24x7 program had a lot of critique for the way fairness creams are marketed in India. The program's panelists and audience agreed that while discrimination against dark skin is a reality in India, advertisers exacerbate the problem. The program ended on an upbeat note with Alyque Padamsee, creative head for "Fair and Lovely" creams, saying that he would now try and launch a cream called "Bright and Lovely," removing the word "fair."
36. Details from website http://www.fairandhandsome.net, accessed 9 November 2008.

37. Interview with Rajan Shahi (August 2008).
38. Interviews with Shailja Kejriwal and Sandiip Sikcand (August 2007).
39. Interview with Shailja Kejriwal (August 2007).
40. Interview with Achint Kaur (August 2007).
41. Pallavi returned to the family fold, chastened and enlightened, in the September–October 2008 episodes of *Kahaani*, begging forgiveness from Parvati. This, however, had less to do with soap narratives than to do with *Kahaani* coming to an end and going off air.
42. Interview with Rajan Shahi (August 2008).
43. Two films that come to mind in this context are Hollywood's *Disclosure* (1994, dir. Barry Levinson) and Bollywood's *Aitraaz* (Objection, 2004, dirs. Abbas–Mastan) that was based on the Hollywood film. Both Demi Moore and Priyanka Chopra, playing the lead roles, are "tamed" at the end of the film. *Aitraaz* has Chopra committing suicide.
44. In referencing how soaps appropriate current issues in their narratives, Rama Bijapurkar told me that while discussing this new turn, Santosh Desai, CEO of Future Brands, and earlier COO of McCann-Erickson, remarked, "now you're telling me that national news is about entertainment, and that soaps are educational!" (Interview with Rama Bijapurkar [August 2008]).
45. It is equally important to know how audiences make sense of such representations. But this falls beyond the scope of this book.

6

The Male Voice

It seems at times ironic that a genre that generally finds reference as a "feminine" genre is equally dominated by the presence of male lead actors. Ronit Bose Roy (Mr Bajaj in *Kasautii,* Mihir Virani in *Kyunki*) is referred to as the "Amitabh Bachchan of television." Producer–director Rajan Shahi calls Alok Nath, who plays the role of *Mamaji* (maternal uncle) Prakash Chand Sharma in *Bidaai,* the "soul of the show." Others like Hiten Tejwani (Karan in *Kyunki,* the new avatar of Anurag on *Kasautii*); Ram Kapoor (Jay Walia in Balaji Telefilms' high TRPs *Kasamh Se,* 9 pm–9:30 pm IST, Zee TV, and from October 2007 for about 6 months, as Jaz Thakral on *Kyunki*); and Alok Nath in *Bidaai* are all actors who are important players in soap stories.

It is well known by now that family, and familial relationships, are the backbone of all soap narratives. Writer Kamlesh Pandey said, "since the basis for soaps is relationships, one needs the men — as husbands, as sons, as brothers-in-law — to show the various relationships."[1] This bears out Robert W. Connell's observation that "masculinity and femininity are inherently relational concepts, which have meaning in relation to each other ... masculinity as an object of knowledge is always masculinity-in-relation" (1995: 44; see also Connell 1987, especially chapters 8–10; Mumby 1998; Gaonkar 2001; Gopalan 2002; Kimmel *et al.* 2004; and Rajan 2006).

Ronit Bose Roy feels that the "soap stories are not woman dominated, but woman centric. But men also have an important role to play."[2] Shailja Kejriwal echoes Roy's sentiments in that "you cannot have women-centric soaps without men. Mihir supports Tulsi, Karan supports Nandini, and Sahil is Ganga's anchor (*Kyunki*); Mr Bajaj supports Prerna (*Kasautii*), Om is the main anchor for Parvati (*Kahaani*)."[3] Sakshi Tanwar strongly feels that in *Kahaani,* "Om's role is always at par with Parvati's. If Parvati is strong at being the decision maker, it is because, most times, she has her husband's support. It is always Om and

Parvati, never the other way around."[4] This chapter examines how masculinities are constructed in relation to femininities in prime time soaps and how demands of the genre make them different from Bollywood cinematic representations.

In her work on soap operas, Christine Geraghty delineates how the question of family and masculinity is different in US and British prime time soaps. Drawing on Laura Mulvey's reevaluation of 1950s melodrama in the films of directors like Douglas Sirk (Mulvey 1978; see also Gledhill 1987), Geraghty deals with how " ... *Dallas, Dynasty* and other US prime time soaps tend to be male melodramas whereas the British soaps tend towards the woman's viewpoint" (1991: 62). Indian soaps draw from Western ones, particularly in terms of spectacle and glamor. But Indian soap narratives follow their own demands, and do not draw this line as clearly as US or British prime time soaps, and narratives overlap as and when the story line demands it. Journalist Shailja Bajpai (2003) makes the astute observation that our soaps, like all soaps, have a focus on the family with "the *saas–bahu* angle to it. Beyond that, Indian soaps have moved in many directions and Ekta Kapoor's serials are very Indian and original in treatment and themes."

The roles of men and women, however, function differently in soap narratives. In Indian prime time soaps, it is important to note, as Shailja Kejriwal says, that "many times men are the catalysts in the narrative, and their actions take the story forward."[5] That said, it is crucial to note that plot lines in soaps develop usually not as a result of a man's villainous intent, or his reckless disregard for his home and family, but as a result of naïve, ill-thought of choices that anyone could make.[6]

Thus, in the May 2008 episodes of *Kahaani*, the narrative moved forward because of Om's naïveté in signing over business papers of the Aggarwal business empire to the unscrupulous Vijay Aggarwal, without once checking that the papers should have read "Aggarwal and Aggarwal Industries," rather than simply "Aggarwal Industries." In so doing, Om signed away the family fortunes to Vijay Aggarwal, thereby setting the stage for the trials and tribulations that followed. The omnipresent sister, Chhaya, found ample opportunity to mock her elder brother Om. The wayward granddaughter, Tanu, found a powerful opportunity to mock Om's stupidity and negligence each time she was chastened for her so-called bold behavior in wanting to become a model, have a boyfriend, drink at parties, etc. Had it not been for the Aggarwal family's penury, the wicked sister-in-law, the second wife of Kamal, Trishna Aggarwal, could not have been rewritten so easily into the narrative as *Kahaani* headed towards a closure (May–October 2008). Trishna, having reentered the Aggarwal family, once again became a cause of strife and problems for every person in the household, and in particular for Parvati, who she outmaneuvered and packed off to a mental asylum for regular electric shocks, and Om, whom she kept drugged on what is peculiarly termed "depression medicines!"

Similarly, in *Kyunki*, it has been Sahil who has been responsible, not once, but twice, for bringing the Virani *parivaar* to the brink of disaster, once in financial terms (episodes of September–December 2007); and from August 2008 onwards, in terms of his own marriage, albeit unknowingly. Sahil's naïveté in dealing with second wife, Trupti, saw the Virani family fortunes signed over entirely to Trupti, who, in turn, turned the entire family out on to the streets. For a while, the family lived in the *chawls* (slums) of Mumbai, till elder son Karan found a way to outsmart Trupti and bring the family back home. From August 2008 onwards, Sahil entered a business partnership with Shiv Singhania despite wife Ganga's protestations. Her protests had a basis in the justified fear that all Shiv actually wanted was to get Ganga back into his life. Sahil, unaware of this, wondered at his wife's protestations. Shiv maneuvered his way into staying in the Virani family home so that he could be physically closer to Ganga.

The narrative of *Bidaai* moved forward in June 2008 because Ranvir Rajvansh placed a telephone call to a number that was incorrect, but which was answered by the dark-skinned sister, Ragini. Since then, the two have spoken many times over the telephone and in September–early October 2008, think they are in love, though they had not met till then. Around this central forward movement of *Bidaai*'s narrative, Ranvir, for several weeks, is represented as unaccepting of Ragini, because she is not fair and lovely. In subplots during this time, we see Malti *bhabi* and Avani's machinations in keeping the lovers apart, Ragini's mother arranging for a boy to see Ragini for marriage, Vasundhara Rajvansh misunderstanding her daughter-in-law, Sadhana. From December 2008 onwards, the narrative again moves forward when Ranvir realizes that Ragini's inner beauty and innate good qualities are actually what are needed most in a life partner. Most importantly, in the episodes of January 2009, it is the mentally challenged Alekh who is the prime mover in *Bidaai*'s narrative. Through a mixture of threat and supplication, Alekh manages to secure his mother, Vasundhara Rajvansh's blessing for Ranvir to marry Ragini.

Mihir, Om, Anurag Basu, and Mr Rishabh Bajaj in the K soaps are all represented as heading their family business empires; this gives them the status as the head of the family. The women of the family too, especially their wives, are always shown to be giving them this respect. So, like US soaps, "on the surface … men appear to be extremely powerful capitalist patriarchs, giving orders, making deals and sacrificing other people …" (Geraghty 1991: 63). This certainly has resonance with the soaps under study, especially those from the Balaji production house. Both Mihir Virani and Om Aggarwal have thrown their wives out of the house when misled by villainous characters. Anurag Basu and Mr Bajaj have taken turns in accusing Prerna of wrongdoings she had never committed.

Perhaps the most dynamic of all the masculine representations was that of the tall, dark and handsome Mr Rishabh Bajaj in *Kasautii* with salt and pepper hair. Ronit Bose Roy, who played this role, told me that "it was initially supposed to be a three month cameo, but the role became so popular, and audience demand to see Mr Bajaj was so great, that he stayed on." Roy also admitted that it was this role which "catapulted him to the big league."[7] In playing the stylish, iconic Mr Bajaj, the older man that young Prerna relied on emotionally and financially, and married, Roy said that he identified with the role that brought him such popularity, where "somehow you feel a character belongs to you, and you belong to a character." He added that "in all the characters he plays, [his] individual traits and style are very much present." He also stated that he does a lot of research about his roles, reads voraciously, and asks various kinds of people for feedback. He added that "my [his] playing Mr Bajaj is what makes Mr Bajaj."[8] This observation is, in all likelihood, true, because Mr Bajaj's role was initially crafted in a negative mold — the successful, older man coming between two younger lovers. That the audience response was so overwhelmingly positive underscores Roy's observation.

When Ekta Kapoor killed off Mr Bajaj in the early months of 2007, *Kasautii*'s story lagged. Audiences clamored for the return of Mr Bajaj. Thankfully, for *Kasautii* audiences (including myself) Mr Bajaj "returned from the dead," so to speak, by the autumn of 2007, exactly as Roy had thought, "not in a simple straightforward way as a loving husband, but in a dramatic re-entry."[9] Mr Bajaj had amnesia when he "returned."

Mr Bajaj was cast in an overtly suave way and represented as worldly and ruthless in his business dealings. He was also decisive in his actions, a go-getter and a risk taker. The success of this image of Mr Bajaj is obviously a deciding factor in crafting Roy's latest role — that of the older man, Dharmaraj Mahiyavanshi, married to a young girl in Balaji Telefilms' new soap, *Bandini*, that started airing on 19 January 2009 on NDTV Imagine. Asked about playing an elderly role, like that of Mr Bajaj in *Kasautii*, Roy is on record saying "I don't play an elderly man, I am an elderly man. I don't know why people think I am 25. But I play a little above my age. But it is not like any other character that I have played before, but it does have a few common traits with Mr Bajaj. He is a wealthy, self-made man who is proud of his achievements" (Pereira 2009).[10]

Kahaani has also constructed men with negative overtones. Sasha, a distant nephew of the Aggarwal clan, has been an integral part of *Kahaani*'s narratives. Always plotting and scheming, even the evil Sasha, with his famous one liner "kill me!," is domesticated by the time *Kahaani* ended in October 2008, having seen the error of his ways and touching his aunt, Parvati's feet. Similarly, Ishan Nanda, aka Chotu, Parvati's grandson when he entered *Kahaani*, was a gangster, cold and calculating in his dealings. Brought up by Sasha, this does not come as a surprise. Such characterizations are the most removed from other constructions of masculinity such as Mihir and Karan in *Kyunki*; Om in *Kahaani*; *Mamaji* in *Bidaai*. One reason for this is that at their respective points of entry into *Kasautii* and *Kahaani*, Mr Bajaj and Ishan were not married men and loving husbands like the others mentioned here. Matrimony and the love of a good woman (Prerna for Mr Bajaj and Gauri for Ishan) seem to domesticate Indian soap heroes as nothing else. In the case of Sasha, it is his aunt Parvati's lifelong example of always doing the right thing and standing by the family that finally redeems him.

But, like in US soaps, it is precisely Mr Bajaj, Sasha and Ishan Nanda's masculinities that get tamed. The reasons are not the same for the taming of JR in *Dallas*, for example. Unlike professional business dealings in US soaps being the reasons for one's downfall (see Geraghty 1991: 62–64); in the Indian psyche, *pyaar aur izzat* (love and respect) for a feminine character conquers all. It is, therefore, Mr Bajaj's near obsession with Prerna where he thinks he is in control, but in actuality is not, that proves to be his taming and containment, if not his downfall. Ishan Nanda, despite all his negative attributes, succumbs to wife Gauri's unquestioning love and faith in him. Add to this a dollop of grandmother Parvati's *sanskar* (tradition) and Ishan is transformed from being a *khatarnak* (dangerous) gangster to landing a job as a bank clerk where he foils an attempt at bank robbery, bringing all the money back after beating up the scoundrels. As husbands, several episodes have shown both Om Aggarwal (*Kahaani*) and Mihir Virani (*Kyunki*) praising their wives, Parvati and Tulsi, respectively, and telling them that all good things in the family have come about because of the wives always doing the right thing and treading the path of truth.

The same domestication holds true for other male characters playing negative roles who depict assertiveness. Ansh and Eklavya in *Kyunki* exhibit more assertiveness than the other heroes in their demands and actions. Each one, however, has a feminine obsession, which ultimately leads to their taming; and in Ansh's case, even death at the hands of his mother Tulsi in *Kyunki* in a much talked about episode.

There are also more passive male characters — the softer Nakul and Lakshya in *Kyunki*, sons of another gentler male character, Sahil. The softer, gentler men do not come off well in their televisual representations, however. Sahil's scheming second wife, Trupti, browbeats him mercilessly, is actually married to another man, Rishabh, but has been bleeding Sahil dry for his money for 23 years (episodes of *Kyunki*, October 2007), and Sahil's ex-wife Ganga is his boss in the firm where he works (episodes of 2007). By the August 2008 episodes of *Kyunki*, Sahil and Ganga are married once again, but Sahil's naïveté continues as he cannot fathom how his new business partner, Shiv Singhania, is trying to pull the wool over his eyes. Singhania is (September–October 2008) plotting to procure Sahil's signatures by treachery, making him responsible for a collapsing construction site. Sahil is unaware, and only Ganga knows and keeps thwarting Shiv's wrongdoings.

Kamal, the devoted younger brother of Om in *Kahaani*, like Ram's younger brother Lakshman in the *Ramayan*, is devoted to the Ram–Sita *jodi* (couple) of Om–Parvati. But he has always played second fiddle to Om, even when he knows that his elder brother is taking incorrect decisions professionally and personally. He has had two failed marriages, and has been shown drinking heavily after his second failed marriage.

In *Bidaai*, it is the powerful matriarch, Vasundhara Rajvansh, not her husband Indrajit Rajvansh, who makes all the decisions in the Rajvansh household. Similarly, the scheming Malti *bhabi*'s husband, Vineet or Vinu, as he is called, is putty in is wife's hands, and very easily led to revolt against his loving parents when Malti puts him up to it, always adding *"jhoot toh main bolti nahin"* (I don't tell lies), when in fact that is the only thing she does.

There is obviously truth in Christine Geraghty's (1991: 64) claim that in soaps "there remains some difficulty … in representing the domesticated man positively." Like *Dallas* and *Dynasty*, soaps such as *Kyunki* and *Kahaani* offer us "… representations of masculinity both out of control and over-controlled" (ibid.).

Women are central to the man's trials and tribulations in several ways. The previous chapter has demonstrated how villainesses in particular, through their ability to understand, facilitate and control relationships, always get the upper hand over men (and other family members) in soap narratives. One way is when they are represented as rivals in the public domain of the business arena, particularly in the K soaps (Komolika, Anurag's ex-wife, for Anurag in *Kasautii*; Sahil's wives Trupti and Ganga, in *Kyunki*; and the gentler Kamal's ex-wives, Trishna and Pallavi, in *Kahaani*. Trishna was also married to Om for some time in *Kahaani*). Just as Alexis in *Dynasty*, this legion of women, when they become ex-wives, take on "the masculine attributes of the hero and return them in spades; she is as brutal, as single-minded and daring as he can ever be with, in the programme's terms, the additional advantage of a woman's expertise in handling emotional issues" (Geraghty 1991: 65).

In prime time soaps, filial relationships are explored only insofar as they are connected to family property disputes. Thus, the fact of so many ex-wives begs the obvious assumption — that the rivalries have their roots in other problems in the personal domain of familial relationships (cf. Geraghty 1991). Komolika's business feud with Anurag had its roots in their failed marriage and her understanding of Anurag's undying passion for Prerna; Trupti and Trishna's rivalry with the Virani and Aggarwal families, respectively, bringing them to the brink of penury and servitude, had its roots in their own weak position as second wives in the family, when the family members clearly preferred the first wives and also kept up relationships with the first wives, welcoming them back for festivals into the household, if not as *bahu*s (daughters-in-law), then as *beti*s (daughters). There have been many episodes for example, when, much to the chagrin of Trupti (Sahil's wife) and Tanya (Karan's wife), Ba and Tulsi have welcomed Ganga (Sahil's ex-wife at the time) and Nandini (Karan's ex-wife at the time) back into the family fold as daughters, even when they did not have any legal relationship with the Virani family. It is this second source of challenge through the family relationships that one needs to explore further (cf. Geraghty 1991).

While admitting that most of the action is centered around the family home, and therefore the story must be set therein, Geraghty (1991: 66) still raises the point of "a slightly absurd situation" in which " … two or three adult sons still [live] under their parents' roof and [bring] their own families to the family dining table." While this may seem absurd in the Western context, it is much more the norm for families in India, especially when there are family run businesses. As Steve Derne (2005: 45) notes, "Indian marriages are structured within larger joint families, that most Indians want love to follow from duty rather than the specialness of the beloved and expect that love should be extended to many in the family, while remaining subordinate to the fear of elders" (ibid.; see also Derne 1994 and 1995). Add to that the fact that most prime time soap stories are set within rich, industrial families, which, often in India, live together in joint families in real life as well. Thus, joint families are portrayed in all the K soaps, as well as in the more recent *Bidaai*.

It is the women — wives, ex-wives, future wives — who create the movement in and out of the family home for purposes of the K soaps' narrative.[11] This is similar to soaps such as *Dynasty* and *Dallas* (cf. Geraghty1991: 66–68). Tulsi and Parvati have left the family home for 18 and 20 years at a stretch and have returned, unquestioned, to reclaim their rightful place. It is Komolika and Aparna in *Kasautii*, Pallavi and Trishna in *Kahaani*, and Nandini, Ganga and Trupti in *Kyunki*, who have "moved in and out of the family through marriage and divorce. The women are thus the outsiders, taking on the family name but potentially threatening the family both when they enter it and when they leave" (ibid.: 67). Drawing on Geraghty's analysis of US soaps (ibid.: 67–68), the two threats that occur due to the in-and-out movements of the women in the K soaps — with the exceptions of Tulsi and Parvati — are those of loyalty to the family and the control of women's sexuality. When the women mentioned above leave the house, most times they receive help from another man who is briefly introduced into the soap's narrative. This raises questions about the women's undivided loyalty to their family.

A more important challenge perhaps to the *parivaar* (family) are issues tied up with questions of sexuality, paternity, inheritance, etc. As Geraghty, speaking about US soaps, astutely observes, "property is the physical manifestation of the family's success; inheritance is the mechanism of its survival" (1991: 69). The *parivaar*'s boundaries ideally must not be crossed, but they often are, by women's transgressive movements, especially those of the villainesses. Pallavi had a brief avatar as Pammi Nanda; Trupti was married to another man, Rishabh, while she was married to Sahil Virani and stayed in the Virani household. Ganga and Nandini, while remaining loyal to the Virani household, have still been outside its boundaries for several years. One exception is the heroine of *Kasautii*, Prerna, who has children with both Anurag and Mr Bajaj.

Men also transgress sexual boundaries. Mihir Virani had an affair with Mandira, which resulted in the birth of their son, Karan (*Kyunki*). Om was married for a while in his amnesiac state to Rishika, and had three daughters with her (*Kahaani*). Kamal had an affair outside his marriage which resulted in the birth of his son, Krishna.

Maternal affection, however, has been showered on the children by women who are not their biological mothers, but have brought them up. Karan is brought up with great love and care as the elder son of the Virani household by Mihir's wife, Tulsi, to the extent that he totally disowns Mandira, his biological mother, and states many times over that Tulsi is his real mother. Pallavi showers love on Krishna who was handed to her as a baby. It is because of her fierce maternal instinct to love and guard Krishna for her own that she comes into conflict with Parvati.

Problems of inheritance have, however, not occurred. The elder son of the family has always inherited the mantle of carrying on the family empire, even if his birth is illegitimate. Thus Karan, aptly named after his character in the *Mahabharat*,[12] heads the Virani family business empire after Mihir; and Krishna heads the Aggarwal family empire after Om. In the Indian context, we can discern in the soaps, "the typical features of a 'patriarchal' kinship ideology" (Moore 1988 cited in Uberoi 2006). Patricia Uberoi rightly argues that this is "an ideology that ... justifies the authority of the patriarch over women and juniors (male and female) in the family ..." (2006: 32). Dissension has been shown when wives or mothers of younger sons, such as Damini and Trupti in *Kyunki*, feel that their husbands and children have always come in second place. Tulsi, however, has always stepped up to say that this is not the case and that all children are treated equally in the family. Though argued in another context, still, such a situation bears out Uberoi's insightful observation that " ... this moral economy of family relations is not based on the ideal of the pursuit of individual self-interest...but rather on the ideals of selflessness ad altruism, duty and sacrifice" (ibid.: 33).

A great deal of " ... the drama (and pleasure) in these programmes comes from the way in which patriarchal power is continually challenged ..." (Geraghty 1991: 63). This is different from the way it is represented in US prime time soaps, where challenges have more to do with work in the professional sphere. In the Indian context, this challenge to patriarchal authority comes from within the domestic sphere, with a wink and nod towards audiences, strategizing from within, rather than from without (cf. Munshi 1998). Therefore, the heroines, especially Tulsi and Parvati, are almost always proved right even if 20 years pass in between and generational leaps occur to introduce new characters, and they return home, vindicated, if not triumphant (because it would not do to be openly triumphant against one's husband). It is as though through their devotion towards their husbands and families that the heroines control their masculine power. There are, of course, occasions where the woman goes clearly against her husband, but always because she is treading the path of truth (*sachhai ki raha par chalna*). The villainesses of course are the most visible symbols of disrupting the patriarchal status quo. They challenge men on their own turf in the public domain professionally by taking over their business empires, and also in the personal sphere due to their liaisons with them, which, in some cases, result in children, thereby increasing their claim on the man, so to speak.

Points of Difference

A few points differentiating constructions of masculinity in Indian prime time soaps from other forms of media must be noted at this juncture. Soaps in India do not explore relationships among men, not even by way of friendship. This is a distinct point of difference with soaps in the West such as *EastEnders*, *Brookside* and even *Dynasty* that co-opted such discourses into their narratives. As Christine Geraghty writes (1991: 157), in the 1980s, "*Dynasty* led the way by putting Steve Carrington's emotional and sexual dilemmas right into the heart of the family serial and, although neither *EastEnders* nor *Brookside* included gays or lesbians among their initial residents, both later introduced gay characters through whom they have tried to deal with specifically gay issues while at the same time involving them in the day-to-day life of the serial." Geraghty notes, however, that "the working through of this new material has not, however, been unproblematic" (ibid.). Regarding representations of same-sex relationships among women, she makes the important point that it is indeed because of the central role of women in soaps that this might be difficult to portray since this would raise several kinds of questions and issues about the role that female bonding plays in traditional soaps (for a fuller discussion, see ibid., especially pp. 157–65).[13] Thus, as she notes, "where soaps have taken up the issues of sexual orientation, it has been almost entirely through male characters" (ibid.: 158).

Bollywood films have been exploring the space of male friendships and bonding over some years now.[14] Films such as *Sholay* (Flames, 1975, dir. Ramesh Sippy), *Dharam Veer* (1977, dir. Manmohan Desai), *Kal Ho Naa Ho* (Maybe There Will Be No Tomorrow, 2003, dir. Nikhil Advani), and *Dostana* (Friendship,

1980 dir. Raj Khosla; and 2008, dir. Tarun Mansukhani) have, as their main focus, stories of male bonding. It must be stressed that with the exception of the film *My Brother Nikhil* (2005, dir. Onir) that openly explored the problems of AIDS in India, Bollywood films have dealt with male friendships covertly, except in song and dance sequences.

The Bollywood film *Dostana*, released on 14 November 2008, has been touted as bringing gay relationships out into the open in Bollywood and exploring this intelligently (Malani 2008; and *Hindustan Times*, 12 November 2008). Defending the film, producer Karan Johar says, "as for the gay jokes, I think it's time for everyone to wake up to reality. I had gay jokes in *Kal Ho Naa Ho* and no one was offended" (Jha 2008). Bollywood's tongue-in-cheek acceptance of the so-called gay theme resulted in the actors of *Dostana*, John Abraham and Abhishek Bachchan, recently winning the award for the best on screen *jodi* (couple) at the January 2009 Nokia Star Screen Awards, presented to them, amidst much laughter, by their real life *jodis* of Bipasha Basu and Aishwarya Rai Bachchan, respectively. Positive commentary followed in the English language print media. I reproduce here excerpts from an article by Maddox in the *Indian Express* dated 16 January 2009: " 'It is an achievement that a film like *Dostana* is redefining what couple-hood means,' says Malini Dabbas, who works in the non-profit sector on issues of health, gender and sexuality. Vikram of Gay Bombay, a self-funded organisation, says *Dostana* is an exception but not the rule. 'One will always have to deal with stereotypes. It is the spirit in which *Dostana* was done that is inspiring. Not only did it take up the subject but did it well. I do not expect Bollywood to do a *Brokeback Mountain* but this comedy is not malicious,' says Vikram. 'Bollywood has to catch up with the prevailing discourses on alternate sexuality. They made a good start with *Fire*, and now *Dostana*,' says queer activist Lesley Esteves, who also believes that even though the film invited people to poke fun at stereotypes of gay men, it did so without offending many gay people." It must be noted, of course, that the lead actors only pretend to be gay in the film in order to rent an upmarket apartment. Still, as the article notes at the end, "one cannot assume that applause at an award function translates into a gay revolution — yet it is a small step in a homophobic society" (ibid.). As noted above, prime time soaps in

India do not delve into relationships between men, not even by way of friendship, much less sexual orientation.

A second point of difference is that, even in a globalizing India, prime time soaps do not construct relationships of Indian men with women of any other nationality. This is another point of difference with, for example Chinese soap operas of the 1990s that involved " ... transnational romances between Chinese men and Russian and American women." Sheldon Lu, writing about soap opera in China, observes that in soaps such as *Russian Girls* and *Foreign Babes*, "there is undeniably a marginalization of the local Chinese woman in favor of the white woman in the racial, transnational politics of Chinese men, whose desire and gaze motivate the flow of the respective narrative ... the imaginary conquest of the white woman is a male defense mechanism, an attempt to do away once and for all with the stereotype and self-perception of inadequate Asian/Chinese masculinity and sexuality" (2000: 40).

We have seen the bias for fair-skinned girls in previous chapters that was the genesis for the production of soaps such as *Saat Phere* and *Bidaai*. Men in Indian prime time soaps, however, are not shown exploring notions of masculinity through the mechanism of (for want of a better word) foreign women. Without getting into too detailed an analysis here on this point (which is also beyond the scope of this book), suffice it to say that *Saat Phere* and *Bidaai* explore the tensions in this discourse more through the problems that dark-complexioned girls face in India, especially in the matrimonial stakes.

A third, and very crucial point of difference is that unlike Bollywood films, women are the central protagonists around whom soap stories revolve. Ekta Kapoor is on record making the important distinction that "[in films] women are taken as the sex symbols and men are the icons, the identifiable characters, the heroes. In television, [it is] exactly the opposite: women are the identifiable characters, the icons, the heroines, the so-called, and the actors. The men have to be the sex symbols!" (Ekta Kapoor, Talk Asia Interview, 2007). Others I interviewed, such as Shailja Kejriwal, Sandiip Sikcand, Rama Bijapurkar, Kamlesh Pandey, and Shobhaa De, stressed that people "fantasize about Bollywood heroines and idealize the heroes; whereas in soaps, it is just the opposite — people fantasize about the men and idealize the women, especially Parvati and Tulsi."[15]

A last word on women fantasizing about soap heroes. Sandiip Sikcand was practically prescient when he told me that "men are very important ... women fantasize about TV heroes, they want to fall in love with TV heroes. These men are good-looking and sexy, like Mr Bajaj and Karan Virani, but they also have values. They are the kind of men women want to marry. Television soaps are about women, and women aspire to be like Tulsi and Parvati; but they want a husband like Mr Bajaj."[16]

Imagine my surprise then, on reading a news item a year later, on 22 September 2008, that reported as follows: "TV tycoon Ekta Kapoor has set the criteria for her ideal life partner saying he should be good-looking, tall and handsome, in short, like Ronit Roy. Ekta spoke when she was asked whether her infamous 'K' factor would be a deciding factor in choosing her husband as well. 'If he is good-looking, tall and handsome, the "K" won't matter. He should be like Ronit — handsome,' she said" (Interview with Ekta Kapoor, 22 September 2008, www.sify.com).

Notes

1. Interview with Kamlesh Pandey (August 2007).
2. Interview with Ronit Bose Roy (August 2007).
3. Interview with Shailja Kejriwal (August 2007).
4. Interview with Sakshi Tanwar (August 2007).
5. Interview with Shailja Kejriwal (August 2007).
6. Bonnie J. Dow (2006) carries out an excellent analysis on similar issues in Hollywood films such as both productions of *Stepford Wives* (1975, dir. Bryan Forbes; and 2004, dir. Frank Oz) and *Fatal Attraction* (1987, director: Adrian Lyne).
7. Interview with Ronit Bose Roy (August 2007).
8. Interview with Ronit Bose Roy (August 2007).
9. Interview with Ronit Bose Roy (August 2007).
10. Asked about the story of the soap, Ronit Bose Roy is on record saying that "*Bandini* is the tale of a young girl who is forced into a marriage of convenience with an elderly man twice her age. It is set against a rural backdrop and it traces the journey of the young girl and her husband" (see Priyanka Pereira's interview with Ronit Bose Roy, *Indian Express*, 17 January 2009).
11. It must be noted that Rajan Shahi, producer–director of *Bidaai*, was clear in that he did not want to deal with multiple marriages in his soaps (interview with Rajan Shahi, August 2007).

12. Karan, who fought on the side of the Kauravas in the epic *Mahabharat*, has long been considered more sinned against than sinning, because he was a half brother of the Pandavas, born from Kunti's union with the Sun God. Kunti also visited Karan, her illegitimate son, on the Kurukshetra battlefield, to beg for the lives of her legitimate Pandava sons. Interestingly, Hiten Tejwani, the actor who plays Karan in *Kyunki*, is also essaying the role of Karan in Ekta Kapoor's production of the *Mahabharata*, starting with the letter "K" like all her productions, titled *Kahani Hamaray Mahabharat Ki*, aired on the newly launched 9X channel from July 2008 onwards.

13. Given Indian prime time soaps, such as the K soaps for instance, it would be difficult to portray same-sex relationships between the generations of women.

14. For a discussion on masculinity in India and in Bollywood films, see Alter (1992); and Derne (2000). For discussions of masculinity in popular culture generally, see for instance Mort (1988); Goulet (1991); Cohen and Hark (1993); Jeffords (1993); Kirkham and Thummin (1993); Tasker (1993); Coltrane and Allen (1994); Simpson (1994); Katz (1995); Leighninger (1997); Hart (2000); Scharrer (2001); Spicer (2001), Good *et al.* (2002); Hunter (2003); Smith and Wilson (2004); Elliott and Elliot (2005); and Gorman-Murray (2006).

15. Interviews with the people mentioned (2007 and 2008).

16. Interview with Sandiip Sikcand (August 2007).

7

Themes and Issues

The soap opera is a constantly evolving form that has to be developed, expanded and renewed. Shailja Kejriwal, with long experience in developing soap stories, said, "since soaps have a never-ending narrative form, it enables us as producers to respond to the development of stories and characters. They have to evolve to remain relevant and they also have to respond, in some way, to social realities of the time."[1] Indeed, as Dorothy Hobson (2003: 107) points out, "all soap operas reflect the time when they are conceived and are first produced, but their capacity to evolve is the secret of their longevity. The fictional reality which is created comes from the ideas which are incorporated into the programme when it is first transmitted, and the reality that constitutes that programme comes from that time." *Kyunki* and *Kahaani* were concept driven soaps introduced during an economically lean period at the time of the IT dot com crash. *Saat Phere* and *Bidaai* deal with the continuing obsession we have in India about a fair-skinned girl. Soaps are thus "... both a diachronic and synchronic approach to the representation of reality and fiction. The historical reality is the history of the soap opera, of the fiction, as well as of the world which is represented" (ibid.).

This chapter will explore how "soap operas explore a practical and social world and the emotional world of their characters and [how these] are handled in the dramas. The history of the genre incorporates norms, values and changing behavior which is a reflection and representation of what is happening in the world outside the soap opera — the world of 'so-called' reality, the 'real world'" (Hobson 2003: 109–10).

We have already noted that the prime time soaps in India examined in this book are produced at a particular juncture in India's economic and socio-cultural history. Prime time soaps started being aired in India at a time when India had gone beyond the (in)famous "Hindu rate of growth"[2] and begun its journey on the path of economic liberalization. Ekta Kapoor's soaps first hit prime time on Star Plus when India was in fact beginning to come to grips with the uncertainties of what happens when the economy starts colliding with the world's global economies, and the soap stories are continuing at a time when India is more surefooted on the global stage. What Jenny Sharpe observes about the film *Monsoon Wedding* (2001, dir. Mira Nair) is true for the Indian landscape of " … [destroying] any image of a nation mired in some premodern space as a traditional land with ancient customs and beliefs. Rather, it reveals a postmodern world in which cell phones and e-mail coexist with age old rituals and occupations" (2005: 59).[3] It is also a moment when visual culture sites of advertising, film and prime time soaps were contributing to consumption-based lifestyles, what Leela Fernandes (2001 and 2007) examines as a shift in the Indian national imaginary towards social mobility through consumerism.

Consumerism and Themes of "Indian-ness"

Bollywood films of the 1990s explored "a range of social issues including shifting gender roles and family conflicts … anxieties over changing lifestyles and consumption patterns, and the links and distinctions between this new middle class and its overseas connections, particularly in the United States and Britain" (Fernandes 2007: 31; see also Dwyer 2000 and Uberoi 2006). Patricia Uberoi, in her insightful analysis of Aditya Chopra's *Hum Aapke Hain Kaun* (1994, dir. Sooraj K. Barjatya), notes that the film effortlessly blended "a haute bourgeois lifestyle seamlessly with religiosity and with traditionalism in rituals … the display of affluence was accepted without guilt …" and the "film's consistent display of the fetishized symbols of middle-class consumerist desire" (2006: 149–50). The same happens in prime time soaps in India. They follow an intricate pattern that are the warp and weft of their stories, weaving together various themes and issues — they foreground discourses of consumerism in a globalizing India, while at the same time threading together discourses of a normative Hindu identity. The spectacle of lavish glamor in soaps — from sets and locations to costumes and accessories — is a source of pleasure for audiences.

Sapna Babul Ka ... Bidaai

28. *Bidaai matrimonial advertisement*

29. Sharma Family L–R: Prakash Chand Sharma,
Kaushalya Sharma, Sadhana, and Ragini

30. Rajvansh Family L—R: Ranvir, Indrajit, Vasundhara, Alekh

31. Ragini and Sadhana

32. Ranvir and Alekh

33. Ragini

34. Ranvir and Prakash Chand Sharma

35. Prakash Chand Sharma, Ragini and Sadhana
with the Taj Mahal in the background

36. Prakash Chand and Kaushalya Sharma
(*Mamaji* and *Mamiji*)

37. Ranvir and Ragini at the Taj Mahotsav

38. Rajan Shahi directing Sara Khan (Sadhana)

39. Rajan Shahi directing Alok Nath (*Mamaji*) and Sara Khan (Sadhana)

40. Rajan Shani directing Sara Khan (Sadhana) — outdoor sets

41. Outdoor sets of *Bidaai*

42. L–R: Kinshuk Mahajan (Ranvir), Parul Chauhan (Ragini), producer–director Rajan Shahi, Sara Khan (Sadhana) and Angad Hasija (Alekh) at *Bidaai* party in Mumbai, August 2008

Saat Phere ... Saloni Ka Safar

43. Saloni

44. Saloni and Nahar

45. L–R: Nahar, Saloni and Neel

46. Saloni and Neel

47. L–R: Aditi *baisa*, Saloni, Tara *bhabi* and Ishan

48. Saloni and Nahar's wedding

49. Saloni, Nahar and family

50. Poster celebrating 700 episodes of *Saat Phere*

This has two important fallouts. First, soaps, as experienced in prime time programming, have become objects of consumption and pleasure; and second, the expensive sets and décor, where festivals and other celebrations regularly take place, contribute to a sense of "Indian-ness."

An important point needs to be made at this juncture. Unlike advertising and Bollywood films, it is *not* the women or their bodies that are commodified and fetishized in soaps, but much more the sets and other accoutrements themselves, such as the fashion and jewelry, richly and lavishly presented, that serve as objects of visual consumption. It is also the lavish lifestyles of the wealthy soap families that serve as objects of consumption. Smriti Z. Irani herself, who plays the role of the iconic *bahu* Tulsi in *Kyunki*, makes the important point that "[she is] not sultry [and has] to make do with housewife type of roles. Unfortunately, I am not a Bipasha Basu or a Katrina Kaif. I am comfortable wearing saris and only *bahus* get to do that" (*Indian Express*, 15 April 2008). Commoditization of TV soaps also takes place through advertisements which punctuate viewing in real time. So, the total experience is pleasurable visually and involves commoditization, but the narrative element dominates.[4]

Expensive sets and décor, where festivals and other celebrations regularly take place, are not only pleasurable to see, but also contribute to a sense of "Indian-ness." For example Karva Chauth is a festival generally celebrated in north India. It has been rendered so popular due to Hindi films and soaps that it is now celebrated in south India as well.[5] Rama Bijapurkar told me that such is the popularity of Karva Chauth thanks to the K soaps that Santosh Desai, who writes a regular column in *Times of India*, told her that "Karva Chauth has become the new Valentine's Day in India."[6] Journalist Vimla Patil notes that "though Karva Chauth is essentially a North Indian festival for married women — who pray for the welfare and long life of their husbands on this day — it has become almost a 'national' festival for Indian women because of its attractive and extremely ornamental portrayal in popular films like *Hum Aapke Hain Kaun, Dilwale Dulhaniya Le Jayenge, Kabhi Khushi Kabhie Gham, Kuch Kuch Hota Hai* and *Hum Aapke Dil Mein Rehte Hain*. Ever since Bollywood films became virtual 'wedding videos,' the observance of Karva Chauth has been glamourised so much, that women of all communities and regions in India have taken a fancy to it and celebrate it in a 'filmi' manner, dressed in the typical Punjabi red and gold *chunaris* worn over bridal *ghagra–cholis* or *sarees*. In more recent times, popular TV serials like *Saas Bhi Kabhi Bahu Thi*, *Kahaani Ghar Ghar Ki* and *Kasautii Zindagi Kay* have also popularised Karva Chauth celebrations" (Patil 2004). It must be added that newer soaps such as *Saat Phere* and *Bidaai* also depict Karva Chauth in detail.

This exchange of fasts and festivities is remarkable in the soap landscape (cf. Patil 2004). If women in south India, as Bijapurkar said, observe Karva Chauth, then women from north India "have discovered *Vat Savitri* — during which women worship the banyan tree to pray for the safety and growth of their families."[7] Vimla Patil (2004) notes that "Ganpati and Gauri, earlier worshipped on a grand scale by Maharashtrians, are now worshipped all over India. Durga Puja ia no longer restricted to Bengal. Baisakhi is celebrated all over India."

Soaps, over several episodes, depict other rituals and festivals as well. Thus, we see the *garba* and *dandiya* in *Kyunki*, the celebrations of Janamashtami in all soaps. Weddings in all films are shown to include that part of the ceremony in which the bridegroom ties the black beaded necklace, the *mangalsutra*, around his bride's neck. The Maharashtrian woman's black beaded *mangalsutra* is worn by all soap women, regardless of which part of India the soap family comes from, thereby making it almost a national symbol.

When I asked Shailja Kejriwal, who was responsible for closely monitoring the K soaps, whether it was necessary to create such continuous representations of celebrating customs and rituals, her reply was that "soap representations do not segregate widows and single women and treat them like second class citizens. If anything, we use the motif of celebrations in bringing women together."[8]

Soaps are also fashion trend setters. It was noted in Chapter 3 how the saris, jewelry, *bindis* (dot on forehead) used by soap heroines have spawned small businesses of tailors and other handicraft makers to churn out copies of what women see on the screen almost on an overnight basis. L. V. Krishnan, CEO of TAM Media Research Pvt. Ltd, told me that "many small businesses of wedding planners and contractors, tailors, jewelry and costume designers have sprung up in the suburbs of Mumbai and Delhi, and also in smaller towns in India. This has a very positive fallout. Thousands of crafts people such as tailors, designers, jewelers, florists, embroiderers, caterers ... find employment."[9]

Similar to the Bollywood films of the 1990s, soaps also conflate an "Indian identity" with a Hindu identity. There is an absence of Muslims, Christians and other religious identities in their narratives as central characters. Arvind Rajagopal makes the important point that "there was no causal relation between economic reforms and *Hindutva* [Hinduness], nor any inherent shared logic. Rather, there was an opportunistic alliance between them, as aspiring middle classes and business elites and a [political] party till recently at the margins of political life sought to maximize their presence. Hindu symbolism had not been absent from public life by any means, but its presence now took on a different ... meaning, signifying a claim to rule public space and brooking no challenges to its dominion" (2001: 3). This is more or less the answer I received when I interviewed producers of soaps.[10] All of them pointed out that "there is no deliberate attempt on their part for this predominance of Hindu identities." One reason given by them is that "two of the first soaps, *Kyunki* and *Kahaani* drew on the Hindu epics of *Ramayan* and *Mahabharat*," and later soaps, even while making no explicit reference to them, continued with the depiction of Hindu characters "because it is easier to show all the festivities associated with the many festivals that Hindus celebrate." We have already seen in Chapter 4 how many festivals are depicted in soaps.

In fact, in the K soaps, almost every week, the elders in the family — Ba in *Kyunki*, Dadi and Ma-ji in *Kahaani* — say "*ghar mein puja rakhi gayi hai*" (special prayers are being held at home). Part of the explanation is that soap narratives are, by definition, continuous and endless, and many times the narrative is made to move forward through a crisis in the family. Crises are also almost endless. Thus each time a crisis occurs, God is invoked, either through the *puja* at home, or by visiting temples and asking for God's help. Innumerable episodes have characters saying *Thakurji, raksha karo; Ma Durga, raksha karo* (God, please protect us; Ma Durga, please protect us).

One has only to read about how the television serialization of the *Ramayan* and *Mahabharat* in the 1980s were received by Indian audiences to know the fervor it aroused in viewers (see, for example Mankekar 1999; Rajagopal 2001; and Kumar 2006). Arvind Rajagopal, in his interviews with viewers of the *Ramayan*, recounts how viewers, not united by any political ideology, could nonetheless identify with the images and themes in the weekly telecasts, and how this serial could "take on an entirely naturalized presence, articulating with existing concerns and familiar symbols" (2001: 146).[11] Even in 2008, after the new channel NDTV Imagine successfully launched a new serialized version of the *Ramayan*, it led to a ratings war on TV, with other channels following suit. Ekta Kapoor's *Kahaani Hamarey Mahabharat Ki* (The Story of Our Mahabharat) was launched on 9X; *Jai Shri Krishna* was launched on Colors; *Jai Maa Durga* on Star Plus; *Shri Ganesh* on Sony; and *Jai Santoshi Maa* on Zee TV.[12]

Shobha Kapoor told me that the depiction of Hindu prayers and rituals in the K soaps "has taught the younger generation about them, since they do not really know about all our festivals or the rituals associated with them." The audience response cell at Balaji bears out the truth of her observation.[13] Chapter 2 has already detailed how all production houses, especially Balaji Telefilms, express their religiosity overtly even in their office spaces. Weaving this aspect into their soap narratives does not really come as a surprise.

Elders in soaps, such as Ba in *Kyunki*, and *Dadi* and Ma-*ji* in *Kahaani*, play the role of *sutradhars* (narrators)[14] of religious stories to the younger generation in the form of oral histories. Episodes of November 2007 in *Kahaani* have Parvati doing her utmost to restore Om's memory and bring him back to the Aggarwal family fold. The soap narrative takes this opportunity to pass on the story, as oral tradition, to the younger generation. Thus the young grandchildren, Tiny and Bheem, come bounding to Ma-*ji* and Vandy *maasi* (maternal aunt) to ask them about the significance of the story of Savitri and Satyavan. The elders speak about the ideal wife, Savitri, asking for the life of her husband, Satyavan, from the god of death, Yamraj. The story is recounted in reference to Parvati's selfless love and dedication to her husband, Om, in showing how she can win over the ultimate victor, death, and bring her husband back to life. Similarly, it is believed that Parvati's dedication will surely triumph, as it does after several episodes, in helping Om regain his lost memory and return to his rightful position in the Aggarwal household. The secondary narrative in

Kahaani at the same time shows the wifely devotion and love of Gauri for her husband, Ishan, who is mentally challenged; Gauri says that if Savitri's *pati dharma* (duty to husband) can bring Satyavan back from the dead, then her pure love can also cure Ishan being mentally challenged. Similarly, episodes of October 2007 have the granddaughter Archita asking Ba in *Kyunki* about the significance of Ganesh Chaturthi and Diwali. Ba explains the significance of Ganesh being the *vighnaharta* (the god who overcomes all troubles) and how all Hindu prayers start with the invocation of Ganesh's name. In explaining the significance of Diwali, the underlying theme of the epics, reiterated in soaps — *sachhai ki jeet buraai par hamesha hoti hai* (truth always triumphs over evil) — is once again brought to the forefront.

Advertising, not to be left behind, has also joined the bandwagon. A recent television advertisement in the summer of 2008 for Tata Sky direct-to-home services shows how many channels on religion are available. The camera then shows a smiling joint family sitting together to watch religious rituals together. The idea is that a family that prays together stays together. Another television advertisement for Reliance mobile phones in India shows a young, newlywed girl who, upon reaching the holy pilgrimage site of Kedarnath, telephones her grandmother so that she can hear the Kedarnath temple's bells as they toll, and the grandmother cradles the telephone and folds her hands in prayer at the sound of the temple bells.

Strong Women and Real Issues

Soaps deal with many real issues that confront us in our daily lives. I will use this section to weave together two separate, yet deeply connected, arguments. By tackling real life issues, soaps provide a glimpse of the social history of the times. Through the handling of these issues, as represented in soaps, I will also present an argument that soap heroines are strong, positive women. This defense of them is necessary because representations of women in soaps, particularly the K soaps, have come in for sustained criticism from journalists, media watch bodies, and activist groups as being "regressive." The "*saas–bahu* sagas" have been criticized by saying that they show situations "where the protagonists' mindsets were 50 years behind the times" (interview with

Shobhaa De, indiantelevision.com, 11 February 2003). Making particular reference to the K soaps, Sujata Moorti (2007) postulates that "the mother-in-law is cast in a negative light for being too demanding, for being too faithful to the anachronistic joint family system and archaic lifestyles. Indeed, her strict adherence to 'tradition' is presented as not just alienating but as causing instability in the family." Analyzing some shows across channels in the 1990s, Divya C. McMillin states that " ... Indian television in the late 1990s perpetuates, across channels, the 1980s stereotypical images of women, images that have their roots in Vedic, colonial and nationalist literature" (2002b: 1). McMillin, however, holds out hope for "more positive television portrayals of women in the 21st century" (ibid.).

Academic focus on prime time soaps in India has so far been, at best, fleeting (see, for instance McMillin 2002b; Ahmed-Ghosh 2003; and Moorti 2007). Anxieties and concerns have been expressed largely by activists and journalists in their columns, interviews and on television talk shows. It is such concerns that I seek to address here.

The K soaps have been around much longer than *Saat Phere* and *Bidaai*. They have dealt with issues of marital rape and the strong stand taken by Parvati and Tulsi against it. In the episodes of February 2005, *Kyunki* dealt with the issue of Tulsi's son, Ansh, who, despite advice and warnings from his mother, still forced himself on his wife, Nandini. This led to an important turning point in *Kyunki*'s narrative when Tulsi shot her own son, Ansh. Tulsi took this extreme step and going immediately to the temple after the shooting, she tells the goddess that she shot Ansh not so much to punish him as to deliver him from evil. She also prayed that the goddess absolve him of his crimes and forgive him. The September 2007 episodes of *Kahaani* showed Parvati dealing with the case of marital rape of a grandson of the family, Pranay, raping his wife, Maithili. In this fight, she had her own daughter, Shruti, against her, as well as most of the Aggarwal family. Only her daughter-in-law, Gunn, was ready to fight the case as a lawyer after 18 years of not practicing law. Seeing Gunn's apprehension, Parvati puts her hand on Gunn's head and says *"sach sabse bara hota hai, hum larengey aur hum jeetengey"* (truth is always the greatest; we will fight and we will win).

Christine Geraghty, in her study of soap operas, rightly observes, "in soaps, competence in the personal sphere is valued and women are able to handle difficult situations well because of it" (1991: 47). Prime time soaps in India handle the woman's dealings in the public sphere through the settings of the programs. Soaps feature the public domain such as offices, factories and court rooms. The distinction between the private and public domains is not always clearly defined for the women protagonists since family and business relationships often fuse together. Within the family business empires as well, such as the Virani (*Kyunki*) and Aggarwal (*Kahaani*) family businesses, "working relationships are often an extension of family and friendships" (cf. Geraghty 1991: chapter 3). Instead of dismissing this as naïve and unrealistic, as is often done, prime time soaps play on the skill and capability of their audience in showing how often the public can duplicate the complexities of the wheeling and dealings in the personal sphere (cf. Brunsdon 1997; and Geraghty 1991). Indian soaps, however, have an extra dimension in their representation of the central woman character in the public domain. When, for instance Parvati brings the case of her grandson, Pranay, to court for marital rape against his wife, Maithili, through the efforts of the newspaper *Avaam Ki Awaaz* despite strong family protest (episodes of *Kahaani*, September 2007), Parvati is highlighting what probably happens in reality in many families in India where women do not come forward for fear of long drawn out court cases and social stigma. *Kahaani*, by foregrounding this issue over several episodes, plays out the complexities of familial and marital relations in the public domain, as well as social comments through a series of sketches of public reaction in India to this story carried in the print media by *Avaam Ki Awaaz*. This can probably be cited as a clear model of Benedict Anderson's view of how "print capitalism" allows "rapidly growing numbers of people to think about themselves and to relate to others ... in an 'imagined political community' of the nation" (1991: 6, 36).

Kyunki also touched upon the controversial issue of euthanasia. In episodes of December 2006, Tulsi's mother-in-law, badly hurt in a car accident and doomed to live her life as a vegetable, begs Tulsi to release her from this pain through the act of mercy killing. After many protestations, Tulsi agrees. This sets her on a direct confrontation path with the Virani family, including, even for once, the ever supportive Ba. When asked why she took up this contentious issue, Ekta Kapoor replied, "I have dealt with social issues in all my soaps. I was always interested in mercy killing; I believe in it and feel it should be legalised, subject to certain laws that make sure people don't misuse it. What I find extremely interesting is the fact that in Hindu mythology, to kill a suffering soul is to give him *moksha* (salvation), or set him free; but by other standards, mercy killing is murder. How do we understand this contradiction? I am definitely taking a clear stand on this" (interview with Ekta Kapoor, *Mid-Day*, 6 November 2005). What is important to note is that both sides of the issue were explored: the act of mercy killing on the one hand, and all the moral and legal issues involved with it through the actions of the Virani family thereafter. Decidedly controversial, Ekta Kapoor still presented the issue in *Kyunki*. The Balaji Telefilms office witnessed crowds of protestors outside their gates after the episode was aired, "protesting against Ekta's showing that mercy killing was an acceptable alternative."[15]

Kyunki, Kahaani and *Bidaai* also take up the issue of mentally challenged people within the family fold. *Kyunki* has Mayank, Damini's son, who is mentally challenged, and in his fixation for Krishnatulsi, ends up raping her to show his love for her. In face of the family's anger, Tulsi has him committed to a mental asylum. She, however, agonizes constantly at the electric shocks being given to an uncomprehending Mayank. In *Kahaani*, Parvati's own grandson, Ishan, is mentally challenged. Family members would rather have him committed, but Parvati wants to keep him at home and make him better through the love and support of the familial structure. In *Bidaai*, Sadhana is married to the mentally challenged Alekh Rajvansh, but grows to love him when she comes to realize that he has a heart of gold. While Alekh lives in fear of his authoritarian mother, he is shown as very close to his brother, Ranvir, and aunt whom he calls *Chhoti Ma* (younger mother). Both are patient and loving with him.

Other uncomfortable issues foregrounded in soaps may well reflect social realities in many families. In *Kahaani*, Shruti is caught with drugs at the airport. Her mother, Parvati, stands by her, completely sure that Shruti has been framed. Shruti, in her turn, protects her mother, Parvati, when Om dies, and older, conservative women of the neighborhood come to the Aggarwal house to cut Parvati's long hair. Shruti steps in and forbids this from happening. In episodes of *Kahaani* in 2008, the young, rebellious granddaughter, Tanu is shown insisting on a career in modeling, and then going on to do drugs and alcohol.

I agree with Rama Bijapurkar's observations when she says "these are not bizarre situations that our soaps depict. Many families have these problems now. Sure, soaps do not explicitly offer solutions to such issues; still, they foreground these uncomfortable matters that we would rather keep in the closet. India, still mostly being a single TV set household, the whole family watches these things together on TV. In so doing, at least a space for discussion is opened up."[16]

Soaps also deal with the constituency of old age romance. In the K soaps, despite having become grandparents, Mihir–Tulsi and Om–Parvati share a tender and loving relationship. A similar situation exists with Prakash Chand Sharma and Kaushalya in *Bidaai*. Soap narratives put these characters into situations where a husband–wife conversation becomes mandatory, all the while solicitous of each other's needs. Indeed, in order to show Ba dying in *Kyunki*, the episodes of the last week that the soap aired, from 3–6 November 2008, had flashbacks to Ba's marriage and happier times, her late husband beckoning her to join him and singing his favorite song "*dheere dheere aare badal, mera bulbul so raha hai, shorgul na macha*" (o clouds and rain, come gently, my nightingale is sleeping, do not be noisy and wake her; from the film *Kismet*, 1943, dir. Gyan Mukherjee). Ba tells Tulsi, "*mujhe tere Babuji ke paas jana hai, woh akele hain, mujhe bula rahe hain*" (I have to go to your Babuji, he is alone and is calling me). She then puts on an antique gramophone with this film song, sits back in her armchair, and listening to their favorite song, passes away peacefully.

We have already noted in Chapters 4 and 5 how *Saat Phere* and *Bidaai* deal with the problems that dark-skinned girls face in India. Rajan Shahi, producer and series director of *Bidaai*, conveys the important message that dark skin is of little importance faced with the greater truth of true beauty and love in simple, elegant ways threaded through the soap's narrative. Episodes of September and October 2008 showed a budding telephone romance between the dark-skinned Ragini and Ranvir Rajvansh. When Ranvir finally sees Ragini at the Taj Mahotsav (episode of

13 October 2008), he is shocked to discover that Ragini is his sister-in-law's sister, someone he had turned down earlier because she was not good looking enough. Shahi uses the figure of Ranvir's mentally challenged elder brother, Alekh, to show Ranvir how wrong he is to make such a judgment. Alekh tells Ranvir that if we depict Lord Krishna, whom we all worship and love, as dark-skinned, then what could possibly be wrong with a dark-skinned complexion? Later episodes show other family members, notably Ranvir's father, advising him that in choosing his life partner, he should pay heed to her inner beauty and strength of character and the love she will have for her husband, because that is true beauty.

Prime time soaps present narratives in which the woman is the central prop, sustaining the family through moments of crisis. Christine Geraghty, in her analysis of British soaps, observes how "this structural role of selfless support is passed on from one generation to another … indeed, the young women seem almost to be in training to pick up the mother's burdens … young girls in the programmes develop into strong women on whom, in their turn, the family relies" (1991: 79). Tulsi and Parvati entered their in-laws' households as young brides and went on to become mothers, mothers-in-law and grandmothers themselves. In the last months of *Kahaani* being on air, Parvati says that she is happy that the reins of the family have been so successfully taken over by Shruti, Gunn and Pragati in the younger generation. When Ba died on 4 November 2008, Tulsi was inconsolable. Ba, however, assured her that she (Tulsi) would now become the large tree that gives shade and protection to the Virani family that Ba earlier was. The 5 November 2008 episode of *Bidaai* has Ragini's prospective mother-in-law already extolling her virtues, saying *"jis ghar mein Ragini aayegi, wahan ke rishton ki bag dor atoot bandhan mein baandh degi"* (whichever house Ragini will come to [as a daughter-in-law], she will tie together relationships into unbreakable bonds).

What is important to note here is that the soap husbands appreciate their wives greatly. There have been many occasions when Om has told Parvati that he loves her because she is strong. In the October 2008 episodes of *Kyunki*, when Tulsi successfully resolves yet another crisis, Mihir tells her lovingly, *"Tulsi, tumne ek baar phir se sachhai ki ladai jeet li hai"* (Tulsi, you have once again successfully won the battle for truth).

It has been noted by analysts that one of the reasons for the success of prime time soaps is "the cultural message of the shows. They celebrate large joint families and traditional women propagating traditional values" (Krishna 2004). This book has tracked how, whether it is the heroines of the K soaps, Saloni in *Saat Phere*, or Sadhana and Ragini in *Bidaai*, the heroines always put the welfare of the family before their own happiness and personal desires. This, of course, is not necessarily always a bad thing. But this is only one part of it. How do soaps handle transition problems for a young *bahu* to the new family of her in-laws? The K soaps have tracked this journey for eight years as Tulsi and Parvati morphed from young daughters-in-law to mothers, then mothers-in-law themselves, and then grandmothers. Zee TV's *Saat Phere* also dealt with "the ever-prevalent subject of a new daughter in law's entry in a household that is different from the one she has been brought up in ... [an issue] we all will be able to identify with" (www.indiantelevision.com, 15 March 2007). Similarly, *Bidaai* also deals with Sadhana's entry into the Rajvansh house-hold as a new *bahu* and her negotiation of this new, un-familiar terrain; and episodes from December 2008 onwards show Ragini's impending entry into the same household as the younger daughter-in-law.

The 5 November 2008 episode of *Saas, Bahu aur Saazish* on Star News had reporters on the sets of *Kyunki* for the episode of Ba's death on 4 November 2008. The reporters interviewed Ba and Tulsi together. They were asked what important message their relationship, portrayed on screen (grandmother-in-law and granddaughter-in-law), sent out to audiences. Stressing the need to respect elders in the family, one of the main concepts on which *Kyunki* was based, Tulsi (Smriti Z. Irani) replied that "*hum ne sab jagah parivaron se kaha hai ki aap ke ghar mein agar koi bada ho, toh unhe apni sahi jagah dijiye*" (we have told families everywhere that if there is an elder person in your family, accord them their rightful place in the family). She added that "*jab Ba ko log raaste par dekhtey hain, toh unka ashirwad letey hain*" (when people see Ba on the streets, they take her blessings). Nivedita Basu, deputy creative head at Balaji Telefilms, had told me the same thing when I met her on fieldwork.

If, in the joint families of soaps, the son does not treat his wife well, who does the mother-in-law support? Who should the *parivaar* be loyal to? In the June–October 2008 episodes of *Kyunki*, all the males of the Virani family are shown allied against Ganga, including her husband, Sahil, because they believe the web of lies presented to them by Shiv Singhania. It is the women of the family who come out openly in support of Ganga. They do not believe Shiv's accusations and rely on the Ganga they have come to know and trust over the years. In the episode aired on 14 October 2008, Tulsi brings Ganga back to the family home, only to be confronted by all the men of the family. She tells the sons of the family "*Ghar ki bahu hai yeh … Jitna adhikaar tum logon ka is ghar par hai, utna hi adhikaar bahuyon ka hai*" (She is the daughter-in-law of this house. As much right as the sons have over this house, daughters-in-law have equal right). Soap heroines are treated like daughters in their in-laws' households. This point is stressed repeatedly, particularly in the K soaps. In one of the last episodes of *Kyunki*, on 4 November 2008, when Ba dies and her will is to be read out, the three daughters-in-law — Ganga, Nandini and Damini — make a pact that no matter what the will's contents reveal, their relationship will not be affected. All these are moments when soaps show how women realize that their interests are collective and one can go forward meaningfully when united.

Stooping to Conquer: Strong Women

a) Soaps as Sites of Contestation

One common overarching factor by now is crystal clear. Lead actresses in soaps — whether positive or negative — are always strong women. Heroines of soap operas in India are also almost always an embodiment of *Shakti* (power/strength).[17] *Shakti*, as defined by Heinrich Zimmer, is "power, ability, capacity, faculty, energy, strength, prowess; regal power; the power of composition, poetic power, genius; the power or signification of a word or term; the power inherent in cause to produce its necessary effect; an iron spear, lance, pike, dart; a sword." He also adds that "Shakti is the female organ; shakti is the active power of a deity and is regarded mythologically, as his goddess-consort and queen" (1946: 25). The feminine aspect of divinity, in Hinduism, *shakti* is the dynamic, energizing aspect. The promos for *Kyunki* and *Kahaani* in the autumnal festival period of Durga Puja, Dussehra and Diwali, in September and October 2007, showed Parvati and Tulsi together, bedecked in all their finery, *puja thalis* in hand, with flowers and lit lamps on the *thalis*, tying the scared red thread around a peepul tree, while the voiceover proclaimed them to be "*nari shakti ke do roop*" (two faces of womanly strength/power). They are, without exception, strong women.[18]

There are good reasons why prime time programming characterizes soap heroines as dominant, strong women. Creative heads and writers recognize that the stories are directed primarily towards women, but *not just* towards them. Slotted for prime time viewing, families are the target since most households in India are still single television set households. A study carried out by TAM (Television Audience Measurement) for ESOMAR (World Association of Opinion and Marketing Research Professionals, formerly European Society for Opinion and Marketing Research) notes that even in urban India, 97 per cent of TV owning households have only one TV set. Hence, "the common image that pops up ... is that of several individuals in the household huddled around a TV set, especially given the fact that about 40% households have a family size of five or more members" (Krishnan *et al.* n.d.: 14). The study further notes that "the most watched programming genre during prime time is that of soaps. Most of the soaps during this time-band have been running since many years ... " (ibid.: 8), and that "the housewife controls the remote during prime time ... " (ibid.: 21).

Rama Bijapurkar argues that "our lives in India are soap operas, we do soap opera living ... your own stories, your mother's stories, your maid's stories ... everyone knows everyone, we live cheek by jowl. Families, particularly the women, watching together find reflections of their own life problems in the soaps."[19] Shailja Kejriwal was clear that in soaps, "we are following women's stories. We could have got into the heads of men, but the social structure is such that what happens to women is far more interesting. A lot of the times, she is not earning, she has to take into account in-laws, kids, and husband. The woman has many more [narrative] tracks to contend with; therefore she is a much 'richer' person for soap stories to go with."[20] She also had an answer for the success of soaps like *Saat Phere* and *Bidaai*. According to her, the problems dark-skinned girls face is "a winning idea" for soaps because "not only is this a real problem in India; it is a woman's story, and also the story of the underdog. Once you have got people rooting for the underdog, then you're on your way ...."[21]

Sandiip Sikcand was clear that soap stories "put the central protagonist in a problem, and then go on to show nothing will break her. We glorify her as a strong persona." He also stressed that "India has an aspirational middle class now, the same holds true for smaller towns. A recent thing going on in *Kahaani* is the talk about 500 crore (episodes of summer 2007); look at the sums we talk about so easily now. To protect the family and its fortunes, Parvati even marries Suyash Mehra when Om is (presumed to be) dead. Tulsi and Parvati don't really exist, but *everyone aspires to have a Tulsi and Parvati in their house.*"[22]

Sikcand put it pithily when he said that "television is a central part of all our lives. In films, you go to see something different. So while films are like *bahaar ka khana* (outside food), TV is like *ghar ka khana* (home cooked food). TV is in your home, so you want to keep soap stories close to the house because *it is the woman who holds the house together.*"[23] Such observations bear out Christine Geraghty's analysis of representation of women in soap operas, where she argues that the "dominant role" that women play in soaps "needs to be studied more broadly in terms of the thematic preoccupations of the programmes and the formal conventions which structure them ... the *powerful representation of women in soaps* comes from the contradictory demands made of them by ... their role as the moral centre of the family ... [and] the way in which narrative action [demands] spectacle and glamour" (1991: 6, emphasis mine).

Rama Bijapurkar notes that "behind the different interpretations of the Indian woman, Parvati and Tulsi are very strong women. They don't take any nonsense from anybody."[24] A writer of soaps herself, Shobhaa De's earlier criticism of the K soaps had turned around by 2008 when I met her. When asked about this change of heart, De told me that she "began wondering about the appeal of the K soaps and why audiences lapped them up." She said that in the course of her travels to Pakistan, "women in Lahore and Islamabad" told her that they had "found answers to many *saas–bahu* problems from Ekta Kapoor's soaps." This led her to wonder that "despite posturing, Ekta has made the matrix of the joint family almost desirable ... there is an almost vicarious contact with what you believe to be your culture." De made the interesting point that "Hindi films are all hero-oriented. If they were otherwise, they would flop. Conversely, all television soaps are heroine-oriented, and if they were otherwise, they would not work."[25] Shailja Kejriwal's opinion is that "women — wives, daughters-in-law, mothers-in-law — find their strength and their 'heroes' in Tulsi and Parvati, just as they found their heroes in Amitabh Bachchan's angry young man persona. Amitabh was larger than life. Tulsi and Parvati are the Amitabh Bachchans of the small screen."[26]

Obviously, everyone does not agree. We have already noted above how there is a general tendency to dismiss soaps and their heroines as portrayed regressively, with stereotypical images of submissive women. For instance *Times of India* carried a report in 2002 stating that "Indian soaps promote gender stereotypes, present an unreal picture of women and do not mirror contemporary urban society. The women mostly are confined to the kitchen, living room, dining room and bedrooms and traditionally dressed. The heroines are shown as selfless virtues, seldom seen in real life. While wives are dressed in traditional suits and saris, girlfriends are fashionably dressed, sometimes in Western clothes, and are far more defiant and carefree in their demeanour ... TV narratives [are prevented] from exploring gender issues in the modern context and ignore the impact such depictions may have on viewers with regard to the family, marriage and individual rights ... the media, especially the broadcast media, is being seen as an instrument of social change and one that is playing a determining role in influencing public attitudes and priorities in South Asian countries" (16 October 2002). This study was carried out by the non-governmental organization, Centre of Advocacy and Research in New Delhi, along with Bangladesh's Proshika and Nepal's Asmita. Together, "they studied the emerging trends in Indian television serials. At the end of their study, they compiled a report on *Regional Initiative on Women and Media*, for which their activists had watched 50 hours and 30 minutes of soap operas. *The aim of the study was to examine the representation of gender in TV fiction with the objective to influence the broadcast media towards a balanced, diverse and nonstereotypical portrayal of women*" (ibid., emphasis mine).

The problem with such analyses is two-fold: one, 50 hours of watching soaps that have been on air for four days of the week over a period of eight years does not exactly permit a representative sampling. Two, and much more importantly, the aim of the study already presupposes the results. There is little room for openness in analyzing soap representations and narratives with such a foregone conclusion.

It is much more rewarding analytically to see *soaps as sites of contestation*. Prime time soaps in India, like soaps worldwide, by their very nature with their multiple plots and endless narratives, do not allow women to be bracketed comfortably into any one slot. Further, the multiple roles women play in soap stories also embodies the many challenges they face in their daily lives.[27] This illuminates what Michel Foucault points out about how "discourse can be both an instrument and effect of power ... a point of resistance and a starting point for an opposing strategy" (1984: 101–102). Taking a Foucauldian approach, my argument locates the subject (here, the woman) not only as constituted and formed by discourse, but also one which resists (1980: 117).

Prime time soap operas also work smoothly within broadcasting imperatives which need to keep audiences watching and TRPs high. Due to their most important slot in programming, prime time soaps manage to maintain a direct relation with the domestic sphere than most other offerings on television.

A close examination makes clear how prime time soaps interact, in intricate and sophisticated ways, with the epics and traditions of Indian folk genres, particularly women's genres including gossip and women's oral culture (see, for instance Kishwar and Vanita 1984; Appadurai *et al.* 1991; Raheja and Gold 1994; Blackburn 1996 and 2008; Thorner and Krishnaraj 2000; Hansen 2000; Claus *et al.* 2003; Uberoi 2006; and Pauwels 2008). Thus, while undoubtedly the *Ramayan* and *Mahabharat* and other cultural traditions in India exert great influence in conveying an "ideal of womanhood,"[28] we would do well to bear in mind Madhu Kishwar's persuasive stance when she acknowledges the hold that such representations have on our psyche, but cautions that "our [Indian] cultural traditions have tremendous potential within them to combat reactionary and anti-women ideas, if we can identify their points of strength and use them creatively" (Kishwar and Vanita 1984: 46).

One way of undertaking such an endeavor is through the working of alternate models. Kathryn Hansen makes such an examination in her article on brave, heroic warrior women, the *"virangana."* Hansen's argument draws on examples of the *virangana* from historical records such as Razia Sultana, Lakshmibai, Rani of Jhansi; from "local legends, folk theatre and popular song" (2000: 28); as well as Hindi cinema. She argues that just as the "warrior queens fought for their homeland; folk heroines defend family honour and sexual purity of women" (Krishnaraj 2000: 28). She comprehensively details how "between the polarities of self-effacing wife and all-powerful mother likes an overlooked and yet important alternative powerful paradigm of Indian womanhood: the *virangana*, the woman who manifests the qualities of *virya* or heroism" (ibid.: 260).

What is important for analysis in the kinds of roles that soap heroines like Parvati, Tulsi, Prerna, Saloni, Sadhana, and Ragini essay on screen is how, like the *virangana*, they also are "dedicated to virtue, wisdom and the defence of her people (in soap stories, the family). Above all, she is a fighter in the struggle with the forces of evil" (Hansen 2000: 261). As we have seen throughout, soap heroines always fight for *sachhai ki jeet buraai par* (the victory of truth over evil). It can be argued that the televisual *virangana*, as exemplified by soap heroines, is a measure of how this paradigm has been successfully incorporated into one genre of popular culture in India — that of prime time soap operas at the beginning of the twenty-first century. My analysis in this book details how Sadhana and Ragini; Prerna; Saloni; but most of all, Parvati and Tulsi, like their sister *virangana*s of yore, define strong women on screen — they are "virtuous *and* strong, powerful and prudent ... and [move] beyond the roles for women prescribed by patriarchal society. [They] transcend and subvert categories which ordinarily divorce power, strength, and independence in women from goodness, charity, and nurturance of others ... *and assert the female potential for power as well as virtue"* (ibid.: 283, emphasis mine).

Regarding the oral culture of women, soap operas in particular " ... deal with subjects that have been of particular concern to women under patriarchy, i.e., domestic matters, kinship and sexuality, but they also do it in a way that does 'minister questions' and acknowledges the contradictions in women's lives. The function of talk in soap opera plots reflects the basis of orality that persists in TV in general, but also embodies an ethos that is characteristic of oppressed groups … soap opera, like women's talk or gossip and women's ballads, are part of a women's culture that exists alongside dominant culture, and that insofar as these women's cultural forms are conscious of their otherness, they are a form of feminine discourse that engenders power for women" (Brown and Barwick 1987; see also Atwood 1971).

In the context of India, academic analyses show how the oral tradition of women's talk and speech genres transcends cultural authority and becomes a medium of resistance (see, for instance Appadurai *et al.* 1991; Raheja and Gold 1994; and Pauwels 2008). Such discussions also provide a crucial link in examining the roles of soap opera heroines. Folk songs and women's other performative discourses in India depict how women speak in multiple voices — sometimes as a wife, sometimes as a mother, sometimes as a sister, and how these highlight the contradictions and ambiguities apparent within a patrilineal kinship system (see also Uberoi 2006, especially chapters 1 and 5).

To illustrate in a parallel fashion, comparisons can be drawn with prime time soaps. Plots and storylines in oral and folklore genres situate the family and relationships within the family as a primary locus of concern, wherein women and women's issues are central. This is similar to the features that that define the genre of Indian prime time soaps as well. In terms of production processes, both are repeated regularly and experienced in real time. There is a pleasure in the recognition of familiar plots, subplots and characters, involving what the viewer already knows and enjoys guessing at. Above all, both genres are heavily dependent on dialog.

In Chapter 4, I have detailed how viewers of soaps find both engagement and distance from soap narratives and characters. Thus, often in soaps, the audience is already privy to what a character in the soap might be unaware of. Two things happen here: different characters in soaps have different bits of knowledge about other characters; and the form of the genre, with its lack of narrative closure, leaves the storyline open to development. This provides a space in which audiences of soaps gossip about how episodes will unfold and about their favorite characters on the show. The everyday characters that we live with in soaps parallel "women's conversations which often juxtapose[s] the day-to-day with an intense interest in other people and relationships; hence gossip about soaps meshes with women's gossip in general" (Brown and Barwick 1987).

Gossip, as a form of conjecture and guesswork, often has "to do with the rules of social behavior for women, can be classified as a type of feminine discourse" (Brown and Barwick 1987). The term "feminine discourse," as being discussed here, reflects how reality is constructed for women in terms of a social order where she is subordinate (cf. Brown 1987), and how "women enjoy gossip in part because talk as opposed to silence is an empowering activity" (Brown and Barwick 1987). Also, gossip helps women to position themselves in relation to other women. In this context, Nancy Chodorow, in a much cited article, has eloquently shown how feminine and masculine identities are constructed differently: " ... in any given society, feminine personality comes to define itself in relation and connection to other people more than masculine personality does. (In psychoanalytic terms, women are less individuated than men; they have more flexible ego boundaries). Moreover, issues of dependency are handled and experienced differently by men and women. For boys and men, both individuation and dependency issues become tied up with the sense of masculinity, or masculine identity. For girls and women, by contrast, issues of femininity or feminine identity are not problematic in the same way. The structural situation of child rearing, reinforced by female and male role training, produces those differences, which are replicated and reproduced in the sexual sociology of adult life" (2001: 81).

Soap heroines, like real life women, care about family, familial and other relationships; and as we have seen, soaps are also dependent on gossip structures, both in their production processes of narrative form, as well as in the consumption processes of gossip amongst their viewers. Gossip lends itself to the creation of verbal and non-verbal codes that women share with each other (cf. Kothari 2005: 300). Furthermore, often times, gossip amongst women is a matter of the private and personal domain, and carried out within environments generally associated with women, such as the hairdressing salon, supermarket, and within houses (Jones 1980; and Johnson and Aries 1983). Similarly, soap opera settings largely make use of the enclosed environment of the family home in which all the action takes place.

Very importantly as well, the "dailiness" of soaps and the pleasures involved in their regularity form part of what Charlotte
Brunsdon (1984) has famously termed "ritual pleasure" (see also
Geraghty 1991). Furthermore, returning to a continuing soap
story is somewhat akin to the pleasure of returning to one's
family home and reflecting upon events and occasions of the
past, a stroll down memory lane so to speak, that find association
with physical, mental and chronological space (cf. Brown and
Barwick 1987).

Analyzing audience responses to *Crossroads*, Dorothy Hobson
writes that "the message is not solely in the 'text' but can be
changed or 'worked on' by the audience as they make their
own interpretation of a programme" (1982: 26). It is extremely
important to make the addition that Mary Ellen Brown and
Linda Barwick make to Hobson's analysis in suggesting that
women, in gossiping about and discussing soaps, establish " ... a
solidarity that operates as a threat to dominant representational
systems because the knowledge of pleasure created by women
for themselves is a denial of pleasure in masculine terms around
which much dominant discourse is constructed, and gossip
and networking are a source of solidarity and group unity for
women around which a political feminine can be constructed and
further developed. Hence gossip, as well as the soaps themselves,
establishes an openness which defies boundaries defined within
patriarchal representational systems."

b) Soaps as Entertainment-Education

The growing trend of entertainment-education shows that prime
time soaps work positively towards social empowerment as
well (see, for instance Nariman 1993; Tufte 2000a, 2000b, and
n.d.; Singhal and Rogers 2002; and Singhal *et al.* 2003). This
development has its roots in the *telenovela*s of Latin America, and
the work of Jesus Martin-Barbero (1993 and 2001) and Nestor
Garcia Canclini (2001 and 2005), whose research inspired focus
on the cultural value of *telenovela*s. This has become a key element
in development communication in general in many areas of the
world, tying in with questions of human rights and cultural
citizenship.

The method of communicating the educational content in entertainment programs such as soap operas is based on the work
carried out by Miguel Sabido in the mid-1970s, who was then

Vice President for Research of the Mexican network, Televisa, and came to be popularly known as the Sabido method.[29] This method was used with regard to the *telenovela* titled *Acompáñame* (Accompany Me). Screened over a period of nine months from 1977–78, five days a week at prime time, the show focused on the issue of family harmony through the personal benefits of family planning. Such was its success that "phone calls to Mexico's national family planning office requesting family planning information increased from zero to an average of 500 a month. Many people calling mentioned that they were encouraged to do so by the television soap opera. More than 2,000 women registered as voluntary workers in the National Program of Family Planning. This was an idea suggested in the television soap opera. Contraceptive sales increased 23 percent in one year, compared to a 7 percent increase the preceding year. More than 560,000 women enrolled in family planning clinics, an increase of 33 percent" (Ryerson n.d.). Following the success of *Acompáñame*, Miguel Sabido developed four additional family entertainment education soap operas for Televisa —*Vamos Juntos* (We Go Together), *Caminemos* (Let's Walk), *Nosotros las Mujeres* (We the Women), and *Por Amor* (For Love).

Similar success stories occurred in Kenya and Tanzania. David Poindexter, then with the Population Institute, helped in the development of two programs, a television series, *Tushauriane* (Let's Talk About It) and a radio series, *Ushikwapo Shikamana* (If Assisted, Assist Yourself), both aired in 1987. The programs were aimed at opening the minds of men to allowing their wives to seek family planning, and effectively linked family size with land inheritance and the resulting ability or inability of children to support their parents in their old age. By the time both series concluded, "contraceptive use in Kenya had increased 58 percent and desired family size had fallen from 6.3 to 4.8 children per woman" (Ryerson n. d.). In Dodoma, Tanzania, Radio Tanzania broadcast a serial melodrama that attracted 55 per cent of the population between the ages of 15–45 in areas of the broadcast. In regions where the show was broadcast, "the percentage of married women who were currently using a family planning method increased by more than one-third, from 26 percent to 33 percent in the first two years of the program, while that percentage stayed flat in the Dodoma area where the program was not broadcast" (ibid.).

Moving over to India, *Hum Log* (We People), which started being telecast in 1984, was India's first social content soap opera (see, for instance Das 1995: 169–89; and Mankekar 1999). Over 17 months of broadcast, the programs achieved ratings of 60–90 per cent of the viewing audience. Research conducted by Arvind Singhal and Everett Rogers (1989a and 1989b) and Arvind Singhal *et al.* (1992) found, through a sample survey, that 70 per cent of the viewers indicated they had learnt, from *Hum Log*, that women should have equal opportunities; 68 per cent had learnt that women should have the freedom to make their personal decisions in life; and 71 per cent had learnt that family size should be limited. Among other things, the program stimulated over 400,000 people to write letters to Doordarshan, the state-run channel, stating their views on the issues being dealt with or asking for help and advice.

A second Indian soap opera, *Humraahi*,[30] went on air on Doordarshan in January 1992, airing at 9 pm on Tuesdays. The focus of the first 52 episodes was on the status of women, with particular attention to age of marriage, age of first pregnancy, gender bias in childbearing and child-rearing, equal educational opportunities, and the right of women to choose their husbands. By May 1992, *Humraahi* was the top rated program on Indian television. A conservative estimate is that it was watched by over 100 million people every week. A study of over 3,000 people in the Hindi-speaking region of India identified numerous significant shifts in attitudes while *Humraahi* was on air, particularly with reference to the ideal age of marriage for women. The shifts in pro-social directions were dramatically greater for viewers than non-viewers (Ryerson n.d.).

c) Prime Time Soap Operas as Persuaders in Empowering Women

Hum Log and *Humraahi* fall much more explicitly in the domain of entertainment-education and social development-oriented programming.

What is exciting and heartening is to see how, despite the criticisms leveled against them, prime time Hindi soap operas, telecast from the year 2000 onwards, particularly the K soaps, play a central role in empowering women. Throughout the book, I have tried to show how prime time soap narratives are so structured as to carry out this role; and how their heroines are represented as strong women, who, when faced with moral dilemmas, or in tackling other problems, deal with them in ways that must undoubtedly resonate with many women who feel that these soaps change the way they see and interact with their world. Recent academic scholarship (Johnson 2001; Scrase 2002; and Jensen and Oster 2007) substantiates my point that television soaps can have the most unexpected effects on the status of women, even in rural India — for the better! I will outline this research, particularly the most recent Jensen–Oster study, in some detail.[31]

The most important point to note about the Jensen–Oster study is that, unlike the soaps of earlier times on Doordarshan which employed social messages directed at audiences, the positive effects they found in their detailed research come from prime time soaps on satellite television. These are different genres of programming.[32]

Robert Jensen and Emily Oster carried out three years, from 2001–2003, empirical research focusing on the "effect of the introduction of cable television in rural areas of India on a particular set of values and behaviors, namely attitudes towards and discrimination against women" (Jensen and Oster 2007: 2). They surveyed "2700 households, each containing a person aged 50 or older," and focused on the four states of "Bihar, Goa, Haryana and Tamil Nadu, and the capital, Delhi" (ibid.: 7). This research notes that "most popular satellite television shows in India portray life in urban settings; further, a wide range of international programs are now available" (ibid.: 2), and that *"the most popular shows tend to be game shows and soap operas. As an example, among the most popular shows in both 2000 and 2007 (based on Indian Nielsen ratings) is Kyunki Saas Bhi Kabhi Bahu Thi ... a show based around the life of a wealthy industrial family* in the large city of Mumbai. As can be seen from the title, the main themes and plots of the show often revolve around issues of family and gender. Among satellite channels, Star TV and Zee TV tend to dominate, although Sony, Star Plus and Sun TV are also represented among the top 20 shows. Viewership of the government channel, although relatively high among those who do not have cable, is extremely low among those who do (and limited largely to sporting events)" (ibid.: 5, emphasis mine).

The authors go on to note that "on issues of gender specifically, television seems to have had a significant impact, since this is an area where the lives of the rural viewers differ greatly from those depicted on most popular shows. By virtue of the fact that the most popular Indian serials take place in urban settings, women depicted on these shows are typically much more emancipated than rural women" (Jensen and Oster 2007: 6).

That increase in exposure to television in general, and its effects on the rural population of India, has been documented. Kirk Johnson's ethnographic fieldwork (2001) in two remote villages in the mountains of western Maharashtra, Danawli and Raj Puri, quotes respondents in his study saying that since television had come to their village, they were having to help their wives with the household chores. Similarly, Timothy Scrase (2002) reports that several of his respondents in West Bengal thought that television might help the cause of women's advancement by making them question their social position.

Thus television, generally speaking, has had positive effects. The significance of the Jensen–Oster study lies in tracking the positive effects that cable television in particular has had.[33] A very important point that it makes is that "in terms of magnitude, the introduction of cable television dramatically decreases the differences in attitudes and behaviors between urban and rural areas — *between 45 and 70 percent of the difference disappears within two years of cable introduction in this sample*" (2007: 3, emphasis mine).

Jensen and Oster's findings show that "after cable is introduced to a village, women are less likely to report that domestic violence towards women is acceptable. They also report increased autonomy (for example, the ability to go out without permission and to participate in household decision-making). Women are less likely to report son preference (the desire to give birth to a boy rather than a girl). Turning to behaviors, we find increases in school enrollment for girls (but not for boys), and decreases in fertility (which is often linked to female autonomy)" (Jensen and Oster 2007: 3).[34]

The authors continue that "it is also *noteworthy* that the large changes observed are accomplished despite there being little or no direct targeted appeals, such as through public service announcements or explicitly socially-oriented programming (such as the 'Sabido Method' soap operas used worldwide). It may be *that cable television, with programming that features lifestyles in both urban and other countries, is an effective form of persuasion because people emulate what they perceive to be desirable behaviors and attitudes, without the need for an explicit appeal to do so"* (Jensen and Oster 2007: 27, emphasis mine).

So, *Kyunki Saas Bhi Kabhi Bahu Thi* has done women, even in rural India, a great deal of good. How did this happen? This is not a new premise. When Doordarshan was launched, one of the guiding principles behind it was that the media can be used as a tool for development. It is a simple postulate. The visual image leaves a lasting imprint in our minds. Especially for those who cannot read or write, television is an effective tool for communication. Wilbur Schramm's thesis (1964) is that the mass media can be used for explaining goals, raising aspirations, and creating a climate for national development. Schramm also indicates that development of the media encourages political democracy with its attempts to involve the public in decision-making processes. Instead of the government forcing changes in lifestyle, the population would become aware of a need that was not satisfied by their present behavior. They would then borrow, or replicate, behavior that would come closer to meeting those needs. Thus, as noted in the previous section, *Hum Log* was the first Indian soap to try out this concept, with a good measure of success (see, for instance Das 1995; and Mankekar 1999).

The Jensen–Oster study underlines what Ekta Kapoor said of the representation of women in soaps. Differentiating between Bollywood film and television soaps, she said of their audiences: "in films, women idolize the men, but on television, it is just the opposite. They fantasize about the men and idolize the women" (*Koffee With Karan*, episode of 27 May 2007, Star One). There may, of course, be other factors contributing to the changes in the lives of the women under study in the Jensen–Oster report. But one thing is certain. Soap operas have been changing the way women see their role in society and in families. It bears remembering that changing expectations is the first step to changing reality.

Writing about the Jensen–Oster study, Wharton Business School professor Joel Waldfogel (2007) noted that "the women of rural India ... should perhaps call the TV the Empowerment Box instead of the Idiot Box." Referring to the same study, columnist Niranjan Rajadhyaksha (2007) wrote that during a visit to Pakistan in 2006, he faced an "array of questions ... on the soap operas churned out by Ekta Kapoor." Further in the article, he correctly notes that "recent research by economists suggests that ... empowered women will help push economic growth to new heights" and points to the fact of television soaps acting as catalysts for change. In a personal observation, thanks to "a brother-in-law who runs a successful Marathi entertainment channel," Rajadhyaksha states that he knows first-hand that "cable television changes the way people behave. The one example is the colors and furniture used in middle-class Maharashtrian homes today. They are the rich modern colors and contemporary furniture depicted in his serials, a far cry from the dull décor of the traditional, middle-class home. Mindsets have changed." I am quoting the conclusion of Rajadhyaksha's text because it bears repeating. Rajadhyaksha admits that "like most urban men, I love to scoff at the family sagas that dominate television in the evening. A former colleague of mine used to argue that we were wrong in the assumption that these serials were regressive in their portrayal of women. She always insisted that beneath the traditionalist garb, Ekta Kapoor serials portrayed remarkably independent women. What Jensen and Oster have found in their research shows that she was right after all. Smriti Irani [Tulsi] and Sakshi Tanwar [Paravti] as drivers of long term economic growth. Now, that's a thought!"

Are heroines like Tulsi and Parvati, bedecked in designer finery with expensive saris and jewelry, changing rural India? The short answer is yes. Writing in a different context on south Indian folktales, A. K. Ramanujan defines "women's tales" as tales recounted by and focused on women. This does not, in any way, exclude men's exposure to them. Ramanujan's analysis (1991: 33–55) is about the theme of separation and suffering, in which the heroine is made a person through the recounting of her tale. He argues, "the whole tale is of her acquiring her story, making a person of her, making a silent person a speaking woman" (ibid.: 42). Such an analysis finds echoes in the episode of 29 October 2008 of *Kyunki*, in which it was said, "*aurat khamosh hai, kamzor nahin*" (women are silent, but not weak).

For the majority of the country, television is the window to the world. Recent academic research (for instance Johnson 2001; Scrase 2002; and Jensen-Oster 2007) clearly demonstrates that rural women admire the independence of strong soap heroines, especially Tulsi and Parvati. The most positive fall-outs are, to my mind, a mother welcoming a girl child because she learnt on prime time soap operas on satellite television that she too can grow up to be a strong woman; and that education is key, so she sends her daughter to school with her brothers.

Notes

1. Interview with Shailja Kejriwal (August 2007).
2. Krishna (1983) cited in Byres (1997).
3. In 2008, India's telecom regulatory authority, TRAI, said that India was all set to "become second largest mobile phone market in the world, after China. The total number of wireless customers in the country touched 250.93 million in February this year, as compared to 260.50 million subscriber base in the US and 540.50 million for China. The US is adding about 2–3 million subscribers in a month where as China is adding around 6–7 million subscribers per month. The country's monthly wireless subscriber addition is highest in the range of 8–9 million a month" ("India to become 2nd largest mobile phone market: TRAI," 24 March 2008, http://news.webindia123.com/news/Articles/India/20080324/916317.html).
4. I am grateful to Patricia Uberoi for making this point (personal communication, October 2008).
5. Rama Bijapurkar also elaborated on this point (interview, August 2008).
6. Interview with Rama Bijapurkar (August 2008).
7. Interview with Rama Bijapurkar (August 2008).
8. Interview with Shailja Kejriwal (August 2007).
9. Interview with L. V. Krishnan (August 2008).
10. Interviews with Shailja Kejriwal, Sandiip Sikcand, Kamlesh Pandey, Sunjoy Waddhwa, Rajan Shahi, and Yash Khanna (2007 and 2008).
11. See Rajagopal (2001), especially pp. 136–47, for a discussion on the popularity of the *Ramayan* serial with viewers.
12. See Kapoor (2008).
13. Interview with Shobha Kapoor and fieldwork at Balaji Telefilms' office (August 2007). It is not an exaggeration to say that I learnt many verses from the *Bhagvad Gita* by heart thanks to their repetition in the K soaps.
14. The term *sutradhar* literally translates to "one who holds the threads." Shanti Kumar writes, "in classical Sanskrit theater, the *sutradhar* is a central figure who combines various generic elements to create a coherent narrative by acting as a producer, a narrator, a director, and even a manipulator of the performance" (2005: 317).

15. Interview with Shobha Kapoor (August 2008).
16. Interview with Rama Bijapurkar (August 2008).
17. The concept of the female goddess in Hinduism as the embodiment of *Shakti* finds expression in the worship of Durga, Kali and Parvati. The relations of Shiv and other male gods with the different incarnations of feminine *Shakti* such as Parvati and Kali provide a wealth of material for ethnological and psychoanalytic analyses. That is, however, outside the scope of this book. For a discussion on these and other aspects, see Doniger O'Flaherty (1973 and 1980). See also Mitter (1995); Lagasse *et al.* (2004) states that "*Shakti*, in Hinduism, name given to the female consorts of male deities. The *Shakti* personifies the dynamic, manifesting energy that creates the universe, while the male god represents the static, unmanifest aspect of the divine reality. The concept is related to that of *prakriti* in Samkhya metaphysics (see Hindu philosophy and of *maya* in Vedanta philosophy. The idea of *Shakti* is prominent in *Tantra* where the *Kundalini* energy (see yoga) is regarded as a goddess, and the theme of male–female polarity is developed. The term *Shakti* is often used to refer to the spiritual partner or consort of a spiritual master, a relationship often without the emotional and sexual components of ordinary marriage." The notions of the mother goddess in Hinduism have often been conflated with the notion of the nation as in the motherland. Bankim Chandra Chatterji (1969) used Durga in his poem "Bande Mataram" to represent the nation and the homeland, mutually constituted, rising to defeat the imperialist British, symbolized by the king. Bipin Chandra Pal wrote, "Durga represents this perfected type of nationhood. She is the soul of National Life and Unity. With her ten hands, she joins all the ten points of the compass in her, symbolising the territorial unity of the Nation's Body" (1911: 174–75). See also Chatterji (1986, 1993, and 1997); and Jordan (1993).
18. Moving for a moment from reel life to real life, I would like to focus on one of the most bitterly fought battles of corporate India in recent years — that for the Reliance empire between Mukesh and Anil Ambani, the two sons of the late industrialist Dhirubhai Ambani. Mukesh Ambani earned his business degree from Stanford University and Anil Ambani studied business as the Wharton Business School. "The dispute drew out Kokilaben Ambani, the mother of two warring brothers, from her role as homemaker to centre stage on two separate occasions. First in 2005, after brokering peace, Kokilaben remarked 'with the blessings of Srinathji (a reference to the Hindu god Krishna), I have … amicably resolved the issues between my two sons, Mukesh and Anil,' she said in a brief statement." Even as recently as August 2008, "the Bombay High Court … suggested that the warring Ambani brothers go back to their mother Kokilaben and

have the dispute settled ... the court said that the dispute between Mukesh Ambani-led Reliance Industries Limited (RIL) and Anil Ambani-led RNRL (Reliance Natural Resources Ltd) might affect the economy. 'Why can't the two brothers go back to the mother and discuss?' asked Justice J. N. Patel" (*Indian Express*, 22 August 2008). My point is to stress the centrality of Kokilaben in the proceedings. The Indian media for weeks hailed her as "Mother India" and several TV channels carried discussions on her role in mediating a business dispute in India's biggest industrial house. Here were two brothers — trained at Stanford and Wharton — each with a host of advisors. Yet, it was finally their mother to whom they listened in settling the dispute that for weeks had being played out in the Indian media by camps from each side. Indeed, the text message doing the rounds in Delhi and Mumbai about the battle between the two Ambani brothers read, "Mukesh: *Mere paas daulat hai; paisa hai; izzat hai. Tumhare pas kya hai?* (I have wealth, money, respect. What do you have?) Anil: *Mere paas MAA hai*" (Mulayam Singh, then [in 2005] chief minister of Uttar Pradesh; Amar Singh of the Samajwadi Party and Amitabh Bachchan, film star — the troika that Anil Ambani is seen with everywhere). The MAA here, of course, has a double entendre, one, meaning mother; and two, because for anyone cognizant with Bollywood, this dialog is one of the best known ones of Hindi cinema, from the hit film *Deewar* (The Wall, 1975, dir. Yash Chopra) — this was the exact conversation between Amitabh Bachchan (elder brother, gangster) and Shashi Kapoor (younger brother, police officer trying to catch the elder brother); the long suffering Ma (mother) in question was played by Nirupa Roy.

I do not have details of people mediating business empire battles in other countries. I would, however, risk saying that it is perhaps only in India that a mother can resolve a dispute when billions of dollars are involved; and where the legal system, instead of deciding on an issue that will affect the Indian economy (see news item above), advises the sons to go back to their mother!

19. Interview with Rama Bijapurkar (August 2008).
20. Interview with Shailja Kejriwal (August 2007).
21. Interview with Shailja Kejriwal (August 2007).
22. Interview with Sandiip Sikcand (August 2007).
23. Interview with Sandiip Sikcand (August 2007).
24. Interview with Rama Bijapurkar (August 2008).
25. Interview with Shobhaa De (August 2008).
26. Interview with Shailja Kejriwal (August 2007).
27. For a further discussion on this see Munshi (2001). For a comparative examination of Urdu television drama serials in Pakistan, see a comprehensive analysis by Shuchi Kothari (2005).

28. For a fuller discussion on the influence of epics on soaps, see Chapter 1.

29. Simply put, the Sabido Method, named after Miguel Sabido who was Vice President for Research at Televisa in Mexico when he developed the process in the 1970s, is a methodology for designing and producing radio and television drama that can win over audiences while imparting messages and values. It is based on character development and plot lines that provide the audience with a range of characters that they can engage with — some good, some not so good — and follow as they evolve and change. Change is key to the Sabido method. Characters may begin the series exhibiting the antithesis of the values being taught, but through interaction with other characters, twists and turns in the plot, and sometimes even outside intervention, come to see the value of the program's underlying message. Veena Das, in her analysis of *Hum Log*, mentions in addition about the Sabido method how "the audience is not to be trusted to decipher the correct message without the aid of a celebrity who is to appear in a brief 30 to 40 second epilogue" (1995: 172). In the case of *Hum Log*, the celebrity was veteran Hindi film actor Ashok Kumar. For a discussion on the Sabido method, see Singhal *et al.* (1992).

30. "Humraahi" literally means co-traveler. In the poetic context in which the term is generally used, it refers to a partner who travels with one along the path of life.

31. As can be understood, the Jensen–Oster study came to the notice not just of academics but also of television producers. I was, in fact, very kindly sent a copy of it by Yash Khanna, Head of Corporate Communications, Star TV.

32. For a fuller discussion on this, see Chapters 1 and 5 in this book.

33. The authors document that as with any ethnographic study, they were "measuring only what is *reported*, rather than directly observing the outcomes" (2007: 19–20).

34. My own earlier work on the effects of television advertisements and beauty pageants acting as tools of empowerment for women underlines the positive effects that television plays in the lives of women (see Munshi 1998, 2001, 2004 and 2008).

8

Conclusion

This book has been written out of a long time interest in examining the pleasures and possibilities of watching prime time soap operas. As a theoretical project, it began for me when, in the years of my postdoctoral work, I started examining artifacts of the media in India such as advertising texts, Bollywood films and beauty pageants. In the intervening years, a great deal has changed. Work on popular culture in western academia has gained respectability, though it took somewhat longer for a similar trend to catch up in India (cf. Uberoi 2006: ix).

From the 1990s onwards, when economic liberalization started in India, it irrevocably changed the face of the media in India. Modernity is indeed, as Arjun Appadurai points out, "at large" (1996). But there is no one modernity, there are "multiple modernities" (Comaroff and Comaroff 1993: xi) and even "alternative modernities" (see, for instance Martin-Barbero 1988; Morley and Robins 1995; Sreberny-Mohammadi 1996; van der Veer 1998; and Munshi 1998). What anthropologists are examining everywhere is that " ... people do not just live the modern, or in the modern. They struggle with it, query it, quarrel with it, and try to get around it and sometimes even out of it" (Robinson 1999: 504). It is a time when contradictions built into the local moral worlds of family and social life in India are negotiating that process between tradition and modernity; when modernity, often times, appears to be negotiated tradition.

It is also a time in which "the goals of individual autonomy and freedom of choice and action are seen to be constrained by a social ethic that demands the deferral of individual self-gratification on behalf of the family" (Uberoi 2006: ix–x). As Patricia Uberoi further notes, the long term effects of these changes still remains to be evaluated, but it is a time wherein representations of women *and* men, as well as the "moral economy of Indian family life [is] subject to particularly intense scrutiny and challenge" (2006: x). I will return to these points in greater detail.

Prime time soaps started being aired from the year 2000 onwards and have been subject to feverish activity in the development of themes and narratives. This book has focused more on the K soaps than on others, a major reason for that being that the K soaps have been around for eight years as compared to the two others — *Saat Phere* and *Bidaai* — which have been on air just from one to three years. Like them or dislike them, there is no denying that *Kyunki* and *Kahaani* redefined prime time viewing in India and remained in the top 10 shows in the TRPs for close to eight years running. As Dipti Nagpaul D'Souza reported in *Indian Express* on 25 October 2008, "it's okay to cast a patronising glance when someone brings up the topic of the soap operas on Indian television, but if you say you don't know who Parvati and Tulsi are, you have to be lying through your teeth. Indian television changed forever when Balaji Television introduced to the audiences the ideal daughter-in-law through its twin shows: *Kahaani Ghar Ghar Kii* and *Kyunki Saas Bhi Kabhi Bahu Thi*. Mothers-in-law sang their praises for daughters-in-law who toiled hard to exceed expectations. As *Kyunki*, following in the tracks of *Kahaani*, prepares to go off air by the year-end, it takes with it the end of an era, for better or worse."[1]

Indeed, it seems like serendipity that the three K soaps dealt with in this book — *Kyunki*, *Kahaani* and *Kasautii* — all wound up by the close of 2008, though *Kyunki* left its narrative open with the question of relocating to another channel in a new avatar. This has provided an unexpected closure to an ongoing saga, perhaps the end of an era of one kind of television production and viewing. A well-timed and critical perspective on this phenomenon is provided by this research.

This book establishes the primary role of the soap opera genre within the television industry in India. Prime time soaps are the flagship programs of television channels and indeed, work as brands for the channels. I have noted how prime time programming requires certain conventions to be followed and how these have developed in the specific context of India.[2] Viewership of prime time soaps remains the highest among all kinds of television programs.

Indian soaps have their origins in a variety of sources, both from India and the West. They draw on the epics of the *Ramayan* and *Mahabharat*, as well as Indian folk genres, including women's genres and oral culture. Soaps incorporate elements of myth, melodrama and realism. They are also influenced by successful US prime time soaps and Bollywood. While impacted by a variety of sources, Indian prime time soaps defy any strict categorization and have their own unique features and specificities. I will revisit them briefly below.

Unlike the West, all content producers in India such as Balaji Telefilms, Sphere Origins and Director's Kut, are largely family-owned and operated. With great passion and commitment to work, in a burgeoning industry that is fast posing a challenge to moviegoing by keeping audiences home for four or five days a week, these companies work incredibly long hours, and sometimes work on a "cut-to-cut" situation, producing episodes for airing that very evening itself. Personally, and within their work space, production houses pay visible obeisance to deities of gods and goddesses, astrology and *vaastu*. This finds reflection in the stories our prime time soaps tell. As we have seen, prayers and celebration of (Hindu) festivals are an integral part of soap narratives.

The ideology of family and the centrality of women are visible not just in the content of all prime time soaps, but also in the production process. Being part of one *parivaar* (family) and the upholding of *parampara* (tradition) is a recurring allusion in soap narratives. One can see and hear it as well among people working in front of and behind the camera, in production houses and television channels, and also on television award shows. Another point of note is that unlike the US, where there are season breaks, our soaps are on air for four sometimes five days a week, throughout the year. In such circumstances, the entire circuit of the relationship between production content houses, television channels and audiences is configured in a much more intimate, hands-on fashion.

This has two important fallouts. Creative heads, both in production houses and in television companies, deal with each other on a daily basis, and keep track of the content that is to be delivered to the audiences, for whom prime time soaps are like the Indian staple diet of *dal–chawal* (rice and lentils). On the other hand, characters in the soaps become like family members for viewers, coming, as they do, into their homes everyday. In addition, television channels and content production houses employ large numbers of women in senior positions. Often, lead female actors command higher salaries than lead male actors. This is quite different from the general situation in Bollywood.

The book has discussed, in detail, the stylistic features of Indian prime time soaps such as the roles of the producer, writers, actors and actresses, costumes, music, etc., as well as the ubiquitous and by now well-understood reference to the term *saas–bahu* in making an allusion to a certain kind of phenomenon and manufacturing publicity. I have also detailed various techniques of representation such as the swish pan shot, thrice repeated, in different colors, at various climactic moments; the "recap–precap" procedure; and the return from the "dead"… which, in Indian soaps, includes plastic surgery to keep pace with new actors entering the show, or the same actors returning with makeovers.[3] Features such as these are distinctive of Indian prime time soaps.

I have analyzed the narrative structure of soaps in the context of their fractured, but never-ending time frames and plot outlines, and how they use formal strategies to allow for a simultaneous engagement and distance for audiences. I have also detailed how the K soaps in particular use the technique of generational "leaps" to introduce new characters and move the narrative forward. I have examined how K soaps have similarities with US soaps such as *Dynasty* and *Dallas* in telling stories of rich, industrial joint families; but how the two recent soaps *Saat Phere* and *Bidaai* deal with problems that dark-complexioned girls face in India. *Bidaai*, in fact, also deals with the reverse discrimination that the fair-skinned, beautiful Sadhana faces in her maternal home with her aunt treating her (at times) badly in order to protect her own daughter, the dark-skinned Ragini. Interestingly, it was these two soaps — *Saat Phere* and *Bidaai* — that were responsible for first dislodging the K soaps from their top positions in the TRPs.

Some reflections on the singularity of Indian prime time soap narratives need reiteration. US prime time soaps and recent Hindi blockbuster films of Aditya Chopra (Yashraj Films) and Karan Johar (Dharma Productions) are lavish in their presentation and spectacle depicting consumption-based lifestyles. Similarly, in Indian prime time soaps, glamorous, expensive lifestyles, reflective of a consumerist, middle-class India, blend seamlessly with discourses of a normative Hindu identity. Add to this an explicit emphasis on embracing so-called "traditional Indian values," *parivaar aur parampara* (family and tradition) — respecting elders, participation in all kinds of (Hindu) ceremonies and festivals, etc. This is, of course, a situation where traditional gender roles and familial relations become a space that is perceived to require protection from so-called corrupting influences of a globalizing, modern India.

A significant rupture with contemporary Bollywood films is how the family space in soaps is patently different from the space of the family in films. Prime time soaps foreground issues and problems that exist in the real world of twenty-first century India and in the lives of families, such as the problems of drugs, marital rape, euthanasia, the mentally challenged, even the very welcome constituency of old age romance. Bollywood has not led in this regard, but only followed, and that too, recently with films that tackle similar issues. In taking up such topics, prime time soaps have helped open up a space for debate and discussion, if not resolution. This is particularly important in the context of India where even now, most families are single TV set families.

Another noteworthy difference with Bollywood is in the representation of masculinity in soaps. Unlike Bollywood films, whose heroes are idolized and heroines fantasized about, exactly the reverse is true in soaps. Here, it is the women who are idealized and men who are fantasized about. I have noted earlier how all the people interviewed in the production process of soaps mentioned this critical difference. Men in soaps are represented as heading the family business empires and, on the surface, appear to be capitalist patriarchs. It is their actions that propel the narrative of soaps forward. But the form of the soap genre, with its primary setting in the family home, domesticates and tames constructions of masculinity. Soaps do not allow the domesticated man to be represented positively (Geraghty 1991: 64). Further, the soap opera's characteristic centrality of women — whether heroines or villainesses — positions women and men as probably more equal than in other forms of art or drama or in any area of real life (Lopate 1977: 50–51).

The soap opera is a theme, as we have seen, that has attracted feminist scholars worldwide because of the soap's characteristic *address* (chiefly) to women viewers, and the centrality of *female characters*. Creative heads of programming certainly recognize this. So, the woman is the central character in soap stories, yes. But she is also constructed within a (greater) joint family, thereby remaining posited within traditional structures of patriarchal hegemony. But even when women are contained within traditional frameworks, we need to remember that "feminist research has relied to a large extent on Michel Foucault's theories of modern power as opposed to sovereign power in explaining hegemonic power structures. In the Foucauldian framework ... we need to think of power as a nexus of conventions, organizations and methods that foster positions of dominance and subordination in a given domain. In the realm of femininity, in particular, we need an analysis of power "from below," as Foucault puts it: an analysis of the mechanisms not which subdue, but rather which multiply and generate our energies, and help in the construction of notions of normalcy and deviance (Foucault 1980: 94, 136 cited in Munshi 1998). In the field of the soap opera, in particular, such discussions have had many interlocutors (see, for instance Ang 1985; Brown 1987; Gledhill 1987; Seiter 1989 and 1999; Geraghty 1991; van Zoonen 1994; Mumford 1995; Brunsdon 1997; Mankekar 1999; McMillin 2002a; Hobson 2003; Abu-Lughod 2004; Spence 2005; Klein 2006; McCabe and Akass 2006; and Lotz 2006).

Discussions encompassing representations of femininity in Indian media in particular are plentiful (see, for instance Krishnan and Dighe 1990; Vasudevan 1991 and 1996; Chakravarty 1993; Zutshi 1993; Rajan 1993; Niranjana *et al.* 1993; Uberoi 1989 and 2006; Mankekar 1999; Munshi 1998, 2001, 2004, and 2008; Robinson 1999; and McMillin 2002b). All these studies focus, in one way or another, on femininity and its negotiations with issues of modernity, the community, and the nation. This is the first book to focus on prime time soap operas in India, their history, narratives, form, and genre, and representations of gender therein.

It is clear by now that *parivaar aur parampara* (family and tradition) are valorized in all prime time soap stories. Even *Saat Phere* and *Bidaai*, which deal with the problems that dark-skinned girls face in India, explicitly foreground their narratives in a joint family arena. As Shailja Kejriwal, who played a key role in conceptualizing the K soaps, puts it, "in real life India [at the turn of the century], it is the family that keeps you grounded, anchored ... safe and stable in an uncertain world. We had to reflect this in our stories."[4]

It is this stress on *parivaar aur parampara* whereby, many times, it appears that constructions of femininity in the Indian media are subsumed within a dominant patriarchal ideology. Prime time soap operas in particular have come in for sustained criticism on this score and their constructions of womanhood have often been termed "stereotyped" and "regressive." A more careful examination, however, reveals that the story is somewhat different. Prime time soap narratives and characterizations situate the central characters of the woman within traditional frameworks. But while seemingly traditional and conventional, these soaps allow for many real conflicts of a globalizing India to be depicted and debated, and also provide many moments of subversion, transgression and rupture.[5]

In the production process, therefore, "even when it appears that women are subjugated and dominated, new spaces are constantly being opened up from where women create their own terms of resistance." At times these appear so minor that they may go unnoticed. But even when tradition and social structures seem unyielding, "the slight displacement of a symbol from its conventional positioning is enough to codify completely different meanings" (Kumar 1994: 21 cited in Munshi 1998: 574). Thus, the ideological needs much closer examination as the "articulation of complex, sometimes contradictory and unevenly determining practices" so that "a theory of struggle *within the ideological* is possible" (Tharu 1989: 127, emphasis in original; see also Krishnan and Dighe 1990).

It is important to remember that these positions are *represented* and *offered* to viewers by allowing them to simultaneously engage and distance themselves from the narratives. Individual viewers may, of course, take up or reject positions offered in soaps. As Christine Geraghty notes, "soaps, perhaps more than any other fictional form available to women, stress the relationship between text and reader; their constructions are dependent on the audience to fulfil their possibilities" (1991: 198).

Women are the central characters in soaps, global or Indian. I have explored, in detail, the various representations of femininity on prime time soaps — as wives, mothers-in-law, daughters-in-law, villainesses, fair- skinned, and dark-skinned. Representations of femininity in soaps provide ruptures from earlier televisual representations (see, for instance Mankekar 1999; McMillin 2002;

and Ahmed-Ghosh 2003).[6] Briefly, unlike the representations of Indian womanhood in earlier works based on the 1990s media landscape, prime time soap stories are set in rich joint families, not middle class households; dowry, the sexuality of daughters, and exploitation of daughters-in-law are not themes in today's soaps. If anything, there is repeated stress how *bahus* (daughters-in-law) are treated like *betis* (daughters) in their in-laws' households. Also, "a woman's sexuality does not, in soap opera, result in her objectification for the male. Rather, it is ... a means of her empowerment in a patriarchal world" (Fiske 1995: 345; see also Brown 1987: 19–20). These may be some of the reasons why women's bodies are not sites of commodification and fetishization in contemporary soaps. Rather, it is the lavish spectacle of the sets, costumes and fashion trends set by the actors and overall glossy presentation that are commoditized.

Prime time soaps represent the familial space as deeply conflicted. This, as we have seen, is unlike the ideal, utopic resolutions of many Hindi films of the 1990s in particular. Part of this, of course, has to do with the necessity of keeping the (technically) never-ending narrative moving. The important point to note is that by representing the family as fraught with discord, jealousy and rivalry, soaps rupture the idealized imaginary of *parivaar aur parampara* even as they attempt to invoke it.[7]

One of the ways in which this is shown is how numerous conflicts are played out around issues of control in the family. This control, exercised largely by women, whether heroines or villainesses, is for control over a man's affections and/or over the *parivaar ki jaidaad* (family fortune). Open, public discussions about money, especially by women, are already a point of departure from Bollywood sensibilities. In our soaps, however, women have no problem with engaging in such discussions. Thus, in *Kahaani*, we have Parvati who married Suyash Mehra and later masqueraded as Janki Devi in order to regain control of the Aggarwal business empire. Mandira and Trupti (*Kyunki*) fought long and hard to gain control of the Virani family fortune. *Bidaai* has the rich Vasundhara Rajvansh making constant allusions to the Rajvansh family business empire and also taking important decisions about the business, such as dismissing her nephew, Naveen, when he cheated the company.

Villainesses in particular fracture notions of the patriarchal ideology. They turn what are often seen as feminine characteristics, often perceived as weaknesses, into a source of strength — through interaction with men in the public, professional sphere of work, and the personal sphere of liaisons with them, some times resulting in the birth of children, through whom they exercise control not just over the man, but also on the larger family. Their ultimate control, as Tania Modleski points out (1982: 97) is not so much over men but over feminine passivity.

In soap opera tradition, control for a man's affections, whether that of husband or son, are constantly played out by women. In *Kyunki*, Tulsi battles with Mandira for the affections of both Mihir, her husband, and Karan, the son, whose biological mother is Mandira, but who has been brought up by Tulsi. In *Kahaani*, Parvati battles Rishika Rai Choudhuri for her husband Om, who during that time is suffering from amnesia. Parvati also fights her sister-in-law, Pallavi, for the affections of Krishna, her nephew whom she treats as her son, as she does not want Pallavi's bad influence to impact his upbringing negatively. In *Bidaai*, Vasundhara Rajvansh does not want the dark-skinned Ragini to marry her fair and handsome son, Ranvir.

When soap stories pick up on these subplots, they play out moments of crisis in the family. As we have noted, fractured narratives and crises are essential for soap opera narratives resisting closure. But very importantly, they also work at two other levels. First, through control over the men and the family fortunes, women assert their control over the family. Second, such crises provide some of the moments when the moral and ethical superiority of soap heroines is established. Their fight is always for *parivaar ki bhalaai* (good of the family) and *sachhai ki jeet* (the triumph of truth). In presenting women characters in soaps in their domestic caring and nurturing roles, always upholding the moral order, the women serve as exemplars of bearers of tradition. They are examples to the younger generation of daughters and daughters-in-law. Rowena Robinson (1999: 503–39) refers to this as the "feminisation of tradition." Thus, Parvati is a role model for daughter Shruti, daughter-in-law Gunn, and even granddaughter Pragati. Tulsi is a role model for daughter Shobha, daughters-in-law Ganga, Damini and Nandini, and granddaughters Bhumi and Archita.

I have noted how women in soaps are also, very crucially, an embodiment of *Shakti*. Through their superhuman powers of forbearance in their ultimate goal of truth and virtue always triumphing, prime time soap operas draw on the melodramatic mode in their representations (see, for instance Brooks 1976; Ang 1985; and Gledhill 1987 and 1992). Extending Christine Gledhill's argument, Indian prime time soap operas make use of the melodramatic mode to "explore terminal conflict between polarized moral forces that run through the social fabric in personal and familiar terms in extending beyond the biological family into areas of social life" (1992: 107). Gledhill further argues that "personalization is melodrama's primary strength. The webs of economic, political and social power in which melodrama's characters get caught up are represented not as abstract forces but in terms of desires which they express con-flicting ethical and political identities and which erupt in the actions and transactions of daily lives" (ibid.: 108).

Heroines in soap operas, such as Parvati, Tulsi, and even the younger Sadhana and Ragini make the unity and harmony of their families their principal and overriding concern and go to any lengths to preserve it. Not only do these women depict unreal and *superhuman* strength in times of adversity (of which there are plenty); they are also positioned as *impossibly ideal* women. Indeed, often, as I have detailed, Parvati and Tulsi are glorified, deified and sacralized in what Patricia Uberoi terms an "elision of the sacred and the secular" (2006: 56).

Everyone I interviewed — executives in production houses, television channels, and even the actresses themselves — pointed out that such a reel life ideal woman is a real life impossibility. That said, they all also stressed that their market research has shown them that "Parvati and Tulsi are icons," much like the hugely successful angry young man persona of Amitabh Bachchan in 1970s Bollywood cinema. Real life women are not like that, but they would like to be. Interestingly, men and in-laws would like them to be perfect as well! Across India, matrimonial adver-tisements underline that the girl should be like Tulsi in *Kyunki*, or Parvati in *Kahaani* (Biswas 2008). In a globalizing India, therefore, with all the perceived, attendant threats of "westernization" and "modernization," the characterization of Tulsi and Parvati is clearly "*aspirational*."[8] Sakshi Tanwar and Smriti Z. Irani, who play the roles of Parvati and Tulsi, respectively, while adding that they are "not perfect" in their real lives, still stressed that they realize the impact their screen characters have. Mindful of their responsibility to their viewers and fans, both are careful about their comportment off screen as well.[9]

Soaps have also been attacked for being mawkishly sentimental and women's weepies. But, as Bruce F. Kawin argues, "to be fair to the picture, however, one must note that it is a *wonderful* melodrama and not at all 'mindless,' especially on its surface. Its intelligence comes not just in its critique of its own genre but also in the care and understanding with which it *realizes* the genre. And if you dismiss soap operas as mawkish entertainments whose only serious project is to sell soap to housewives, what you are probably dismissing is the audience. There is nothing inherently dumb about an infinite structure or an open-ended narrative, and there is something extremely interesting about a form that allows you to follow a set of characters from day to day." Soaps address "many of the concerns of middle class women, and sees them ... as having to make the important decisions about how families are run and how moral and societal values are to be reconciled. The 'weepie' adds to this worldview the formulaic element of the noble sacrifice. None of this is trivial" (1992: 511–12, emphasis in original).

Such a representation is a complex, multi-layered one. While this ideal woman apparently seems to fit comfortably into the mold of patriarchal discourse, a closer examination makes clear that, if anything, such representations pose a threat to such notions. Women's strength of tolerance for all kinds of troubles heaped upon them — incessantly and consecutively through episodes of weeks and months — positions them as superhuman beings. Parvati and Tulsi have, on occasion, been "punished" by their respective families. They have either been sent to jail or thrown out of the family home. Sadhana married the mentally challenged Alekh Rajvansh in order to save her uncle's (who had brought her up) home. Ragini was prepared to sacrifice her own happiness by not marrying Ranvir because their families were unhappy with the match.

On the face of it, all this appears as the soap opera's narrative capitulation to patriarchal discourses. But the unflinching, uncompromising capacity to suffer endlessly and and follow the right moral path — *sachhai ka saath dena* (always siding with the truth) even when faced with familial displeasure — permits soap heroines to assume a strong and powerful position that, in fact, questions patriarchal authority. Parvati stood alone and gave Shruti away in marriage, when normally the father, Om, should have done so, because she was convinced of the correctness of her decision. Tulsi took the extreme steps of killing her own son, Ansh, for marital rape; and agreeing to euthanasia for her mother-in-law, Savita, when nobody in the family, even the usually helpful Ba, supported her. But Tulsi was convinced she was doing the right thing.

By always giving precedence to ethics and morality in doing the right thing, such representational ideals challenge accepted wisdom about women's roles and responsibilities, particularly within the context of joint families. Their moral righteousness elevates them in their families, even with respect to male family members. Men, and even elders in the family, look to Parvati and Tulsi for advice and guidance. In addition, since the soap opera genre resists narrative closure, the villainesses scheme and fight on and on. The women therefore — both heroines and villainesses — not only *challenge* gendered roles, they also, often, *surpass* them. In addition, these women (the heroines in particular) test hegemonic discourses from within the domestic space of the family, rather than in the generally recognized masculine sphere of paid work outside domestic confines.[10]

As we can see, therefore, prime time soap operas "articulate and explore the tensions, ambiguities and dissonances embedded in the moral economy of Indian family life, linked to the challenges of nationhood, citizenship and modernity … " (Uberoi 2006: 33). It is clear that no attempt is made to change the larger social superstructure. Still, as I have detailed, such representations of femininity in prime time soaps does help change " … the individual's sense of power with respect to the world she lives in. Her *significance* is re-scaled to *epic proportions*; she wears spectacular tradition on her sleeve and forehead as she sallies forth to protect what is deemed to be hers. The content, which is what most critics focus on, is not key. It is her *expanded* sense of self that is vital. What changes is her ability to believe in her own power and change in her real life comes as a consequence" (Desai 2007, emphasis mine).[11]

The intricate and refined interaction of soaps with epics, and with traditions of Indian folk genres, particularly women's genres including gossip and oral culture, also highlight moments of feminine discourse and contestation that are powerful and pleasurable for women. These pleasures are based " ... on a validation of women's skills in the personal sphere and a reworking of those values so that they operate ... in the public sphere" (Geraghty 1991: 195; see also Brunsdon 1997).

I have also examined how prime time soaps on cable television have played a significant and persuasive role towards betterment in the lives of rural women in India. What is important to remember is that unlike soaps of the 1990s, aired on the state-run channel Doordarshan, with more targeted appeals towards improvement in social conditions, this has been accomplished by prime time soaps on private satellite channels with little, or no direct targeted appeals. Soap women struggle with the demands that their various roles place upon them within the matrix of family and personal relationships. Prime time soaps also present "a version of a universal 'female condition' which cuts across age, race and class and allows women to recognise each other across these barriers. It is this essentialism that is both a source of pleasure and problem in soaps. It allows for reassurance, support, recognition of common problems ... '' (Geraghty 1991: 196).

A close, careful examination of the cultural significance of soap stories in constructing spaces of resistance thus shows us that prime time soaps, examined as sites of contestation, need to be appreciated as areas for domination *and* resistance, affirmation *and* denial (cf. Munshi 1998; and Krishnan and Dighe 1990). A couple of observations bear repeating here. First, that "to speak in an alternative voice is already to assert an objectivity and be active in the creation of one's own world" (Kumar 1994: 19); and second, making sense of representations necessitates grounding analysis in its historical context and acknowledging the "subversions, elaborations, hybridizations, transformations, realignments or reappropriations that do take place within oppositional discourses" (Tharu 1989: 128).

Future Directions: Some Thoughts

The soap opera genre, like any other genre, is not fixed, but fluid and evolving. New features and trends are continuously emerging.

It is far too early to guess where the latest changes will lead, or which, in retrospect, will turn out to be the most important in redefining the parameters of the genre. It is also possible to be mistaken about such projections.[12] Still, it is tempting to imagine how this might play out in the future.

Scholars of soap opera in the West (Gledhill 1997; and Geraghty 2005) have posed the question whether the range of soap opera has expanded beyond being labeled simply as "women's fiction." Christine Gledhill notes the "increasing centrality of male characters and, second, the increasing intrusion into soap opera of features from male-oriented genres" (1997: 379). She buttresses her argument by stating how " ... *Dallas* incorporates elements of the western in its representation of the Southfork ranch, while both *Brookside* and *EastEnders* [draw on] elements of crime drama for stories involving male characters" (ibid.). This is one trend that has not so far occurred in prime time soaps in India. There is no similar movement towards incorporating specifically male-oriented features in Indian soap stories.

Some trends and directions that soap operas in India now seem to be taking are outlined briefly below. Prime time programming, with a bid to increase audience share to include the younger generation, are introducing a host of younger characters into their narratives. Shailja Kejriwal, Sandiip Sikcand and Yash Khanna called this "an effort to draw in India's Gen-Next."[13] The K soaps introduced young members of the family with generational "leaps"; *Bidaai* and *Saat Phere* have many young actors playing pivotal lead roles.

Another recent development in Indian soap opera storytelling seems to hint at the direction in which it may develop in the near future: the creation of crossover narratives between shows and characters that move from one soap to another. For instance characters from one show sometimes "visit" another show. The K soaps, at the time of Dussehra and Diwali celebrations, have at times shown a few episodes in which characters from *Kyunki, Kahaani* and *Kasautii* have all come together for a celebration in the Virani or Aggarwal household. *Bidaai*, in its one hour special episode on the grand festival of the Taj Mahal, the Taj Mahotsav, on 13 October 2008, had Prerna (the heroine from *Kasautii*) perform a dance number on stage, though she was referred to by her real name, Shweta Tiwari. Still, audiences first connected with her as Prerna from *Kasautii.* When Star Plus aired the last episode of *Kyunki* on 6 November 2008, the narrative took an unexpected turn when Parvati from *Kahaani* entered the frame to inform Tulsi that the Virani family had broken apart due to her intervention five years ago. The last shot was of the two iconic *bahus* of the small screen face-to-face with each other, leaving the question of *Kyunki* continuing in a new avatar on a new channel. In January 2009, Rajan Shahi's two soaps on Star Plus, *Bidaai* and *Yeh Rishta Kya Kehlata Hai* (What Is This Relationship Called) had characters from each show talking to the other. So we had Prakash Chand Sharma (*Bidaai*) inviting the Maheshwari family (*Yeh Rishta ...*) for Ragini's wedding to Ranvir. As Laura Stempel Mumford asks in this context, "if characters can travel regularly from one soap to another, expanding the idea of what constitutes a community, their movements also force us to ponder exactly what constitutes a soap opera and where its limits lie" (1995: 135). Such crossover narratives remind us of the potential power of such shifts in redefining the genre of prime time soaps in India.

A third visible trend is locating soap narratives outside the metropolis of Mumbai. The K soaps set their narratives in Mumbai, but Ekta Kapoor's new soap *Bandini* on NDTV Imagine is set in a small village in Gujarat. *Bidaai* is set in Agra (Uttar Pradesh), and Rajan Shahi's newest *Yeh Rishta Kya Kehlata Hai* is set in Udaipur (Rajasthan). After the success of *Saat Phere*, Sunjoy Waddhwa's new successful soap on Colors TV, *Balika Vadhu* (Child Bride), is set in Rajasthan. Palampur, in the state of Himachal Pradesh, is the setting for *Raja Ki Ayegi Baraat* (Raja's Marriage Procession Will Come), while *Santaan* (Child/Offspring) is set in Kanpur (Uttar Pradesh).

Star Plus' Senior Creative Director Vivek Bahl, who earlier worked on *Saat Phere* for Zee TV, "heads the team that caters to small town viewers who want reaffirmation and big city viewers with 'reverse aspirations' " (Bamzai 2008). Bahl is on record saying, "these new shows deal with more realistic characters and everyday issues," and setting them in small towns "gives a rawness to the characters and a freshness to the viewers" (ibid.). Thus, adds Bahl, "*Yeh Rishta Kya Kehlata Hai* seeks to build the concept of love within the traditional setting of an arranged marriage. It creates a quintessential contrast to the world around us where marriages are losing their sanctity and turning into relationships of convenience" (*Indian Express*, 12 January 2009).

Even Ekta Kapoor of the K soaps has incorporated new concepts into her soap narratives, *Bandini* and *Kitani Mohabbat Hai*, that started airing on prime time on NDTV Imagine from 19 January 2009. Shailja Kejriwal remarks of these, "[*Bandini*] is the story of a young girl who is forced into a marriage of convenience with an elderly man twice her age ... [it is a] volatile story of age, class and caste divide." *Kitani Mohabbat Hai* is a "frothy love story [of] two completely opposite individuals ... the backdrop and settings are distinct from each other and unique in their own right" (ibid.).

This demand for a different, new kind of content and setting is being driven by the inescapable fact of viewership increasing in the smaller towns of India. Research commissioned by Starcom Worldwide, carried out by the Hansa Research Group, shows that of cable households that grew from 41 million in 2002 to the current 68 million, the growth comes from towns with a population of less than one million (from 70–72 per cent) and more than one million (8–9 per cent). By contrast, the growth of cable households in metros has declined from 23 per cent to 19 per cent (report of Hansa Research Group, 2003, www.indiantelevision. com). Thus, "sixty per cent of the audience share for *Bidaai* comes from smaller towns of the Hindi heartland" (Bamzai 2008), and it would not be an exaggeration to say that it is perhaps the same for Colors' *Balika Vadhu*.

The difference from earlier soaps lies in the geographical space where the narrative unfolds (a move away from big cities to smaller towns); the way the narrative is developed, without, for instance generational "leaps"; and the various stylistic modes of the form. Rajan Shahi pointed out the importance of doing away with the "swish pan shot" and replacing it with the "ten second shot" where the camera remains on the actor's face.[14] Very importantly, in trying to locate the chief reason for the success of the newer soaps, Shahi and Sunjoy Waddhwa, referring to their productions *Bidaai* and *Yeh Rishta Kya Kehlata Hai*, and *Saat Phere* and *Balika Vadhu*, respectively, stressed "the simplicity and high emotional quotient of the stories." Interestingly, Shailja Kejriwal, in an interview in February 2009, echoes their view about Ekta Kapoor's new soap on NDTV Imagine, *Bandini*, saying that "the USP (unique selling point) has to be its simplicity, and the way in which the simple tale is said without being pretentious ... if you observe [*Bandini*] very carefully, you can see that Ekta has tried her best to stay away from showing unnecessary negativity through the characters. Even though the basic concept is closer to her usual style, of a girl with good values meeting a boy who is rich, she has also provided a good overlap of emotions and has tried to be different" (interview with Srividya Rajesh, 2 February 2009, www.India-Forums.com).

What remains the same with earlier soaps, however, is that the new, TRP-topping soaps like *Bidaai* and *Balika Vadhu*, and the more recent *Yeh Rishta* ... and *Bandini*, once again locate the woman within the traditional framework of joint families. It will be exciting to see how this will play out as their narratives continue to develop. Such terrain provides rich potential for research.

Trends and shifts outlined briefly above raise interesting questions about how both content producers and television channels are reacting to prevailing social concerns.[15] I have noted in detail that the K soaps were conceptualized during a time of economic hardship in India due to the IT dot com crash. India, now firmly attached to global economic swings, has been witnessing negative economic fallout since the last months of 2008. Add to that the fierce competition between production houses and channels for viewership that drives the demand for constant novelty.

As Ella Taylor correctly observes (1989: 3), "like all storytelling, television speaks to our collective worries and to our yearning to improve, redeem or repair our individual and collective lives, to complete what is incomplete ... television comments upon and orders, rather than reflects, experience, highlighting public concerns and cultural shifts." How will creative heads at both ends of the spectrum, in content production houses and television channels, conceptualize their developing soap narratives from here on?

In pondering the future of soap operas, it is instructive to remember Christine Geraghty's observation that "the body of work, which associated women and soap opera, has to be read in the context of feminist politics in which notions of, for instance, 'women's space' had particularly strategic connotations. It is not necessary to deny that soaps have been, and in certain situations still are, women's fiction, in order to *tell other stories* based on different research into soaps" (2005: 318, emphasis mine).

The story of prime time soap operas in India has only just begun. But in the few short years of its existence, it has already opened up a large space where are they are discussed and debated, critiqued and celebrated. Soap stories rebuff easy answers, require ongoing reexamination and reinterpretation, and demand constant heightened interaction from both producers and audiences. It is in these possibilities and future developments that the strength and power of soaps lies.

Notes

1. The daily newspaper *Mumbai Mirror* on 8 November 2008 carried out a small ethnographic study of three women who had never missed a single episode of *Kyunki* in its eight-year run. I reproduce here some excerpts: "Over the last eight years the success of *Kyunki* ... which spawned a whole slew of *saas–bahu* sagas changed the face of Indian television and also the way we often spell. Hundreds and thousands of families spent their evening following the never-ending travails of the Virani family. *Mumbai Mirror* located three women who had not missed a single episode of the serial and what its end means to them ... Seventy-year-old Juhu housewife Beena Lalwani has not missed a single episode of *Kyunki*... Come high or hell water, family functions or marriages, she has stayed loyal to the Viranis — the Lalwanis could take a backseat. If, by chance her family obligations got in the way she ensured that she caught up with the repeat telecast in the afternoons. 'I am addicted to the serial, I can't do without watching it,' she says ... The shock value of the serial drove her to watch the serial. 'There were so many twists and turns and I especially liked where the episode froze ...' The concept of nightlife is alien for 45-year-old Harsha Kardam-Chitalia. For the last years, her nightlife revolved around the Viranis. 'On the rare occasion I had to go out I watched the repeat run the next afternoon. I remember once I went to the US for 45 days and was so anxious about missing the serial that I made my son find a website that showed the serial 12 hours later. I then watched it on his laptop' ... No prizes for guessing which character Harsha loved most. 'Tulsi, of course,' she says. 'I liked her confidence and her readiness to make sacrifices for the family. I think every family needs at least one *bahu* like that to keep the joint family system alive. She was very close to my heart. She handled adverse conditions so well' ... Shevantibai Dattaram Maule, a maid based at Malad, is so

upset by the news of *Kyunki*... going off air that she stopped watching the serial in protest five days before it actually went off air. In eight years she had never missed an episode ... 'We changed our dinner timings to suit the serial timing I couldn't bear to see the final...[now] I will go to sleep early, though I don't know if I will be able to sleep without watching *Kyunki* ...'"

2. There are also many regional prime time soap operas, but that falls outside the purview of this book, which has focused on the GEC sector of Hindi prime time programming.

3. These features are more particular of the K soaps, and also *Saat Phere* with the "dead" Nahar (Saloni's husband) who has now (December 2008 onwards) returned as an ascetic to help Saloni's family. Rajan Shahi's *Bidaai* is the only exception.

4. Interview with Shailja Kejriwal (August 2007).

5. Scholar, filmmaker and activist Shohini Ghosh, when interviewed about the so-called *saas–bahu* soaps, said that in these soaps, "Extra-marital relationships, non-monogamy, surrogate motherhood and a variety of erotic tensions are engaged with. These transgressive ideas can be engaged with precisely because the soaps work on many registers — the most overt being the seemingly conventional" (see Raaj 2008).

6. This has been dealt with in detail in Chapter 5.

7. As mentioned earlier, I am indebted to Shohini Ghosh for making this astute observation.

8. Interviews with Shailja Kejriwal, Sandiip Sikcand, Yash Khanna, L. V. Krishnan, Kamlesh Pandey, Nivedita Basu, Sakshi Tanwar, and Smriti Z. Irani (2007 and 2008).

9. Interviews with Sakshi Tanwar and Smriti Z. Irani (2007).

10. There are exceptions, of course, when Parvati was shown as taking over the reins of the Aggarwal business empire. Prerna (*Kasautii*) has been shown as a working woman.

11. Women in prime time soaps, termed *behenji*s in a recent article, "'upholds traditional values and embodies contemporary concerns,' says Akhila Sivdas, of Center of Advocacy and Research '...she is not regressive. She is packaged in a way where she is assertive, individualistic. She confronts problems, articulates them, gangs up with other women to permit a female bonding, and this lends an appeal amongst women viewers who see some hope in a patriarchal society. The surging, in-your-face *behenji*dom is a backlash against the sanctimonious, chicken and smug mostly English-speaking middle-class of the past,' says Sivdas. Today's upwardly mobile are running to fill the vacuum left behind by the transition from feudal to modern. They may disturb the status quo but they do not build new value systems'" (Gopinath 2006). This is a change in

attitude on the part of the Center for Advocacy and Research, New Delhi. In 2002, its stance was critical of the K soaps in particular (see Chapter 7 for details). By 2007, however, its stand seems to be to take a more positive outlook on the K soap heroines in particular. Two things in addition need to be noted here: 1. The term *behenji* is a carry over from the 1970s. When used on college campuses, it could mean many things. Cruel and insensitive, it was a term used for girls who were perceived to be conservative, wore salwar kameez (a form of dress with a tunic and loose trousers) rather than trousers and T-shirts, perhaps had oil in their hair, and an accent from the hinterland. *Behenji* literally means sister (*behen*) with the suffix of *ji* (sign of respect). The other term was BTM, for *behenji*-turned-mod (mod = modern). The term *behenji* has now come to mean other things. In Indian politics, currently, the term is used to refer to Mayawati, the powerful chief minister of Uttar Pradesh. See, for example Bose (2008).

12. Laura Stempel Mumford provides a similar argument for soap operas in the West. See Mumford (1995), especially chapter 6.
13. Interviews (2007 and 2008).
14. Interview with Rajan Shahi (August 2008).
15. There are other trends as well. For instance in a first for Indian television, we have a spin-off of court TV in Star Plus' *Aap Ki Kachehri Kiran Ke Saath* (Your Court with Kiran), anchored by India's first woman police officer (now retired), Kiran Bedi. There are also more reality shows, such as *Khatron ke Khiladi* (Player with Danger) on Colors TV, anchored by Bollywood superstar Akshay Kumar. Both these shows feed off the image of the people anchoring them. Research carried out by industry watch body Assocham shows that working women in India fear for their safety. This, in turn, is the basis for Zee TV's new crime based series called *Monica Mogre Case Files*, which started airing from 10 January 2009 on weekends at 8:30 pm. (See Bamzai 2008). I cannot enter into too much detail regarding other shows on television as that would fall outside the focus of this book, i.e. that of prime time soap operas.

Appendix 1:
Tracking the Growth of Television in India

Television in India has grown in a certain economic, political and social mediascape.[1] Post-Independence, in 1947, television was supposed to be a medium of education rather than entertainment. In 1959, a pilot television center broadcast twice a week from the capital, Delhi, to rural areas. It was only by 1965 that TV had become a daily service and Doordarshan began to increase its transmission time and reach (see Deodhar 1991; Ninan 1995; Shah 1997; Gupta 1998; Melkote *et al.* 1998; Ohm 1999; Butcher 2003; and Mehta 2008).

The 1970s was a period of transition and Doordarshan's scope and audience numbers both registered an increase. India's indigenous satellite program called SITE (Satellite Instructional Television Experiment) was also launched at this time, with the chief purpose of spreading development messages on literacy, health and agricultural programs, known as *Krishi Darshan*. Sales of TV sets, as reflected by licenses issued to buyers, were, however, just 676,615 until 1977 (http://www.indiantelevision. com/indianbrodcast/history/historyoftele.htm).

There were two points in time in the 1980s that can be marked out as moments that were critical in the development of television, the first in the 1980s when color TV was introduced by Doordarshan, coinciding with the televising of the 1982 Asian Games (Asiad) which India hosted. It then proceeded to rapidly install transmitters nationwide for terrestrial broadcasting. Doordarshan branched out with three main services: the national network, Doordarshan, DD-1; the metropolitan entertainment channel, DD-2; and regional language satellite channels. Ananda Mitra observed that at this time, Doordarshan articulated television watching "as a dominant national practice" (1993: 43). During the 1980s, private enterprise was not allowed to set up TV stations or to transmit TV signals.

Real change, however, was to follow. Economic liberalization of the Indian economy in the 1990s had a tremendous impact on the media industries, particularly that of television. India went from having two state-controlled channels prior to 1991 to over 50 by 1996, over 300 by 2006, and 427 in August 2008, and counting (http://www.indiantelevision.com/indianbrodcast/history/historyoftele.htm; Mehta 2008: 59; TAM India figures August 2008). Nalin Mehta observes that "while the Indian government was forced to adapt to satellite television as an agent of global capitalism, it certainly did not give up control over television easily or voluntarily. It simply lost control ... unlike many developed economies, where capitalism brought in television and the state regulated it, in India, the state ushered in television and it is capitalism that is now pushing it, with the state staggering behind as it tries to catch up" (2008: 60).

In 1991, Hong Kong based Star TV launched its satellite broadcast in countries of Asia and the Middle East. Though India was not its main target, the network's success in India surprised even its own managers (Tucker cited in Page and Crawley 2001: 77). The year 1999 saw the emergence of Subhash Chandra's Zee TV. When 1998 ended, Zee TV was valued at hardly a quarter of a billion dollars. By the end of 1999, its valuation was a stupendous $677 billion (http://www.indiantelevision.com/news analysis/newsletter/030100/special030100.htm).

In 1999, channels continued to proliferate at an incredible rate, and new channels such as Lashkara, Gurjari, Vatsa Music, ETC, Channel Oxygen, ITV, Alpha Marathi, Alpha Bengali, Alpha Punjabi, Prabhat, Sony Max, DD Sports, DD News, Surya TV, Nickelodeon, Hallmark, Jain News, Kermit, Animal Planet, Fashion TV, MCM, as well as several others debuted on the Indian TV scene (http://www.indiantelevision.com/news#analysis/newsletter/030100/special 030100.htm).

Some important facts at the turn of the century were the introduction of regional language channels in Bengali, Marathi, Punjabi, Gujarati, etc. Many channels — the Star TV network, Discovery, Animal Planet, TV5, and FTV — went digital. Sports, news, and movie programming saw rapid development (http://www.indiantelevision.com/news#analysis/newsletter/030100/special 030100.htm).

The year 2000 saw the beginnings of successful game shows on television, the most successful of which was *Kaun Banega Crorepati* (*KBC*, Who Wants To Be a Millionaire), hosted by Bollywood superstar Amitabh Bachchan on Star Plus. It was also a year that saw successful women emerging on the television scene — both in production houses and television channels. This was the year Ekta Kapoor's *Kyunki Saas Bhi Kabhi Bahu Thi* was launched on the same day as *KBC*, and a few months later, *Kahaani Ghar Ghar Ki* was also launched. These two soaps have been the longest running on Indian prime time television. This was the year that India's first television online portal — http://www.indiantelevision.com — was launched. Regional language channels and niche channels also continued to expand (see http://www.indiantelevision.com/ye2k/y2ka.htm for details).

The following graphs track the growth of television channels and viewership for the period from the close of the previous century to the current date.

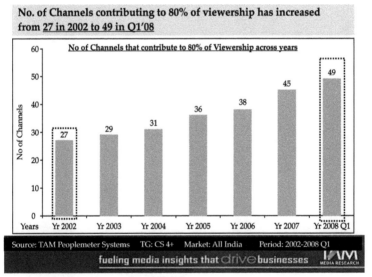

Courtesy: TAM Media Research Pvt. Ltd

Hindi and Regional Mass have been the major Genres although advent of newer Channel Genres have lead to more fragmentation

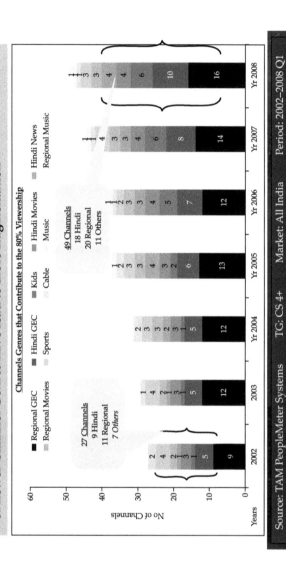

Source: TAM PeopleMeter Systems   TG: CS 4+   Market: All India   Period: 2002–2008 Q1

fueling media insights that drive businesses

Courtesy: TAM Media Research Pvt. Ltd

Finally, according to a study carried out in 2007 by Pricewater-house Coopers for the Federation of Indian Chambers of Commerce and Industry (FICCI), the Indian media and entertainment (M&E) industry is expected to grow at 18 per cent compound annual growth rate (CAGR) to reach Rs 1 trillion by 2011 from its present size of Rs 437 billion.

The report points out that growing demand coupled with technological advancements, policy initiatives taken by the Indian government to encourage the inflow of investment, and initiative by private media companies will be the key drivers for the E&M industry. The industry has been forecast to out-perform economic growth in each year till 2011. Of this, the television industry is projected to grow by 22 per cent, from Rs 191 billion to Rs 519 billion by 2011.

Key Overall findings[2]
Current size: Rs 437 billion
Projected size by 2011: Rs 1 trillion
CAGR: 18%
Growth achieved in 2006 over 2005: 20%

Television
Current size: Rs 191 billion
Projected size by 2011: Rs 519 billion
CAGR: 22%

Filmed entertainment
Current size: Rs 85 billion
Projected size by 2011: Rs 175 billion
CAGR: 16%

Print media
Current size: Rs 128 billion
Projected size by 2011: Rs 232 billion
CAGR: 13%

Radio
Current size: Rs 5 billion
Projected size by 2011: Rs 17 billion
CAGR: 28%

Music
Current size: Rs 7.2 billion
Projected size by 2011: Rs 8.7 billion
CAGR: 4%

Live entertainment
Current size: Rs 9 billion
Projected size by 2010: Rs 19 billion
CAGR: 16%

Out-of-home advertising
Current size: Rs 10 billion
Projected size by 2010: Rs 21.5 billion
CAGR: 17%

Internet advertising
Current size: Rs 1.6 billion
Projected size by 2010: Rs 9.5 billion
CAGR: 43%

Notes

1. For a theoretical discussion, see Appadurai 1990.
2. Source: http://www.indiantelevision.com/headlines/y2k7/mar/mar238.php.

Appendix 2
TAM (Television Audience Measurement) Ratings

This is a sample rating taken from two time periods in TAM measurement data since soaps started being broadcast. The date covers the time period of 2000–2008.

TAM Ratings in 2008

TAM Ratings for the Week of 12/10/2008—18/10/2008

Star Plus regains the Top position in all C&S homes					
Channel	Date	Day	Start Time	Programme	TVR
Star Plus	13-Oct-08	Mon	9:00 PM	BIDAYI	6.25
Colors	16-Oct-08	Thu	7:59 PM	BALIKA VADHU	4.69
Zee TV	13-Oct-08	Mon	9:00 PM	KASAMH SE	3.02
Colors	14-Oct-08	Tue	8:30 PM	JAI SHRI KRISHNA	2.96
Star Plus	13-Oct-08	Mon	8:31 PM	KIS DESH MEIN HAI MERAA DIL	2.83
Star Plus	14-Oct-08	Tue	7:59 PM	RAJA KI AAYEGI BAARAT	2.81
Star Plus	13-Oct-08	Mon	9:59 PM	DIWALI RISHTON KI	2.68
Star Plus	12-Oct-08	Sun	8:00 PM	AAJAA MAHI VAY-GRAND SHAADI	2.61
Sun TV	12-Oct-08	Sun	7:36 PM	TMF ANACONDAS THE HUNT FOR	2.52
Star Plus	17-Oct-08	Fri	8:00 PM	NACH BALIYE 4	2.48

Source: http://www.indiantelevision.com/tvr/indextam.php4
Accessed 25 October 2008

TAM Ratings for the Week of 15/06/2008–21/06/2008

Star Plus regains monopoly in C&S homes					
Channel	*Date*	*Day*	*Start Time*	*Programme*	*TVR*
Star Plus	19-Jun-08	Thu	9:00 PM	BIDAYI	4.04
Star Plus	17-Jun-08	Tue	9:00 PM	BIDAYI	4
Star Plus	18-Jun-08	Wed	9:00 PM	BIDAYI	3.82
Star Plus	19-Jun-08	Thu	10:31 PM	KYUNKI SAAS BHI KABHI BA	3.76
Star Plus	16-Jun-08	Mon	10:30 PM	KYUNKI SAAS BHI KABHI BA	3.75
Star Plus	16-Jun-08	Mon	8:59 PM	BIDAYI	3.67
Star Plus	19-Jun-08	Thu	8:31 PM	KIS DESH MEIN HAI MERAA DIL	3.65
Star Plus	18-Jun-08	Wed	8:30 PM	KIS DESH MEIN HAI MERAA DIL	3.54
Star Plus	18-Jun-08	Wed	10:31 PM	KYUNKI SAAS BHI KABHI BA	3.51
Star Plus	17-Jun-08	Tue	8:31 PM	KIS DESH MEIN HAI MERAA DIL	3.43
Source: http://www.indiantelevision.com/tvr/indextam php4? startperiod =15/06/2008&endperiod=21/06/2008 Accessed 25 October 2008					

TAM Ratings for the Week of 27/01/2008–02/02/2008

Zee TV's Banoo Main Teri Dulhaan on top					
Channel	*Date*	*Day*	*Start Time*	*Programme*	*TVR*
Zee TV	31-Jan-08	Thu	7:59 PM	BANOO MAIN TERI DULHAAN	4.7
Zee TV	30-Jan-08	Wed	8:00 PM	BANOO MAIN TERI DULHAAN	4.6
Star Plus	29-Jan-08	Tue	10:28 PM	KYUNKI SAAS BHI KABHI BA	4.5
Zee TV	29-Jan-08	Tue	7:59 PM	BANOO MAIN TERI DULHAAN	4.5
Star Plus	30-Jan-08	Wed	10:27 PM	KYUNKI SAAS BHI KABHI BA	4.2
Zee TV	1-Feb-08	Fri	7:58 PM	BANOO MAIN TERI DULHAAN	4.2
Star Plus	31-Jan-08	Thu	10:30 PM	KYUNKI SAAS BHI KABHI BA	4.1
Star Plus	28-Jan-08	Mon	10:30 PM	KYUNKI SAAS BHI KABHI BA	4.1
Star Plus	29-Jan-08	Tue	9:59 PM	KAHAANI GHAR GHAR KI	4.0
Star Plus	27-Jan-08	Sun	8:00 PM	14TH ANNUAL STAR SCREEN AWARD	4.0

Source: http://www.indiantelevision.com/tvr/indextamphp4?startperiod
=27/01/2008&endperiod=02/02/2008
Accessed 25 October 2008

TAM Ratings in 2007

TAM Ratings for the Week of 11/11/2007—17/11/2007

				Thanks to Cricket...DD1 occupies the Top 3 in all C&S homes	
Channel	*Date*	*Day*	*Start Time*	*Programme*	*TVR*
DD1	15-Nov-07	Thu	6:43 PM	L/T IOC CUP-07 4 ODI PAK/IND	8.3
DD1	11-Nov-07	Sun	1:12 PM	L/T IOC CUP-07 3 ODI IND/PAK	5.8
DD1	11-Nov-07	Sun	8:54 AM	L/T IOC CUP-07 3 ODI IND/PAK	5.6
Star Plus	13-Nov-07	Tue	10:31 PM	KYUNKI SAAS BHI KABHI BA	4.5
Star Plus	14-Nov-07	Wed	10:28 PM	KYUNKI SAAS BHI KABHI BA	4.3
Neo Sports	15-Nov-07	Thu	6:43 PM	L/T IOC CUP-07 4 ODI PAK/IND	4.2
DD1	15-Nov-07	Thu	2:27 PM	L/T IOC CUP-07 4 ODI PAK/IND	4.1
Star Plus	13-Nov-07	Tue	9:58 PM	KAHAANI GHAR GHAR KI	4.1
Star Plus	12-Nov-07	Mon	10:31 PM	KYUNKI SAAS BHI KABHI BA	4.0
Zee TV	12-Nov-07	Mon	8:00 PM	BANOO MAIN TERI DULHAAN	3.8

Source: http://www.indiantelevision.com/tvr/indextamphp4?startperiod =11/11/2007&endperiod=17/11/2007
Accessed 25 October 2008

TAM Ratings for the Week of 10/06/2007—16/06/2007

		Star Plus retains monopoly in C&S homes			
Channel	*Date*	*Day*	*Start Time*	*Programme*	*TVR*
Star Plus	14-Jun-07	Thu	10:00 PM	KAHAANI GHAR GHAR KI	5.3
Star Plus	12-Jun-07	Tue	10:40 PM	KYUNKI SAAS BHI KABHI BA	5.2
Star Plus	11-Jun-07	Mon	10:36 PM	KYUNKI SAAS BHI KABHI BA	4.9
Star Plus	13-Jun-07	Wed	10:39 PM	KYUNKI SAAS BHI KABHI BA	4.8
Star Plus	14-Jun-07	Thu	10:33 PM	KYUNKI SAAS BHI KABHI BA	4.7
Star Plus	13-Jun-07	Wed	10:03 PM	KAHAANI GHAR GHAR KI	4.6
Star Plus	12-Jun-07	Tue	10:08 PM	KAHAANI GHAR GHAR KI	4.6
Star Plus	11-Jun-07	Mon	10:04 PM	KAHAANI GHAR GHAR KI	4.5
Star Plus	15-Jun-07	Fri	8:59 PM	PRITHVIRAJ CHAUHAN	3.6
Zee TV	15-Jun-07	Fri	9:58 PM	SAREGAMAPA CHALLENGE 2007	3.5

Source: http://www.indiantelevision.com/tvr/indextamphp4?startperiod
=10/06/2007&endperiod=16/06/2007
Accessed 25 October 2008

TAM Ratings in 2006

On 13 September, 2006, it was reported that "the top drivers of Zee TV, *Saat Phere* (Sphere Origins) and *Kasamh Se* (Balaji Telefilms) continue to deliver good ratings for the channel as per the data. *Saat Phere* leads the 9:30 pm slot with 6.55 TVR (recorded on 1 September)" (Source:http://www.indiantelevision.com/headlines/y2k6/sep/sep116.htm – accessed on 18 November 2008).

TAM Ratings for the Week of 15/10/2006—21/10/2006

MAX gatecrashes Star Plus party					
Channel	*Date*	*Day*	*Start Time*	*Programme*	*TVR*
Star Plus	16-Oct-06	Mon	10:33 PM	KYUNKI SAAS BHI KABHI BA	7.9
Star Plus	19-Oct-06	Thu	10:30 PM	KYUNKI SAAS BHI KABHI BA	7.3
Star Plus	17-Oct-06	Tue	10:32 PM	KYUNKI SAAS BHI KABHI BA	7.3
Star Plus	18-Oct-06	Wed	10:30 PM	KYUNKI SAAS BHI KABHI BA	6.3
Star Plus	16-Oct-06	Mon	9:57 PM	KAHAANI GHAR GHAR KI	6.1
Star Plus	19-Oct-06	Thu	9:58 PM	KAHAANI GHAR GHAR KI	6.0
MAX	15-Oct-06	Sun	6:46 PM	L/T ICC CHM.TRO. ENG/IND	5.8
Star Plus	17-Oct-06	Tue	9:58 PM	KAHAANI GHAR GHAR KI	5.8
Star Plus	17-Oct-06	Tue	8:28 PM	KASAUTII ZINDAGII KAY	5.3
Star Plus	15-Oct-06	Sun	9:00 PM	PRITHVIRAJ CHAUHAN	5.2

Source: http://www.indiantelevision.com/tvr/indextamphp4?startperiod =15/10/2006&endperiod=21/10/2006
Accessed 18 November 2008

Zee TV's Soaps in December 2006 in TAM Ratings

					Zee TV'S Top 4 Keep it in the hunt	
Serial No.	*Rank*	*Date*	*Day*	*Start Time*	*Programme*	*TVR*
1	13	13/12/2006	Wed	9:29 PM	SAATH PHERE	5.4
2	22	14/12/2006	Thu	9:30 PM	SAATH PHERE	4.8
3	27	12/12/2006	Tue	9:30 PM	SAATH PHERE	4.3
4	31	14/12/2006	Thu	8:59 PM	KASAMH SE	3.9
5	33	13/12/2006	Wed	8:59 PM	KASAMH SE	3.8
6	35	14/12/2006	Thu	7:59 PM	BANOO MAIN TERI DULHAAN	3.7
7	36	12/12/2006	Tue	8:59 PM	KASAMH SE	3.6
8	38	15/12/2006	Fri	9:30 PM	SAATH PHERE	3.5
9	40	11/12/2006	Mon	9:29 PM	SAATH PHERE	

Source: http://www.indiantelevision.com/tvr/telemeter/telechanneltam.php4?ch=Zee%20TV&startperiod=10/12/2006&endperiod=16/12/2006 Accessed 18 November 2008

TAM Ratings for the Week of 15/01/2006—21/01/2006

Channel	Date	Day	Start Time	Programme	TVR
Star One regains monopoly in C&S homes					
Star Plus	18-Jan-06	Wed	10:28 PM	KYUNKI SAAS BHI KABHI BA	8.3
Star Plus	16-Jan-06	Mon	10:28 PM	KYUNKI SAAS BHI KABHI BA	8.3
Star Plus	17-Jan-06	Tue	10:28 PM	KYUNKI SAAS BHI KABHI BA	8.1
Star Plus	17-Jan-06	Tue	9:59 PM	KAHAANI GHAR GHAR KI	7.6
Star Plus	19-Jan-06	Thu	10:30 PM	KYUNKI SAAS BHI KABHI BA	7.6
Star Plus	16-Jan-06	Mon	9:59 PM	KAHAANI GHAR GHAR KI	7.5
Star Plus	19-Jan-06	Thu	10:00 PM	KAHAANI GHAR GHAR KI	7.5
Star Plus	19-Jan-06	Thu	8:30 PM	KASAUTII ZINDAGII KAY	7.4
Star Plus	20-Jan-06	Fri	8:29 PM	KASAUTII ZINDAGII KAY	7.4
Star Plus	18-Jan-06	Wed	9:59 PM	KAHAANI GHAR GHAR KI	7.4

Source: http://www.indiantelevision.com/tvr/indextam php4?startperiod
=15/01/2006&endperiod=21/01/2006
Accessed 18 November 2008

TAM Ratings in 2005

TAM Ratings for the Week of 13/11/2005–19/11/2005

Channel	Date	Day	Start Time	Programme	TVR
Star One regains monopoly in C&S homes					
Star Plus	17-Nov-05	Thu	10:30 PM	KYUNKI SAAS BHI KABHI BA	9.4
Star Plus	14-Nov-05	Mon	10:30 PM	KYUNKI SAAS BHI KABHI BA	9.2
Star Plus	15-Nov-05	Tue	10:30 PM	KYUNKI SAAS BHI KABHI BA	8.5
Star Plus	16-Nov-05	Wed	10:30 PM	KYUNKI SAAS BHI KABHI BA	8.3
Star Plus	13-Nov-05	Sun	9:00 PM	KAUN BANEGA CROREPATI 2	8.0
Star Plus	14-Nov-05	Mon	10:00 PM	KAHAANI GHAR GHAR KI	8.0
Star Plus	17-Nov-05	Thu	8:30 PM	KASAUTII ZINDAGII KAY	7.8
DD Sports	19-Nov-05	Sat	6:43 PM	L/T PEPSI CUP 2ODI SA/IN	7.8
Star Plus	15-Nov-05	Tue	10:00 PM	KAHAANI GHAR GHAR KI	7.6
Star Plus	17-Nov-05	Thu	9:59 PM	KAHAANI GHAR GHAR KI	7.5

Source: http://www.indiantelevision.com/tvr/indextamphp4?startperiod
=13/11/2005&endperiod=19/11/2005
Accessed 18 November 2008

TAM Ratings for the Week of 13/02/2005—19/02/2005

Star Plus regains monopoly in C&S homes					
Channel	*Date*	*Day*	*Start Time*	*Programme*	*TVR*
Star Plus	14-Feb-05	Mon	10:30 PM	KYUNKI SAAS BHI KABHI BA	11.3
Star Plus	16-Feb-05	Wed	10:31 PM	KYUNKI SAAS BHI KABHI BA	11.2
Star Plus	15-Feb-05	Tue	10:30 PM	KYUNKI SAAS BHI KABHI BA	10.7
Star Plus	17-Feb-05	Thu	10:29 PM	KYUNKI SAAS BHI KABHI BA	10.2
Star Plus	14-Feb-05	Mon	10:00 PM	KAHAANI GHAR GHAR KI	10.2
Star Plus	17-Feb-05	Thu	8:31 PM	KASAUTII ZINDAGII KAY	10.1
Star Plus	16-Feb-05	Wed	10:00 PM	KAHAANI GHAR GHAR KI	10.0
Star Plus	15-Feb-05	Tue	9:59 PM	KAHAANI GHAR GHAR KI	9.8
Star Plus	14-Feb-05	Mon	8:29 PM	KASAUTII ZINDAGII KAY	9.3
Star Plus	16-Feb-05	Wed	8:29 PM	KASAUTII ZINDAGII KAY	9.3

Source: http://www.indiantelevision.com/tvr/indextamphp4?startperiod =13/02/2005&endperiod=19/02/2005
Accessed 18 November 2005

TAM Ratings in 2004

TAM Ratings for the Week of 19/12/2004–25/12/2004

	Star Plus regains monopoly in C&S homes				
Channel	*Date*	*Day*	*Start Time*	*Programme*	*TVR*
Star Plus	21-Dec-04	Tue	10:30 PM	KYUNKI SAAS BHI KABHI BA	11.3
Star Plus	22-Dec-04	Wed	10:30 PM	KYUNKI SAAS BHI KABHI BA	11.3
Star Plus	23-Dec-04	Thu	10:30 PM	KYUNKI SAAS BHI KABHI BA	11.3
Star Plus	20-Dec-04	Mon	10:30 PM	KYUNKI SAAS BHI KABHI BA	10.9
Star Plus	22-Dec-04	Wed	8:30 PM	KASAUTII ZINDAGII KAY	10.5
Star Plus	23-Dec-04	Thu	8:30 PM	KASAUTII ZINDAGII KAY	10.2
Star Plus	22-Dec-04	Wed	10:00 PM	KAHAANI GHAR GHAR KI	10.2
Star Plus	21-Dec-04	Tue	10:00 PM	KAHAANI GHAR GHAR KI	9.9
Star Plus	20-Dec-04	Mon	10:00 PM	KAHAANI GHAR GHAR KI	9.7
Star Plus	20-Dec-04	Mon	8:30 PM	KASAUTII ZINDAGII KAY	9.6

Source: http://www.indiantelevision.com/tvr/indextamphp4?startperiod =19/12/2004&endperiod=25/12/2004
Accessed 18 November 2008

TAM Ratings for the Week of 18/04/2004–24/04/2004

Star Plus regains monopoly in C&S homes					
Channel	*Date*	*Day*	*Start Time*	*Programme*	*TVR*
Star Plus	20-Apr-04	Tue	11:01 PM	KYUNKI SAAS BHI KABHI BA	10.9
Star Plus	19-Apr-04	Mon	10:30 PM	KAHAANI GHAR GHAR KI	10.8
Star Plus	19-Apr-04	Mon	11:00 PM	KYUNKI SAAS BHI KABHI BA	10.7
Star Plus	21-Apr-04	Wed	11:00 PM	KYUNKI SAAS BHI KABHI BA	10.2
Star Plus	20-Apr-04	Tue	10:30 PM	KAHAANI GHAR GHAR KI	10.2
Star Plus	22-Apr-04	Thu	10:30 PM	KAHAANI GHAR GHAR KI	10.1
Star Plus	22-Apr-04	Thu	11:01 PM	KYUNKI SAAS BHI KABHI BA	9.9
Star Plus	21-Apr-04	Wed	10:30 PM	KAHAANI GHAR GHAR KI	9.9
Star Plus	19-Apr-04	Mon	9:00 PM	KASAUTII ZINDAGII KAY	9.0
Star Plus	21-Apr-04	Wed	9:00 PM	KASAUTII ZINDAGII KAY	9.0

Source: http://www.indiantelevision.com/tvr/indextamphp4?startperiod =18/04/2004&endperiod=24/04/2004
Accessed 18 November 2008

TAM Ratings in 2003

TAM Ratings for the Week of 14/12/2003–20/12/2003

Star Plus regains monopoly in C&S homes					
Channel	Date	Day	Start Time	Programme	TVR
Star Plus	17-Dec-03	Wed	8:30 PM	KASAUTII ZINDAGII KAY	10.4
Star Plus	18-Dec-03	Thu	10:31 PM	KYUNKI SAAS BHI KABHI BA	9.9
Star Plus	16-Dec-03	Tue	8:30 PM	KASAUTII ZINDAGII KAY	9.8
Star Plus	18-Dec-03	Thu	8:31 PM	KASAUTII ZINDAGII KAY	9.7
Star Plus	15-Dec-03	Mon	8:30 PM	KASAUTII ZINDAGII KAY	8.9
Star Plus	18-Dec-03	Thu	10:01 PM	KAHAANI GHAR GHAR KI	8.9
Star Plus	15-Dec-03	Mon	9:59 PM	KAHAANI GHAR GHAR KI	8.9
Star Plus	15-Dec-03	Mon	10:29 PM	KYUNKI SAAS BHI KABHI BA	8.8
Star Plus	16-Dec-03	Tue	10:30 PM	KYUNKI SAAS BHI KABHI BA	8.8
Star Plus	17-Dec-03	Wed	10:00 PM	KAHAANI GHAR GHAR KI	8.7
Source: http://www.indiantelevision.com/tvr/indextamphp4?startperiod =14/12/2003&endperiod=20/12/2003 Accessed 18 November 2008					

TAM Ratings for the Week of 18/05/2003—24/05/2003

Star Plus regains monopoly in C&S homes					
Channel	*Date*	*Day*	*Start Time*	*Programme*	*TVR*
Star Plus	21-May-03	Wed	8:31 PM	KASAUTII ZINDAGII KAY	10.5
Star Plus	19-May-03	Mon	8:29 PM	KASAUTII ZINDAGII KAY	9.8
Star Plus	22-May-03	Thu	8:31 PM	KASAUTII ZINDAGII KAY	9.6
Star Plus	19-May-03	Mon	9:00 PM	DES MEIN NIKLA HOGA CHAN	9.5
Star Plus	20-May-03	Tue	8:30 PM	KASAUTII ZINDAGII KAY	9.1
Star Plus	22-May-03	Thu	10:31 PM	KYUNKI SAAS BHI KABHI BA	8.8
Star Plus	20-May-03	Tue	10:29 PM	KYUNKI SAAS BHI KABHI BA	8.3
Star Plus	19-May-03	Mon	10:00 PM	KAHAANI GHAR GHAR KI	8.1
Star Plus	19-May-03	Mon	10:31 PM	KYUNKI SAAS BHI KABHI BA	8.0
Star Plus	20-May-03	Tue	9:00 PM	KEHTA HAI DIL	7.8

Source: http://www.indiantelevision.com/tvr indextamphp4? startperiod
=18/05/2003&endperiod=24/05/2003
Accessed 18 November 2008

TAM Ratings in 2002

TAM Ratings for the Week of 17/11/2002–23/11/2002

				Star Plus regains monopoly in C&S homes	
Channel	*Date*	*Day*	*Start Time*	*Programme*	*TVR*
Star Plus	18-Nov-02	Mon	10:01 PM	KAHAANI GHAR GHAR KI	10.56
Star Plus	21-Nov-02	Thu	10:30 PM	KYUNKI SAAS BHI KABHI BA	10.27
Star Plus	19-Nov-02	Tue	9:59 PM	KAHAANI GHAR GHAR KI	10.19
Star Plus	20-Nov-02	Wed	10:30 PM	KYUNKI SAAS BHI KABHI BA	9.79
Star Plus	19-Nov-02	Tue	10:29 PM	KYUNKI SAAS BHI KABHI BA	9.67
Star Plus	20-Nov-02	Wed	10:00 PM	KAHAANI GHAR GHAR KI	9.48
Star Plus	21-Nov-02	Thu	10:01 PM	KAHAANI GHAR GHAR KI	9.25
Star Plus	18-Nov-02	Mon	10:32 PM	KYUNKI SAAS BHI KABHI BA	9.05
Star Plus	18-Nov-02	Mon	8:31 PM	KASAUTII ZINDAGII KAY	8.79
Star Plus	20-Nov-02	Wed	8:30 PM	KASAUTII ZINDAGII KAY	8.36

Source: http://www.indiantelevision.com/tvr/indextamphp4?startperiod =17/11/2002&endperiod=23/11/2002
Accessed 18 November 2008

TAM Ratings for the Week of 27/01/2002–02/02/2002

It's a Star Show All The Way in Cable & Satellite Homes					
Channel	*Date*	*Day*	*Start Time*	*Programme*	*TVR*
Star Plus	29-Jan-02	Tue	10:01 PM	KAHAANI GHAR GHAR KI	9.92
Star Plus	29-Jan-02	Tue	10:29 PM	KYUNKI SAAS BHI KABHI BAHU THI	9.88
Star Plus	28-Jan-02	Mon	10:00 PM	KAHAANI GHAR GHAR KI	9.66
Star Plus	28-Jan-02	Mon	10:29 PM	KYUNKI SAAS BHI KABHI BAHU THI	9.53
Star Plus	30-Jan-02	Wed	10:30 PM	KYUNKI SAAS BHI KABHI BAHU THI	8.82
Star Plus	31-Jan-02	Thu	10:30 PM	KYUNKI SAAS BHI KABHI BAHU THI	8.72
Star Plus	31-Jan-02	Thu	10:00 PM	KAHAANI GHAR GHAR KI	8.55
Star Plus	30-Jan-02	Wed	10:00 PM	KAHAANI GHAR GHAR KI	8.38
Star Plus	29-Jan-02	Tue	8:30 PM	KASAUTII ZINDAGII KAY	6.37
Star Plus	1-Feb-02	Fri	9:00 PM	KHULLJA SIM.SIM	6.18

Source: http://www.indiantelevision.com/tvr/indextamphp4?startperiod
=27/01/2002&endperiod=02/02/2002
Accessed 18 November 2008

TAM Ratings in 2001

TAM Ratings for the Week of 23/12/2001–29/12/2001

It's a Star Show All The Way in Cable & Satellite Homes					
Channel	*Date*	*Day*	*Start Time*	*Programme*	*TVR*
Star Plus	27-Dec-01	Thu	10:30 PM	KYUNKI SAAS BHI KABHI BA	10.75
Star Plus	25-Dec-01	Tue	10:30 PM	KYUNKI SAAS BHI KABHI BA	10.31
Star Plus	26-Dec-01	Wed	10:29 PM	KYUNKI SAAS BHI KABHI BA	10.15
Star Plus	27-Dec-01	Thu	10:00 PM	KAHAANI GHAR GHAR KI (F)	9.28
Star Plus	24-Dec-01	Mon	10:29 PM	KYUNKI SAAS BHI KABHI BA	8.97
Star Plus	25-Dec-01	Tue	10:00 PM	KAHAANI GHAR GHAR KI (F)	8.94
Star Plus	24-Dec-01	Mon	10:00 PM	KAHAANI GHAR GHAR KI (F)	8.55
Star Plus	26-Dec-01	Wed	9:59 PM	KAHAANI GHAR GHAR KI (F)	8.33
Star Plus	28-Dec-01	Fri	9:00 PM	KHULLJA SIM.SIM	6.45
Star Plus	25-Dec-01	Tue	9:00 PM	KAMZOR KADII KAUN	6.11

Source: http://www.indiantelevision.com/tvr/indextamphp4?startperiod
=23/12/2001&endperiod=29/12/2001
Accessed 18 November 2008

TAM Ratings for the Week of 12/08/2001—18/08/2001

It's a Star Show All The Way in Cable & Satellite Homes					
Channel	*Date*	*Day*	*Start Time*	*Programme*	*TVR*
Star Plus	13-Aug-01	Mon	10:31 PM	KYUNKI SAANS BHI KABHI B	10.8
Star Plus	14-Aug-01	Tue	10:31 PM	KYUNKI SAANS BHI KABHI B	10.1
Star Plus	13-Aug-01	Mon	10:01 PM	KAHAANI GHAR GHAR KII	9.6
Star Plus	16-Aug-01	Thu	10:30 PM	KYUNKI SAANS BHI KABHI B	9.6
Star Plus	14-Aug-01	Tue	10:01 PM	KAHAANI GHAR GHAR KII	9.3
Star Plus	16-Aug-01	Thu	10:00 PM	KAHAANI GHAR GHAR KII	9.2
Star Plus	15-Aug-01	Wed	10:32 PM	KYUNKI SAANS BHI KABHI B	8.5
Star Plus	15-Aug-01	Wed	10:04 PM	KAHAANI GHAR GHAR KII	8.5
Star Plus	15-Aug-01	Wed	9:02 PM	KAUN BANEGA CROREPATI	7.0
Star Plus	17-Aug-01	Fri	9:01 PM	KHULJA SIM SIM	6.4

Source: http://www.indiantelevision.com/tvr/indextamphp4?startperiod
=12/8/2001&endperiod=18/8/2001
Accessed 18 November 2008

TAM Ratings for the Week of 07/05/2001—13/05/2001

		All TV Homes		
Rank	*Channel*	*Programme*	*Start time*	*TVR*
1	Star Plus	KYUNKI SAAS BHI KABHI BAHU THI	10:31 PM	10.7
2	Star Plus	KAHAANI GHAR GHAR KI	10:02 PM	9.0
3	Star Plus	KAUN BANEGA CROREPATI	9:00 PM	5.8
4	Sun TV	CHITHTHI	9:35 PM	4.7
5	Zee TV	MEHNDI TERE NAAM KI	8:31 PM	4.5
6	Zee TV	AMANAT	8:30 PM	4.4
7	Zee TV	KOSHISH ... EK AASHAA	8:32 PM	4.1
8	Star Plus	KALASH	8:00 PM	3.9
9	Star Plus	KORA KAAGAZ	9:00 PM	3.5
10	Sony	HEENA	9:30 PM	3.2

Source: http://www.indiantelevision.com/tvr/indexorgarch php4? startperiod=7/5/2001&endperiod=13/05/2001
Accessed 18 November 2008

TAM Ratings in the Year 2000

2000's Top Shows In All Cable and Satellite Homes

Rank	Date	Day	Programme	Channel	Genre	Duration	Start-End	TVR	Channel Share
1	19/10/00	Thursday	Kaun Banega Crorepati 64	Star Plus	Game Show - G/T/Q‡‡		21:00:08-22:04:14	20.15	49.32
2	3/2/2000	Thursday	Amanat	Zee TV	**Serials** - Drama Soap	40	20:32:28-21:12:22	9.15	29.12
3	13/12/00	Wednesday	Kyunki Saas Bhi Kabhi Bahu Thi 30	Star Plus	**Serials** - Drama Soap		22:28:59-22:58:35	8.43	31.61
4	23/10/00	Monday	Sawaal Dus Crore Ka	Zee TV	**Game Show** -G/T/ Q‡*‡	66	20:30:23-21:33:17	7.97	28.07
5	14/01/00	Friday	Heena	Sony	**Serials** - Drama Soap	33	20:59:22-21:32:29	7.46	24.54
6	9/2/2000	Wednesday	C I D	Sony	**Serials** - M/A /T‡	34	21:36:14-22:10:16	6.68	22.47
7	3/2/2000	Thursday	X-Zone	Zee TV	**Serials** - M/A /T‡	56	21:12:41-22:08:16	6.24	18.89

(Continued)

(*Continued*)

Rank	Date	Day	Programme	Channel	Genre	Duration	Start-End	TVR	Channel Share
8	18/09/00	Monday	Koshish...Ek Aashaa	Zee TV	**Serials** - Drama Soap	44	20:29:44-21:13:56	6.22	21.52
9	30/06/00	Friday	Aashirwad	Zee TV	**Serials** - Drama Soap	38	20:32:15-21:10:36	6.13	22.7
10	19/10/00	Thursday	Kahaani Ghar Ghar Ki	Star Plus	**Serials** - Drama Soap	27	22:05:11-22:32:12	6.11	19.39
11	13/09/00	Wednesday	Mehndi Tere Naam ki	Zee TV	**Serials** - Drama Soap	47	20:30:24-21:17:06	5.81	20.24
12	12/3/00	Sunday	Pepsi Cup-2000 ODI(IND VS SA)L	DD1	**Sports**-Cricket	53	13:06:55-14:00:24	5.69	25.71
13	31/12/00	Sunday	Eternal Asha Aaj Kal Aur Hamesha	Sony	**Serials**- Comedy Serials	253	19:59:53-24:12:25	5.4	15.57
14	11/1/00	Tuesday	Basera	Zee TV	**Serials** - Drama Soap	36	20:58:38-21:34:58	5.04	16.87
15	15/10/00	Sunday	ICC-Knockout 2000-Live	DD1	**Sports**-Cricket	239	12:00:50-15:59:43	4.59	17.28

16	9/1/00	Sunday	Chinna Pappa Periya Pappa	Sun TV	**Serials-** Comedy Serials	26	19:32:16-19:58:11	4.49	12.51
17	18/10/00	Wednesday	Chiththi	Sun TV	**Serials** - Drama Soap	28	21:37:26-22:05:45	4.45	7.9
18	14/10/00	Saturday	Dreamgirls	Sony	**Film Based**-Film Based Program	195	20:02:44-23:17:39	4.25	16.36
19	5/12/00	Tuesday	Kora Kaagaz	Star Plus	**Serials** - Drama Soap	27	20:31:15-20:58:38	4.08	15.43
20	29/12/00	Friday	Kalash	Star Plus	**Serials** - Drama Soap	29	19:59:50-20:28:58	4	15.87

†*‡ denotes (Game/Talk/Quiz)
‡ denotes (Mystery/Adventure/Thriller)

Source: http://www.indiantelevision.com/datamonitor/y2k/cs.htm Accessed 18 November 2008

Note: The first soap, *Kyunki Saas Bhi Kabhi Bahu Thi*, started being telecast from 3 July 2000 onwards; and *Kahaani Ghar Ghar Ki* started being telecast from 16 October 2000 onwards.

Appendix 3
Synopses of Soap Operas

Note: The following are synopses of the soaps discussed in the book. Given that the K soaps were on air from 7–8 years, with multiple plots and subplots, five generations of characters, and innumerable twists and turns, their narratives defy summarization. Thus, the synopses are far from being comprehensive. My aim, in the circumstances, is to highlight, as best is possible, some of the main events. They are also listed chronologically, as they started airing on television. The narratives of *Saat Phere* and *Bidaai*, still on air, have been brought up to date till the beginning of February 2009.

Kyunki Saas Bhi Kabhi Bahu Thi (3 July 2000–6 November 2008, Star Plus, Monday–Thursday, 10:30 pm–11 pm IST)

The story of *Kyunki* revolves around the rich industrialist family of the Viranis who live together in the family home called Shanti Niketan. The story began with three generations of the Viranis living together. Govardhan Virani and his wife Amba (Ba) are the elders in the household. They have three sons: Mansukh, married to Savita; Himmat, married to Daksha; and Jamnadas (JD), married to Gayatri. Mansukh–Savita's sons are Mihir and Hemant; Himmat–Daksha have a son, Chirag, and a daughter, Suhasi; JD–Gayatri have a son, Hemant, and a daughter, Sejal. The daughters-in-law, Savita, Daksha and Gayatri do not accord the respect she deserves to Amba, their mother-in-law.

Originally engaged to Payal, Mihir breaks off his engagement to marry Tulsi, the daughter of the family *pujari* (priest), against the wishes of his mother. Payal's enmity with Tulsi continues and she plots to marry Hemant and enter the Virani family. After her marriage, Tulsi starts taking a stand in grandmother-in-law Amba's defence, underlining the need to show respect to elders in the family. This is the beginning of the lifelong bond between Tulsi and Ba. Pragna, the sister of the Viranis, comes to stay in her natal home but, with the exception of Tulsi, is humiliated by others in the family. From the beginning, therefore, Tulsi is shown as always doing the right thing and fighting, on the side of truth, for justice. In addition, Tulsi manages to do this without creating strife and tension in the family.

Mihir has to leave to take care of the Virani family's factories in Aligarh. Tulsi is pregnant at this time. There is an accident at the factory and Mihir dies. The family is shattered, but Savita's attitude towards her pregnant daughter-in-law changes to a more positive note now. A son, Gautam, is born to Tulsi, who Tulsi gives to her sister-in-law, Aarti, to bring up because Aarti cannot have children of her own. Aarti, however, due to family misunderstandings, goes away to Australia with the child, Gautam, and her husband. Anupam Kapadia, the financier of the Aligarh project, steps in to save it, and gradually falls in love with Tulsi and wants to marry her. We discover that Mihir is alive but has amnesia. He is being helped by a doctor called Mona (actual name Mandira) who starts falling in love with him. Mihir begins to recall his past as vague, disjointed memories. The day arrives for Tulsi's marriage to Anupam. Just before the *kanyadaan* (giving away of the daughter in marriage), Tulsi's eyes alight on Mihir. Gradually Mihir regains his lost memory, but Mandira is not willing to let go of him and continues to call and meet him. She tells him that she is pregnant with their child. Around the same time, Mihir discovers that Tulsi is also pregnant again, and this time, Tulsi gives birth to their daughter, Shobha. Payal's charade is exposed to the Virani family thanks to JD having taped her conversations. Mandira continues to try and gain Mihir's affections.

With a generational leap of 20 years, many new characters and storylines are introduced in the soap. Gautam returns from Australia as a spoilt young man, but is reformed due to Tulsi's example. He marries Damini. Shobha, Mihir–Tulsi's daughter, gets married to the son of Payal Mehra, Tulsi's first arch enemy. It is also revealed that Mihir and Mandira have an illegitimate son, Karan, who returns from Australia, to (initially) take revenge on the Viranis for not having supported his mother. Over time, Karan is converted and becomes Tulsi's greatest support. From here on, he always stands allied with Tulsi against his biological mother, Mandira.

Problems between various sons and their wives of the fourth generation start. Sahil divorces Ganga to marry Trupti. Karan loves Nandini. She, however, is married at the time to Ansh, Tulsi's long-lost son. Ansh is a thoroughly rotten apple who is killed by his mother, Tulsi, for marital rape against Nandini. Pregnant from the rape, Karan and Nandini get married, and Bhoomi is born. But Nandini goes into a coma; her best friend Tanya steps in to take care of the child, and ends up marrying Karan. When Nandini comes out of her coma, she finds out that Tanya and Karan are married, but that she is now pregnant with Karan's child. We find out much later in the story that they have a son, Parth, but who is abducted. It is around the issue of Parth that the soap aired its last episode. Tanya and Karan have a son, Manthan, and Tanya is deeply in love with Karan whose heart, however, is forever in Nandini's keeping. Tulsi is jailed for three years for killing Ansh.

Mandira is jailed for her nefarious activities after being found out by son Karan. She and her friend, Meera, plot against the Viranis. Meera, too, falls in love with Mihir. In the initial stages, Savita, Tulsi's mother-in-law, is allied with them against Tulsi. But she learns of their plans. Stunned, she reveals the truth to the Viranis. Mandira and Meera cause an accident in which Savita is badly hurt. The Viranis must go to London to attend a wedding. All of them do so, but Tulsi stays back to be with her mother-in-law. It is at this time that Savita, who will remain paralyzed the rest of her life, begs Tulsi to perform euthanasia. After much deliberation and many tears, Tulsi does so. The Virani family, on their return, however, blame Tulsi for killing Savita and throw her out of the house.

Heartbroken and alone, Tulsi goes to Benares. Here she rescues, and adopts, a little girl whom she brings up and names Krishnatulsi (KT). We once again have a generational leap here and Tulsi returns home, after many "almost" meetings with Mihir and Karan. Back at Shanti Niketan, now there is a fifth generation. KT and Lakshya, the son of Sahil and Ganga, fall in love. Lakshya, however, has been brought up by Sahil's second wife, Trupti, who is a schemer and plotter. Ansh's son, Eklavya, brought up Damini, is also in love with KT. During the festival of Holi, Damini's mentally challenged son, Mayank, rapes KT. Mayank is sent to a mental asylum, something Damini never forgives Tulsi for. Suspicion falls on Eklavya, who vows to take revenge, and does by tricking KT into marrying him when she thinks it is Lakshya she is getting married to. Tanya is also angry at Tulsi for continuing to welcome Nandini into the house.

It is revealed that Sahil's wife Trupti has been married all along to another man, with whom she now plots to take over the Virani family business. Turned out into the streets, the Viranis live in a Mumbai chawl for a while, till Karan outmaneuvers Trupti and brings everyone back to Shanti Niketan.

The trio of Trupti, Damini and Tanya have Tulsi committed to a mental asylum. In an accident here, Tulsi is badly injured and presumed dead (exit Smriti Z. Irani from the role of Tulsi). However, Tulsi returns with a new face (enter Gautami Gadgil). After some time, she establishes that she is the real Tulsi and only her face has changed due to plastic surgery. We later find out that the second Tulsi is not the real one, but is actually the wife of Jaz Thakral and mother of Billy Thakral. Exit the fake Tulsi, and the "return" of the real Tulsi (Smriti Irani) into the soap once again.

With this return, Tulsi is now fighting Vaidehi, Lakshya's wife, who is actually Trupti's pawn of Trupti. Vaidehi is sowing discord in the family and as always, Tulsi continues saving the family, all the while telling Vaidehi that she too will come around at the end. Lakshya finds out about his wife's machinations and says that he will maintain a married front only for the family's sake, but will have no real relationship with her.

In the meantime, we see that Karan and Nandini are married once again and Tanya, who became "blind," has stepped out of the storyline, being knocked down by a car, and then later rescued, we do not see by whom. Nandini is now determined to locate her long-lost son, Parth. Sahil and Ganga, who have remarried, also face trials with the entry of Shiiv Singhania, who is obsessed in his love for Ganga. Tulsi assures both daughters-in-law, Nandini and Ganga, that they are daughters of the house and that she will support them in their respective causes. Mihir is shown as suffering from Alzheimer's; he keeps forgetting things.

Ba makes her will with Tulsi as the witness, and some time later, dies. When the contents of Ba's will are revealed, that her property should be given to Karan–Nandini's son Parth, Gautam–Damini, Sahil–Ganga, and, surprisingly for the viewers, even Karan–Nandini (Parth's parents) leave home. The last episode shows a temporal leap forward of five years to Tulsi's birthday. Mihir and Tulsi are now living alone, and a young girl (new character in the soap) named Sugandhi stays with them and cares for them. The sons and daughters-in-law have come to wish Tulsi on her birthday. Tulsi goes to meet a mysterious person who will give her news of Parth. The episode concludes, in a very open-ended way, with the unknown person turning out to be none other than *Kahaani Ghar Ghar Ki*'s Parvati, who tells Tulsi that it is indeed she who had made contact with Ba and she has Parth in her keeping. The last shot remained frozen on the faces of the two iconic heroines of the small screen, Tulsi and Parvati.

Kahaani Ghar Ghar Kii (16 October 2000– 9 October 2008, Star Plus, Monday–Thursday, 10 pm–10:30 pm IST)

The story revolves around five generations of the Aggarwal family who live together in Aggarwal House. There is *Babuji* (Father/Grandfather) who has two sons from his first wife — Om and Gaurav. His second wife is *Ma-ji* (Mother), and together, they have five children — Ajay, Kamal, Chaaya, Preeti, and Sonali. *Ma-ji*, however, loves Om best of all. Om is referred to as Ram, who (most times) can never do anything wrong. He is the dutiful son, husband and father. He loves everyone dearly and especially Parvati, his wife. Parvati is the iconic *bahu* (daughter-in-law) of this soap, Loving, dutiful, self-sacrificing, she will do anything for the Aggarwal family, and the family looks up to her for everything. But she never does anything that she does not deem to be just, truthful and for the good of the family. Together, Om and Parvati are referred to as *Ram–Sita ki jodi* (the Ram–Sita couple).

Om and Parvati have a daughter, Shruti. Gaurav, Om's younger brother, is married to Shilpa. His daughter Sonu is not Shilpa's child, though the latter loves Sonu as her own. Kamal is devoted to Om and Parvati. For him they can do no wrong, especially Parvati *bhabi* (elder sister-in-law). Chhaya, the only sister, is married, but spends most of her time in her parents' household, stirring up trouble. An elder, unmarried aunt, Vandy *maasi* (maternal aunt), also lives in the same house.

Pallavi, one of the villainesses in this soap, is supposed to marry Ajay, but the latter walks out of the marriage at the last minute.

At this point, Parvati decides that it will be better all around if Pallavi marries Kamal. It is this which creates the first major rift between the two *bahu*s (daughters-in-law). Kamal has an affair with another woman who bears him a son, Krishna. This son is brought up by Pallavi who, after her initial hesitation, loves Krishna as if he is her own. Pallavi, however, keeps scheming against the Aggarwal family and finally divorces Kamal. Parvati takes over Krishna's upbringing in the Aggarwal household. This becomes the biggest bone of contention between Parvati and Pallavi. Ajay is married to Avantika and they have a daughter, Monalika, who has been shown with negative characteristics. Pallavi and Monalika plot against the Aggarwals, especially Parvati.

A family friend, Khushi, gets raped by a cousin Deven, and Parvati has him placed behind bars. His fiancée, Mallika aka Ambika, enters the Aggarwal household, creates havoc and gets thrown out. Sasha, one of the central negative characters in the soap, is the son of one of the brothers who had raped Khushi, and who had subsequently been jailed. Herein lie the roots for Sasha's hatred of Parvati.

Om's younger brother, Ajay is murdered by his wife Avantika. After a long investigation, Avantika finally gets caught. Mallika, who has married Sanjay Doshi (Parvati's ex-fiancé) has a son, Aryan, who falls in love with his parents' arch rival's daughter, Shruti. Om opposes this marriage, but after many twists and turns, Parvati gives Shruti away in marriage to Aryan. In order to bring Sanjay Doshi and Mallika's machinations to light, Parvati takes on another avatar, and, for a brief period, another actress (Jaya Sil) plays the role of Parvati. The truth is, of course, revealed and the original Parvati (Sakshi Tanwar) returns. Shruti divorces Aryan.

We discover that Shruti is not Om and Parvati's biological offspring. Due to great confusion during riots, babies were swapped, and Gayatri is actually Om and Parvati's daughter. This comes out at a late stage. Enter Sameer who loved Gayatri, but she turned him down. Sameer and Shruti get married, but it is discovered that pregnancy will endanger Shruti's life. Gayatri, however, is pregnant with Sameer's son, Ishan aka Chotu (who enters the soap much later). Nephew Krishna is married to a lawyer, Gunn. They have a daughter, Pragati. Krishna is killed, but Gunn is pregnant with their second child.

Kamal's second wife is Trishna. But prior to getting married to Trishna, we find out that Trishna was mentally disturbed and Om had married her because Trishna's father had begged him to do so to save her life. Apparently a good character, Trishna turns out to be one of the biggest villainesses.

Shruti decides to take a risk and get pregnant. Gunn is also pregnant around this time. When the children are born, Shruti gives her daughter, Tanu, to Gunn; and takes her cousin Sonu's son, Pranay, as her own, because she is convinced that Sameer wants a son to replace the lost Chotu. Only Shruti, Sonu and Gunn know about this arrangement which Parvati accidentally finds out about. The seeds for a future problem are sown.

Om "dies." A few years later, Parvati is forced into the situation of marrying Suyash Mehra to save the family fortunes. Mehra's sons love Parvati as their own mother. Mehra also loves her deeply, as is confirmed much later in the story. Parvati is wrongly framed by Trishna and is sent to jail for killing her husband Om and nephew Krishna. Trishna manages to secure even Shruti's help in this. Parvati "dies" in the jail.

After 18 years, Parvati returns as Janki Devi with her mentor Narayani Devi to take revenge on Trishna and Rajeshwari, Suyash Mehra's first wife, and a close friend of Trishna's. On reaching Mumbai, Narayani Devi buys the Aggarwal house. Narayani Devi introduces her daughter, Janki Devi/Parvati to the whole world at a party Everyone is shocked seeing Janki Devi who looks exactly like Parvati. Rajeshwari and Trishna plan to prove that Janki Devi is actually Parvati but are foiled in their efforts by Janki Devi/Parvati. Parvati also threatens Shruti that she will reveal the truth of Pranay's birth to him. But saddened by the pain of separating a mother from her child, she reunites Pranay and Shruti. Pranay is married to Maithili, but Pranay's violent behavior towards her forces her to take a stand against him and send him to jail. Parvati helps Maithili in this endeavor. Maithili loves Aditya, one of Suyash Mehra's sons, but cannot be with him since she is Pranay's wife. Aditya ends up being married to Garima, one of Om and Rishika's daughters.

It is revealed that it was Suyash Mehra who was actually helping Parvati all these years. He had sent Narayani Devi to guide Parvati, though Parvati is unaware of this. Parvati comes to know that her daughter Gayatri is dead and that her son, Ishan aka Chotu, has been abducted by his nanny. The only link she has is a photograph of Chotu and his nanny together. Parvati/ Janki Devi gets Pragati married to Ankit, much against the wishes of Trishna. Parvati and her daughter Shruti now plot against Trishna, who unknowingly confesses her crime and is caught by the police and put behind bars. Parvati finally comes back to her family and is accepted by everyone. She regains her identity of Parvati Om Aggarwal.

To prepare for the re-entry of the "dead" Om, the story takes the Aggarwal family to visit Benares to get a new idol of Lord Ram. In Benares, Parvati is thrown into the Ganga river, but is saved by none other than Om. He does not recognize Parvati since he has lost his memory and is now known as Rishabh, husband to Rishika Rai Choudhuri, and father of their three daughters. Happy just to see Om alive, Parvati decides not to uproot him from his new life. But she discovers that Rishika keeps medicating Om so that he will not remember his past. Om and Parvati also keep meeting each other by coincidence and Om realizes that he shares a strong bond with Parvati. Parvati decides to get Om back to Aggarwal house and challenges Rishika that she will remind Om about his past life. When Parvati is caught in a fire, she refuses to come out, convinced that if Om sees her in danger, he will recollect his past life. Her belief obviously comes true, as Om recollects his past and returns to his Parvati and the family. Finally once again, the Aggarwal family is complete with Om's return.

But troubles have not yet ceased. Vijay Aggarwal arrives from London and tricks Om into signing over the Aggarwal family business to him. Vijay Aggarwal also introduces the young, orphaned Aditi who treats Parvati as her own mother. Parvati's grandson, pretending to be mentally challenged, is introduced into the Aggarwal house by Pallavi. It turns out that Chotu has been brought up by Sasha and Pallavi, but Parvati decides to redeem him. He is married to Gauri who wants to help Parvati in curing him of his mental illness. Shruti is bitter about her mother, and encourages Tanu in her desire to follow a career in modeling against the family's wishes. Tanu is murdered. Om is accused of Tanu's murder, but Parvati takes the blame on herself. It is finally resolved that Vijay Aggarwal killed Tanu. He is jailed, the misunderstandings with Shruti are resolved, and she is brought back into the family fold. Trishna once again schemes against Parvati and has her committed to a mental asylum. At this point, earlier arch rivals, Pallavi and Sasha, call upon the help of the younger generation of Pragati, Chotu, Aditi, and Aditya, one of Suyash Mehra's sons, to have Parvati released from prison and nurse her back to health. Pallavi and Sasha have seen the error of their ways and want to repent. Returning to the Aggarwal house, Parvati, with the help of these family members, finally traps Trishna, who is now jailed. *Kahaani* ends with the Aggarwal family reunited once again.

Kasautii Zindagi Kay (29 October 2001–28 February 2008, Star Plus, Monday–Thursday, 8 pm–8:30 pm IST)

Anurag Basu and Prerna Sharma are the children of two great friends. Both their fathers hope that one day their children will get married. Initially hesitant, Anurag and Prerna meet at college and gradually fall in love. Anurag's mother, Mohini, does not want her son to marry Prerna, whose family is less wealthy than the Basu family. Anurag and Prerna consummate their love, but soon afterwards Anurag is forced by his mother to marry Komolika. Prerna discovers she is pregnant and has a son, who is named Prem. Komolika is also pregnant, but she aborts the child. Soon afterwards, we find out about Komolika being deceitful and vicious; her only interest is the Basu family fortune. She also has another husband. Anurag divorces her, and Komolika vows to take revenge on both Anurag and Prerna.

Mr Rishabh Bajaj is a very rich businessman. Prerna and Anurag decide to marry. Komolika takes over Anurag's property with Bajaj's help. Anurag and his family are left destitute. Prerna requests Mr Bajaj to have mercy on the Basu family. He agrees, but on the condition that Prerna has to have a paper marriage with him. Sacrificing herself for the Basu family, Prerna agrees. After marriage, Prerna grows close to Mr Bajaj's three children from his previous marriage — Vishakha, Tushar and Kuki, who is blind. The children and Mr Bajaj grow deeply fond of Prerna. Mr Bajaj's ex-wife now enters the scene and tries to murder him. She also lies to Prerna that Mr Bajaj never divorced her, so Prerna and Mr Bajaj's marriage is not real. Prerna marries Anurag and the couple stays happily for a while. Prerna still misses her stepchildren and does whatever she can for them.

Meanwhile, Komolika returns and marries Anurag's cousin Shubroto (who is secretly jealous of his elder brother). It is also revealed that Mr Bajaj is not dead; his ex-wife keeps this a secret from everyone. He comes back, still in love with Prerna, who continues to help him as a friend and takes care of his children. This causes Anurag to be jealous. Their fights scale new heights when Prem is kidnapped and Mr Bajaj is wrongly accused of the kidnapping (the real kidnapper is Subroto). Anurag and Prerna finally get Prem back. However, he is extremely ill and dies. Prerna, at this point, gets pregnant again but Anurag claims that she cheated on him and says that it is actually Mr Bajaj's child. Anurag and Prerna get divorced, each blaming the other for Prem's death. Anurag now has a new woman in his life, his secretary, Aparna. His mother hastens to get Anurag married to Aparna. Soon afterwards, Prerna gives birth to a daughter, Sneha. Anurag at first believes that Sneha is his daughter, but a faked DNA test proves otherwise and some photographs of Bajaj and Prerna together enrage Anurag further. Mr Bajaj has a brief liaison with his ex- sister-in-law, Madhavi.

Eight years pass. Prerna returns to Mumbai with eight-year-old Sneha who is the apple of her eye. Mr Bajaj also adores the child. Sneha goes to school in Mumbai where she meets a girl named Diya. She visits Basu House, but nobody guesses her to be Anurag's daughter. Anurag, who is depressed by his son Prem's death, has withdrawn into a shell but is soon won over by his daughter who resembles him in many ways. Sneha finds out that her father is Anurag and goes to meet him but he dismisses her claim and humiliates her. She leaves his house, crying. In an attempt to console her, Prerna says that her father is actually Mr Bajaj. Hurt by Anurag's rejection, Prerna becomes engaged to Mr Bajaj so that Sneha can have a father. She finds out that Sneha has leukemia and the only thing that can cure her is the bone marrow of a sibling. As Prem is dead and Anurag and Prerna have no other children, Prerna swallows her pride and asks Anurag for help. Prerna and Anurag, each now married to other people, have another child, a son, whom they name Prem once again.

Soon afterwards, Aparna's first husband, Debu, enters the picture. He helps Aparna kill Anurag on the night of Karva Chauth. Aparna, who inherits all of Anurag's property, treats the Basu family very badly. It is soon revealed that Debu actually saved Anurag's life, and he requests Anurag to look after his and Aparna's son, Shravan, which Anurag promises to do. Frightened by Anurag's "ghost," Aparna finally confesses her crime to a roomful of reporters. At a family ceremony, Prerna gives the year-old Prem to Anurag to hold, who, in turn, mistakenly hands the baby to Komolika who kidnaps him. Prerna is livid and distraught and blames Anurag. Shattered and gulity, Anurag goes abroad with Shravan.

Twenty years pass. Anurag returns to India, where now, Prerna and Mr Bajaj are happy with their five children. They also have a daughter together by the name of Kasak. At this point, a whole string of misunderstandings occur involving Kasak, Sneha, Shravan, and Tanisha, another friend. Shravan thinks that Prerna killed Aparna, and to punish Prerna, he leaves a pregnant Kasak at the altar and marries Tanisha instead. Kasak has a miscarriage. Now we find out that Tanisha is Mr Bajaj's daughter from his brief fling with Madhavi.

A jealous, drunk Anurag causes a car crash for Prerna and Mr Bajaj, and both go into coma. Prerna recovers with retrograde amnesia and doctors advise that it is better to let her believe that she is still married to Anurag and their first son, Prem, is still alive. At this point, Anurag's friend from his London days, Sampada (often called Sam) comes into the picture. Sam is in love with Anurag. Aparna returns, and Prerna regains her memory but pretends that she still has not in order to trap Anurag into admitting that he tried to murder Mr Bajaj. Anurag admits as much and Prerna gets him sent to jail. Mr Bajaj's brother, Mahesh, a lawyer, enters the picture, and together with Prerna, figures out that it was actually Aparna who had caused the accident. Mr Bajaj awakens from his coma.

Now Yudi, a spoilt young man, enters the scene. Yudi is actually Prerna–Anurag's second son, Prem, whom Komolika had kidnapped. Prerna vows to reform Yudi back to Prem in a month's time. Yudi makes life very difficult for everyone. In addition, Mukti, Prerna's driver's daughter, who has been raised by

Prerna as her own, also enters the narrative. Mukti starts falling in love with Prem, who is dismissive of her. Still, in a moment of weakness, they spend a night together. At a party, Mukti is drugged and raped by none other than Sharad, her best friend, Sneha's husband. Everyone is now aligned against Mukti. Mr Bajaj asks Mahesh to defend Sharad; the latter confesses to Mahesh that he has indeed raped Mukti. Mahesh tells this to Sharad's father, who wants his son released. Sharad's mother tries to do the right thing but is stopped by her husband. Sneha finds proof in Prem's office and after the court's judgment, stops Sharad outside and confronts him. Unaware that he is being taped, he shoves Sneha aside violently, and she miscarries. Prem realizes his mistake and proposes to Mukti, but she turns him down.

A new subplot is added when Prerna finds out about Mr Bajaj's son, Tushar, being married to a young British girl, Doris, whom no one in the family knows about. Another new character, villainess Debonnita, is introduced into the story. After a series of misunderstandings, Sneha accidentally shoots her mother-in-law. Prerna takes the blame upon herself. Mr Bajaj overhears a conversation between Anurag and Prerna and misunderstands them, thinking Prerna still loves Anurag. Prerna goes to jail in order to save her daughter, Sneha. When Prerna returns from jail, she finds that Prem has cheated Mr Bajaj of his money. Mr Bajaj and his children are nowhere to be found.

Sam asks Prerna to stay in Basu House, but her insecurities regarding her husband, Anurag, and his relationship with Prerna, continue to grow. Mukti's marriage is fixed, but Prem convinces her to come back to him. Mukti, however, is killed on her wedding night in a car accident, and Prem ends up severely mentally disturbed. Mr Bajaj returns, but does not meet Prerna because he thinks she still loves Anurag. Sneha intervenes to get Mr Bajaj and Prerna together, who live together happily for a while.

The next crisis occurs when Prerna realizes that Anurag and Mr Bajaj are trying to organize her life, without asking for her opinion or taking her feelings into consideration. She cuts off all relationships with both men, and goes with Prem to Panchmeshwar to have him treated. Here, she spies a girl, Devaki, who looks exactly like Mukti, and figures that Devaki will work as Prem's "treatment," instead of electric shocks. Devaki, however, is evil. Mr Bajaj knows this, but does not tell anyone in order to save Prem. The wedding night accident is re-enacted, and Prem recovers. Prem and Devaki spend a night together, but she leaves him. Prem later starts becoming friends with his grandmother's physiotherapist, Palchin. Very soon thereafter, Shravan and his wife Tanisha, who is pregnant, are in a car accident for which Prem is held responsible. The family is divided: Prerna, Anurag, Shravan, Sneha, and Kasak support Prem; while Mr Bajaj, Sampada, Tushar, Kuki, and Vishakha side with Tanisha. Prem and Tushar fight over property and when Prerna sides with Tushar, Prem vows to hate her and Mr Bajaj forever. Palchin is engaged to be married, but when her fiancé leaves her, Prem steps in and marries her in order to save her honor.

We are told that Kasak deliberately caused Tanisha's miscarriage and then later offers to be a surrogate mother because she wants to carry Shravan's child. On finding out, an enraged Shravan hits Kasak, who falls and miscarries. She is taken to hospital, where she dies, blaming Shravan. Mad with grief, Mr Bajaj makes off with a gun to avenge his daughter's death. Mr Bajaj and Anurag confront each other with guns in their hands as Prerna looks on from a distance, unable to stop them. A gunshot is heard and Mr Bajaj falls dead and the gun falls at Prerna's feet. She grabs the gun and, believing Anurag to be her husband's killer, shoots him. We come to know that it is Sampada who has killed Mr Bajaj.

Sampada vows to destroy Prerna, who now has lost all faith in love. The Basu company collapses without Anurag, and his mother is hospitalized because she is declared insane. Prerna opens a new school in Panchmeshwar, called the Rishabh Bajaj Gurukul. Boys and girls are kept separated, and Prerna's proposition is that no student should be allowed to fall in love, most of all any of her grandchildren.

Pratham Mittal, a rich businessman, now enters the scene, who actually is Anurag Basu after extensive plastic surgery. Sam is scared that he will discover that she killed Mr Bajaj. Prerna's eldest granddaughter, called P2 (Prerna the 2nd) falls in love with Saksham, but is scared of telling Prerna, who is now called Big P by the grandchildren. A series of misunderstandings and mishaps ensue with this new generation of grandchildren. Suffice it to say that Sam gets Saksham killed, but of course Prerna is blamed for this. A little later, with Sam out of the way, the children pressurize Prerna to marry Anurag. But on the wedding day, Mr Bajaj returns with amnesia. But we realize that he does not actually have amnesia, and is suffering under the misapprehension that Anurag and Prerna tried to kill him off. So he allies with Komolika, who once again has reappeared, against the Anurag–Prerna duo. He, however, finds out that Komolika has been playing him all along and begs forgiveness from Anurag and Prerna. Mr Bajaj and Prerna are reunited. But peace does not reign for long, as Komolika shoots Mr Bajaj in the head on Prerna and Mr Bajaj's wedding anniversary.

After a three-year leap, we see Prem writing a book on the trials of life, *Kasautii Zindagi Kay*. After finishing the book, he visits a memorial whereby we see that Palchin died in an accident while conveying a message that Devaki is alive. Prem and Devaki are now reunited. Devaki calls Prem for the book release, but Prem first goes to a mental asylum where Mr Bajaj is admitted, who he brings along to the book release. There he recounts what really happened that fateful night. We come to know that after Mr Bajaj was shot in his head by a bullet by Komolika, he was taken to a hospital by Prerna and underwent surgery. Anurag came to the hospital to tell Prerna that he would take one last step to finish Komolika. On a snowy night, Anurag met Komolika at the top of a cliff, Prerna following him. Komolika and Anurag fought on the cliffside; Prerna rushed to save Anurag, and was shot by Komolika. Prerna fell off the cliffside and died. But Komolika fell off as well. Anurag stayed the night cradling Prerna's body, and died as well due to the extreme cold.

The last episode of *Kasautii* shows Prerna and Anurag in their spiritual form in front of their son Prem's memorial, pledging that love (*prem*) lives on forever.

Saat Phere ... Saloni Ka Safar
(October 2005–Present, Zee TV,
Monday–Thursday, 9:30 pm–10 pm IST)

The website of Sphere Origins, the content production house of *Saat Phere*, states: "*Saat Phere* is a story of a girl's struggles against the stigmas forced upon her by society and her quest for her unique identity. Although India has progressed in various fields of technology, science & education, discrimination against women remains the root cause of regression in many societies in India leading to degradation of women. One such story is that of Saloni, a dark complexioned 24-year-old girl. Saloni's talent is overshadowed by her complexion. Faced with such a situation, Saloni is determined to not let society's will be imposed upon her and ruin her life and has the will, spirit and the courage to embarkl upon the journey to search for her own unique identity" (http://www.sphereorigins.com).

A simple, dark-complexioned, middle-class girl, Saloni, is loved by her father, Narpat Singh. Her mother, Ambika, prefers the fair sister Shubhra, and brother Samar. Saloni's mother fixes her engagement with Kunjan Pratap Singh, whom Saloni refuses to marry due to his suspect character. Saloni's close friend, Neel, goes to the city to make his career. Saloni sees Neel being attacked on TV and follows him to the city to save him. She participates in a talent hunt to earn money for Neel's treatment. On her return home, however, her mother refuses to accept her back into the house, but due to the intervention of Gayatri *bua* (paternal aunt), problems are resolved.

Shubhra spies Nahar Singh, a Rajput, at a club in a sword fight and falls in love with him. Ambika tries to fix Shubhra's marriage with Nahar. But Nahar and his Tara *bhabi* (elder sister-in-law) choose Saloni over her sister, Shubhra. At the engagement, Neel returns and tells Nahar that Saloni actually loves him. Asked by Nahar, Saloni cries and asks him to trust her. At the instigation of sister-in-law Kaveri, Shubhra runs away with Karan and sleeps with him before marriage. But Karan leaves Shubhra alone with Somesh, who runs away from his house to save herself.

During the henna ceremony of Saloni's marriage, Shubhra discovers she is pregnant, and plots with Kaveri to ruin Saloni's wedding. To recover her sister's pictures, Saloni, all covered up, goes to Somesh's hotel room. After Nahar and Saloni's marriage, Saloni is arrested for Somesh's murder before their marriage can be consummated, because her anklet was found at the crime scene. This problem is resolved. Neel marries Shubhra, but the latter continues to carry on her affair with Karan. When Neel finds out, he leaves her, and Shubhra marrying Kunjan Pratap Singh, who was earlier engaged to Saloni.

Kuki *kaki* (paternal aunt), villainess, joins Nahar's family and tells Saloni about Nahar's first marriage to Chandni, who, Kuki *kaki* says, has been murdered by Nahar. Initially shocked, Saloni determines to get to the truth of the matter. Tara *bhabi*, dressed as Chandni, gets Kuki *kaki* to confess that it is she who killed Chandni, not Nahar.

Nahar and Saloni are happily married till Yug enters the family. Yug, unbeknown to all, is Neel's pawn in the household, and helps Saloni find a job as a singer. Saloni is compelled to work to take care of her brother's treatment. Yug sows suspicion in Nahar's mind about his relationship with Saloni.

At this point, the narrative goes through many twists and turns. Abhi, the son of Saloni's aunt Manno *bhabi*, arrives on the scene, but after a while it is discovered that he is a traitor and not really her son. He marries Nahar's sister Pia and rapes her, but is finally thrown out. Now Urvashi (Tara's sister) comes back and blackmails Saloni, who is pregnant, telling her that she will give the baby back to the family only if Saloni gets out of Nahar's life. Saloni acquiesces, but is of course in trouble and is thrown out of the house. Aditi, Nahar's elder sister, finds out the truth. Urvashi kills Aditi by tampering with her car brakes. Saloni loses her memory, but Nahar finds out the truth. Urvashi's plans are foiled.

It is discovered that Saloni's father, Narpat Singh, had had an affair with Shyama, and he has an illegitimate daughter, Kalika, from that liaison. Kalika is married to Kshitij, Nahar's cousin; together they plan to destroy Nahar's family. Kalika tries to instigate everyone in the family against Saloni, and also sister Shubhra's mother-in-law against her.

During the celebrations of Saloni's pregnancy, there are inauspicious omens. There is an accident, and as Saloni rushes to save someone, she loses her baby. No one has the courage to tell her the truth, but later in the hospital, Saloni overhears the nurses talking and finds out. But the baby, as we later find out, is alive. Coming home, Saloni treats Adwitiya, Tara's offspring, as her child. Needless to say, Kalika works on Tara, instigating her against Saloni. Heartbroken, Saloni starts working as a volunteer in a school. Picking up a crying child here, Saloni is unaware she is holding her own daughter, now named Saawari. A drunk man accuses Saloni of trying to steal "his" child; Nahar pays him off.

Kshitij and Kalika try to frame Nahar for stealing the family fortunes, but in a fight with each other, Kalika kills Kshitij. Nahar is arrested for Kshitij's murder and sentenced to death. Finding our from Nahar's cell mate as to how he was framed, Saloni works to save Nahar.

When Saloni and Nahar come home, Shyama, by now ashamed and fed up of her daughter Kalika's villainous ways, makes it clear that Narpat did not know she was pregnant with Kalika. At this point, Kalika confesses that she had paid the doctor to put a dead baby in place of Saloni's own baby. In the meantime, the drunk foster father of Saawari wants to place her in a brothel for some money, does not succeed, and leaves the baby in a truck.

Nahar is diagnosed with cancer and is treated by his friend, doctor Varun, who, however, is in cahoots with Urvashi, and is actually killing Nahar slowly instead of curing him. The narrative is now at the stage when Nahar has died. But we see Nahar's doppelganger, Swami Amritanand, a holy man with many spiritual powers. He is requested by Manno *bhabi* and Saloni to help the grieving family since his face is the same as Nahar's. And so the story goes on ...

Sapna Babul Ka ... Bidaai
(8 October 2007–present, Star Plus, Monday–Friday, 9 pm–9:30 pm IST)

Bidaai is the story of two families in Agra, the city famous for that symbol of eternal love, the Taj Mahal. One family is that of Prakash Chand Sharma (*Mamaji*, maternal uncle), his wife, the dark-skinned Kaushalya (*Mamiji*), their daughter Ragini, their son Vineet and his wife, Malti, and Kaushalya's mother (*Naniji*). They live in "Kaushalya Niwas". The Sharmas are an upper middle-class family. The second family is the rich, industrialist Rajvansh family, with Indrajit Rajvansh and his wife, Vasundhara Rajvansh (*Badi Ma*, elder mother); his younger brother Satyen and his wife Ambika (*Choti Ma*, younger mother); Indrajit–Vasundhara's sons, Alekh and Ranvir and daughter Dolly; Satyen–Ambika's son Naveen, his wife Avani and their two children, Guni and Pratham. Vasundhara is fair and Ambika is dark. Indrajit and

Vasundhara have a stormy relationship, whereas Satyen–Ambika's relationship is a loving one. In general, nobody in the Rajvansh household goes against Vasundhara's wishes. The concept revolves around the fair skin/dark skin thesis. It is the story of the two cousins, Sadhana, who is fair and beautiful, and her cousin, Ragini, attractive, but dark-complexioned. On her part, Vasundhara Rajvansh lays great store by fair skin and good looks. Sadhana's father goes overseas and leaves her in the care of Prakash Chand Sharma. Society's approach of favoring Sadhana because of her good looks and mistreating Ragini because she is dark and not so good-looking leads to *Mamiji* differentiating between her daughter Ragini and Sadhana, who starts feeling cursed for her good looks. In the beginning, her mother, *Naniji* (maternal grandmother) also keeps telling Kaushalya to beware because otherwise Ragini's future will be poisoned by the beautiful Sadhana. The two sisters, however, love each other unconditionally, and the younger Sadhana calls Ragini *jiji* (elder sister).

Vasundhara Rajvansh enters into an agreement with Sadhana that she will marry her elder son, the mentally challenged Alekh; and in return, she will have Ranvir married to Ragini. Sadhana agrees to do this because otherwise her *Mamaji's* house will be sold off. Without informing anyone of the true reason, she gets married to Alekh. Everyone is very upset and annoyed and think Sadhana has married for money. Ragini is, however, sensitive enough to know that there must be a good reason for Sadhana's decision, and she finds out and informs the family. Sadhana is welcomed back into *Mamaji's* house.

In the meantime, Ranvir falls in love with Sonia, who is beautiful but is a two-timer. At Sadhana and Alekh's wedding reception, Vasundhara Rajvansh, making sure that Sadhana can overhear, tells Ranvir about marrying Ragini. Ranvir reacts negatively, saying that Ragini is not suitable for him. Later, however, Sadhana brings to light Sonia's scheming ways and the relationship between Ranvir and Sonia comes to an end.

Sadhana is caring and sensitive of Alekh and she manages to make him better than before. Referring to his wife as *dost* (friend), Alekh grows very attached to her. She fulfils all her duties as daughter-in-law impeccably. Satyen and Ambika are very loving towards her as well as Alekh and Ranvir. Their own son, Naveen, however, has an eye on the main chance and he and his wife, Avani, are more flattering of Vasundhara Rajvansh because they know it is she who is the de facto head of the family.

Vineet works at the Rajvansh family's offices but does not tell his parents about it. Malti and Avani are friends, their only interest being in plotting, scheming and creating trouble for Sadhana and Ragini. They enjoy the misunderstandings and strife that they create in their respective households.

One day Ranvir makes a telephone call that Ragini answers at the dance school where she goes for training. The "wrong number" phone conversations continue and, without setting eyes on one another, the two fall in love through their phone conversations. Sadhana accidentally finds out that Ragini and Ranvir are the two unknown phone friends. She is overjoyed and is also sure that when Ranvir finds out, he will marry her *jiji* (elder sister). The two decide to meet at the Taj Mahotsav (grand festival of the Taj Mahal) where Ragini will perform on stage. Malti and Avani manage to discover the identities of the two phone friends and decide to stir up trouble. Avani tells *Badi Ma* Vasundhara, who is enraged. In the meantime Ragini's grandmother, *Naniji*, also fixes a match for Ragini with Shishir, who is the only son of his parents. Shishir and his family like Ragini a lot.

When Ranvir and Ragini finally discover each other's true identities, they are shocked. Ranvir leaves the theater and cannot come to terms with the fact that it is Ragini whom he has been fallen in love with over the phone. His mother also does nothing to lessen his angst, and everyone blames Sadhana for plotting to bring her sister into the Rajvansh family fold. This is not true, of course, but Vasundhara Rajvansh spares no opportunity for insulting the Sharmas for what she perceives to be an attempt on their part to ensnare her son. Ragini is heartbroken and decides to get engaged to Shishir. A confused Ranvir decides to go to Switzerland, but at the airport, overhearing an old couple talking about the importance of the inner qualities of true beauty, realizes that he actually loves Ragini.

In the meantime, Naveen has been defrauding the family business for a large sum of money and frames Vineet for the fraud. Vineet goes to jail. The Sharma family is distraught, and Malti is shocked at her friend Avani's complicity in this wrongdoing. Ranvir comes to the Sharma home and pledges that he will clear Naveen's name. He then goes to Delhi, brings back the true culprit and presents him to the Sharmas just as Ragini's engagement to Shishir is about to take place. Shishir, however, realizing that Ragini and Ranvir love each other, steps aside.

Both families now try to convince the respective mothers — Vasundhara Rajvansh and Kaushalya Sharma — to give their blessings to Ranvir and Ragini's marriage, but both mothers are unrelenting. Kaushalya goes and meets Vasundhara Rajvansh to say that she does not want her daughter to be a daughter-in-law where Sadhana is. Ranvir and Ragini decide that they will only get married if their mothers bless the union. Alekh first takes a knife to threaten his mother for preventing Ranvir from marrying his *dost* Ragini, but then falls at her feet and begs for her permission. Overcome by the son who has never really communicated with her before, Vasundhara Rajvansh gives her permission. The family is overjoyed and Vasundhara is also happy at the love and warmth her sons give her. She still worries, however, about what people will say when they see Ranvir and Ragini together. Kaushalya, on the other hand, worries incessantly about Ragini not being treated at par if she marries into the same household as the beautiful Sadhana. Still, upon persuasion from *Mamaji*, her mother and the now chastened Malti, she agrees to the union.

Vasundhara's and Kaushalya's fears bear fruit when people are overheard commenting on how dark and ugly Ranvir's future bride is. At the pre-wedding ceremonies, one of Vasundhara's friends, Sheetal, also speaks insultingly about Ragini. Ranvir steps in and says that for him, Ragini is the most beautiful person and that true beauty comes from within. Back at the Rajvansh mansion, Ambika tries to reassure Vasundhara that she should not worry about people who are not well-wishers. Vasundhara gets angry with her, and it is now that Ambika's husband, Satyen, steps in and shouts at Vasundhara. He tells her that Ambika has always suffered in this house and while people do not know it, actually Ambika is Vasundhara's own elder sister. Totally by chance, Sadhana overhears this conversation, as does *Mamiji* who had dropped by for a visit. *Mamiji*'s fears for history repeating itself for Ragini now become acute. She accuses Sadhana of knowing these facts, Sadhana denies it, and *Mamiji* speaks to her very harshly. *Mamaji* is horrified and apologizes to Sadhana who says that *Mamiji* has brought her up like a mother and she does not mind being scolded by her mother. Vasundhara and Ambika also come to know that Kaushalya and Prakash Chand Sharma know that they are really sisters and that Kaushalya fears greatly that Sadhana might ill-treat Ragini, just as Vasundhara has done Ambika. Sadhana and Ragini reassure Kaushalya that no similar rift will ever occur between them. *Mamiji* remains unconvinced.

Ranvir and Ragini get married and Ragini's *bidaai* takes place, and she enters the Rajvansh family as their newest *bahu*. And so the story goes on ...

Bibliography

Abu-Lughod, Lila. 2004. *Dramas of Nationhood: The Politics of Television in Egypt*. Chicago: Chicago University Press.

Afghanistan News Center. 2008. "Hit Indian Soap Opera Pulled from Afghan TV." 21 April. http://www.afghanistannewscenter.com/news/2008/april/apr212008.html#5. Accessed 18 September 2008.

Ahmed-Ghosh, Huma. 2003. "Writing the Nation on the Beauty Queen's Body: Implications for a 'Hindu' Nation," *Meridians: Feminism, Race, Transnationalism*, vol. 4 (1): 205–27.

Allen, Robert, C. 1985. *Speaking of Soap Operas*. Chapel Hill, North Carolina: University of North Carolina Press.

——(ed.).1995. *To Be Continued … Soap Operas Around the World*. London and New York: Routledge.

Alter, Jospeh S. 1992. *The Wrestler's Body: Identity and Ideology in North India*. Berkeley: University of California Press.

Amar, Charu. 2008. "From *bahu*s to bombshells," *Times of India*. 8 August.

Anderson, Benedict. (1983) 1991. *Imagined Communities: Reflections on the Origins and Spread of Nationalism*. London: Verso.

Ang, Ien. 1985. *Watching Dallas: Soap Opera and the Melodramatic Imagination*. London: Methuen.

——. 1991. *Desperately Seeking the Audience*. London: Routledge.

——. 1996. *Living Room Wars: Rethinking Media Audiences for a Postmodern World*. London: Routledge.

Appadurai, Arjun. 1981. "The Past As A Scarce Resource," *Man*, n.s., vol. 16 (2): 201–19.

——. 1990. "Disjuncture and Difference in the Global Cultural Economy," *Public Culture*, vol. 2 (2): 1–24.

——. 1996. *Modernity At Large: Cultural Dimensions of Globalization*. Minneapolis: University of Minnesota Press.

Appadurai, Arjun, Frank J. Korom and Margaret A. Mills (eds). 1991. *Gender, Genre and Power in South Asian Expressive Traditions*. Philadelphia: University of Pennsylvania Press.

Appadurai, Arjun, Frank J. Korom and Margaret A. Mills. 1991. "Introduction." in Arjun Appadurai, Frank J. Korom and Margaret A. Mills (eds), *Gender, Genre and Power in South Asian Expressive Traditions*, pp. 3–32. Philadelphia: University of Pennsylvania Press.

Armbrust, Walter. 1996. *Mass Culture and Modernism in Egypt*. New York: Cambridge University Press.

Askew, Kelly and Richard R. Wilk. 2002. *The Anthropology of Media: A Reader*. Malden, MA, USA; Oxford, UK; and Victoria, Australia: Blackwell Publishing.

Atwood, Margaret. 1971. *Power Politics*. New York: Harper and Row.

Babb, Lawrence A. 1981. "Glancing: Visual Interaction in Hinduism," *Journal of Anthropological Research*, vol. XXXVII/4: 387–401.

Bakshi, Amba Batra. 2008. "This Sperm Counts," *Outlook India*. 3 November.

Bamzai, Kaveree. 2008a. "Small Town Winners," *India Today*. 25 January.

———. 2008b. "Life After Death," *India Today* group online. 19 November. http://www.itgo.in/index.php?option=com_content&task=view&id=16918&sectionid=2&secid=10. Accessed 27 January 2009.

Barthes, Roland. 1975. *The Pleasure of the Text*. New York: Hill and Wang.

Bartky, David Scott. 2008. *Grooming Secrets for Men: The Ultimate Guide to Looking and Feeling Your Best*. iUniverse, inc.

Beck, B. E. F. 1989. "Core Triangles in the Folk Epics of India," in Stuart H. Blackburn, P. J. Claus, J. B. Flueckiger, and Susan S. Wadley (eds), *Oral Epics in India*, pp. 155–75. Los Angeles: University of California Press.

Bijapurkar, Rama. 2007. *We Are Like That Only: Understanding the Logic of Consumer India*. New Delhi: Penguin Books India.

———. 2008a. "Janata Has Given Thumbs Up!," *Economic Times*. 3 March.

———. 2008b. "Consumer Syndrome," *The Week: Anniversary Special*. 28 December.

Biswas, Premankur. 2008. "Saas, Bahu and Revolution," *Indian Express*. 4 November.

Blackburn, Stuart. 1996. *Inside the Drama House: Rama Stories and Shadow Puppets in South India*. Los Angeles: University of California Press.

———. 2008. *Himalayan Tribal Tales: Oral Tradition and Culture in the Apatani Valley*. Brill Academic Publishers.

Blackburn, Stuart H. and J. B. Flueckiger. 1989. "Introduction," in Stuart H. Blackburn, P. J. Claus, J. B. Flueckiger, and Susan S. Wadley (eds), *Oral Epics in India*, pp. 1–14. Los Angeles: University of California Press.

Booth, Gregory D. 1995. "Traditional Content and Narrative Structure in the Hindi Commercial Cinema," *Asian Folklore Studies*, vol. 54: 169–90.

Bose, Ajoy. 2008. *Behenji: A Political Biography of Mayawati*. New Delhi: Penguin Books India.

Brooks, Peter. (1976) 1985. *The Melodramatic Imagination: Balzac, Henry James, Melodrama and the Mode of Excess* (2nd edn). New Haven, CT: Yale University Press.

Brosius, Christiane. 2005. *Empowering Visions: The Politics of Representation in Hindu Nationalism*. London: Anthem Press.

Brosius, Christine and Melissa Butcher (eds). 1999. *Image Journeys: Audio–Visual Media and Cultural Change in India*. New Delhi: Sage Publications.

Brown, Judith M. 2007. *Global South Asians: Introducing the Modern Diaspora.* New Delhi: Cambridge University Press.

Brown, Mary Ellen. 1987. "The Politics of Soaps: Pleasure and Feminine Empowerment," *Australian Journal of Cultural Studies*, vol. 4 (2): 1–25.

———(ed.).1990. *Television and Women's Culture.* London: Sage Publications.

———. 1994. *Soap Opera and Women's Talk: The Pleasure of Resistance.* London: Sage Publications.

Brown, Mary Ellen and Linda Barwick. 1987. "Fables and Endless Genealogies: Soap Opera and Women's Culture," *Continuum: The Australian Journal of Media and Culture*, vol. 1 (2): 71–82. http://wwwmcc.murdoch.edu.au/ReadingRoom/1.2/Brown.html. Accessed 16 October 2008.

Brown, William J. and Michael J. Cody. 1991. "Effects of a Prosocial Television Soap Opera in Promoting Women's Status," *Human Communication Research*, vol. 18 (1): 114–42.

Brunsdon, Charlotte. 1981. " 'Crossroads': Notes on Soap Opera," *Screen*, vol. 22 (4): 32–37.

———. 1984. "Writing About Soap Opera," in L. Masterman (ed.), *Television Mythologies*, pp. 82–87. London: Comedia.

———. 1990. "Problems with Quality," *Screen*, vol. 22 (4): 32–37.

———. 1997. *Screen Tastes: Soap Opera to Satellite Dishes.* London: Routledge.

——— 1997 " 'Crossroads': Notes on Soap Opera," reprinted in Charlotte Brunsdon (ed.), *Screen Tastes: Soap Opera to Satellite Dishes*, pp. 13–18. London: Routledge.

———. 2000. *The Feminist, the Housewife and the Soap Opera.* Oxford: Oxford University Press.

Budge, Belinda. 1988. "Joan Collins and the Wilder Side of Women: Exploring Pleasure and Representation," in Lorraine Gamman and Margaret Marshment (eds), *The Female Gaze: Women as Viewers of Popular Culture*, pp. 102–11. London: The Women's Press.

Butcher, Melissa. 2003. *Transnational Television, Cultural Identity and Change: When STAR Came to India.* New Delhi: Sage Publications.

Canclini, Nestor Garcia. 2001. *Consumers and Citizens: Globalization and Multicultural Conflicts.* Trans. George Yudice. University of Minnesota Press.

———. 2005. *Hybrid Cultures: Strategies for Entering and Leaving Modernity.* Trans. Christopher L Chiappari and Silvia L. Lopez. University of Minnesota Press.

Cantor, M. G. and S. Pingree. 1983. *The Soap Opera.* Beverly Hills, CA: Sage Publications.

Chakrabarty, Dipesh. 1992. "Provincializing Europe: Postcoloniality and the Critique of History," *Cultural Studies*, vol. 6 (3): 337–57.

Chakravarti, Uma. 1988. "Beyond the Altekerain Paradigm: Towards a New Understanding of Gender Relations in Early Indian History," *Social Scientist*, vol. 16 (8): 44–52.

Chakravarty, Sumita. 1993. *National Identity in Indian Popular Cinema, 1947–1987*. Austin: University of Texas Press.

Challapalli, Sravanthi. 2002. "All's Fair in this Market," *Business Line* online. 5 September. http://www.thehindubusinessline.com/catalyst/2002/09/05/stories/2002090500040300.htm. Accessed 8 March 2007.

Chatterji, Bankim Chandra. 1969. *Bankim Rachanavali*. Calcutta: Sahitya Samsad.

Chatterjee, Partha. 1986. *Nationalist Thought and the Colonial World: A Derivative Discourse*. London: Zed Books.

———. 1989. "The Nationalist Resolution of the Women's Question," in Kumkum Sangari and Sudesh Vaid (eds), *Recasting Women: Essays in Colonial History*, pp. 233–53. New Delhi: Kali for Women.

———. 1993. *The Nation and its Fragments: Colonial and Postcolonial Histories*. Princeton, N.J.: Princeton University Press.

———. 1997. "On Religious and Linguistic Nationalisms: The Second Partition of Bengal," in Ranabir Samaddar (ed.), *Reflections on Partition in the East*, pp. 35–58. New Delhi: Vikas Publishing House.

Chodorow, Nancy. (1974) 2001. "Family Structure and Feminine Personality," in Darlene M. Juschka (ed.), *Feminism in the Study of Religion: A Reader*, pp. 81–105. Continuum International Publishing Group. Reprinted from M. Z. Rosaldo and L. Lamphere (eds), 1974. *Women, Culture and Society*, pp. 43–66. Stanford: Stanford University Press.

Chopra, Anupama. 1997. "Bollywood: Bye-Bye Bharat," *India Today*, pp. 53–54. 1 December.

———. 2002. *Dilwale Dulhaniya Le Jayenge*. London: British Film Institute.

Chopra, Anupama and Nandita Chowdhury. 1999. "New Blood: The New Bollywood Brigade," *India Today*. 28 June.

Chua Beng Huat and Koichi Iwabuchi (eds). 2008. *East Asian Pop Culture: Analysing the Korean Wave*. Hong Kong: Hong Kong University Press.

Claus, Peter J., Sarah Diamond and Margaret A. Mills (eds). 2003. *South Asian Folklore: An Encyclopedia — Afghanistan, Bangladesh, India, Nepal, Pakistan, Sri Lanka*. London: Routledge.

Cohen, Steven and Ina Rae Hark (eds). 1993. *Screening the Male*. Routledge.

Coltrane, Scott and Kenneth Allan. 1994. "'New' Fathers and Old Stereotypes: Representations of Masculinity in 1980s Television Advertising," *Masculinities*, vol. 2 (4), Winter: 43–66.

Comaroff, Jean and John Comaroff (eds). 1993. *Modernity and its Malcontents: Rituals and Power in Post-Colonial Africa*. Chicago: University of Chicago Press.

Connell, Robert W. 1987. *Gender and Power: Society, the Person, and Sexual Politics*. Stanford: Stanford University Press.

———. 1995. *Masculinities*. Berkeley: University of California Press.

Creeber, Glen (ed.). 2001. *The Television Genre Book*. London: British Film Institute.

Culler, Jonathan. 1976. *Saussure*. London: Fontana.

Das, Veena. 1981. "The Mythological Film and its Framework of Meaning: An Analysis of *Jai Santoshi Ma*," *India International Centre Quarterly*, special issue on "Indian Popular Cinema," vol. 8 (1): 43–55.

———. 1995. "On Soap Opera: What Kind of Anthropological Object Is It?," in Daniel Miller (ed.), *Worlds Apart: Modernity Through the Prism of the Local*, pp. 169–89. London: Routledge.

Deodhar, P. S. 1991. *The Third Parent*. New Delhi: Vikas Publishing House.

Derne, Steve D. 1994. "Structural Realities, Persistent Dilemmas, and the Construction of Emotional Paradigms: Love in Three Cultures," in William Wentworth and John Ryan (eds), *Social Perspectives on Emotion*, vol. 2, pp. 281–308. Greenwich, CT: JAI Press.

———. 1995. *Culture in Action: Family Life, Emotion and Male Dominance in Banaras, India*. Albany: SUNY Press.

———. 2000. *Movies, Masculinity and Modernity: An Ethnography of Men's Filmgoing in India*. Westport, CT: Greenwood Press.

———. 2005. "The (Limited) Effect of Cultural Globalization in India: Implications for Culture Theory," *Poetics*, vol. 33: 33–47. Elsevier.

———. 2008. *Globalization on the Ground: New Media and the Transformation of Culture, Class and Gender in India*. Sage Publications.

Desai, Santosh. 2007. "Good Reel Models Don't Always Mean Change," *Times of India*. 15 October.

Deshpande, Satish. 2003. *Contemporary India: A Sociological View*. New Delhi: Penguin Books India/Viking.

Dissanayake, Wimal (ed.). 1993. *Melodrama and Asian Cinema*. Cambridge: Cambridge University Press.

Doniger O'Flaherty, Wendy. 1973. *Asceticism and Eroticism in the Mythology of Shiva*. London: Oxford University Press.

———. 1980. *Women, Androgynes and Other Mythical Beasts*. Chicago: University of Chicago Press.

Dornfeld, Barry. 1998. *Producing Public Television, Producing Public Culture*. Princeton, N. J.: Princeton University Press.

Dow, Bonnie J. 1996. *Prime Time Feminism: Television, Media Culture, and the Women's Movement since 1970*. Philadelphia: University of Pennsylvania Press.

———. 2006. "The Traffic in Men and the Fatal Attraction of Postfeminist Masculinity — Conversation and Commentary," *Women's Studies in Communication*, vol. 21 (9) Spring: 113–31. Also available at http://arapaho.nsuok.edu/~aldridga/dow.pdf.

D'Souza, Dipti Nagpaul. 2008. "The End of A Beginning," *Indian Express*. 25 October.

Dudrah, Rajinder Kumar. 2006. *Bollywood: Sociology Goes to the Movies.* New Delhi: Sage Publications.

Dudrah, Rajinder and Jigna Desai (eds). 2008. *The Bollywood Reader.* England: Open University Press.

Dusenbery, Verne A. 1997. "The Poetics of Politics and Recognition: Diaspora Sikhs in Pluralist Polities," *American Ethnologist*, vol. 24 (4): 738–85. November.

Dwyer, Rachel. 2000. *All You Want Is Money, All You Need Is Love.* New York: Cassell.

———. 2006. *Filming the Gods: Religion and Indian Cinema.* London and New York: Routledge.

———. 2007. "Bollywood Bourgeois," in Ira Pande (ed.), *India at 60: Towards a New Paradigm*, pp. 222–31. India: Harper Collins.

Dwyer, Rachel and Christopher Pinney (eds). 2000. *Pleasure and the Nation: History, Consumption and Politics of Public Culture in India.* New Delhi: Oxford University Press.

Dwyer, Rachel and Divia Patel. 2002. *Cinema India: The Visual Culture of Hindi Film.* London: Reaktion Books.

Dyal, R. 1992a. *"CTV: Glitter or Gloom — Public Perceptions of and Reactions to Multi-Channel CTV in India."* New Delhi: Indian Institute of Mass Communication.

———. 1992b. *"Satellite Broadcasting and CTV: A Study on CTV in Five Cities in India."* New Delhi: Indian Institute of Mass Communication.

Eck, Diana. 1985. *Darsan: Seeing the Divine Image in India.* Chambersberg, PA.

Eickelman, Dale F. 2008. "Gender and Religion in the Private and Public Spheres," in Kazoo Ohtsuka and Dale F. Eickelman (eds), *Crossing Boundaries: Gender, the Public and the Private in Contemporary Muslim Societies*, pp. 135–50. Studia Culturae Islamicae no. 89, MEIS series number 5. Tokyo: Research Institute for Languages and Cultures of Asia and Africa.

Eickelman, Dale F. and Jon W. Anderson (eds). (1999) 2003. *New Media in the Muslim World: The Emerging Public Sphere.* Bloomington and Indianapolis: Indiana University Press.

Elliott, Richard and Christine Elliott. 2005. "Idealized Images of the Male Body in Advertising: A Reader-Response Exploration," *Journal of Marketing Communications*, vol 11 (1): 3–19. March.

Ellis, John. 1999. "From Visible Fictions: Broadcast TV as Sound and Image," in Leo Braudy and Marshall Cohen (eds), *Film Theory and Criticism* (5th edn), pp. 395–404. New York: Oxford University Press.

Elsaesser, Thomas. 1987. "Tales of Sound and Fury: Observations on the Family Melodrama," in Christine Gledhill (ed.), *Home Is Where the Heart Is: Studies in Melodrama and the Women's Film*, pp. 43–69. London: British Film Institute.

Enloe, Cynthia. 1989. *Bananas, Beaches and Bases: Making Feminist Sense of International Politics*. Berkeley: University of California Press.

——. 2000. *Maneuvers: The International Politics of Militarizing Women's Lives*. Berkeley: University of California Press.

Federation of Indian Chambers of Commerce and Industry (FICCI) — Arthur Andersen. 2001. Report on *Indian Entertainment Industry: Envisioning for Tomorrow*.

Fernandes, Leela. 2000. "Restructuring the New Middle Class in Liberalizing India," *Comparative Studies of South Asia, Africa and the Middle East*, vol. 20 (1): 88–104.

——. 2001. "Rethinking Globalization: Gender and the Nation in India," in Marianne DeKoven (ed.), *Feminist Locations: Global and Local, Theory and Practice*, pp. 147–67. Piscataway, N. J.: Rutgers University Press.

——. (2006) 2007. *India's New Middle Class: Democratic Politics in an Era of Economic Reform*. New Delhi: Oxford University Press.

Feuer, Jane. 1984. "Melodrama, Serial Form and Television Today," *Screen*, vol. 25 (1): 4–16. January/February.

——. (1987) 1992. "Genre Study and Television," in Robert C. Allen (ed.), *Channels of Discourse, Reassembled: Television and Contemporary Criticism*, pp. 138–59. Chapel Hill: University of North Carolina Press.

Fiske, John. 1987. *Television Culture*. London: Methuen.

——. 1995 "Gendered Television: Femininity," in Gail Dines and Jean M. Humez (eds), *Gender, Race and Class in Media: A Text-Reader*, pp. 340–47. Thousand Oaks, CA: Sage Publications.

Flocker, Michael. 2003. *The Metrosexual Guide to Style: A Handbook for the Modern Man*. Da Capo Press.

Foucault, Michel. 1980. *Power/Knowledge*. New York: Pantheon.

——. 1984. *The History of Sexuality: An Introduction*, vol. I. Harmondsworth: Penguin Books.

Frith, Simon. 1982. *Sound Effects: Youth, Leisure and the Politics of Rock n' Roll*. New York: Pantheon.

Gaonkar, Dilip P. 1999. "On Alternative Modernities," *Public Culture*, special issue on "Alter/Native Modernities," vol. 11 (1): 1–18.

——(ed.). 2001. *Alternative Modernities*. Durham, N. C.: Duke University Press.

Ganguly-Scrase, Ruchira and Timothy J. Scrase. 2009. *Globalisation and the Middle Classes in India: The Social and Cultural Impact of Neoliberal Reforms*. London and New York: Routledge.

Ganti, Tejaswani. 1999. "Centenary Commemorations or Centenary Contestations? Celebrating a Hundred Years of Cinema in Bombay," *Visual Anthropology*, special issue on "Indian Cinema," vol. 11 (4): 399–419.

——. 2004. *Bollywood: A Guidebook to Popular Hindi Cinema*. London: Routledge.

Geraghty, Christine. 1981. "The Continuous Serial: A Definition," in Richard Dyer (ed.), *Coronation Street*. London: British Film Institute.
——. 1991. *Women and Soap Opera: A Study of Prime Time Soaps.* Cambridge: Polity.
——. 1995. "Social Issues and Realist Soaps: A Study of British Soaps in the 1980s/1990s," in Robert C. Allen (ed.), *To Be Continued ... Soap Operas Around the World*, pp. 66–80. London: Routledge.
——. 2003. "Aesthetics and Quality in Popular Television Drama," *International Journal of Cultural Studies*, vol. 6 (1): 25–45.
——. 2005. "The Study of Soap Opera," in Janet Wasko (ed.), *A Companion to Television*, pp. 308–23. Malden, MA: Blackwell Publishing.
Ghosh, Amitav. 1989. "The Diaspora in Indian Culture," *Public Culture*, vol. 2 (1): 73–78.
Ghosh, Shohini. 1999. "The Troubled Existence of Sex and Sexuality: Feminists Engage with Censorship," in Christiane Brosius and Melissa Butcher (eds), *Image Journeys: Audio–Visual Media and Cultural Change in India*, pp. 233–60. New Delhi: Sage Publications.
Gillespie, Marie. 1995. *Television, Ethnicity and Cultural Change*. London: Routledge.
Ginsburg, Faye D., Lila Abu-Lughod and Brian Larkin (eds). 2002. *Media Worlds: Anthropology on New Terrain*. Berkeley and Los Angeles: University of California Press.
Gledhill, Christine (ed.). 1987. *Home Is Where the Heart Is: Studies in Melodrama and the Women's Film*. London: British Film Institute.
——. 1987. "The Melodramatic Field: An Investigation," in Christine Gledhill (ed.), *Home Is Where the Heart Is: Studies in Melodrama and the Women's Film*, pp. 5–42. London: British Film Institute.
——. 1992. "Speculations on the Relationship between Soap Opera and Melodrama," *Quarterly Review of Film and Video*, vol. 14 (1–2): 103–24.
——. 1997. "Genre and Gender: The Case of Soap Operas," in Stuart Hall (ed.), *Representation: Cultural Representations and Signifying Practices*, pp. 337–86. London: Sage Publications.
Gopalan, Lalitha. 2002. "On Fire," in Peter X. Feng (ed.), *Screening Asian Americans*, pp. 293–98. New Brunswick, N. J.: Rutgers University Press.
Gokulsing, Moti K. 2004. *Soft-Soaping India: The World of Indian Televised Soap Operas*. Trentham Books.
Gokulsing, Moti K. and Wimal Dissanayake (eds). 2009. *Popular Culture in a Globalised India*. Routledge.
Good, G. E., M. J. Porter and M.G. Dillon. 2002. "When Men Divulge: Portrayals of Men's Self-Disclosure in Prime Time Situation Comedies," *Sex Roles*, vol. 46 (11–12): 419–27. June.
Gopinath, Vrinda. 2006. "The Behenji Backlash," *Indian Express* online. 17 September. http://www.indianexpress.com/story/12807.html. Accessed 21 September 2007.

Gorman-Murray, A. 2006. "Queering Home or Domesticating Deviance?: Interrogating Gay Domesticity through Lifestyle Television," *International Journal of Cultural Studies*, vol. 9 (2): 227–47.

Goulet, Robert G. 1991. "Life With(out) Father: The Ideological Masculine in Rope and Other Hitchcock Films," in Walter Raubicheck *et al.* (eds), *Hitchcock's Rereleased Films: From Rope to Vertigo*. Detroit: Wayne State University Press.

Grewal, Inderpal. 1994. "The Postcolonial, Ethnic Studies, and the Diaspora: The Contexts of Ethnic Immigrant/Migrant Cultural Studies in the US," *Socialist Review*, vol. 24 (4), Fall: 45–74.

Grewal, Inderpal and Caren Kaplan. 2001. "Global Identities: Theorizing Transnational Studies of Sexuality," *GLQ: A Journal of Lesbian and Gay Studies*, vol. 7 (4): 663–79.

Gripsrud, Jostein. 1995. *The Dynasty Years: Hollywood, Television and Critical Media Studies*. London: Routledge.

Guha-Thakurta, Tapati. 1991. "Women as 'Calendar Art' Icons: Emergence of Pictorial Stereotypes in Colonial India," *Economic and Political Weekly*, vol. 26 (43), WS: 91–99.

Gupta, Nilanjana. 1998. *Switching Channels: Ideologies of Television in India*. New Delhi: Oxford University Press.

Hall, Stuart. 1996. "Cultural Identity and Cinematic Representation," in Houston A. Baker Jr, Manthia Diawara and Ruth H. Lindeborg (eds), *Black British Cultural Studies*, pp. 210–22. Chicago: University of Chicago Press.

—— (ed.). 1997. *Representation: Cultural Representations and Signifying Practices*. London: Sage Publications.

Hall, Stuart, Dorothy Hobson, Andrew Lowe, and Paul Willis (eds). (1980) 1991. *Culture, Media, Language: Working Papers in Cultural Studies, 1972–79*. London: Routledge.

Halliday, Jon. 1971. *Sirk on Sirk*. London: Secker and Warburg.

Hansen, Kathryn. 2000. "The *Virangana* in North Indian History: Myth and Popular Culture," in Alice Thorner and Maithreyi Krishnaraj (eds), *Ideals, Images and Real Lives: Women in Literature and History*, pp. 257–87. Hyderabad: Orient Longman.

Hart, Kylo-Patrick R. 2000. "Representing Gay Men on American Television," *Journal of Men's Studies*, vol. 9 (1), Fall: 59–79.

Hindustan Times. 2008. "Dostana — Taking Male Bonding To A New High." 12 November.

Hayward, Jennifer. 1997. *Consuming Pleasures: Active Audiences and Serial Fictions from Dickens to Soap Opera*. Kentucky: The University Press of Kentucky.

Hobson, Dorothy. 1982. *Crossroads: The Drama of a Soap Opera*. London: Methuen.

——. 2003. *Soap Opera*. Cambridge: Polity.

Hogan, Patrick Colm. 2008. *Understanding Indian Movies: Culture, Cognition, and the Cinematic Imagination.* Austin: University of Texas Press.

Hunter, L. 2003. "The Celluloid Cubicle: Regressive Constructions of Masculinity in 1990s Office Movies," *Journal of American & Comparative Cultures,* vol. 26 (1): 71–86. March.

India Today. 2006. 31 December.

Indian Express, The. 2008a. 13 April.

———. 2008b. "Interview with Smriti Irani." 15 April.

———. 2008c. "Court Tells Wrangling Ambanis to Go to Mother Kokilaben." 22 August.

———. 2009. "A Full House." 12 January.

Iyer, Meena. 2008. "Hollywood Still Accounts for Only 5% of Indian Market," *Times of India* online. 4 November. http://timesofindia. indiatimes.com/India/Hollywood_still_accounts_for_only_5_of_ Indian_market/articleshow/3670666.cms. Accessed 4 November 2008.

Jain, Kajri. 1997. "Producing the Sacred: The Subjects of Calendar Art," *Journal of Arts and Ideas,* vol. 30 (1): 63–88.

———. 2002. "More Than Meets the Eye: The Circulation of Images and the Embodiment of Value," *Contributions to Indian Sociology,* n.s., vol. 36 (1 and 2): 33–70.

Jain, Ravindra K. 1997. "A Civilisational Theory of Indian Diaspora and its Global Implications," *Eastern Anthropologist,* vol. 50 (3–4): 347–55.

Jayaram, N., S. L. Sharma and Yogesh Atal. 2004. *The Indian Diaspora: The Dynamics of Migration.* London and New Delhi: Sage Publications.

Jayawardena, Kumari. 1986. *Feminism and Nationalism in the Third World.* London: Zed Books.

Jayawardena, Kumari and Malathi De Alwis. 1996. *Embodied Violence: Communalizing Women's Sexuality in South Asia.* London and New Jersey: Zed Books.

Jeffords, Susan. 1993. *Hard Bodies: Hollywood Masculinity in the Reagan Era.* New Brunswick, N. J.: Rutgers University Press.

Jeffrey, Robin. 2000. *India's Newspaper Revolution: Capitalism, Technology and the Indian Language Press.* Palgrave Macmillan.

Jensen, Robert and Emily Oster. 2007. "The Power of TV: Cable Television and Women's Status in India," 30 July. Available on http://home. uchicago.edu/~eoster/tvwomen.pdf. Accessed 17 August 2007.

Jha, Subhash K. 2008. "Kahaanii Romeo aur Juliet Kii," *Mumbai Mirror* online. 16 September. http://www.mumbaimirror.com/net/mmpaper. aspx?page=article&sectid=12&contentid=20080916200809160350236 41dd44c5ff&pageno=1. Accessed 18 September 2008.

———. 2008. "Dostana is a Clean Happy Watch: Karan Johar," *Hindustan Times.* 15 November.

Jhally, Sut and Justin Lewis. 1992. *Enlightened Racism: The Cosby Show, Audiences and the Myth of the American Dream.* Boulder, CA: Westview Press.

John, Binoo K. 2007. *Entry From Backside Only: Hazaar Funds of Indian-English*. New Delhi: Penguin Books India.

Johnson, Fern L. and Elizabeth J. Aries. 1983. "The Talk of Women Friends," *Women's Studies International Forum*, vol. 6 (4): 353–61.

Johnson, Kirk. 2001. "Media and Social Change: The Modernizing Influences of Television in Rural India," *Media, Culture & Society*, vol. 23 (20): 147–69.

Jones, Deborah. 1980. "Gossip: Notes on Women's Oral Culture," *Women's Studies International Quarterly*, no. 3: 193–98.

Jordan, Michael. 1993. *Encyclopedia of Gods: Over 2,500 Deities of the World*. New York: Facts on File.

Kakar, Sudhir. 1982. *The Inner World*. Oxford: Oxford University Press.

Kandiyoti, Deniz. 1996. *Gendering the Middle-East: Emerging Perspectives*. Syracuse: Syracuse University Press.

Kapoor, Coomi. 2008. "India Diary: Ancient Epics Fuel New Ratings War." 7 July. http://thestar.com.my/columnists/story.asp?file=/2008/7/7/columnists/indiadiary/21745136. Accessed 5 November 2008.

Katz, Jackson. 1995. "Advertising and the Construction of Violent White Masculinity," in Gail Dines and Jean M. Humez (eds), *Gender, Race and Class in Media: A Text Reader* (2nd edn), pp. 133–41. Thousand Oaks, CA: Sage Publications.

Kaur, Raminder and Ajay J. Sinha (eds). 2005. *Bollyworld: Indian Cinema through a Transnational Lens*. New Delhi: Sage Publications.

Kawin, Bruce F. 1992. *How Movies Work*. University of California Press.

Kilborn, Richard. 1992. *Television Soaps*. London: Batsford.

Kimmel, Michael, Jeff R. Hearn and Robert W. Connell (eds). 2004. *Handbook of Studies on Men and Masculinities*. Sage Publications.

Kinsley, David R. 1988. *Hindu Goddesses: Visions of the Divine Feminine in the Hindu Religious Tradition*. Los Angeles: University of California Press.

Kirkham, Pat and Janet Thumim (eds). 1993. *You Tarzan: Masculinity, Movies and Men*. London: Lawrence and Wishart.

Kishwar, Madhu. n.d. "When India Missed the 'Universe,'" *Manushi*. http://www.sawnet.org/books/writing/beauty.html. Accessed 3 January 2008.

Kishwar, Madhu and Ruth Vanita (eds). 1984. *In Search of Answers: Indian Women's Voices from Manushi*. London: Zed Books.

Klein, Allison. 2006. *What Would Murphy Brown Do? How the Women of Prime Time Changed Our Lives*. Emeryville, CA: Seal Press.

Kong, Lily. 2001. "Mapping 'New' Geographies of Religion: Politics and Poetics in Modernity," *Progress in Human Geography*, vol. 25 (2): 211–33.

Kothari, Shuchi. 2005. "From Genre to Zanaana: Urdu Television Drama Serials and Women's Culture in Pakistan," *Contemporary South Asia*, vol. 14 (3): 289–305. September.

Kripalani, Coonoor. 2001. "Coming of Age: Bollywood Productions of the Nineties," *Asian Cinema*, vol. 12, Spring–Summer: 29–48.

Krishnan, L. V., Trevor Sharot, Sharan Sharma, and Akash Chawla. n.d. "Reincarnating TAM Panelists to Understand Channel Surfing." *ESOMAR*.

Krishna, Raj. 1983. "Growth, Investment and Poverty in Mid-Term Appraisal of Sixth Plan," *Economic and Political Weekly*. 19 November. Cited in T. J. Byres. 1997. "Introduction: Development Planning and the Interventionist State versus Liberalization and the Neo-Liberal State: India, 1989–1996," in T. J. Byres (ed.), *The State, Development Planning and Liberalisation in India*. New Delhi: Oxford University Press.

Krishnaraj, Maithreyi. 2000. "Permeable Boundaries," in Alice Thorner and Maithreyi Krishnaraj (eds), *Ideals, Images and Real Lives: Women in Literature and History*, pp. 1–34. Hyderabad: Orient Longman.

Krishnadas, K. C. 2001. "U.S. Slowdown Batters India's Software Industry," 17 October. http://www.eetimes.com/story/career/newsfeatures/OEG20011017S0075. Accessed 24 October 2008.

Krishnan, Prabha and Anita Dighe. 1990. *Affirmation and Denial: Construction of Femininity on Indian Television*. New Delhi: Sage Publications.

Kuhn, Annette. 1987. "Women's Genres," in Christine Gledhill (ed.), *Home Is Where the Heart Is: Studies in Melodrama and the Woman's Film*, pp. 339–49. London: British Film Institute.

Kumar, Nita (ed.). 1994. *Women as Subjects: South Asian Histories*. New Delhi: Stree.

Kumar, Shanti. 2005. "Innovation, Imitation, and Hybridity in Indian Television," in Gary R. Edgerton and Brian G. Rose (eds), *Thinking Outside the Box: A Contemporary Television Genre Reader*, pp. 314–35. Lexington, Kentucky: The University Press of Kentucky.

———. 2006. *Gandhi Meets Primetime: Globalization and Nationalism in Indian Television*. Chicago: University of Illinois Press.

Kurup, Saira. 2009. "Kyunki Brazil Loves the Saas–Bahu Saga," *Times of India*. 1 March.

Lagasse, Paul, Lora Goldman, Archie Hobson, and Susan R. Norton (eds). 2004. *The Columbia Encyclopedia* (6th edn). The Gale Group and New York: Columbia University Press.

Lakshmi, Rama. 2008a. "In India's Huge Marketplace, Advertisers Find Fair Skin Sells," *Washington Post* online. 27 January. http://www.washingtonpost.com/wp-dyn/content/article/2008/01/26/AR2008012601057_pf.html. Accessed 3 March 2008.

———. 2008b. "Finally Ekta Has Found Her Krishna," *Times of India*. 19 June.

Lalwani, Vickey. 2008. "End of Kahaani," *Mumbai Mirror*. 6 September.

de Lauretis, Teresa. 1987. *Technologies of Gender: Essays on Theory, Film and Fiction*. Bloomington: Indiana University Press.

Larkin, Brian. 1997. "Indian Films and Nigerian Lovers: Media and the Creation of Parallel Modernities," *Africa*, vol. 67 (3): 406–39.

Leech, Geoffrey. 1974. *Semantics*. Harmondsworth: Penguin Books.

Leighninger, Robert D. 1997. "The Western as Male Soap Opera: John Ford's Rio Grande," *Journal of Men's Studies*, vol. 6 (2), Winter: 135–48.

Liebes, Tamar and Elihu Katz. 1989. "On the Critical Ability of TV Viewers," in Ellen Seiter, H. Borchers, G. Kreutzner, and E. M. Warth (eds), *Remote Control*. London: Routledge.

Livingstone, Sonia M. 1990. *Making Sense of Television: The Psychology of Audience Interpretation*. Oxford: Pergamon.

Lopate, Carol. 1977. "Daytime Television: You'll Never Want to Leave Home," *Radical America*, vol. 2: 3–51.

Lotz, Amanda D. 2006. *Redesigning Women: Television after the Network Era*. Urbana and Chicago: University of Illinois Press.

Lozano, Elizabeth. 1992. 'The Force of Myth on Popular Narratives: The Case of Melodramatic Serials," *Communication Theory*, vol. 2 (3): 207–20.

Lozano, Elizabeth and Arvind Singhal. 1993. "Melodramatic Television Serials," *Communications: The European Journal of Communication*, vol. 18 (1): 115–27.

Lu, Sheldon H. 2000. "Soap Opera in China: The Transnational Politics of Visuality, Sexuality and Masculinity," *Cinema Journal*, vol. 40 (1): 25–47.

Lutgendorf, Philip. 1990. "Ramayan: The Video," *The Drama Review*, vol. 34 (2), Summer.

——. 1991. *The Life of a Text: Performing the Ramcaritmanas of Tulsidas*. Berkeley: University of California Press.

——. 1995. "All in the 'Raghu' Family: A Video Epic in Cultural Context," in Lawrence A. Babb and Susan S. Wadley (eds), *Media and the Transformation of Religion in South Asia*, pp. 217–53. Philadelphia: University of Pennsylvania Press.

——. 2006. "Is There an Indian Way of Filmmaking?," *International Journal of Hindu Studies*, vol. 10 (3): 227–56. December.

McCabe, Janet and Kim Akass (eds). 2006. *Reading Desperate Housewives: Beyond the White Picket Fence*. London and New York: I. B. Tauris.

McMillin, Divya C. 2002a. "Choosing Commercial Television's Identities in India: A Reception Analysis," *Continuum: Journal of Media and Cultural Studies*, vol. 16 (1): 135–48.

——. 2002b. "Ideologies of Gender on Television in India," *Indian Journal of Gender Studies*, vol. 9 (1): 1–26.

Makdisi, Saree. 1995. " 'Postcolonial' Literature in a Neocolonial World: Modern Arabic Culture and the End of Modernity," *Boundary*, vol. 22 (1), Spring: 85–115.

Maddox, Georgina. 2009. "Abhishek and John Win 'Best Couple' at Star Screen Awards," *Indian Express*. 16 January.

Malhotra, Sheena and Tavishi Alagh. 2004. "Dreaming the Nation: Domestic Dramas in Hindi Film Post-1990," *South Asian Popular Culture*, vol. 2 (1): 19–37.

Mani, Lata. 1998. *Contentious Traditions: The Debate on Sati in Colonial India*. Berkeley: University of California Press.

Mankekar, Purnima. 1999. *Screening Culture, Viewing Politics: An Ethnography of Television, Womanhood, and Nation in Postcolonial India*. Durham, N. C.: Duke University Press.

Manuel, Peter. (1997) 1998. "Music, Identity, and Images of India in the Indo-Caribbean Diaspora," *Asian Music*, vol. XXIX (1), Fall/Winter: 17–35.

Martin-Barbero, Jesus. 1988. "Communication from Culture: The Crisis of the National and the Emergence of the Popular," *Media, Culture & Society*, vol. 10: 447–65.

———. 1993. *Communication, Culture and Hegemony: From Media to Mediations*. London: Sage Publications.

———. 2001. *Al Sur de la Modernidad: Comunicación, Globalización y Multiculturalidad*. Instituto Internacional de Literatura Iberoamericana.

Mazzarella, William. 2003. *Shoveling Smoke: Advertising and Globalization in Contemporary India*. Durham, N. C.: Duke University Press.

Mehta, Nalin. 2008. *India on Television: How Satellite News Channels Have Changed the Way We Think and Act*. India: Harper Collins.

Mehta, Pratap Bhanu. 2006. "Identity Dilemmas in a Globalizing World," in David Kelly (ed.), *India and China in a Globalizing World*. Singapore: Scientific Publishing.

Melkote, S., P. Shields and B. C. Agarwal (eds). 1998. *International Satellite Broadcasting in South Asia*. New York and Oxford: University Press of America.

Mercer, John and Martin Shingler. 2004. *Melodrama: Genre, Style and Sensibility*. Wallflower Press.

Mid-Day. 2005. "Interview with Ekta Kapoor." 6 November.

Mishra, Vijay. *Bollywood Cinema: Temples of Desire*. London and New York: Routledge.

Mitra, Ananda. 1993. *Television and Popular Culture in India: A Study of the Mahabharat*. New Delhi: Sage Publications.

Mitter, Sara. 1995. *Dharma's Daughters: Contemporary Indian Women and Hindu Culture*. New Brunswick, N. J.: Rutgers University Press.

Modleski, Tania. 1982. *Loving with a Vengeance: Mass Produced Fantasies for Women*. New York: Methuen.

Mort, Frank. 1988. "Boys Own?," in R. Chapman and J. Rutherford (eds), *Male Order: Unwrapping Masculinity*, London: Lawrence and Wishart.

Moore, Henrietta L. 1988. *Feminism and Anthropology*. Minneapolis: University of Minnesota Press.

Moorti, Sujata. 2007. "Imaginary Homes, Transplanted Traditions: The Transnational Optic and the Production of Indian Television," *Journal of Creative Communications*, vol. 2 (1–2): 1–21. Also available online at http://web.mit.edu/cms/events/mit2/Abstracts/Moortipaper.pdf. Accessed 21 September 2007.

Morley, David. 1988. *Family Television: Cultural Power and Domestic Leisure.* London: Routledge.

Morley, David and Kevin Robins. 1995. *Spaces of Identity: Global Media, Electronic Landscapes and Cultural Boundaries.* London: Routledge.

Motihar, Jhilmil. 2008. "Trend-Setting Style Statements," *India Today*, 33rd Anniversary Special Issue, pp. 148–50. 29 December.

Mulvey, Laura. 1978. "Notes on Sirk and Melodrama," *Movie*, no. 25, Winter.

———. 1987. "Notes on Sirk and Melodrama," in *Home Is Where the Heart Is: Studies in Melodrama and the Women's Film*, pp. 75–82. London: British Film Institute.

Mumby, Dennis K. 1998. "Organizing Men: Power, Discourse and the Social Construction of Masculinity(s) in the Workplace," *Communication Theory*, vol. 8: 164–83.

Mumford, Laura Stempel. 1995. *Love and Ideology in the Afternoon.* Bloomington: Indiana University Press.

Munshi, Shoma. 1997. "'Women of Substance'": Commodification and Fetishization in Contemporary Advertising within the Indian Urban-scape," *Social Semiotics*, vol. 7 (1): 37–53.

———. 1998. "Wife/Mother/Daughter-in-Law: Multiple Avatars of Home-maker in 1990s Indian Advertising," *Media Culture & Society*, vol. 20 (4): 573–93.

———. (ed.). 2001. *Images of the 'Modern' Woman' in Asia: Global Media, Local Meanings*, Richmond, Surrey: Curzon Press.

———. 2001a. "Introduction," in Shoma Munshi (ed.), *Images of the 'Modern' Woman' in Asia: Global Media, Local Meanings*, pp. 1–16. Richmond, Surrey: Curzon Press.

———. 2001b. "Marvellous Me: The Beauty Industry and the Construction of the 'Modern' Indian Women," in Shoma Munshi (ed.), *Images of the 'Modern' Woman' in Asia: Global Media, Local Meanings*, pp. 78–93. Richmond, Surrey: Curzon Press.

———. 2004. "A Perfect 10: Modern and Traditional — Representations of the Body in Beauty Pageants, and the Visual Media in Contemporary India," in Satadru Sen and James H. Mills (eds), *Confronting the Body: The Politics of Physicality in Colonial and Post-Colonial India*, pp. 162–82. London: Anthem Press.

———. 2008. "*Yeh Dil Maange More…* (This Heart Wants More…) Television and Consumer Choices in a Global City," in Peter van der Veer and Christophe Jaffrelot (eds), *Patterns of Middle Class Consumption in India and China*, pp. 263–76. New Delhi: Sage Publications.

Nandy, Ashis. 1980. "Woman versus Womanliness in India: An Essay in Cultural and Political Psychology," in Ashis Nandy (ed.), *At the Edge of Psychology: Essays in Politics and Culture*, pp. 32–46. New Delhi: Oxford University Press.

Nariman, Heidi Noel. 1993. *Soap Operas for Social Change: Toward a Methodology for Entertainment-Education Television*. Westport, CT: Praeger Publishers.

Neale, Steve. 1980. *Genre*. London: British Film Institute.

———. 1986. "Melodrama and Tears," *Screen*, vol. XXVI/6: 6–22.

Newcomb, Horace. 1974. *TV: The Most Popular Art*. New York: Anchor Books.

Newcomb, Horace and Paul M. Hirsch. 1983. "Television as a Cultural Forum: Implications for Research," *Quarterly Review of Film Studies*, vol. 8 (3): 45–55.

Nigam, Divya. 2007. *Women in Advertising: Changing Perceptions*. DGM Icfai Books.

Ninan, Sevanti. 1995. *Through the Magic Window: Television and Change in India*. New Delhi: Penguin Books.

———. 2007. "The Public Address System," in Ira Pande (ed.), *India at 60: Towards a New Paradigm*, pp. 244–53. India: Harper Collins.

Niranjana, Tejaswini, P. Sudhir and Vivek Dhareshwar (eds). 1993. *Interrogating Modernity: Culture and Colonialism in India*. Calcutta: Seagull Books.

Nochimson, Martha. 1992. *No End to Her: Soap Opera and the Female Subject*. Berkeley and Los Angeles: University of California Press.

Nowell-Smith, Geoffrey. 1987. "Minelli and Melodrama," in Christine Gledhill (ed.), *Home Is Where the Heart Is: Studies in Melodrama and the Women's Film*, pp. 70–74. London: British Film Institute.

Ohm, Britta. 1999. "Doordarshan: Representing the Nation's State," in Christiane Brosius and Melissa Butcher (eds), *Image Journeys: Audio–Visual Media and Cultural Change in India*, pp. 69–98. New Delhi: Sage Publications.

Ojha, Abhilasha. 2007. "Topsy Turvy at Balaji House," *Business Standard Weekend*. 13 October.

Page, David and William Crawley. 2001. *Satellites over South Asia: Broadcasting Culture and the Public Interest*. New Delhi: Sage Publications.

Pal, Bipin Chandra. 1911. *The Soul of India: A Constructive Study of Indian Thoughts and Ideals*. Calcutta: Choudhury and Choudhury.

Parekh, Bhikhu C., Gurharpal Singh and Steven Vertovec (eds). 2003. *Culture and Economy in the Indian Diaspora*. London: Routledge.

Patil, Vimla. 2004. "Women's Affairs," *The Tribune* online. 31 October. http://www.tribuneindia.com/2004/20041031/women.htm#1. Accessed 30 November 2007.

Pauwels, Heidi Rika Maria (ed.). 2008. *Indian Literature and Popular Cinema: Recasting Classics*. London: Routledge.

———. 2008. *The Goddess as Role Model: Sita and Radha in Scripture and on Screen*. Oxford University Press.

Pereira, Priyanka. 2009. "Talking Point with Ronit Roy," *Indian Express*. 17 January.

Phadnis, Atul and Myleeta Aga. 2008. "Race for GEC Number 3," *The Brand Reporter* online. 16–31 August. http://www.mediae2e.com/news50.html. Accessed 16 October 2008.

Pinney, Christopher. 1995. "An Authentic Indian 'Kitsch': The Aesthetics, Discrimination and Hybridity of Popular Hindu Art," *Social Analysis*, vol. 38: 88–110.

Prasad, M. Madhava. 1998. *Ideology of the Hindi Film: A Historical Construction*. New Delhi: Oxford University Press.

Raaj, Neelam. 2008. "Saas, Bahu and 'the End,'" *Times of India*. 26 October.

Radway, Janice M. 1987. *Reading the Romance: Women, Patriarchy and Popular Literature*. London: Verso.

Raheja, Gloria Goodwin and Ann Grodzins Gold. (1994) 1996. *Listen to the Heron's Words: Reimagining Gender and Kinship in North India*. New Delhi: Oxford University Press.

Rai, Amit S. 1995. "India On-line: Electronic Bulletin Boards and the Construction of a Diasporic Hindu Identity," *Diaspora: A Journal of Transnational Studies*, vol. 4(1), Spring: 31–58.

Rajadhyaksha, Niranjan. 2007. "Saas, Bahu and Economy," *The Wall Street Journal* online. 15 August. Available at http://www.livemint.com/2007/08/15002253/Saas-bahu-and-Economy.html. Accessed on 17 August 2007.

Rajagopal, Arvind. 1999. "Thinking about the New Middle Class: Gender, Advertising and Politics in an Age of Globalisation," in Rajeswari Sundar Rajan (ed.), *Signposts: Gender Issues in Post-Independence India*, pp. 57–100. New Delhi: Kali for Women.

———. 2001. *Politics after Television: Hindu Nationalism and the Reshaping of the Public in India*. Cambridge University Press.

Rajan, Gita. 2006. "Constructing-Contesting Masculinities: Trends in South Asian Cinema," *Signs: Journal of Women in Culture and Society*, vol. 31 (4): 1099–1124.

Ramanujan, A. K. 1990. "Is There an Indian Way of Thinking?: An Informal Essay," in McKim Marriott (ed.), *India Through Hindu Categories*, pp. 41–58. New Delhi: Sage Publications.

———. 1991. "Toward a Counter System: Women's Tales," in Arjun Appadurai, Frank J. Korom and Margaret A. Mills (eds), *Gender, Genre and Power in South Asian Expressive Traditions*, pp. 33–55. Philadelphia: University of Pennsylvania Press.

Rao, Anjali. 2007. "Ekta Kapoor Talk Asia Interview." 29 March. http://edition.cnn.com/2007/WORLD/asiapcf/03/27/talkasia.kapoor.script/index.html. Accessed 19 April 2008.

Ray, Sangeeta. 2000. *En-Gendering India: Woman and Nation in Colonial and Postcolonial Narratives*. Durham, N. C.: Duke University Press.

Rester, Aaron. n.d. *Darshan, Television and Media Theory in India*. Available online at http://aaronrester.net/writings/televisionRamayanpaperCCL.pdf. Accessed 7 October 2008.

Reuters India. 2008. "TV Soap Addicts Vexed by Reruns on Indian Channels." 13 November. http://in.reuters.com/article/topNews/idINIndia-36487520081113. Accessed 13 November 2008.

Robinson, Rowena. 1999. "Interrogating Modernity, Gendering 'Tradition:' *Teatr* Tales from Goa," *Contributions to Indian Sociology*, vol. 33 (3): 503–39.

Roy, Piysuh. 2007. "I Can Do Without Tulsi," *Indian Express* online. 1 April. http://www.indianexpress.com/story/27163.html. Accessed 3 April 2007.

Ryerson, William. n.d. "Sixteen Myths About Population: Part 5 — The Centrality of Motivation." http://www.populationpress.org/essays/essay-myths5.html. Accessed 20 December 2008.

Sangari, Kumkum and Sudesh Vaid (eds). 1989. *Recasting Women: Essays in Colonial History*. New Delhi: Kali for Women.

Sarkar, Tanika. 2001. *Hindu Wife, Hindu Nation: Community, Religion and Cultural Nationalism*. New Delhi: Permanent Black.

Sarkar, Tanika and Urvashi Butalia (eds). 1995. *Women and Right-Wing Movement: Indian Experiences*. London and New Jersey: Zed Books.

de Saussure, Ferdinand. (1916) 1974. *Course in General Linguistics*. London: Fontana.

Schramm, Wilbur. 1964. *Mass Media and National Development: The Role of Information in the Developing Countries*. Stanford: Stanford University Press.

Scharrer, E. 2001. "Tough Guys: The Portrayal of Hypermasculinity in Aggression in Televised Police Dramas," *Journal of Broadcasting & Electronic Media*, vol. 45 (4): 615–34.

Scrase, Timothy. 2002. "Television, the Middle Classes and the Transformation of Cultural Identities in West Bengal, India," *Gazette: The International Journal for Television Studies*, vol. 64 (40): 323–42.

Seiter, Ellen. 1999. *Television and New Media Audiences*. USA: Oxford University Press.

Seiter, Ellen *et al.* (1989) 1991. "Don't Treat Us Like We're So Stupid and Naïve: Towards an Ethnography of Soap Opera Viewers," in Ellen Seiter, H. Borchers, G. Kreutzner, and E. M. Warth (eds), *Remote Control*, pp. 223–47. London: Routledge.

Shah, Kunal M. 2008a. "Code of Conduct," *Mumbai Mirror* online. 15 February. http://www.mumbaimirror.com/net/mmpaper.aspx? page=article&sectid=12&contentid=2008021520080215025403279cb89 7ac6&pageno=1. Accessed 15 September 2008.

——. 2008b. "Ekta Kapoor snubbed!," *Mumbai Mirror*. 12 August.

——. 2008c. "Ekta to Sue Actresses," *Mumbai Mirror*. 13 August.

Sharpe, Jenny. 2005. "Gender, Nation and Globalization in Monsoon Wedding and Dilwale Dulhaniya Le Jayenge," *Meridians: Feminism, Race, Transnationalism*, vol. 6 (1): 55–81.

Shukla, Sandhya. 1997. "Building Diaspora and Nation: the 1991 Cultural Festival of India," *Cultural Studies*, vol. 11 (2): 296–315. 1 May.

Silverstone, Roger. 1989. "Let Us Then Return to the Murmuring of Everyday Practices: A Note on Michel de Certeau, Television and Everyday Life," *Theory, Culture & Society*, no. 6: 77–94.

Simpson, Mark. 1994. *Male Impersonators: Men Performing Masculinity*. Cassell.

Singhal, Arvind and Everett Rogers. 1989a. *India's Information Revolution*. New Delhi: Sage Publications.

——. 1989b. "Prosocial Television for Development in India," *Public Communication Campaigns*, pp. 331–50. California. Cited in Veena Das. 1995. "On Soap Opera: What Kind of Anthropological Object Is It?," in Daniel Miller (ed.), *Worlds Apart: Modernity Through the Prism of the Local*, pp. 169–89. London: Routledge.

Singhal, Arvind, Everett Rogers and W. Brown. 1992. *Entertainment Telenovelas for Development: Lessons Learnt About Creation and Implementation*. Sao Paulo, Brazil: International Association for Mass Communication Research.

Singhal, Arvind and Everett Rogers. 2002. "A Theoretical Agenda for Entertainment-Education," *Communication Theory*, vol. 12 (2): 117–35.

Singhal, Arvind, Michael J. Cody, Everett Rogers, and Miguel Sabido (eds). 2003. *Entertainment-Education and Social Change: History, Research and Practice*. New York: Lawrence Erlbaum.

Sirk, Douglas and Jon Halliday. 1972. *Sirk on Sirk (Cinema One)*. Viking.

Smith, G. M. and P. Wilson. 2004. "Country Cookin' and Cross-Dressin': Television, Southern White Masculinities, and Hierarchies of Cultural Taste," *Television New Media*, vol. 5 (3): 175–95.

Somaaya, Bhawana. 2008. *Fragmented Frames: Reflections of a Critic*. New Delhi: Pustak Mahal.

Sonawala, Dipti and Viral Shah. 2008. "Saas boo-hoo!," *Mumbai Mirror*. 8 November.

D'Souza, Dipti Nagpaul. 2008. "The End of a Beginning," *Indian Express*. 25 October.

Spence, Louise. 2005. *Watching Daytime Soap Operas: The Power of Pleasure*. Middletown, CT: Wesleyan University Press.

Spicer, Andrew. 2001. *Typical Men: The Representation of Masculinity in Popular British Cinema*. London and New York: I. B. Tauris.

Sreberny-Mohammadi, Annabelle. 1996. "The Global in the Local in International Communications," in James Curran and M. Gurevitch (eds), *Mass Media and Society*, (2nd edn), pp. 177–203. London: Edward Arnold.

Stam, Robert and Ella Shohat. 1994. *Unthinking Eurocentrism: Multiculturalism and the Media*. London and New York: Routledge.

Stempel Mumford, Laura. 1995. *Love and Ideology in the Afternoon: Soap Opera, Women and Television Genre*. Bloomington and Indianapolis: Indiana University Press.

Stevens, Paul and Rahul Sapra. 2007. "Akbar's Dream: Moghul Toleration and English/British Orientalism," *Modern Philology*, vol. 104 (3): 379–411.

Sullivan, Nancy. 1993. "Film and Television Production in Papua New Guineas: How Media Become the Message,"*Public Culture*, vol. 5 (3): 533–56.

Sullivan, Tim. 2003. "Clarifying Beauty in India," *The Philadelphia Inquirer*. 10 August.

Sunder Rajan, Rajeswari. 1993. *Real and Imagined Women: Gender, Culture, and Postcolonialism*. New York: Routledge.

TAM Media Research Pvt. Ltd. 2008. Graphs and data provided by L. V. Krishnan, CEO, TAM Media Research Pvt. Ltd.

Tasker, Yvonne. 1993. *Spectacular Bodies: Gender, Genre and the Action Cinema*. London and New York: Routledge.

Taylor, Ella. 1989. *Prime-Time Families: Television Culture in Postwar America*. Berkeley: University of California Press.

Thapan, Meenakshi. 2009. *Living the Body: Embodiment, Womanhood and Identity in Contemporary India*. Sage Publications.

Tharu, Susie. 1989. "Thinking the Nation Out: Some Reflections on Nationalism and Theory," *Journal of Arts and Ideas*, no. 17–18: 81–90.

Timberg, Bernard. 1984. "The Rhetoric of the Camera in Television Soap Opera," in Horace Newcomb (ed.), *Television: The Critical View*. New York: Oxford University Press.

Times of India, The. 2002. "Soap Operas Paint Unreal Picture of Women." 16 October. http://timesofindia.indiatimes.com/articleshow/25349005. cms. Accessed 16 October 2007.

———. 2008a. "Smriti is Bravehearted." 14 May.

———. 2008b. "Real life, soap ishtyle." 6 June. http://timesofindia. indiatimes.com/Entertainment/TV_Buzz/Real_life_soap-ishtyle/ articleshow/3102105.cms. Accessed 6 June 2008.

———. 2008c. "New Channels A Threat?" 24 October.

———. 2008d. "Ekta Kapoor's Bad Patch." 29 October.

Tharu, Susie. 1989. "Response to Julie Stephens," in Ranajit Guha (ed.), *Subaltern Studies VI: Writings on South Asian History and Society*, pp. 126–31. New Delhi: Oxford University Press.

Thomas, Rosie. 1995. "Melodrama and the Negotiation of Morality in Mainstream Hindi Film," in Carol A. Breckenridge (ed.), *Consuming Modernity: Public Culture in a South Asian World*, pp. 157–82. Minneapolis: University of Minnesota Press.

Thorburn, David. 1976. "Television Melodrama," in Richard Adler and Douglass Cater (eds), *Television As A Cultural Force*. New York: Praeger.

Thorner, Alice and Maithreyi Krishnaraj (eds). 2000. *Ideals, Images and Real Lives: Women in Literature and History*. Hyderabad: Orient Longman.

Tufte, Thomas. 2000a. *Living With the Rubbish Queen: Telenovelas, Culture and Modernity in Brazil*. Luton: University of Luton Press.

——. 2000b. "The Popular Forms of Hope: About the Force of Fiction Among TV Audiences in Brazil," in Ingunn Hagen and Janet Wasko (eds), *Consuming Audiences? Production and Reception in Media Research*, pp. 275–99. New Jersey: IAMCR/Hampton Press.

——. n.d. http://www.portalcomunicacion.com/catunesco/esp/3/down/tufte/tufte_telenovelas.pdf. Accessed 16 December 2008.

Tummala-Narra, Pratyusha. 2007. "Skin Color and the Therapeutic Relationship," *Psychoanalytic Psychology*, vol. 24: 255–70.

Uberoi, Patricia (ed.). 1996 *Social Reform, Sexuality and the State*. New Delhi: Sage Publications.

——. 1996. "Introduction: Problematising Social Reform, Engaging Sexuality, Interrogating the State," in Patricia Uberoi (ed.), *Social Reform, Sexuality and the State*, pp. ix–xxvi. New Delhi: Sage Publications.

——. 2006. *Freedom and Destiny: Gender, Family and Popular Culture in India*. New Delhi: Oxford University Press.

United Press International. 2001. "India's Software Export Growth Slips." 8 November. http://www.highbeam.com/doc/1G1-79861491.html. Accessed 24 October 2008.

Valaskivi, Katja. 2000. "Being Part of the Family? Genre, Gender and Production in a Japanese TV Drama," *Media, Culture & Society*, vol. 22: 309–25.

van der Veer, Peter. 1998. "The Global History of Modernity," *Journal of the Economic and Social History of the Orient*, vol. 41 (3): 285–94.

van Zoonen, Liesbet. 1994. *Feminist Media Studies*. London: Sage Publications.

Vasudevan, Ravi. 1991. "The Cultural Space of a Film Narrative: Interpreting *Kismet* (*Bombay Talkies*, 1943)," *Indian Economic and Social History Review*, vol. 28 (2): 171–85.

——. 1996. " 'You Cannot Live in Society — and Ignore It': Nationhood and Female Modernity in Andaz," in Patricia Uberoi (ed.), *Social Reform, Sexuality and the State*, pp. 83–108. New Delhi: Sage Publications.

Vasudevan, Ravi. 2000. "The Politics of Cultural Address in a 'Transitional' Cinema: A Case Study of Popular Indian Cinema" in Christine Gledhill and Linda Williams (eds), *Reinventing Film Studies*, pp. 130–64. London: Hodder Arnold.

Vertovec, Steven. 2000. *The Hindu Diaspora: Comparative Patterns*. London: Routledge.

Visweswaran, Kamala. 1997. "Diaspora by Design: Flexible Citizenship and South Asians in U.S. Racial Formations," *Diaspora: A Journal Transnational Studies*, vol. 6 (1), Spring: 5–29.

Waldfogel, Joel. 2007. "Where TV Is Good for You," *Washington Post* online. 26 August. Available at http://www.washingtonpost.com/wp-dyn/content/article/2007/08/24/AR2007082401222.html. Accessed 27 September 2007.

Warhol, Robyn R. 1998. "Feminine Intensities: Soap Opera Viewing as a Technology of Gender," *Genders*, vol. 28. Available online at http://www.genders.org/g28/g28_intensities.html. Accessed 5 October 2007.

West, Ed. 2006. *Male Grooming: Every Bloke's Guide to Looking Great.* Summersdale.

Willeman, Paul. (1972) 1973. "Towards an Analysis of the Sirkian System," *Screen*, vol. 13 (4), Winter: 128–34.

——. (1978) 1979. "The Films of Douglas Sirk," *Screen*, vol. 12 (2), Winter.

Zimmer, Heinrich. 1946. *Myths and Symbols in Indian Art and Civilization.* New York: Pantheon.

Zutshi, Somnath. 1993. "Women, Nation and the Outsider in Contemporary Hindi Cinema," in Tejaswini Niranjana, P. Sudhir and Vivek Dhareshwar (eds), *Interrogating Modernity: Culture and Colonialism in India*, pp. 83–142. Calcutta: Seagull Books.

Websites of Indian Television and Films

Amar, Tuhin. n.d. "An Interview with Rajan Shahi." http://www.indiantelevision.com/interviews/rajan.htm. Accessed 21 October 2008.

Bajpai, Shailja. 2003. "Once You Start Censoring, There Is No End To It." 4 November. http://www.indiantelevision.com/perspectives/y2k3/shailaja.htm. Accessed 6 June 2007.

Bijoy, A. K. 2006. "Saat Phere: The Dark Girl Theory — A Case Study on the Show that Powered Zee TV's Charge to the 2nd Spot in Hindi GEC Space." 12 August. http://indiantelevision.com/special/y2k6/saatphere.htm. Accessed 21 October 2008.

Dubey, Richa. 2005. "Big Fight is in Hindi GEC Middle Rung." 25 January. http://www.indiantelevision.com/special/y2k8/channel_special_report.php. Accessed 31 October 2008.

Entertainment One India online. n.d. "NDTV Imagine Ties Up With Balaji Telefilms." http://entertainment.oneindia.in/television/top-stories/news/2008/imagine-balaji-tie-up-151008.html. Accessed 9 January 2009.

Gmagazine.com. 2005. "Shailja Kejriwal interview." 19 May. http://www. discusstv.com/forums/lofiversion/index.php/t1599.html. Accessed 16 October 2007.

Hansa Research Group. 2003. *Consumer Awareness and Attitude Research on Conditional Access System.* June. http://www.indiantelevision.com/ spotlight/y2k3/StarSight_files/frame.htm. Accessed 27 January 2009.

http://www.balajitelefilms.com

http://caminhodasindias.globo.com

http://www.fairandhandsome.net. Accessed 9 November 2008.

http://www.indiantelevision.com/aboutus.htm. Accessed 29 September 2008.

http://www.indiantelevision.com/headlines/y2k7/mar/mar238.php. Accessed 16 October 2008.

http://www.indiantelevision.com/indianbrodcast/history/historyoftele. htm. Accessed 16 October 2008.

http://www.indiantelevision.com/news_analysis/newsletter/030100/ special030100.htm. Accessed 16 October 2008.

http://www.indiantelevision.com/ye2k/y2ka.htm. Accessed 16 October 2008.

http://www.indiantellyawards.com/y2k5/index_pop.htm. Accessed 29 September 2008.

http://www.rajshri.com/zee/saatphere/index.asp. Accessed on 25 September 2007.

http://www.sphereorigins.com

http://www.televisionpoint.com/news2008/newsfullstory.php?id =1200398692. "Star Plus' Bidaai becomes most popular show." 15 January 2008. Accessed 16 January 2008.

http://www.tellychakkar.com/y2k5/july/29jul/interview_om.php. Accessed 14 September 2008.

http://www.zee-tv.com/Zee_Serial.aspx?zsid=56. Accessed 25 September 2007.

Jain, Ankit. 2008. "Kahaani Ghar Ghar Kii to Go Off Air on October 09." 25 September. http://www.televisionpoint.com/news2008/newsfullstory. php?id=1222353423. Accessed 25 September 2008.

Joshi, Aparna and Trupti Ghag. 2003. 'Changing Storylines — On The Fast Track to Success." 23 July. http://www.indiantelevision.com/ perspectives/y2k3/trackchange.htm. Accessed 24 October 2008.

Kapoor, Reena Thapar. 2008. "It's All About Money!," *Times of India* online. 1 October. http://movies.indiatimes.com/News__Gossip/ Television_News/Its_all_about_money/articleshow/3547992.cms. Accessed 1 October 2008.

———. 2008a. "Ekta Loses the K Touch," *Times of India* online. 3 November. http://movies.indiatimes.com/News__Gossip/Television_News/Ekta_ loses_the_K_touch/articleshow/3659470.cms. Accessed 3 November 2008.

Kotian, Ashwin, Ashwin Pinto and Vickey Lalwani. 2003. "Comedy of Errors." 29 August. http://www.indiantelevision.com/perspectives/y2k3/comedymain.htm. Accessed 28 October 2008.

Krishna, Sonali. 2004a. "Gripping Twists in the Tale Take *Kyunki* … to All-Time Ratings High." 26 October. http://www.indiantelevision.com/headlines/y2k4/oct/oct238.htm. Accessed 24 October 2008.

——. 2004b. "A Tale of 3 Ks: A Case Study on How The 3 Most Celebrated Shows Retained Their Premier Position Over Four Years," 5 November. http://www.indiantelevision.com/special/y2k4/3ks.htm. Accessed 31 October 2008.

——. 2005. " 'Star Parivaar' Tops Ratings with 13.6 TVR." 10 June. http://www.indiantelevision.com/headlines/y2k5/june/june128.htm. Accessed 16 October 2007.

Lalwani, Vickey. 2003a. "Interview with Balaji Belefilms Creative Director Ekta Kapoor." 29 May. http://www.indiantelevision.com/interviews/y2k3/executive/ektakapoor.htm. Accessed 16 October 2007.

——. 2003b. "Balaji Telefilms: Kahaani Aurat Kii." 9 September. http://www.indiantelevision.co.in/perspectives/y2k3/balaji.htm. Accessed 16 October 2007.

——. 2003c. "Interview with Balaji Telefilms' CEO Shobha Kapoor." 9 September. http://www.indiantelevision.com/perspectives/y2k3/interview/shobhaakapoor.htm. Accessed 16 October 2007.

——. 2003d. "The *Kahaani* Thickens … After 20 Years." 1 October. http://indiantelevision.com/special/y2k3/kahaani.htm. Accessed 16 June 2007.

Lookhar, Mayur. 2008a. "Nahar to Die But There's a Twist …." 15 October. http://www.tellychakkar.com/y2k8/oct/15oct/news_highlight.php. Accessed 16 October 2008.

——. 2008b. "Rajshri Quits *Saat Phere*." 23 October. http://www.telly chakkar.com/y2k8/oct/23oct/news_rajshri.php. Accessed 24 October 2008.

Maheshwari, Neha. 2008. "It's Not 'Fair:' Parul and Vibha on Their 'Dark' Days." 4 January. http://www.tellychakkar.com/y2k8/jan/4jan/news_vibha.php. Accessed 14 September 2008.

Malani, Gaurav. 2008. "Dostana" film review, *Times of India*. 14 November. http://movies.indiatimes.com/moviereview/3711873.cms. Accessed 14 November 2008.

Mitra, Anjan. 2005. "Indian television dot com's interview with Star Group CEO Michelle Guthrie." 29 November. http://www.indiantelevision.com/interviews/y2k5/executive/michelle.htm. Accessed 30 October 2008.

Rajesh, Srividya. 2009. "Ekta Has Evolved A New Style for Herself! – Shailja Kejriwal" 2 February. http://www.india-forums.com/tellybuzz/article.asp?id=3959. Accessed 3 February 2009.

Sengupta, Ananya. 2005. "Director's Cut ...." 28 September. http://www.tellychakkar.com/y2k5/sept/28sep/dir_cut_rajan.php. Accessed 19 August 2008.

———. 2006. "What Makes *Saat Phere* Tick." 22 May. http://www.tellychakkar.com/y2k6/may/22may/reviews_saat.php. Accessed 18 September 2007.

Sengupta, Jayalakshmi. 2007. "Ekta Kapoor's Show Is a Hit in Kabul: Conservative Afghanistan Thrives on a Diet of Tulsi, Parvati and Prerna." 5 December. http://buzz18.in.com/features/tv/ekta-kapoors-show-is-a-hit-in-kabul/28645/0. Accessed 28 October 2007.

Sharma, Mandvi. 2008. " 'Kyunki' ... It's Another Channel?,", *Times of India* online. 6 November. http://timesofindia.indiatimes.com/Entertainment/Kyunkii_its_another_channel/articleshow/3677273.cms. Accessed 6 November 2008.

Sultana, Nasrin. 2008. "Star Plus Surges Well Ahead of Zee TV." 12 April. http://www.indiantelevision.com/headlines/y2k8/apr/apr165.php. Accessed 28 October 2008.

Thapar Kapoor, Reena. 2008. "Kyunki ... Nears Its End." 30 October. http://movies.indiatimes.com/News__Gossip/Television_News/Kyunki_nears_its_end/articleshow/3651473.cms. Accessed 31 October 2008.

2001. "Ekta Kapoor rounds off *Asiaweek's* Power 50 List." 11 June. http://www.indiantelevision.com/headlines/y2k1/june/june10.htm. Accessed 16 October 2007.

2001. "Star Plus' Two Hit Soaps Mop Up Top 8 Slots On Ratings Charts: TAM Data." 6 June. http://www.indiantelevision.com/headlines/y2k1/june/june5.htm. Accessed 24 October 2008.

2001. "An Interview with Ashok Pandit." 3 August. http://www.indiantelevision.com/interviews/director/ashok.htm. Accessed 20 October 2008.

2001. "An Interview with Raman Kumar." 16 August. http://www.indiantelevision.com/interviews/director/raman.htm. Accessed 20 October 2008.

2002. "Balaji Hunts for Fresh Talent in Mass Auditions." 30 September. http://www.indiantelevision.com/headlines/y2k2/sep/sep150.htm. Accessed 31 October 2008.

2003. "Indiantelevision.com's Interview with Scriptwriter Shobhaa De." 11 February. http://www.indiantelevision.com/interviews/y2k3/writer/shobhade.htm. Accessed 6 November 2008.

2004. "Interview with Shailja Kejriwal", 7 September. http://www.indiantelevision.com/interviews/y2k4/executive/Shailja_kejriwal.htm. Accessed on 16 September 2008.

2004. "On New Year's Eve, Still Star Plus' Soaps That Ruled." 12 January. http://www.indiantelevision.com/headlines/y2k4/jan/jan82.htm. Accessed 24 October 2008.

2004. "Saas, Bahu aur Saazish captures number 1 slot in the afternoon band." 3 December. http://www.indiantelevision.com/headlines/y2k4/dec/dec29.htm. Accessed 21 January 2008.

2005. "Shailja Kejriwal Interview." 2 March. http://www.discusstv.com/forums/lofiversion/index.php/t1599.html. Accessed 16 September 2008.

2005. "After Months of Acrimony, An Outbreak of Brotherly Love at Reliance," India Knowledge at Wharton: Strategic Management website. 13 July. http://knowledge.wharton.upenn.edu/india/article.cfm?articleid=4043&CFID=34145705&CFTOKEN=32352555&jsessionid=a8305184d3a2453e2f29. Accessed 7 October 2007.

2005. "Kiran Karmarkar Unplugged." 29 July. http://www.tellychakkar.com/y2k5/july/29jul/interview_om.php. Accessed 14 September 2007.

2006. "Retrospectives: Hamara Bajaj." 5 June. http://sriyansa.wordpress.com/2006/06/05/retrospectives-hamara-bajaj. Accessed 24 October 2008.

2006. "Kyunki Saas Bhi Kabhi Bahu Thi, Ready for Leap!" 6 June http://www.televisionpoint.com/news2006/newsfullstory.php?id=1149602422. Accessed 19 April 2007.

2006. "*Kyunki Saas*: Meet Gen Next." 7 June. http://specials.rediff.com/movies/2006/jun/07sld1.htm. Accessed 11 July 2007.

2007. "Zee to Ramp Up 10:30 pm Slot with 'Teen Bahuraaniyaan.'" 15 March. http://www.indiantelevision.com/headlines/y2k7/mar/mar198.php. Accessed 20 October 2008.

2007. *Koffee with Karan,* Star One, episode of 27 May.

2008. "India to become 2nd largest mobile phone market: TRAI." 24 March. http://news.webindia123.com/news/Articles/India/20080324/916317.html. Accessed 4 November 2008.

2008. Interview with Smriti Z. Irani, *Indian Express* online. 13 April. http://www.indianexpress.com/story/296205.html. Accessed 15 April 2008.

2008. "Smriti's Absence Made No Difference to TRP Ratings: Ekta Kapoor," interview with Ekta Kapoor. 21 April. http://in.movies.yahoo.com/news-detail/23913/Smritis-absence-no-difference-TRP-ratings-Ekta-Kapoor.html. Accessed 18 May 2008.

2008. " 'Ekta' 'K' Keeps Coming Back to Us," *Times of India* online. 4 June. http://timesofindia.indiatimes.com/Entertainment/TV_Buzz/Ekta_K_keeps_coming_back_to_us/articleshow/3096164.cms. Accessed 6 June 2008.

2008. "Finally Ekta Kapoor has Found Her Krishna," *Times of India* online. 19 June. http://timesofindia.indiatimes.com/Entertainment/Finally_Ekta_has_found_her_Krishna_/articleshow/3141855.cms. Accessed 19 June 2008.

2008. "Balaji Snaps Ties with Star, to Buy Back 25.99%." 19 August. http://www.indiantelevision.com/headlines/y2k8/aug/aug169.php. Accessed 26 October 2008.

2008. "*Bidaai* turns full circle." 5 September. http://www.tellychakkar. com/y2k8/sep/5sep/news_bidaai.php. Accessed 16 October 2008.

2008. Interview with Shona Urvashi. 12 September. http://www. screenindia.com/news/Saas-bahu-aur-sensex/359690/. Accessed 22 September 2008.

2008. Review of *Saas, Bahu aur Sensex*. 19 September. http://www. realbollywood.com/news/2008/09/saas-bahu-aur-sensex-review. html. Accessed 22 September 2008.

2008. Review of *Saas, Bahu aur Sensex*. 19 September. http://entertainment. oneindia.in/bollywood/reviews/2008/saas-bahu-aur-sensex-review-190908.html. Accessed 22 September 2008.

2008. "Ekta Kapoor wants a husband like Ronit Roy." 22 September. http:// sify.com/movies/bollywood/fullstory.php?id=14763560 and http:// movies.ndtv.com/newstory.asp?slug=Ekta+Kapoor+wants+a+husban d+like+Ronit+Roy&id=ENTEN20080066253. Accessed 22 September 2008.

2008. "Colors Notches 217 GRPs, Stands Strong on 3rd Spot." 25 September. http://www.indiantelevision.com/headlines/y2k8/sep/sep266.php. Accessed 26 September 2008.

2008. "After Bidaai, Rajan's Next." 13 October. http://www.tellychakkar. com/y2k8/oct/13oct/news_bidai.php. Accessed 13 October 2008.

2008. "Balaji Telefilms Moves Court Against Star on '*Kyunki*.'" 20 October. http://www.indiantelevision.com/headlines/y2k8/oct/oct190.php. Accessed 20 October 2008.

2008. "Balaji and Star at Loggerheads." 20 October. http://www.telly chakkar.com/y2k8/oct/20oct/news_highlight.php. Accessed 20 October.

2008. "Balaji Telefilms terminates Star unit terms Kyunki Saas … " *Times of India* online. 20 October. http://timesofindia.indiatimes.com/India/ Star_terminates_Kyunki_Saas_/articleshow/3618563.cms. Accessed 20 October 2008.

2008, "Star terminates 'Kyunki': Balaji," *Indian Express* online. 20 October. http://www.indianexpress.com/news/star-terminates-kyunki-balaji/375621/. Accessed 20 October 2008.

2008. "Balaji Telefilms Ropes in Puneet Kinra as Group CEO." 24 October. http://www.indiantelevision.com/headlines/y2k8/oct/oct241.php. Accessed 24 October 2008.

2008. "Balaji Telefilms Q2 slips 31% to Rs 181 million." 25 October. http:// www.indiantelevision.com/headlines/y2k8/oct/oct265.php. Accessed 25 October 2008.

2008. "What a Cracker! Dhamakas and Diffusions." 25 October. http:// www.tellychakkar.com/y2k8/oct/25oct/feature6.php. Accessed 25 October 2008.

2008. "*Kyunki* to shift to 9X?" 25 October http://www.tellychakkar.com/ y2k8/oct/25oct/grapevine_kyunki.php. Accessed 25 October 2008.

2008. "*Kyunki* Special," *Saas, Bahu aur Saazish*, Star News. 5 November 2008.

2008. "66.54 Million C&S Homes in India: IRS." 8 November. http://www. indiantelevision.com/headlines/y2k8/nov/nov94.php. Accessed 8 November 2008.

2008. "Dabur Ropes in Sakshi Tanwar as Brand Ambassador for Sanifresh Shine." 17 December. http://www.indiantelevision.com/mam/headlines/y2k8/dec/decmam61.php. Accessed 17 December 2008.

2008. "357 Private TV Channels Uplink from India." 24 December. http://www.indiantelevision.com/headlines/y2k8/dec/dec235.php. Accessed 25 December 2008.

2009. "*Bidaai* fetches a TRP of 8.69." 10 January. http://www.tellychakkar. com/y2k9/jan/10jan/news_bidaai.php. Accessed 16 January 2009.

Index